FIFTY YEARS OF THE DIVORCE REFORM ACT 1969

The enactment of the Divorce Reform Act 1969 was a landmark moment in family law. Coming into force in 1971, it had a significant impact on legal practice and was followed by a dramatic increase in divorce rates, reflecting changes in social attitudes.

This new interdisciplinary collection explores the background to the 1969 Act and its influence on law and society. Bringing together scholars from law, sociology, history, demography, literature and film, it reflects on the changes to divorce law and practice over the past 50 years, and the changing impact of divorce on different people in society, particularly women.

As such, it offers a 'biography' of this important piece of legislation, moving from its conception and birth, through its reception and development, to its demise. Looking to the future, and to the new law introduced by the Divorce, Dissolution and Separation Act 2020, this collection suggests ways for evaluating what makes a 'good' divorce law.

This brilliant collection gives insight not only into this crucial piece of legislation, but also into a key period of societal change.

Fifty Years of the Divorce Reform Act 1969

Edited by
Joanna Miles
Daniel Monk
and
Rebecca Probert

•HART•
OXFORD • LONDON • NEW YORK • NEW DELHI • SYDNEY

HART PUBLISHING

Bloomsbury Publishing Plc

Kemp House, Chawley Park, Cumnor Hill, Oxford, OX2 9PH, UK

1385 Broadway, New York, NY 10018, USA

29 Earlsfort Terrace, Dublin 2, Ireland

HART PUBLISHING, the Hart/Stag logo, BLOOMSBURY and the Diana logo are trademarks of Bloomsbury Publishing Plc

First published in Great Britain 2022

A catalogue record for this book is available from the British Library.

A catalogue record for this book is available from the Library of Congress

ISBN: HB: 978-1-50994-788-1
ePDF: 978-1-50994-790-4
ePub: 978-1-50994-789-8

Typeset by Compuscript Ltd, Shannon

FOREWORD

LADY HALE

This is, as the editors explain, the biography of an Act of Parliament, a new way of tracing the life-story of a piece of legislation from its beginnings to its end. The Divorce Reform Act was thought revolutionary when it was passed in 1969. No longer was divorce to be based on the theory of an innocent and a guilty party but on the irretrievable breakdown of the marriage. No longer had marital misconduct to be proved; this was still a possible basis for divorce but so was no-fault separation. But the Act has run its course and is soon to be replaced by another Act of Parliament in which marital conduct and separation do not feature at all: something which would have been unthinkable when the 1969 Act was passed. The story of how the Act came into being and how it has fared since is a story that needs to be told and a very good read it is too.

I am one of that dwindling band of lawyers who remember what life was like both before the Divorce Reform Act 1969 came into force in 1971 and from then until the advent of the so-called 'special procedure', which by 1977 had transferred almost all undefended divorces from being heard on evidence before a judge in open court to being scrutinised on paper in private. Before the Act, I remember the odd defended divorce in which my pupil master appeared in the High Court. I saw the President of the Family Division deny a divorce to a woman with a long catalogue of obviously true complaints against her husband but none of them deemed individually or collectively serious enough to amount to cruelty. I remember appearing very early in my career as a barrister in two undefended divorces in the county court – shortly after these had been transferred from the High Court, where they were heard by county court judges sitting as Commissioners and addressed as 'My Lord' rather than 'Your Honour'. This move was obviously unpopular with those judges, but even more unpopular with members of the Bar who had made a good living from appearing for petitioners, for which they could charge High Court rather than county court fees. Worse still, drafting petitions was no longer a monopoly of the Bar and could be done by solicitors, as mine had been, or even by the parties themselves. The judge made my life as difficult as he possibly could, finding nit-picking fault with the petitions, before doing the inevitable and granting the divorces. This can only have added to the stress and humiliation felt by my poor clients at this most anxious time in their lives. Yet the result was always a foregone conclusion. We knew that from the way the evidence was given. The general rule when taking witnesses through their evidence in chief is that they must not be asked leading questions. The general rule in undefended divorces was that all the questions must be leading, so as to get through them as quickly as possible and avoid the risk that the petitioner might say the wrong thing; however, the one leading question we could never ask was 'do you live at XX address?'; instead, we had to ask 'where do you live?' No-one ever told me why.

Then the 1969 Act came into force and I had another ghastly experience. Before the Act, it was standard practice to apply for costs against the respondent, usually granted because by definition the respondent had been guilty of marital misconduct. After the Act, for the first time, a person whose marital conduct was beyond reproach could be divorced against their will after five years of separation. So I was instructed to go along and resist a claim for costs made against my blameless client. I was all fired up to protest at the injustice of making him pay for a divorce which he did not want and for which he could not be blamed. The wind was taken out of my sails by experienced counsel for the petitioner who blandly told that judge that my presence was unnecessary because he was not going to pursue the claim. I have never forgiven myself for not leaping to my feet and applying for his client to pay my client's costs.

These farcical hearings were soon abandoned, but not all undefended cases were disposed of under the special procedure. When I started sitting as a part time county court judge in 1984, my first two cases were undefended divorces. They had to be heard in open court because the registrar had refused to certify that the basis for a divorce was made out. They were both founded on the allegation that the respondent had behaved in such a way that it was unreasonable for the petitioner to live with him. Clearly the registrar in that particular court expected petitioners to put up with much more than did registrars in other courts. I had no problem granting the decrees. But I might have had a problem in the one defended divorce which came my way as a Judge in the Family Division of the High Court. The wife's allegations were very like those made by Mrs Tini Owens some 20 years later. We sat through two days of evidence before her husband realised that defending the divorce was not going to save his marriage and conceded defeat. This was just before his counsel was due to cross-examine their daughter, who had given evidence in favour of her mother. I took a deep breath and persuaded myself that the allegations were enough to fulfill the behaviour complaint. The cruelty of doing otherwise was not to be borne.

This book traces the story of the background to the Act, how it came to be passed, how it has worked in practice, and how the case for replacing it has become unanswerable. It is full of fascinating insights and by-ways. It shows how important it was that the group convened by the Archbishop of Canterbury swiftly adopted the principle of irretrievable breakdown of marriage and equally swiftly agreed with the Law Commission to abandon their proposed 'inquest' into each marriage in favour of a list of five possible ways of showing breakdown. It shows how implementation of the Act was held up for two years because feminist campaigners like Edith Summerskill had pleaded the cause of the many dependent housewives who might now be divorced against their will by their errant 'Casanova' husbands.

An adventurous Matrimonial Property Bill was withdrawn so that the Law Commission could complete its proposals on financial remedies. These became the Matrimonial Proceedings and Property Act 1970, which came into force in 1971 alongside the 1969 Act, and greatly enhanced the courts' powers to protect the financially dependent spouse. Then as now there were two sorts of feminism – that which saw the route to equality through employment and equal pay and that which saw the need to compensate women for the dependent role which they had been obliged to embrace. It is possible, of course, to believe that both are necessary.

It shows how the allegations made in a divorce petition have always been a formula designed, not to tell the true story of how the marriage has broken down, but to fulfill whatever the law requires to ground a divorce – in the olden days and initially under the Act, particularised allegations of marital misconduct, especially in cruelty and then behaviour petitions, but now reduced to a few bullet points making generalised allegations, not listing incidents, on a form which encourages brevity. It shows how judicial scrutiny and its attendant moral judgment (always a problem and potentially exposing the judiciary to charges of hypocrisy) has been replaced by a bureaucratic exercise, checking whether the form has been properly filled in, and whether an acceptable case has been described, not whether it is true or even plausible. It shows how the fact relied on to prove that the marriage has irretrievably broken down is chosen, not to represent the real reason for the breakdown, but for practical reasons, such as the need to get a speedy divorce or the desire to avoid the name calling involved in relying on conduct rather than separation. In short, it makes an unanswerable case for the Divorce, Dissolution and Separation Act 2020, which will remove any reliance on conduct or on separation. The new scheme is remarkably similar to, but even more radical than, the scheme which the Law Commission of which I was a member recommended in 1990. Its time has come.

But there are many more riches in this book. There are insights into how divorce was portrayed in mid-20th century films, including of course, the most famous non-divorce film of all time, *Brief Encounter*. There are insights into how divorce has been portrayed in novels over the life-time of the Act, the focus shifting from the court room to the lawyers, not always to the latter's advantage, and from the one who wants the divorce to the one who doesn't. There are insights into how the media have reacted to those few divorce cases which do reach the public eye (intriguingly, two of the most famous involved a wife called Brenda). There are insights into divorce and royalty – from the constitutional significance of the marital history of Henry VIII, and of the desire of Edward VIII and Princess Margaret to marry divorced persons, to the normalisation of divorce (and remarriage) as an incident of typical family life even among the 'family on the throne'. No-fault divorce has been legitimised despite the Queen's earlier opposition. The emphasis now is on divorcing responsibly rather than not divorcing at all.

But there will still be challenges once the 2020 Act comes into force. There are families, in particular Muslim families, who conduct their marriages and divorces outside the framework of the secular law, to the disadvantage of many wives. There are same sex marriages and civil partnerships in which the patterns of relationship both before and after divorce may be rather different and suggest a different approach to dissolution from the hetero-normative. There is the human rights framework which has featured surprisingly little in the divorce debates to date but should do so: a rap on the knuckles for the Supreme Court here, which missed a trick in *Owens v Owens*, by not declaring the present law incompatible with the Convention rights. *Mea culpa* but judges usually only decide the cases which the parties argue before them, rather than introduce a completely new case which has not been argued. In any event, the case had the desired effect of reinforcing the need for the law to change. The new law reflects the aspirations of those who campaigned for earlier reforms and had to settle for the compromise reflected in the 1969 Act. But this book shows how a combination of procedural change, judicial attitudes, and public opinion has made that compromise redundant. I hope that it will be read by anyone who is interested in how attitudes to divorce and family life have changed over the life-time of the Act, and not just by the lawyers.

ACKNOWLEDGEMENTS

As editors we are indebted to all of our authors for their generous intellectual contributions. We also want to thank the Society of Legal Scholars for funding the workshop in 2018 from which this collection emerged and the School of Law at Birkbeck, University of London for hosting the event and further support. Finally, thanks to our editor at Bloomsbury, Sasha Jawed our copy-editor, Catherine Minahan and to their colleagues Tom Adams, Sinead Moloney, and Peter Warren for their assistance throughout the project.

CONTENTS

PART THREE
TELLING STORIES ABOUT DIVORCE AND MARRIAGE

PART FOUR
CONTEMPORARY PERSPECTIVES AND CHALLENGES

LIST OF CONTRIBUTORS

Rosemary **AUCHMUTY**, Professor of Law, University of Reading.

Samia **BANO**, Reader in Family Law and Law, Multiculturalism and Rights, School of Law, SOAS, University of London.

James **BROWN**, Research Fellow, Department of Politics, Birkbeck, University of London.

Carmen **DRAGHICI**, Reader in Law, The City Law School, City, University of London.

John **EEKELAAR**, Emeritus Fellow of Pembroke College, Oxford.

Lady **HALE**, Former President of the Supreme Court of the United Kingdom.

John **HASKEY**, Visiting Senior Research Fellow, Department of Social Policy and Intervention, University of Oxford.

Brian **HEAPHY**, Professor of Sociology, School of Social Sciences, University of Manchester.

James **HODGSON**, Research Associate, Department of Sociology, Morgan Centre, Manchester University.

Joanna **MILES**, Professor of Family Law and Policy, University of Cambridge.

Daniel **MONK**, Professor of Law, Birkbeck, University of London.

Rebecca **PROBERT**, Professor of Law, University of Exeter.

Rosie **SINCLAIR**, Senior Lecturer in Law, University of Chester.

Sharon **THOMPSON**, Reader in Law, Cardiff, University.

Liz **TRINDER**, Professor of Socio-Legal Studies, University of Exeter.

PART ONE

Introduction

1

'Irretrievably Broken'? Introducing the Life-Story of the Divorce Reform Act 1969

JOANNA MILES, DANIEL MONK AND REBECCA PROBERT

I. The 1969 Act: What It Did and Said, In Short

By any measure, the passage of the Divorce Reform Act 1969 was a landmark moment in family law. It had a significant impact on legal practice and saw a dramatic increase in divorce. It also had symbolic significance, reflecting changes in social attitudes. But the law's inherent tensions also exhibited prevailing contestations about public morality, conflicting ideals of citizenship and ambivalence about the reforms. And alongside and in keeping with the other key 'permissive' reforms of the era (in particular, the decriminalisation of abortion and 'homosexuality' in 1967), radical change went hand in hand with a degree of continuity.

The Act, codified quite soon after its enactment into Part I of the Matrimonial Causes Act 1973, enshrined the principle that a divorce could be granted if the marriage had 'broken down irretrievably'. Before the Act's passage, almost all divorces had been granted on one of three fault-based grounds: adultery, cruelty and desertion.[1] Of these, cruelty and desertion had only been available as grounds for divorce for a little over 30 years.[2] Previously, adultery had been the sole basis on which a husband could divorce his wife. Wives, perhaps unexpectedly, had had three additional grounds to choose from; however, as these were rape, sodomy and bestiality, this hardly put them in a privileged position.[3] Moreover, before 1923, a wife was not able to obtain a divorce on the basis of her husband's adultery without

[1] A fourth ground, 'incurable insanity' was little used in practice but, as discussed in Section III, significant as a matter of principle.

[2] As a result of the Matrimonial Causes Act 1937. On the passage of the 1937 Act, see Herbert (1937), Kahn-Freund (1937), Redmayne (1993), and see further in Section III.

[3] While rape, sodomy and bestiality are often described as factors that would, in addition to a husband's adultery, entitle a wife to a divorce, they were technically separate grounds (see Matrimonial Causes Act 1857, s 27) and as such survived the abolition of the need to establish an aggravating factor.

establishing an additional aggravating factor: incest, bigamy, cruelty or desertion.[4] And before 1858 there been no option of obtaining a divorce from a court at all: ending a valid marriage had required a private Act of Parliament.

Of course, the 1969 Act did not allow for divorce on the basis of breakdown alone, even where it was accepted by all, the court included, that the marriage had broken down irretrievably.[5] That would have been too big a step to take – tantamount to divorce by consent and on unilateral demand. Instead, breakdown had to be proved by one of five facts, which – perhaps surprisingly – did not need to be proved to have been a *cause* of the breakdown.[6]

Admittedly, three of those five facts bore more than a passing resemblance to the old grounds for divorce, although two were subtly modified to align with the new principle of breakdown. Adultery was no longer sufficient alone: it had to be intolerable for the petitioner to live with the respondent.[7] Cruelty became 'behaviour' – not, it should be emphasised, 'unreasonable behaviour' but the fact that the respondent had 'behaved in such a way that the petitioner cannot reasonably be expected to live with him'.[8] Desertion alone remained unmodified, but this hardly mattered given the two new 'separation' facts. It was expected that the need to establish desertion would fade away, since a separation for an equivalent period of time – two years – would suffice to establish breakdown if the respondent consented to the divorce. Both elements of this were radical innovations at the time. Separation had long been proposed as an alternative ground for divorce, but regularly rejected. Consent, meanwhile, was so diametrically opposed to the principle of the matrimonial offence that, until 1963, an agreement between the parties that both wanted a divorce might well be deemed collusion and thus absolutely bar a divorce and, post-1963, still justified a court in exercising its discretion to refuse a divorce.[9] Under the new law, absent the respondent's consent, the petitioner would have to show five years' separation to establish breakdown. So, it was anticipated that if a marriage had broken down, a divorce would be available, sooner or later, without the need to prove any particular conduct by the respondent. This was a big change.

II. This Collection: What It Aims to Do

The aim of this interdisciplinary collection is to explore the background to the 1969 Act, its impact on law and society, and changing perceptions and experiences

[4] Matrimonial Causes Act 1857, s 27: on the double standard in divorce, see Probert (1999a) and on its removal by the Matrimonial Causes Act 1923, see Probert (1999b), Russell (2019).

[5] *Buffery v Buffery* [1988] 2 FLR 365.

[6] *Stevens v Stevens* [1979] 1 WLR 885.

[7] Divorce Reform Act 1969, s 2(1)(a); see now Matrimonial Causes Act 1973, s 1(2)(a).

[8] Divorce Reform Act 1969, s 2(1)(b); see now Matrimonial Causes Act 1973, s 1(2)(b), and see further Miles, ch 8 of this volume.

[9] Matrimonial Causes Act 1963, s 4.

of divorce over the past 50 years. This book had originally been intended to mark, in 2019, the 50th year of the Divorce Reform Act 1969 – then (given the delay enforced by the global pandemic) of the 50th anniversary, in 2021, of its coming into force. Planning commenced in 2017, at which point longstanding calls for a new law were far from certain to succeed. But the enactment of the Divorce, Dissolution and Separation Act 2020, due to come into force in April 2022, turned what had been planned as an 'anniversary' into a 'funeral' (or, if you prefer, a wake!).

As these key life-stage metaphors suggest, reflecting on one statute – from its origins to its demise – can be thought of as a form of legal biography. The concept of a Biography of a Statute is a relatively new one, building on a broader movement away from thinking of biography as applying only to human subjects but as a frame for thinking about cities, artefacts and objects. Most recently, it has been applied as a conceptual method for exploring another key transformative statute from the late 1960s, the Abortion Act 1967.

In defending the adoption of a biographical approach to a statute, Sheldon et al identify three major implications:

> First, it foregrounds a basic socio-legal insight: that law is a living thing, which needs to be studied as it is interpreted and takes effect in practice, rather than merely as it exists on the statute books. Even where a statute's text remains unchanged, its acquisition of legal meaning is an ongoing process, which involves interpretative work; development and consolidation of received understandings; evolving practices; and moments of challenge, rupture, and revision. Such evolution in meaning inevitably both reflects and influences the shifting broader social and institutional contexts within which a law is read, understood and applied. Second, a statute – and particularly one characterised by considerable controversy – also acquires a broader social and symbolic meaning, which stands in no necessary relationship either to the intention of its drafters or to its doctrinal meaning, as developed by lawyers. The stories told about a law – and what that law represents in broader cultural terms – can and will evolve, whilst at times revealing roots which go deep into its history. Finally, the subject of a biography can offer a window through which to study aspects of the world evolving around it.[10]

In the case of divorce reform, those other aspects of the world implicated in divorce law's biography include Anglicanism, feminism, creative artists, politics and parliamentarians, the judiciary, the divorcing public (as a whole and sub-groups within it), the general public, those working in therapeutic professions and others. And so, in telling the life-story of the Divorce Reform Act 1969, we inevitably glimpse aspects of the life-stories of those other institutions, ideologies, groups and individual actors.

These implications or qualities of biography as a framework capture both individually and collectively the diverse perspectives and insights offered by the

[10] Sheldon et al (2019) 19–20.

authors of the contributions presented here. In its origins, applications and representations, and from the accounts of some of its advocates and fiercest critics (in 1969 and since), the Divorce Reform Act 1969 has always been a statute with many audiences, extending far beyond the individual couples whose marriages are ending. We hope in this book to give some sense of the richness of the Act's 'life', with a diverse range of contributions from scholars of history, sociology, film criticism and demography, as well as lawyers and from both established scholars – many of whom have been teaching the Act to students over many years – and younger scholars born decades after the Act itself came to life. That said, while this collection is far wider than an 'official' account or biography, we do not claim to offer a definitive or comprehensive biographical account, rather a collection of snapshots of particular moments, representations and reflections, many of which in turn reflect something of the biographies of the individuals involved. There are issues that we do not address, or touch on only briefly, that deserve more attention – notably, the de-legalisation of divorce over time, with the removal of legal aid, the promotion of mediation as a forum for resolving the (far more consequential) ancillary issues arising on divorce, and the experiences of different social groups/classes and of those who increasingly do not interact with any family justice system professional in securing their divorce and addressing its implications.[11] As with all rich lives, there is space for many biographies of the life of the 1969 Act. But we hope that readers will enjoy the diverse, thought-provoking perspectives offered in this collection, and that it will serve as a resource for scholars in the future who, inevitably, will bring new perspectives to bear on the past.

In the rest of this introductory chapter, we first apply Sheldon et al's prescription by digging into the deep legal historical roots of the 1969 reform, examining in more detail the fundamental shift from the 'matrimonial offence' to the breakdown principle. We then describe briefly aspects of the practical experience of the 1969 divorce law in action, in particular highlighting the critical and arguably even more transformative role of the so-called 'special procedure' that was introduced in the mid-1970s for the efficient, essentially administrative dispatch of uncontested divorces, and the growing dissatisfaction with the 1969 law's operation that culminated in the enactment of the new divorce legislation that is – to put it bluntly – scheduled to kill off the subject of this biography and begin a new statutory life-story. This basic book-work is intended to bring up to speed readers not familiar with the essential legal history of divorce law or who may want a refresher, and to set the scene for the chapters that follow. We then introduce the contributions to this collection and the inter-twined themes of biography and narrative (doctrinal, fictional, strategic), continuity and change, gender and religion that weave their way through the life-story of the 1969 Act.

[11] Maclean and Eekelaar (2016, 2019); Barlow et el (2017); Mant and Wallbank (2017).

III. The Big Theoretical Shift: From Offence to Breakdown

We begin with the legal history necessary to locate the 1969 Act in the longer trajectory of divorce law and theory in England and Wales.

In establishing the principle that a divorce could be granted if the marriage had 'broken down irretrievably', the 1969 Act finally abolished the idea that a divorce could only be obtained upon proof by the petitioning spouse that the respondent spouse had committed a 'matrimonial offence'. To appreciate the significance of this, we need to delve deep into history.

The concept of the 'matrimonial offence' had originated in the jurisprudence of the ecclesiastical courts – which, of course, did not recognise the concept of a divorce at all, at least not in the modern sense of a decree terminating a valid marriage. While elsewhere across Europe, the Protestant Reformation had marked the rejection of 'the sacramental and indissoluble nature of marriage',[12] in England and Wales marriage had remained indissoluble (notwithstanding the matrimonial antics of Henry VIII, whose three defunct marriages were in fact annulled not dissolved[13]), even if it was no longer regarded as a sacrament.

The ecclesiastical courts were able to grant divorces *a vinculo matrimonii*, but these were annulments and so required it to be shown that there was an impediment to the marriage that had prevented it from coming into being in the first place.[14] The ecclesiastical courts were also able to grant divorces *a mensa et thoro* – that is, from bed and board. These permitted the parties to live separately but not to remarry. Such permission to live apart was not granted lightly. The importance attached to spouses' living together is underlined by the sanctions and remedies available where they did not: the ecclesiastical courts could order those living separately to do penance and to reconcile, and an abandoned spouse could obtain an order for restitution of conjugal rights to compel the other's return.[15] Against this background, it was inevitable that the mere fact that the parties were deeply unhappy together and wished to live apart was insufficient to justify a separation: only if one of them was guilty of adultery or cruelty could an order be made.

In the light of the later history of divorce, it is important to note that the law of divorce *a mensa et thoro* applied to husbands and wives on equal terms.[16] This, of course, is not the same as saying that it was equally *available*, given other inequalities. Nor, indeed, was equal use made of it: few husbands petitioned on the basis

[12] Cornish et al (2019) 355. See also Witte (2012).
[13] See further Monk, ch 10 of this volume.
[14] Stone (1990).
[15] On the action for restitution of conjugal rights, see Douglas (2018). As Waddams (2000) notes, whether this was effective is unknown. On the attitude of the ecclesiastical courts to agreements for separation, see Parker (2015).
[16] Bailey (2003).

of cruelty. But the option was available to them. And the idea that adultery alone was a matrimonial offence applied equally to husbands and wives. There was no requirement for a wife to show anything other than her husband's adultery to justify an order's being made in her favour.[17]

Moreover, although it is often claimed that only 'life-threatening' cruelty would suffice,[18] this is a misleading contraction of Sir William Scott's exposition in *Evans v Evans*.[19] What Scott actually said was that it was necessary to establish that there was a 'danger to life, limb, or health', and that in assessing the threat there must be a 'reasonable apprehension of bodily hurt'.[20] That said, the judicial definition of what constituted cruelty was markedly more restrictive than individuals' own definitions.[21] An order could also be refused if there was evidence that the petitioner had condoned or connived at the respondent's adultery, if there had been collusion between the parties to invent facts or simply smooth the path to separation, or if the respondent established that the petitioner was also guilty of adultery.[22]

The one thing a decree *a mensa et thoro* could not do, of course, was to permit the parties to remarry. In the absence of any *court's* being able to declare that a valid marriage was at an end and permit the parties to remarry, the only (legal) option to achieve that objective was to petition Parliament to pass a private Act doing so. A precedent was set by the case of Lord Roos in 1670.[23] His concerns were primarily dynastic: faced with the prospect of his title's being inherited by a son who was in fact not his own but was presumed in law to be so by virtue of his marriage to the mother, he obtained a private Act of Parliament declaring his adulterous wife's children by another man to be illegitimate.[24] He then – more controversially – obtained a further private Act that would allow him to remarry. For present purposes, the significance of this lies not just in how this established that such a thing was possible, but also in how it was different from the approach of the ecclesiastical courts. It was not a matter of the adultery of Lord Roos' wife being regarded as a matrimonial offence, but rather its being the reason for his lack of legitimate heirs.[25]

[17] In practice, a number did petition on the basis of both adultery and cruelty, but this is a reflection of their marriages, not the requirements of the law.

[18] Stone (1990) 192.

[19] (1790) 1 Hag Con 35; 161 ER 466, 467.

[20] ibid 468.

[21] For a nuanced assessment of what was regarded as cruelty in the 18th century, see Bailey and Giese (2013).

[22] This latter defence was known as 'recrimination'.

[23] Probert (2011). There are earlier contenders to be considered the first divorce – on which see Stone (1990) – but these are associated with the uncertainty engendered by the Reformation as to whether remarriage was possible.

[24] An Act for the illegitimation of the Children of the Lady Anne Roos, Parliamentary Archives, HL/PO/PB/1/1666/18&19C2n21.

[25] On the dynastic dimension of the divorces that followed in the late-17th and early-18th centuries, see Wolfram (1985), Bearman (2010), Probert (2011).

Inevitably, one precedent led to another. Over time, the significance of adultery shifted from its implications for succession to the relationship of the parties,[26] the process for obtaining a divorce became standardised,[27] and issues of connivance and collusion were taken into account in deciding whether an Act should be passed in any given case, just as they were in the ecclesiastical courts.[28] The case of Jane Campbell Addison – whose husband had run off with her sister – also established that it was possible for a divorce to be granted to a wife.[29] Given that her sister's husband had already been granted a parliamentary divorce, it would have been difficult to have refused her petition. However, like the Roos case before it, it was a precedent that brought its own constraints. Incestuous adultery being relatively rare, it was another 39 years before another wife, a Mrs Battersby, managed to convince Parliament that her husband's combination of adultery and bigamy warranted a divorce.[30]

This underlines the significance of the fact that the process of granting a parliamentary divorce had originated in dynastic concerns and developed incrementally, rather than being based on the ecclesiastical concept of the matrimonial offence. The ecclesiastical courts, as noted above, had treated adultery as being equally and sufficiently serious whether it was committed by the husband or the wife. In moral terms, this was clearly true. Equally clearly, when viewed from the perspective of succession to property and titles, male adultery was of far less significance.

The second key difference between the concept of the matrimonial offence as applied in the ecclesiastical courts and the divorces granted by Act of Parliament was that the latter were solely focused on adultery. There was never any question of one being granted on the basis of cruelty.

By the mid-nineteenth century, there was increasing criticism of the fact that the right to remarry was available only to those who could afford to pay for the cost of obtaining a private Act of Parliament.[31] At the same time, the idea that a marriage, validly entered into, could be ended other than by death still remained unthinkable for many. And many of those who accepted the possibility of divorce drew on scriptural authority to argue that it should only be available in cases of adultery.

The pragmatic solution was to present the proposed reform as one of procedure rather than principle. Under the Matrimonial Causes Act 1857, divorce would be available from a civil court, but only on the same grounds on which parliamentary divorces had been granted, not on the wider grounds on which a

[26] Trumbach (1978), Stone (1990), Shaffer (2014).

[27] The person seeking a divorce by private Act of Parliament had to have obtained a divorce *a mensa et thoro* in the ecclesiastical courts and damages for criminal conversation in the Court of Kings Bench. On the latter, see Staves (1982), Stone (1990).

[28] Anderson (1984); Probert, Bailey and Shaffer (2013).

[29] See Wright (2004).

[30] Wolfram (1985).

[31] The cost of obtaining a divorce by private Act of Parliament has been much debated in the literature – see eg Anderson (1984), Wolfram (1985), James (2012).

divorce *a mensa et thoro* had been available. The latter remedy was to remain available, but rebranded judicial separation and removed from the jurisdiction of the ecclesiastical courts.[32] At the same time, however, the principles upon which the ecclesiastical courts had acted were to remain relevant, with the 1857 Act directing the new court to give relief on the basis of principles that were as 'nearly as may be' those previously applied by the ecclesiastical courts.[33] Collusion, connivance and condonation were all absolute bars to a divorce, and the fact that the petitioner had also committed adultery a discretionary one.

Since our focus here is on the concept of the matrimonial offence, this is not the place for a detailed analysis of the passage, operation and impact of the Matrimonial Causes Act 1857.[34] Suffice it to say that the number of divorces increased, as one would expect. Whereas prior to 1858 the number of divorces *a mensa et thoro* had outnumbered parliamentary divorces by five to one, divorces outnumbered separations from the outset under the 1857 Act and the gap widened steadily.[35]

Attempts to move away from the concept of the matrimonial offence proved difficult. A divorce reform Bill was put forward in 1902 by Earl Russell, who was himself embroiled in a long-running and scandalous matrimonial dispute with his first wife, in the course of which – in 1901 – he was imprisoned for bigamy.[36] The Bill proposed that divorce should be available to either a husband or a wife on the grounds of cruelty, a sentence of penal servitude of more than three years, lunacy, living apart for three years or separation for one year plus the consent of the other party. It was rejected without debate, the Lord Chancellor stating that the idea of divorce after a period of separation was an insult to the House of Lords.[37] What is clear from this failed attempt at reform is how deeply rooted was the idea of divorce as punishment for a guilty act, and this explains the long-standing stigma attached to divorce: it was always intended to be so.

Judges, however, exasperated by the 'inconsistencies, anomalies and inequalities amounting almost to absurdities' of the law,[38] added their weight to calls for reform. In 1909, a Royal Commission was set up to consider the possibility of such reform, under the chairmanship of Gorell Barnes, the President of the Family

[32] In addition, desertion for two years was added as a ground for judicial separation.

[33] Matrimonial Causes Act 1857, s 22.

[34] The literature on all of these aspects is vast. On the passage of the Act, see Woodhouse (1959), Stetson (1982), Shanley (1982), Wolfram (1985), Stone (1990), Kha and Swain (2016), Cornish et al (2019). On its operation and impact see Savage (1992, 2011), Probert (1999a), Wright (2004).

[35] Stone (1990).

[36] See Sumner Holmes (1999). Russell was not insensitive to the view that might be taken of his introducing such Bill, remarking that 'Your Lordships no doubt recollect among the fables of your youth the fable of a fox without a tail, and I have felt until the present moment that if I were to introduce any Bill dealing with the subject of divorce I should be exposed to misconstruction, and my attempt to alter the law would be regarded as not entirely disinterested. That objection no longer applies, and I am therefore emboldened to present this Bill for your Lordships' consideration.' *Hansard*, HL Deb 1 May 1902, vol 107, col 389.

[37] *Hansard*, HL Deb 1 May 1902, vol 107, col 408.

[38] *Dodd v Dodd* [1906] P 189.

Division. Its report, published in 1912, was based on rigorous research and extensive evidence. All 12 of its members agreed that the grounds for divorce should be equalised. Nine also recommended that the grounds should be extended to include cruelty, desertion, insanity, habitual drunkenness or imprisonment under a commuted death sentence. The debate had narrowed somewhat since 1857: when the desirability of enacting the recommendations of the majority was debated, no one actually argued that divorce should not be allowed at all. Nonetheless, 11 years were to elapse before the Matrimonial Causes Act 1923 allowed wives to petition for divorce on the ground of adultery alone,[39] and a further 14 years before the Matrimonial Causes Act 1937 extended the grounds for divorce to include the majority of those suggested by the 1912 Commission.

The 1937 Act allowed many marriages that had long ceased to exist as a matter of fact to be legally terminated. In 1938 and 1939, over half of all divorces were granted on the new grounds of desertion or cruelty,[40] and the *de jure* duration of the marriages that were being dissolved was considerably longer than had been the case in 1937.[41] But the modest increase in the number of divorces that followed its passage was to be dwarfed by the still greater increase that followed the Second World War. For some, this increase was seen as demonstrating the need for reform, emphasising that marriage was a solemn undertaking and divorce a correspondingly serious act that needed to be hedged around with due dignity.[42] The need to reconcile dignity with efficiency – and the fact that there were simply not enough High Court judges (to whom the jurisdiction was reserved) to deal with the number of divorces that flowed through the courts, notionally as 'trials', though commonly undefended – led, as so often, to a compromise.[43] From 1 January 1947, county court judges were renamed Special Commissioners of Assize for the purpose of granting divorces and allowed to wear different robes for the day – until, as Stephen Cretney put it, 'like Cinderella, they returned to reality as the clock struck midnight'.[44] (This charade was ended when the Matrimonial Causes Act 1967 granted jurisdiction to the county courts to deal with undefended divorces.) For others, however, the increase undermined the link between fault and divorce, since it was clear that 'many marriages had been subject to great strain without any real culpability on the part of the spouses'.[45]

With the introduction of legal aid removing the remaining financial barriers to obtaining a divorce,[46] for the first time the occupational status of divorcing

[39] For the reasons for this delay, see Probert (1999b).

[40] Rowntree and Carrier (1958).

[41] Phillips (1988).

[42] See eg the Report of a Committee of Inquiry on Procedure in Matrimonial Causes (1947) Cmnd 6945.

[43] Cretney (2003); Bradley (1976).

[44] Cretney (2003) 284.

[45] Chester (1977).

[46] Legal Aid and Advice Act 1949. Of course, this only dealt with the cost of obtaining the divorce itself, not the wider costs of ending the marriage. On these costs for women in particular see further Auchmuty, ch 4 of this volume and Thompson, ch 6 of this volume.

couples reflected that of society in general.[47] Yet resistance remained to widening the grounds for divorce. A Bill proposing a new ground of seven years' separation met with opposition from both the Church of England and the Mothers' Union. It passed its Second Reading but was withdrawn upon the promise that a new Royal Commission would be established to review the law.[48]

By the late 1960s, however, the principle that a divorce should be allowed only where a matrimonial offence had been committed – and the dichotomy between the 'innocent' petitioner and the 'guilty' respondent that such a principle assumed – had already been undermined by a number of developments.

First, there was in fact already one no-fault-based ground. The Matrimonial Causes Act 1937 had allowed divorce on the basis of the incurable insanity of the respondent. While negligible as a ground in terms of the number invoking it, it was nonetheless highly significant in signalling that Parliament had accepted the principle that there were grounds that justified ending a marriage even where neither party was at fault.

Second, the 'innocence' of the petitioner was becoming ever less relevant. The courts had become increasingly willing to exercise their discretion in favour of petitioners who had committed a matrimonial offence,[49] and increasingly reluctant to find that there had been collusion between the parties.[50] In 1963, a new Act made collusion merely a discretionary bar to divorce, rather than an absolute one.[51]

Third, the guilt of the respondent was also becoming less relevant. In some cases, it was barely tested at all: the trial process for undefended divorces was described as working on a 'slot machine principle'.[52] Even where guilt was relevant and required proper proof, the increasingly expansive interpretation of what constituted 'cruelty' meant that 'guilty' no longer seemed an appropriate adjective for many respondents. Despite repeated assertions that divorce should not be allowed for mere incompatibility, divorce was allowed for an increasingly wide range of behaviour, including nagging[53] and sulking.[54] Considerable ingenuity was exercised in modifying the requirement that the relevant conduct had been 'aimed at' the other spouse,[55] and the requirement itself was finally rejected by the House of Lords in *Gollins v Gollins*.[56] Indeed, much of the post-war general public supported divorce based on mere incompatibility. Public opinion data gathered in 1949 as part of the 'Little Kinsey' study, conducted as an adjunct to the Mass

[47] Rowntree and Carrier (1958).
[48] *Hansard*, HC Deb 9 March 1951, vol 485, col 926; Royal Commission (1956).
[49] See eg *Bull v Bull* [1965] 2 WLR 1048.
[50] See eg *Gorst v Gorst* [1952] P 94.
[51] Matrimonial Causes Act 1963, s 4; see further Auchmuty, ch 4 of this volume.
[52] Harvey (1953).
[53] See eg *Atkins v Atkins* [1942] 2 All ER 637; *Usmar v Usmar* [1949] P 1.
[54] See eg *Lauder v Lauder* [1949] P 227.
[55] See eg *Squire v Squire* [1949] P 51; *Kaslefsky v Kaslefsky* [1951] P 38.
[56] [1964] AC 644.

Observation Survey (MOS), found that 57 per cent of the representative 'street sample'[57] 'more or less approve of divorce' essentially just on grounds of incompatibility. The researchers remarked

> It seems likely that many people are unaware that this principle of divorce on grounds of simple incompatibility, which so many of them recommend, is not recognised by the law; if they did realise this their feelings might be stronger.[58]

Against this background, it was logical for reformers to try to think about divorce in a different way. And by the mid-1960s a shift had occurred not only in wider public opinion, but also crucially within parts of the establishment that had fiercely resisted reform throughout the post-war period – most clearly in the conclusions of the promised Royal Commission (the Morton Commission).[59] For example, arch-conservative Geoffrey Fisher, Archbishop of Canterbury from 1945, was succeeded in 1961 by a younger and notably more forgiving Michael Ramsay. In 1966, Ramsay set up a group to consider the grounds for divorce. This in due course published *Putting Asunder*, which recommended the replacement of the doctrine of the matrimonial offence by the breakdown principle.[60] The matter was taken up by the newly created Law Commission, which agreed that marriages that had irretrievably broken down should be terminated 'with the maximum fairness and the minimum bitterness, distress and humiliation'.[61] However, they considered the suggestion in *Putting Asunder* that breakdown should be ascertained by judicial inquest to be impracticable. The alternative of adding grounds to permit divorce by consent or separation proving unpalatable, a compromise was worked out whereby breakdown would have to be proved by one of five facts.

The breakdown principle was widely approved. The Mothers' Union, so firm in their resistance to earlier proposals for reform, did not oppose it. A poll by the *Sunday Times* showed that 72 per cent of those it had interviewed were in favour. The press coverage was mostly favourable: even the *Daily Mail* – reporting recent national opinion polling under the headline 'Not far enough … That's your verdict on the Divorce Bill' – wrote that 'It's not often that a Bill to alter the law so accurately reflects a change in public opinion as yesterday's Divorce Reform Bill.'[62] The Government lent its support by allowing parliamentary time,[63] always the most significant obstacle to a Private Member's Bill, to finish the deliberations. The Divorce Reform Act duly passed into law on 22 October 1969 and came into force on 1 January 1971.

[57] As distinct from MOS participants, who were generally more progressive than the average person: Stanley (1995) 123.

[58] ibid ch 6 and 131.

[59] Royal Commission (1956).

[60] *Putting Asunder: A Divorce Law for Contemporary Society* (London, SPCK, 1966). See further Sinclair, ch 5 of this volume.

[61] Law Commission (1966) para 15.

[62] *Daily Mail* (16 January 1968) 6.

[63] The first iteration of the Bill, promoted by William Wilson MP in 1967, was given no time in the Lords; the second, successful attempt – with an identical Bill – was promoted by Alec Jones MP in 1968/69. See Lee (1974) generally on the parliamentary history of the Bill.

IV. The New Procedure: From Public to Private

The new divorce law was one primarily to be administered at county court level. A study into the operation of the divorce process in three county courts in 1973 found that they acted with dispatch, with 85 per cent of cases taking less than 10 minutes. The parties who were interviewed clearly neither wanted to be there nor felt that the details of the divorce should be public: they acknowledged that they were nervous at having to appear in court and felt that they should not be listening to the details of other people's divorces.[64]

In 1973, the new 'special procedure' allowed a divorce to be granted purely on the basis of documentary application and evidence, without either of the parties needing to attend court.[65] Initially limited to those petitions based on the fact of two years' separation and the respondent's consent, and within that group restricted to childless couples, from April 1977 it was extended to all undefended divorces. In practice, this meant that it applied to about 99 per cent of all divorces.[66] As Stephen Cretney argued, this procedural change was perhaps more significant than the reform of the substantive law itself.[67]

As had been the case with earlier reforms, these administrative changes were necessary to deal with the increase in the number of petitions for divorce; notably, legal aid for undefended divorces was removed at the same time.[68] But, arguably, they also reflected the spirit of the 1969 Act in according privacy to divorcing couples.[69] After all, if blame was no longer part of divorce law then public shame was equally inappropriate. This contrasted starkly with the Victorian and early-twentieth-century ethos that the publicity attendant on divorce under a doctrine of matrimonial offences performed important educative and deterrent functions protecting the (public) institution of marriage.[70] Divorce's affective history of 'stigma' and 'shame', while distinct and more complex, was evolving alongside the law.

However, whilst doubtless the privacy of the special procedure was welcomed by most couples, it did pose something of a problem for anyone seeking to analyse the operation of the law. With few cases appearing in the law reports, there was little to bridge the gap between large-scale empirical studies and media reports of the very few defended cases that did come to court. Michael Freeman presciently predicted that 'we will have a text-book account of the rules which will gradually lag further and further behind the law in action'.[71]

[64] Elston, Fuller and Murch (1975).
[65] See further Trinder, ch 9 of this volume.
[66] Westcott (1981).
[67] Cretney (2003), 165.
[68] The policy change was announced by the Lord Chancellor in *Hansard*, HL Deb 15 June 1976, vol 371, cols 1210–46, discussed by Freeman (1976).
[69] Davis and Murch (1977).
[70] See Savage (1998).
[71] Freeman (1976) 258.

V. Critical Evaluation from the 1980s to the 2010s: Irretrievably Broken

Fifty years on, however, there was a clear consensus that the 1969 Act was itself irretrievably broken. From the late 1980s, important research[72] and intensive law reform activity[73] had already very nearly led to fundamental reform via the Family Law Act 1996. This would have introduced a no-fault, no-fact, notification + 'period of reflection and consideration' divorce regime. But that Act was never brought into force for complex reasons unrelated to the adoption of the basic no-fault policy.[74] While calls for reform never eased up, the issue came firmly back on the agenda in the 2010s, when a major new research study led by Liz Trinder – echoing and amplifying findings of the earlier research in the 1980s – demonstrated the ease with which the facts could be established where the divorce was undefended (making the practical experience of the law not far off divorce by mutual consent, under cover of whichever fact was relied on), the confusion created by the law's not requiring any causal or other relationship between the fact established and the breakdown of the marriage, and the pragmatic orientation of the law's practical operation, focused on streamlining the process, reducing costs and minimising harm.[75] It was also shown – again, not for the first time – that the need to establish facts could create unnecessary conflict between the parties, as well as a sense of unfairness where the respondent had no realistic means of disproving the allegations made.[76] As Liz Trinder and Mark Sefton concluded in their analysis of the few attempts to defend divorce, the system in place already 'amounts to unilateral divorce on demand, but concealed within an expensive and potentially harmful fault-based law'.[77] All this simply undermined the 'objectives of a good divorce law' that the Law Commission had identified back in 1966 and that had (supposedly) informed the design of the 1969 Act.[78]

At the same time, the saga of Tini Owens' attempt to free herself from her marriage illustrated starkly to the general public the emptiness of the law's breakdown principle: that a petitioner who was unable to establish one of the five facts would be unable to obtain a divorce even if the marriage had broken down.[79] Mrs Owens, who had herself earlier had an affair, sought to divorce her husband of 40 years on the basis of the 'behaviour' fact. Her initial petition contained 'appropriately anodyne'[80] allegations, typical of the mild behaviour allegations that

[72] Davis and Murch (1988).
[73] Law Commission (1988), (1990); Lord Chancellor's Department (1993), (1995).
[74] For discussion, see Miles, George and Harris-Short (2015) 190–95.
[75] Trinder et al (2017).
[76] Trinder and Sefton (2018).
[77] ibid 82.
[78] Law Commission (1966) para 15.
[79] As was clear as a matter of law: *Buffery v Buffery* [1988] 2 FLR 365.
[80] *Owens v Owens* [2018] UKSC 41 [10], Lord Wilson giving the lead judgment.

any family lawyer would expect to pass through the system without difficulty.[81] Ahead of the one-day trial, Mrs Owens reinforced her petition with more detailed particulars of 27 specific allegations of what was characterised as moody, argumentative, disparaging conduct,[82] four of which (elected by the wife) were explored at trial.[83] To near-universal surprise, the petition was not only defended but successfully so, the trial judge being unpersuaded that Mr Owens' behaviour was such that Mrs Owens could not reasonably be expected to live with him (notwithstanding the fact that she was not doing so and clearly had no intention of returning). She would have to wait for five years of separation to clock up. The well-established interpretation of the Act that had underpinned the trial judge's verdict, was – albeit with some serious misgivings[84] – upheld by the Court of Appeal and Supreme Court, both of which more or less quietly noted the growing calls for reform.[85]

Mr Owens was that rare combination: a spouse who had both the desire and the emotional and financial resources to defend the divorce all the way to the bitter end. But the press had little time for this staunch defence of the institution of marriage, never mind of the individual marriage, coming out strongly in favour of Mrs Owens, whose plight elicited sympathy – even in the pages of the *Daily Mail*.[86] While Jan Moir's column deplored calls for no-fault divorce reform, concluding that '[The fate of Mrs Owens] is awful, but it is also right. In a throwaway society, some things must remain sacred',[87] the *Mail Online* carried a strong condemnation of the law by divorce solicitors, headlined 'Divorce laws are an "abomination" and "like slavery", says top lawyer'.[88]

The general, if not universally-held view,[89] supported by robust research data, was that the 1969 divorce law was itself irretrievably broken.

[81] See Trinder, ch 9 of this volume, on the 'habitual narratives' constructed for such petitions.

[82] [2018] UKSC 41 [18].

[83] ibid [19].

[84] In particular, from Lady Hale ([2018] UKSC 41 [50]), who was concerned that the presentation of the case at trial precluded a proper analysis of the cumulative impact of the alleged behaviours, and Hallett LJ in the Court of Appeal ([2017] EWCA Civ 1912 [99]), who described her judgment as being made 'with no enthusiasm whatsoever'.

[85] In the Court of Appeal, Munby P ([2017] EWCA Civ 182 [98]) and in the Supreme Court, Lord Wilson ([2018] UKSC 41 [45]).

[86] In the preceding three decades, the *Daily Mail* had been very vocal in its opposition to other attempted law reforms that, in its eyes, risked undermining the institution of marriage.

[87] *Daily Mail* (27 July 2018), 'Divorce should not be as easy as ending a gym membership'.

[88] See at www.dailymail.co.uk/news/article-5990015/Unhappily-married-woman-loses-Supreme-Court-fight-divorce.html.

[89] The numerical weight of opinion in response to the Ministry of Justice consultation opposed reform, thanks to a 'surge of late responses' right at the end of the consultation period, apparently prompted by religious groups encouraging supporters to send standard-form objections. In response, see Ministry of Justice (2019) 19, 'While we acknowledge views on the religious aspect of marriage vows, these are matters of conscience for the individuals in the marriage and are not matters that concern the legal requirements for divorce. Opposition to reform by Christian groups must be seen alongside the views of respondents more generally, who were broadly supportive of our proposals to reduce conflict.'

The combination of the Trinder research, the *Owens* decision and its reception, and a Private Member's Bill promoted by Baroness Butler-Sloss, a previous President of the Family Division,[90] created an irresistible impetus for reform, to which the Government very quickly acceded.[91] The resulting passage of the Divorce, Dissolution and Separation Act 2020 signals the end of the compromise that was struck in 1969 and the beginning of a new chapter in the history of divorce law. Whilst the nominal ground for divorce will remain the irretrievable breakdown of marriage, this will be proved not by reference to any 'facts' regarding the parties' relationship, but simply by one or both parties' stating that the marriage has broken down irretrievably. That statement will be taken as conclusive evidence – against which no defence can be mounted – on which divorce must be granted should one or both parties confirm, no less than 20 weeks later, that they wish the application to proceed, the final order being made no less than six months after the initial application. 'Irretrievable breakdown', yes – but not as we have known it for the last 50 years.

VI. The Themes and Narratives of this Collection

Having sketched the longer history and future of divorce law in England and Wales within which the 1969 Act sits, we now introduce the reflections on the Act's life-story – and the lives of some of those entangled with it – offered by contributors to this collection.

The remainder of this introductory Part of the collection includes a chapter from John Haskey, the pre-eminent statistician and demographer of the field, who has been analysing the use of the Act for many decades. In 'Divorces by Fact Proven Over the Past Half Century in England and Wales: The Historical Context, Statistical Trends and Future Prospects', Haskey charts the shifting fortunes of the Act's five 'facts'. There are dangers of reading too much into the use of the facts – whether as evidence of the reality of the causes of marital breakdowns or of the parties' own possible narratives.[92] But there are nevertheless good reasons to examine the choice of the facts relied on as legal evidence to support the ground of irretrievable breakdown. First, it shows various empirical predictions about the impact of the Act to have been wrong, and arguably thereby unmasks the ideological views of those who made such predictions. Longstanding trends challenge the idea that the Act can be held responsible for increasing rates of divorce. And the often-marked differences in applications by husbands and wives to a certain extent help to complicate reductive readings about the Act's gendered impact. The overall

[90] Divorce (etc) Law Review Bill [HL] 2017–19.
[91] Ministry of Justice (2018).
[92] See further Trinder, ch 9 of this volume.

picture is a messier one: a 'Casanova's charter'[93] possibly for some husbands, but more a tool of liberation for many women.

Three points stand out from the analysis, and these re-emerge as constant themes throughout the collection. First, Casanova's charter fears aside, the centrality of gender as a frame of reference for evaluating the Act is clear from the very real differences between the choices of fact by husbands and wives. As Haskey demonstrates, social class is also an important factor, albeit less explored. Second, despite the Act's introduction of no-fault separation facts, both adultery and 'behaviour' – perhaps surprisingly, and not predicted – have remained remarkably popular and resilient, their popularity doubtless boosted by the ease and speed of the special procedure for undefended cases. Third, while the *law* has remained unchanged, Haskey's analysis demonstrates fluctuating and shifting *uses* of the five facts, an indication of changing values and attitudes over time. Looking forward to a world under the 2020 Act, Haskey helpfully provides suggestions for what to look out for and how to read new practices, as compared with those under the 1969 Act.

In Part Two of the collection – entitled '*Background*', borrowed from one of the films discussed in its first chapter – four commentators revisit the period before the enactment of the 1969 Act. In exploring the contexts that gave rise to the demand for reform and some of the spirited resistance to it, this Part's long view underscores the necessity of viewing the Act as a reform that, while enacted in the 'permissive' late 1960s, had its roots in preceding generations. In doing so, it complements and digs deeper into Haskey's helpful reminder that the rate of divorce was increasing rapidly *before* the Act. The contributors to this Part are not seeking to replay past struggles but to identify both continuities and change in the shape of debates about divorce over the time, whilst also examining some of the personalities involved in public and parliamentary discourse on divorce.

Stories have always played a key role in highlighting the need for divorce reform. In 1854, Charles Dickens' *Hard Times* depicted the plight of factory worker Stephen Blackpool, married to an alcoholic wife who has deserted him but who returns at intervals to pawn his scanty furniture, and pleading for advice on how he might free himself and marry again. In the 1930s, Evelyn Waugh and AP Herbert satirised the so-called 'hotel divorces' that involved a gentleman in supplying the necessary 'evidence' of adultery by being found in a hotel bedroom with a woman other than his wife.[94]

Picking up that fictional baton but exploring a different creative genre, James Brown, film and social theorist, opens this Part with 'Dynamic Impasse: Divorce and British Film in the Mid-Twentieth Century'. Demonstrating clearly how, like

[93] See further Thompson, ch 6 of this volume; and Thompson (2021) on Edith Summerskill MP's deployment of this concept.

[94] Or at least, a woman who was not recognisable as his wife. The solicitor in Waugh's *A Handful of Dust* (1935) reported a 'particularly delicate case involving a man of very rigid morality and a certain diffidence. In the end his own wife consented to go with him and supply the evidence. She wore a red wig. It was quite successful.'

law, films at once reflect and are part of society, his reading of films from the mid-1930s to the mid-1950s strikingly reveals how unresolved and ambivalent debates were at these times, and how key this earlier period is to understanding the tension and contradictions that informed the 1969 Act. Progressive reforms may appear inevitable with hindsight – but the reality may have been rather more complex. In contrast to political debates explored by other contributors here, the films present a far less didactic, more complex and open-ended view, even when on the surface appearing aligned to pro- or anti-reform agendas.

For example, the first film examined, *One More River* (1934), on one level a plea for legal reform and an indictment of prevailing double-standards, also speaks to the problematic intertwining of legal narratives (in particular here law's preoccupation with sex) with individuals' own narratives. The analysis of later films also shows how the double-standards for husbands and wives continued, long after the achievement of formal legal equality in divorce law. Films made during and shortly after the Second World War often served to represent marital breakdown and divorce as symptoms of difficult times. But while films rarely made explicit demands for reform, the psychological cost of 'respectability' is there to see. Brown's reading of *Brief Encounter* (1945) demonstrates clearly how filmmakers often make space for – indeed require – the viewer to reach a judgement about the morality of the parties' actions or desires.

In films of the 1950s, *No Place for Jennifer* (1950) and *Background* (1953), the focus turns to the effect of divorce on children. Here again, ambiguity seeps through, despite the message that modern understandings of welfare uncompromisingly cohere with traditional marital values and a 'duty first' approach that reflects the findings of the Morton Commission of that time.[95] It is not always easy to see how the couples portrayed can reconcile, and the new emphasis on parental responsibility (and guilt) – as opposed to spousal duty – intentionally or not opens the door to alternative possibilities. Moreover, Brown reminds us that the sometimes complicated personal lives of the people behind the films, the writers, directors and actors, were themselves testament to the reshaping of possibilities.[96]

Gender is a key frame of reference in the films explored by Brown, both regarding double-standards in love and sexual relations and regarding psychological welfare. The gender theme continues in the next chapter by Rosemary Auchmuty, feminist legal scholar and longstanding critical commentator on the institution of marriage, but moves from passion and propriety to property. Foregrounding the harsh economic realities and inequalities of divorce, in 'Feminism, Property and Divorce Law Reform in the 1960s', Auchmuty examines the ambivalence of feminist engagements with divorce reform in the period from the 1950s up to the 1969

[95] Royal Commission (1956).

[96] And so those actors and others were linked to the legal profession: for example, Sir Robin Dunn, who features significantly as a judge in the examination of the behaviour fact by Miles, ch 8 of this volume, had – as a barrister – represented Vivien Leigh in her divorce from Laurence Olivier.

Act, asking 'Was easier divorce *really* positive for women? Was it something that feminists actively sought, supported or welcomed, or was it positive only because it provided a catalyst for efforts to dismantle women's dependence?' In asking, as well as in attempting to answer, these key questions, she identifies the importance of longstanding tensions and ambivalences within feminist thinking and, crucially, the uses of strategic activism between those who focused on challenging women's dependence *on marriage* and those who sought to provide women with protection for the consequences of their dependency *in marriage*. Auchmuty juxtaposes these concerns with examples of far-from-feminist male supporters of divorce. Bringing economics into play troubles individualistic liberal accounts. Change and continuity are evident here, as the conflicts Auchmuty explores in this period to a certain extent reflect current debates about financial remedies on divorce, prenuptial agreements and cohabitation reform.[97] As well as detailing the oft-overlooked statutory reform initiatives regarding matrimonial property attempted prior to the 1969 Act, Auchmuty's account also brings into the frame the contributions of women from those earlier periods who have also been overlooked: Eirene White, Joan Vickers, Edith Summerskill, Hannah Gavron, Marghanita Laski, Eleanor Rathbone, Joan Lester, Lena Jeger – lives all deserving of far more attention.

Continuing the run-up to the 1969 debates, the next chapter brings into play another key recurrent concern in this arena: religion, which, like feminism, might be invoked both against and in favour of reform. Family law scholar Rosie Sinclair, in '*Putting Asunder* – Reappraised', examines the influence of the Church of England through a detailed examination of the role of the Archbishop's Group of church leaders that brought about a profound and hugely significant shift in the approach of the Church of England that in turn had a significant enabling and practical impact on the 1969 Act. Just as Auchmuty's analysis of feminist opposition to reform challenges uncomplicated assumptions about the progressive nature of reform, so Sinclair challenges equally simplistic assumptions that the Act can be explained solely as a manifestation of 'secularisation' and throws light on the resilience of fault in legal, as well as individual and social narratives.

The significance of *Putting Asunder* has long been appreciated. But Sinclair's detailed analysis of the individual participants in the Group makes clear that the report reflected more than a broad establishment perspective but a particularly Anglican one; that the tensions and compromises reflected not simply a balancing act between church traditions and demands of a more permissive age but deep-seated tensions *within* the Church of England between evangelicals and traditional moralists who grappled with 'duty' as a foundation of marriage. Sinclair's exploration then enriches the analysis by encompassing the contributions of Christian parliamentarians in the debates on the Divorce Reform Bill. Viewed from the Anglican perspective, unsullied by a negotiated compromise with external pressures and realities, Sinclair concludes that the authors of *Putting Asunder* would be

[97] On the former, see Heenan (2020), Miles and Hitchings (2018), Eekelaar (2018).

dismayed about the 2020 reforms and new law. Again, the idea of tension within the Church on social issues is not new: the ambivalences and conflicts portrayed here mirror and provide a helpful long view on contemporary debates about issues such same-sex marriage, marriage formalities, gender equality and trans rights.

Sinclair and Auchmuty both highlight the role played by individual participants in the reform debates, and in the next chapter one particular woman, encountered briefly in Auchmuty's contribution, takes centre stage. In 'Behind Casanova's Charter: Edith Summerskill, Divorce and the Deserted Wife', legal academic Sharon Thompson analyses the impact of feminist opponent of divorce reform, Edith Summerskill. Identified at the time as one of the leading opponents of the Act, Summerskill – who famously coined the expression 'a Casanova's Charter' to describe the Act – has been portrayed in later accounts as puritanical, anti-divorce and old-fashioned. Thompson's account, based on new archival research and interviews, challenges these readings, demonstrating not only how Summerskill gave a voice to deserted wives by fighting for their financial protection, but also that her arguments were premised on a decidedly modern view of marriage, within which women were to be treated as fully equal partners. Placed in the broader context of the development of financial remedy law, her views, far from being old-fashioned, were before their time and had important implications for all wives, not just those perceived (by themselves or others) as 'deserted'.

The contributions to this first section of the collection set the scene for thinking about the application of the 1969 Act. The Act from its genesis not only effected important changes in the law, but was also a symbolic text that provoked and had projected onto it a myriad of investments, meanings, desires, expectations, fears and hopes – not all of which would be met. It was the product of a melée of (troubling?) progressive narratives, complex feminist and Christian responses, and a rich cast of individual participants.

The contributors to Part Three – 'Telling Stories about Divorce and Marriage' – explore the diverse forms of legal consciousness in the narratives required by the Act, and how they interacted with, reflected and reinforced shifting ideas of divorce more widely.

Like Part Two, this Part begins with an exploration of fictional representations of divorce. But the stories told of and under the 1969 Act were rather different from those told by the novelists of the 1930s and film-makers before and after the War. In 'Divorced from Reality? Literary Depictions of the Legal Process for Ending a Marriage, 1971–2021', Rebecca Probert, family lawyer and legal historian, examines over 50 novels and short stories, and asks how novelists tell stories about the end of marriages in an era in which the possibility of divorce is no longer really in doubt and in which it has very largely become a desk-based exercise with no courtroom drama to enliven the plot. One of her key findings is that divorce has not in any way become less interesting to novelists – marital relations are just as much a vehicle for ethical and social commentary as they were for the Victorians. Rather, divorce has become normalised within the stories, part of the backstory for the analysis of an intimate relationship and in some contexts of the wider blended family relationships. The very ordinariness of the manner in which divorce is represented is a powerful indicator of the removal of social stigma. Indeed, in some examples, Probert demonstrates how novelists sometimes overstate the extent to which divorce has become prevalent; a reminder of the value of Haskey's statistical analysis as a necessary counterbalance to thinking about fiction as much as policy. While the drama of the courtroom, so popular with representations of law more widely, is no longer present, law is still present in the novels, but it is the parties' legal advisers – the solicitors – who now become the focus of the fictional parties' engagement with the law. As Probert demonstrates, law – through the role of lawyers – is often cast in a negative manner: expensive, inaccessible, arcane and exacerbating bitterness, again reflecting both specific and general criticisms of family law and the legal system more widely. These are longstanding concerns – continuity goes hand in hand with change here. As Probert shows, while novelists are alive to the artificiality of law (albeit now something of a background issue), the move away from difficulties of proving adultery in open court and a shift in stories from the troubles of the spouse who wants the divorce to the predicament of the spouse who does not, both reflect legal realities. But what matters to the novelists is happiness and the human heart: the emotional response. Love is on trial and romanticism is alive and well.

From the stories told by novelists, the focus turns to law's divorce narratives via detailed analysis of the application and changing fortunes of the facts introduced by the Act. In different ways, the next two chapters throw light on law's own artificiality and fictions.

In 'Judging Matrimonial Behaviour', legal academic Joanna Miles explores the development of judicial discourse on the marital relationship through the lens of the 'behaviour' fact, which, as Haskey's analysis shows, was long the most popular basis for divorce, both under the 1969 Act and in the guise of its precursor 'cruelty' ground. Miles examines the unenviable task that the law imposed on the judges required to interpret and apply the law, and public reaction to this, as manifested by newspaper coverage of 'scandalous' cases and – in one notable instance – of the private lives of judges who decided them.

Her analysis reveals the extent to which divorce – as much in law as in literature and film – provides stories that both feed the public's continuing fascination with the contested nature of marital expectations and stimulate public debate about them and the role that the law (and so individual judges) should have in policing them. Some cases had a prurient entertainment value that the press cheerfully exploited. Indeed, generations of family law students have had their education enlivened by such tales, and whilst most academics might applaud the advent of no-fault divorce in 2022, they might regret that the subject will in consequence be less fun to teach. But those cases – those sad stories about the broken marriages of publicly named individuals – provided an opportunity for wider public discussion about modern marriage that the general public might otherwise have been too embarrassed to engage in. A key theme that emerges from examination of the judges' deliberations is the extent to which the behaviour fact compelled them to grapple with changing understandings of gender relations in marriage. These legal texts provide a rich source, often overlooked by commentaries in other disciplines, about changes and continuities in ideals of masculinity; not surprisingly, it was the behaviour of men that was most often in the spotlight. This is most evident in cases where the judicial task – undertaken almost exclusively by men, at least in the reported case law – reveals an urge to civilise other men by way of thinly veiled 'character assassinations' of husbands deemed to have engaged in unreconstructed or ungentlemanly male behaviour.

So, one paradox of the Act in this regard, made evident by Miles's analysis, is that whilst the Act was informed in part by a liberal reconfiguring of the role of the state in relation to private family relations, it nevertheless created a framework that necessitated the exposure and dissection of the minutiae of marital relations. Divorce under the 1969 Act, especially in the context of the behaviour fact, clearly asserted that marriage (and divorce law) had a public function and aroused legitimate public interest as a social institution. The concept of 'fault' (implicit in the vast majority of behaviour petitions) might not be missed, but it prompted discussions and played a role that the new law – substantively as well as procedurally privatised, given the abandonment of any 'facts' – will not.

The importance of appreciating the extent to which the operation of the Act required and enhanced the law's ability to create a compelling narrative, albeit a shifting one contingent on changing attitudes, is brought to the fore once again in the next contribution, 'Telling Tales? Establishing Irretrievable Breakdown under the Matrimonial Causes Act 1973', by Liz Trinder, family law academic and principal investigator in the *Finding Fault* research study[98] that was highly influential in making the case for the 2020 reform. Complementing the novels, case law and media stories of the previous chapters, Trinder's analysis draws on a rich seam of data not easily available: 300 'statements of case' from a nationally-representative sample of undefended cases from 2014/15 collected for the study.

Law in all areas requires a narrative construct – family law is not unique in that respect. But divorce law and practice is a field where that practice is most evident and invasive of the parties' private lives, as law's stories can be compared with and rub up against those of the media, novelists and film makers, as well as the stories of the parties themselves. Trinder's analysis acknowledges that, of course, this is not something fundamentally new in divorce law practice – echoing Brown's films, the history of detectives in 'hotel divorce' adultery cases pre-1969 is a vivid example. What *was* new under the 1969 Act and the special procedure was the move away from the courtroom, and so, like Probert, Trinder reveals what happens to law's story-telling once undefended divorce became paper-based. Her findings highlight how divorce practice, while still notionally framed within an inquisitorial process, set within an adversarial family justice system, became an administrative task based on formulaic and ritualised narratives. Trinder's contribution is a

[98] Trinder et al (2017).

reminder of the day-to-day, routine nature of the vast majority of divorces, which is quite distinct from the cases explored by Miles and the focus of some of the novels explored by Probert on the personal ramifications of that process. It is not that one narrative is more or less authoritative. Rather, we need to acknowledge all of them and accept that they complicate any simple reading of the Act: over its life-course, the Act has always had different audiences, contrasting private and public impacts, and administrative as well as symbolic functions.

The closing contribution of Part Three introduces another perspective that emphasises both the significance of the deep roots of much earlier matrimonial practices and the more recent challenge of how to understand the place of 'judgement' within a divorce law and practice for which doctrinal and theological fault have become increasingly less relevant. In 'Royal Divorces and the Remaking of Marriage and Monarchy', legal scholar Daniel Monk adds to the personal stories of campaigners, judges, parties in reported cases, and fictional husbands and wives from earlier chapters with accounts of some of the most familiar divorces in British history. Taking seriously the function of 'melodrama' as manifested by these cases reinforces the significance of public discourse and contested narratives of divorce as sites for evaluating and making sense of what marriage means in society.

Taking a long view, Monk demonstrates how royal divorces have at different times played a constitutional role, a symbol of the changing relationship between the Crown and the People as much as that between husbands and wives. And, complementing Sinclair's chapter, he highlights the significance and complexity of Anglicanism and how the Monarchy, like the Church of England, has both resisted and at the same time enabled and played a role in legitimising the 'ordinariness' of divorce as a life-stage, and so contributed to the conditions of possibility for the change that the 2020 Act will bring.

In Part Four, 'Contemporary Perspectives and Challenges', the final contributions to the collection introduce three new lenses or frameworks for thinking about divorce, all of which have posed questions for policymakers in the recent past, but which, albeit in different ways, may become more significant.

We begin with a chapter about human rights. In 'Divorced from Human Rights? English Divorce Law under Human Rights Scrutiny', human rights lawyer Carmen Draghici criticises the relative absence of human rights arguments in political debates – and legal argument – about divorce. Since the enactment of the Human Rights Act 1998, human rights have taken centre-stage in many legal debates, but they have been notable for their absence in liberal arguments for reform that were key to the 1969 Act.

Draghici makes a compelling case not only for the relevance of rights, but also as to the incompatibility of the 1969 Act with both the right to respect for family life (Article 8) and the right to marry (Article 12), and suggests that the Supreme Court missed an opportunity in *Owens*[99] to apply these provisions and affirm that denying someone a divorce – keeping someone in a marriage against their will – is

[99] [2018] UKSC 41.

an unjustifiable interference with their rights. The advent of the 2020 Act may make the immediate relevance of the argument seem largely academic. But rights-speak remains a powerful discourse that should have a central place when considering future challenges facing policymakers, as the next chapter demonstrates.

Religion has been a recurring theme in the collection; Sinclair and Monk both consider the role of the Church of England, and it surfaces more obliquely in other chapters. But alongside the formal – and zealously-guarded – role of the Church of England in parliamentary debates about divorce reform (and in the solemnisation of marriages in England and Wales), other religious groups grapple not only with the possibility of divorce and the basis on which it should be made available (as a matter of religious law), but also with having to reconcile state law with practices and traditions that, to varying degrees, conflict with English law. The Catholic prohibition of divorce was a key factor in the Irish Referendum about divorce in 2019, and the Matrimonial Causes Act 1973 since 2002 has included a provision designed to assist wives in religious marriages (particularly Jewish women) to obtain a religious divorce from their husbands alongside the civil divorce and so fully to recover their ability to remarry.[100] Both contexts present human rights challenges that Draghici's framework has much to offer.

But the focus of discussion of religious divorce in this collection is the British Muslim community. In 'British Muslim Communities, Islamic Divorce and English Family Law', scholar of family law and multiculturalism, Samia Bano, draws upon anthropological and sociological research to explore women's experience of divorce within British Muslim communities in recent decades, where religious law principles and procedures may be of far greater significance to their lives than whatever English law has to say about their position. As Bano explains, under Sharia law, whilst the husband is free to grant unilateral divorce – the *talaq* – at any point, wives' access to divorce is controlled either by the delegation of that right to them by their husbands in the original marriage contract, the *nikah*, or by their need to resort to the authority of a Sharia Council to determine whether and on what basis a divorce may be granted.

A key focus of Bano's analysis is the role of Sharia Councils as forums for resolving disputes arising from Muslim marriages and marital breakdown. The Councils have a role both where the couple's marriage is recognised by English law and where it is not. In the former case, civil divorce and its remedies are available, but the couple may also wish to secure a religious divorce. In the latter case, where the couple have a religious-only marriage, not recognised by current English law even as a void marriage, a Sharia Council is their only resort for dispute resolution if that marriage breaks down. The vulnerabilities of women in the latter group, denied access to the matrimonial courts, are particularly acute and a key issue in the Law Commission's current work on the law governing the formalities for creating marriage.[101] But Bano also argues that, whilst the Councils provide an essential

[100] Matrimonial Causes Act 1973, s 10A.
[101] See Law Commission (2020).

service for Muslim women, who are thereby afforded more control of their marital status than Jewish women (who have no forum to which they can resort when the husband refuses to grant a *get*), many of these women are not well served by the Councils' 'privatised'/alternative divorce resolution system. She highlights research findings that raise concerns about the Councils' focus on reconciliation and mediation, in which gender inequalities and other imbalances of power may remain unaddressed and where – in the absence of any enforcement mechanisms – there is heavy reliance on both parties' assent to give effect to the outcomes prescribed. The individualistic liberal framework has always had its limitations, but these are revealed starkly in a pluralistic society where people's lived experiences are moulded, enabled and often conditional upon membership of a group.

One area where the impact of liberal human rights arguments has been most evident in family law is the gradual recognition of same-sex relationships. In 1969, same-sex marriage was not just impossible but unimaginable. The only references to homosexuality in divorce law, and the only one in early family law textbooks, was in the context of 'unnatural offences'.[102] But there are parallels between the partial decriminalisation of male same-sex activity by the Sexual Offences Act 1967 and the 1969 Act. While the two Acts, initiated as Private Member's Bills, are rightly seen as landmarks of the 'permissive' era, they both had their roots in earlier decades. And while the Wolfenden Commission in 1957, unlike the Morton Commission,[103] opted for a more liberal approach to its subject matter, both statutes were products of carefully negotiated compromises: the decriminalisation of gay sex and the move away from 'fault' and the identification of the 'guilty party' in divorce were both partial, leading to later campaigns for further reform and for a more comprehensive fundamental break with conservative and religious tenets. Paradoxically, one of the compromises in the 1967 Act was the limiting of permissible male homosexual activity to *two* people; what might now look like celebration of 'serial' monogamy, however impermanent, demonstrates how laws look different to different ages. But the concern or taboos around sex re-emerged in debates about the Civil Partnership Act 2004 and the Marriage (Same Sex Couples) Act 2013, in which adultery was restricted to heterosexual relations (and not available as a basis for civil partnership dissolution). This issue, which flags a recurring tension about 'sameness' and 'difference' in debates between feminists, is more fully explored by sociologists Brian Heaphy and James Hodgson in the final chapter, 'Dissolution, Divorce and Changing Practices of Commitment'.

The introduction of same-sex marriage and divorce reform were both resisted by those concerned to protect the institution of marriage and supported by those who want to modernise and in doing so 'save' the institution. Heaphy and Hodgson's review of the sociological literature about divorce, including the limited literature about same-sex dissolution/divorce, offers a perspective from which to look beneath these, often ideological, arguments, and instead to trace

[102] Bromley (1957).
[103] Royal Commission (1956).

changes in patterns of commitment. From this grounded view, they suggest that divorce is nowadays best viewed as an 'ordinary' aspect of the changing institution of marriage, as opposed to being indicative of its ultimate demise. Perhaps unsurprisingly, their findings echo the normalisation of divorce found by Probert in novelists' accounts. However, the boundaries of ordinariness are inevitably fluid. Sustaining an amicable – indeed close – relationship post-divorce is a distinctive feature of research about same-sex couples. Heaphy and Hodgson leave open the question whether heterosexual couples might move towards this model of post-divorce amicability (one that might even entail 'conscious uncoupling', as one famous celebrity divorcée had it[104]) as an aspect of embracing more fully egalitarian relations, freed of the adversarial divorce culture – something that heterosexual civil partners might particularly be expected to do.[105] Conversely, they ask whether same-sex relations will in future adopt more of the established 'norms' of heterosexual couples.

In concluding, Heaphy and Hodges look to the future and offer a methodological framework for a nuanced, reflective engagement with the experiences of couples ending their relationships, one in which they highlight the importance of attentiveness to the longer 'biography' of a relationship as much as the process of ending it.

VII. Conclusion

Biographies of individuals on the whole end with the death of the subject. The same is true here. We have enacted the death rites for the 1969 Act once before – in the mid-1990s when the Family Law Act 1996 regime nearly replaced it – but, to adopt the phrase attributed to Mark Twain, reports of its relatively youthful death then turned out to be greatly exaggerated. Now longer in the tooth, albeit scarcely middle-aged in human terms, the big social reform that some considered to be behind its time in 1969 is due to make way for its twenty-first-century successor, contained in the 2020 Act.

Much like the successive manifestations of Dr Who, the new law will be known by the same name – the Matrimonial Causes Act 1973, which the 2020 Act amends. But while – as with the Doctors – the outward appearance of this new divorce law is very different from that which it replaces, it will arguably simply enshrine in law an altogether more humane version of the divorce by mutual consent and on unilateral demand that many divorcing couples have in substance enjoyed over much of the last 50 years, certainly since the advent of the special procedure for uncontested divorces in the 1970s. Writing almost a century ago, philosopher

[104] The expression deployed by Gwyneth Paltrow, with much press and social media commentary, to describe her separation from her musician husband Chris Martin in 2014.

[105] After the Civil Partnerships, Marriages and Deaths (Registration, etc) Act 2019.

Bertrand Russell – younger brother of the Earl Russell of the 1902 Bill, whose progressive ideas about sex and marriage proved controversial[106] – noted a difficulty in framing laws on divorce: 'whatever the laws may be, judges and juries will be governed by their passions, while husbands and wives will do whatever may be necessary to circumvent the intentions of the legislators'.[107] That observation was as true of the 1969 Act as it was of the divorce laws that preceded it. But the latitude of the 2020 Act makes it hard to see that spouses will need to engage in any doubtful or unintended behaviours to secure the divorces that they want in future. We have, it seems, reached the end of a long road to full legal (if not economic) autonomy around the decision to divorce.

So with that profound reform imminent, this collection prompts reflection both on the limitations of the 1969 reform, and on how the new law reflects earlier reformers' aspirations. Our contributors all conclude with reflections about the new era of divorce law that the implementation of the 2020 Act heralds, emphasising in different ways that no-fault divorce creates a space for new forms of story-telling. Taken together, we hope that readers will agree that the contributions to this volume provide a rich assortment of perspectives for telling the myriad of stories surrounding the 1969 Act. And in looking both backwards and forwards, it provides a resource for those interested in learning about the past as much as for those seeking to find ways to understand the entanglement of law, emotion and judgement (if, no longer, legal judgments) as we move into a new era of fault-free divorce.

References

Anderson, S (1984) 'Legislative Divorce – Law for the Aristocracy?' in GR Rubin and D Sugarman (eds), *Law, Economy and Society* (Abingdon, Professional Books Ltd).

Bailey, J (2003) *Unquiet Lives: Marriage and Marriage Breakdown in England, 1660–1800* (Cambridge, Cambridge University Press).

Bailey J and Giese, L (2013) 'Marital cruelty: reconsidering lay attitudes in England, *c.* 1580 to 1850' 18(3) *The History of the Family* 289.

Barlow, A, Hunter, R, Smithson, J and Ewing, J (2017) *Mapping Paths to Family Justice: Resolving Family Disputes in Neoliberal Times* (Basingstoke, Palgrave Macmillan).

Bearman, R (2010) 'Divorce by Act of Parliament: the case of Francis Loggin of Butlers Marston' 14 *Warwickshire History* 202.

Bradley, D (1976) 'Realism in Divorce Law', *New Law Journal* 1204.

Bromley, P (1957) *Family Law*, 1st edn (London, Butterworth and Co).

Chester, R (1977) 'England and Wales' in R Chester (ed), *Divorce in Europe* (New York, Springer).

[106] Szreter and Fisher (2010) 327.

[107] Russell (1929) 233.

Cornish, W, Banks, S, Mitchell, C, Mitchell, P and Probert, R (2019) *Law and Society in England, 1750–1950* (Oxford, Hart Publishing).

Cretney, S (2003) *Family Law in the Twentieth Century: A History* (Oxford, Oxford University Press).

Davis, G and Murch, M (1977) 'The Implications of the Special Procedure in Divorce' 7 *Family Law* 71.

—— (1988) *Grounds for Divorce* (Oxford, Clarendon Press).

Deech, R (1990) 'Divorce Law and Empirical Studies' 106 *Law Quarterly Review* 229.

Douglas (2018) *Obligation and Commitment in Family Law* (Oxford, Hart Publishing).

Eekelaar, J (2018) 'The financial consequences of divorce: Law and reality' 32 *Australian Journal of Family Law* 28.

Elston, E, Fuller, J and Murch, M (1975) 'Judicial Hearings of Undefended Divorce Petitions' 38 *Modern Law Review* 609.

Freeman, M (1976) 'Divorce Without Legal Aid' 6 *Family Law* 255.

Gibson, C (1994) *Dissolving Wedlock* (London, Routledge).

Harvey, CP (1953) 'On the State of the Divorce Market' 16 *Modern Law Review* 129.

Heenan, A (2020) 'Neoliberal autonomy and financial remedy reform: lessons from Sweden' 32 *Child and Family Law Quarterly 263.*

Herbert, AP (1937) *The Ayes Have It* (London, Methuen).

Horstman, A (1985) *Victorian Divorce* (London, Routledge).

James, D (2012) 'Parliamentary Divorce, 1700–1857' 31 *Parliamentary History* 169.

Kahn-Freund (1937) 'The Matrimonial Causes Act 1937' 1 *Modern Law Review* 231.

Karminski, S (1959) 'Family Law' in M Ginsberg (ed), *Law and Opinion in England in the Twentieth Century* (London, Stevens & Sons).

Kha, H and Swain, W (2016) 'The Enactment of the Matrimonial Causes Act 1857: The Campbell Commission and the Parliamentary Debates' 37 *Journal of Legal History* 303.

Law Commission (1966) *Reform of the Grounds of Divorce: The Field of Choice* Law Com No 6 (London, HMSO).

—— (1988) *Facing the Future: A Discussion Paper on the Ground for Divorce*, Law Com No 170 (London, HMSO).

—— (1990) *The Ground for Divorce*, Law Com No 192 (London, HMSO).

—— (2020) *Getting Married: A Consultation Paper on Weddings Law*, Law Com CP 247 (London, TSO).

Lee, BH (1974) *Divorce Law Reform in England* (London, Peter Owen).

Lord Chancellor's Department (1993) *Looking to the Future – Mediation and the Ground for Divorce*, Cm 2424 (London, HMSO).

—— (1995) *Looking to the Future – Mediation and the Ground for Divorce*, Cm 2799 (London, HMSO).

Maclean, M and Eekelaar, J (2016) *Lawyers and Mediators: The Brave New World of Services for Separating Families* (Oxford, Hart Publishing).

—— (2019) *After the Act: Access to Family Justice after LASPO* (Oxford, Hart Publishing).

Mant, J and Wallbank, J (2017) 'The Mysterious Case of Disappearing Family Law and the Shrinking Vulnerable Subject: The Shifting Sands of Family Law's Jurisdiction' 26 *Social and Legal Studies* 629.

Miles, J, George, R and Harris-Short, S (2015) *Family Law: Text, Cases, and Materials*, 4th edn (Oxford, Oxford University Press).

Miles, J and Hitchings, E (2018) 'Financial remedy outcomes on divorce in England and Wales: Not a "meal ticket for life"' 32 *Australian Journal of Family Law* 43.

Ministry of Justice (2018) *Reducing Family Conflict: Reform of the Legal Requirements for Divorce* (London, MOJ), available at consult.justice.gov.uk/digital-communications/reform-of-the-legal-requirements-for-divorce/ (last accessed 19 July 2021]).

—— (2019). *Reducing Family Conflict: Government response to the consultation on reform of the legal requirements for divorce* (London, MOJ), available at consult.justice.gov.uk/digital-communications/reform-of-the-legal-requirements-for-divorce/ (last accessed 19 July 2021]).

Parker, M (2015) 'The draft Nuptial Agreements Bill and the abolition of the common law rule: "swept away" or swept under the carpet?' 27 *Child and Family Law Quarterly* 63.

Phillips, R (1988) *Putting Asunder: A History of Divorce in Western Society* (Cambridge, Cambridge University Press).

Probert, R (1999a) 'The Double Standard of Morality in the Divorce and Matrimonial Causes Act 1857' 28 *Anglo-American Law Review* 73.

—— (1999b) 'The Controversy of Equality and the Matrimonial Causes Act 1923' 11 *Child and Family Law Quarterly* 33.

—— (2011) 'The Roos case and modern family law' in S Gilmore, J Herring and R Probert (eds), *Landmarks in Family Law* (Oxford, Hart Publishing).

Probert, R, Bailey, J and Shaffer, J (2013) *A Noble Affair: The Remarkable True Story of the Runaway Wife, the Bigamous Earl, and the Farmer's Daughter* (Kenilworth, Takeaway).

Redmayne, S (1993) 'The Matrimonial Causes Act 1937: A Lesson the Art of Compromise' 13 *Oxford Journal of Legal Studies* 183.

Rheinstein, M (1972) *Marriage Stability, Divorce and the Law* (Chicago, IL, University of Chicago Press).

Rowntree, G and Carrier, N (1958) 'The Resort to Divorce in England and Wales, 1858–1957' 11 *Population Studies* 188.

Royal Commission (1956) *Report of Royal Commission on Marriage and Divorce*, Cm 9678 (London, HMSO).

Russell, B (1929) *Marriage and Morals* (London, Allen & Unwin).

Russell, P (2019) 'Matrimonial Causes Act 1923' in E Rackley and R Auchmuty (eds), *Women's Legal Landmarks: Celebrating the History of Women and Law in the UK and Ireland* (Oxford, Bloomsbury).

Savage, G (1988) 'Divorce and the Law in England and France Prior to the First World War' 21 *Journal of Social History* 499.

—— (1992) '"Intended Only for the Husband": Gender, Class, and the Provision for Divorce in England, 1858–1868' in K Ottesen Garrigen (ed), *Victorian Scandals: Representations of Gender and Class* (Athens, OH, Ohio UP).

—— (1998) 'Erotic Stories and Public Decency: Newspaper Reporting of Divorce Proceedings in England' 41 *The Historical Journal* 511.

—— (2011) 'They Would if They Could: Class, Gender, and Popular Representation of English Divorce Litigation, 1858–1908' 36 *Journal of Family History* 173.

Shaffer, J (2014) 'Bastardy and Divorce Trials, 1780–1809' in R Probert (ed), *Cohabitation and Non-marital Births in England and Wales, 1600–2012* (Basingstoke, Palgrave Macmillan).

Shanley, ML (1982) '"One Must Ride Behind": Married Women's Rights and the Divorce Act of 1857' 25 *Victorian Studies* 348.

Sheldon, S, Davis, G, O'Neill, J and Parker, C (2019) 'The Abortion Act (1967): A biography' 39 *Legal Studies* 18.

Simon, J (1965) 'The Seven Pillars of Divorce Reform' 62 *Law Society Gazette* 344.
Stanley, L (1995) *Sex Surveyed, 1949–1994: from Mass Observation's 'Little Kinsey' to the National Survey and the Hite Reports* (London, Taylor & Francis).
Staves, S (1982) 'Money for Honor: Damages for Criminal Conversation' 11 *Studies in Eighteenth-Century Culture* 279.
Stetson, D (1982) *A Woman's Issue: The Politics of Family Law Reform in England* (London, Greenwood Press).
Stone, L (1977) *The Family, Sex and Marriage in England 1500–1800* (London, Weidenfeld & Nicolson).
—— (1990) *The Road to Divorce: A History of the Making and Breaking of Marriage in England* (Oxford, Oxford University Press).
—— (1995) *Uncertain Unions and Broken Lives: Marriage and Divorce in England, 1660–1857* (Oxford, Oxford University Press).
Sumner Holmes, A (1999) '"Don't Frighten the Horses": the Russell Divorce Case' in G Robb and N Erber (eds), *Disorder in the Court: Trials and Sexual Conflict at the Turn of the Century* (London, Macmillan).
Szreter, S and Fisher, K (2010) *Sex before the Sexual Revolution: Intimate Life in England 1918–1963* (Cambridge, Cambridge University Press).
Thompson, S (2021) 'Against divorce? Revisiting the charge of the Casanovas charter' 33 *Child and Family Law Quarterly* 193.
Trinder, L, Braybrook, D, Bryson, C, Coleman, L, Houlston, C and Sefton, M (2017) *Finding Fault? Divorce Law and Practice in England and Wales* (London, Nuffield Foundation).
Trinder L and Sefton, M (2018) *No Contest: Defended Divorce in England and Wales* (London, Nuffield Foundation).
Turner, D (2002) *Fashioning Adultery: Gender, Sex and Civility in England, 1660–1740* (Cambridge, Cambridge University Press).
Trumbach, R (1978) *The Rise of the Egalitarian Family* (New York, Academic Press).
Waddams, S (2000) 'English Matrimonial Law in the Eve of Reform' 21 *Journal of Legal History* 59.
Witte Jr, J (2012) *From Sacrament to Contract: Marriage, Religion, and Law in the Western Tradition* (Westminster, John Knox Press).
Wolfram, S (1985) 'Divorce in England 1700–1857' 5 *Oxford Journal of Legal Studies* 155.
Woodhouse, MK (1959) 'The Marriage and Divorce Bill of 1857' (1959) 3 *American Journal of Legal History* 273.
Wright, D (2004) '"Well-Behaved Women Don't Make History": Rethinking Family, Law, and History Through an Analysis of the First Nine Years of the English Divorce and Matrimonial Causes Court (1858–1866)' 19 *Wisconsin Women's Law Journal* 211.

2

Divorces by Fact Proven Over the Past Half Century in England and Wales: The Historical Context, Statistical Trends and Future Prospects

JOHN HASKEY*

I. Introduction

The Divorce Reform Act 1969 came into effect on 1 January 1971 and heralded the introduction of – or, perhaps more accurately, the first step towards – 'no-fault' divorce, the sole ground for divorce being the irretrievable breakdown of marriage that could be established by 'proving' one or more facts. These facts were: adultery; behaviour; desertion; separation for two years (with the respondent consenting to divorce); and separation for five years (without the consent of the respondent).[1] For every divorce granted under the 1969 Act, the 'fact proven' was recorded. This chapter is devoted to a statistical analysis of those facts and what they can tell us about the past, present and future of divorce law.

Inevitably, analysing statistics on the fact proven cannot provide an insight into the circumstances of individual cases. More importantly, it is acknowledged that the declared 'fact' may be more of a reflection of the strategy adopted to obtain divorce rather than the true reason why the marriage ended – indeed, the law does not require that the fact relied on be a cause of the breakdown.[2] Nevertheless, the statistics do illuminate how the legal framework has been used in practice.

Section II of the chapter sets the 1969 Act in its historical context by examining patterns of divorce from the end of the nineteenth century. The annual numbers of divorces and their increases and decreases will be considered, along with the

* The author particularly wishes to thank, for their helpful and constructive comments and advice for improving the draft, Professor Chris Barton, John Eekelaar and the editors of this volume. The author alone is responsible for any error of fact or interpretation, and for the opinions expressed. Thanks are also due to the Department of Social Policy and Intervention, University of Oxford, for providing a range of facilities, and to the Bodleian Library for access to relevant publications.

[1] See Miles, Monk and Probert, ch 1 of this volume.

[2] *Stevens v Stevens* [1979] 1 WLR 885.

relative proportions of divorces granted to husbands and wives. Section III focuses on the period immediately before and after the implementation of the 1969 Act in order to highlight the extent of both continuity and change, and includes consideration of the relative numbers of husbands and wives who went on to remarry after divorce. The longer-term implications of the Act are considered in Section IV, including how patterns in fact proven changed after 1978.

Sections V and VI look to the future. The Divorce, Dissolution and Separation Act received Royal Assent in 2020, and is due to come into force in April 2022. One consequence of the new law's being entirely 'fault-free' is that there will be no information on the basis on which divorce is sought, let alone the reason. There will, nonetheless, continue to be useful indicators from which inferences can be drawn, and Section VI therefore considers the data on which future demographers will be able to draw. Finally, Section VII, Conclusions, provides an overview of the factors influencing the statistics, thereby recognising their limitations for possible interpretation.

II. Divorce Law and Statistics before 1969: The Historical Context

The pattern and use of the law following the 1969 Act can usefully be viewed within a longer time horizon in order to draw parallels and make contrasts. Figure 2.1 traces, from just before the start of the twentieth century, the annual number of decrees (which includes, besides dissolutions of marriage, a relatively small component of decrees of nullity) and also the proportion of all decrees that were petitioned for by, or granted to, wives and husbands. The number of decrees is shown as a solid continuous black line, and it may be seen how large the increase in divorce has been, although there have been two prolonged periods of declining annual numbers.

At around 1900, the number of divorces was only around 500 per year, growing to just under 600 per year just before the First World War (whose duration is shown as a band in Figure 2.1). From 1857, when civil divorce first became possible, the sole ground for divorce had been adultery, and a woman could only petition for divorce on her husband's adultery if he had committed one or more additional matrimonial offences. Not surprisingly, the majority of decrees were sought by husbands, reaching 77 per cent of all decrees obtained in 1920, the largest proportion recorded in the entire period of 118 years to date. In 1923, with women's rights having gained prominence as a political issue, the additional requirements for petitioning wives were abolished. The proportion of decrees awarded to wives rose from 44 per cent in 1923 to 63 per cent in 1925, a proportion which would not be exceeded for some 50 years.[3]

The problem still remained that many couples whose marriages had broken down could not divorce (unless willing to engage in collusion and perjury)

[3] Haskey (1986c).

Figure 2.1 Percentage of decrees by party petitioning*/party granted decree,† and annual number of decrees, 1898–2017, England and Wales

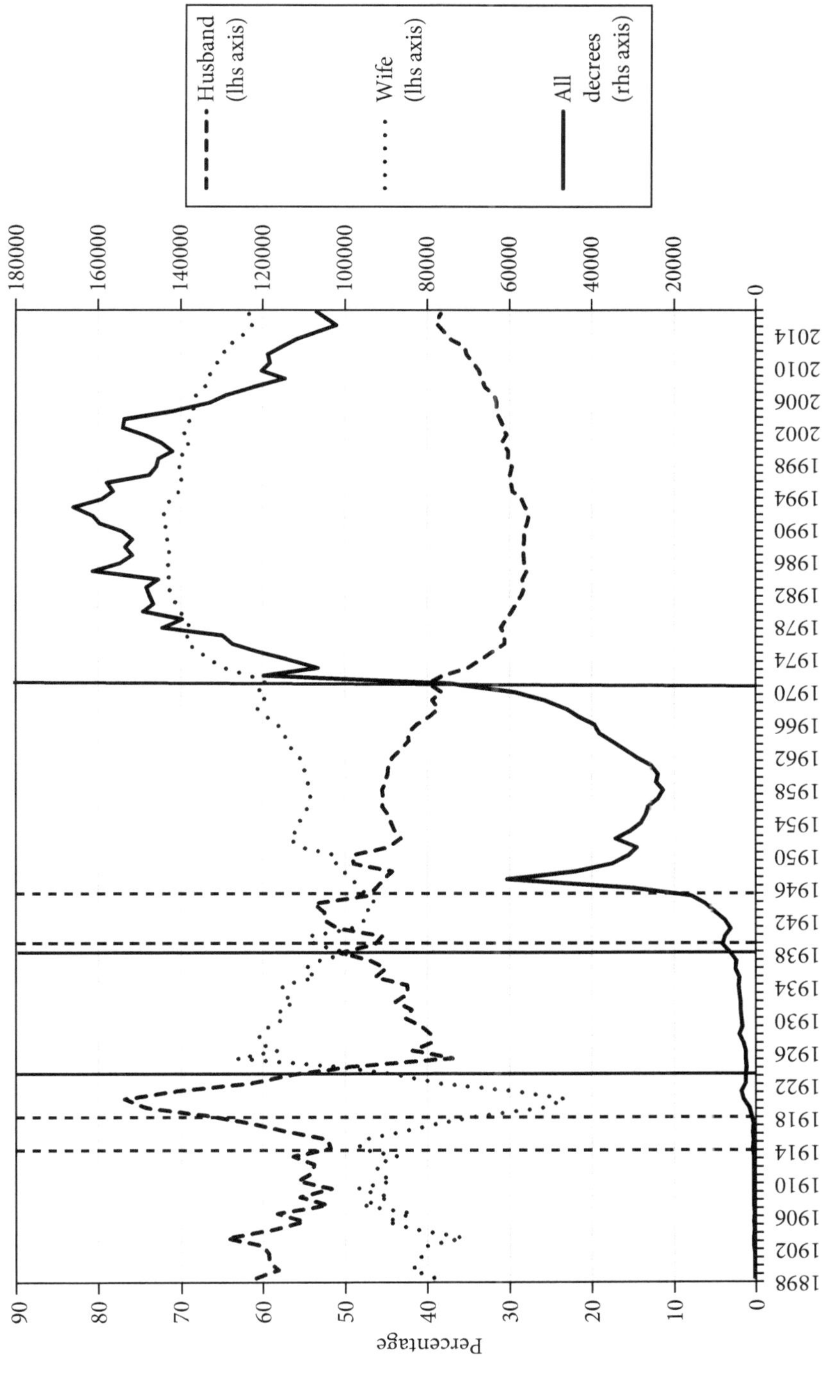

*up to and 1956; †1957 and on.

because neither spouse had committed adultery. During the late 1920s and early 1930s, there were calls for reform to allow divorces to be granted on a wider range of grounds. The Matrimonial Causes Act 1937,[4] enacted in 1938, did just that, the main new grounds being desertion and cruelty.

The number of divorces rose in 1938 and 1939, but after the post-war surge in divorces in 1947, the annual number declined substantially until 1958, forming a decade-long dip. Despite the changes in the annual numbers of divorces, the numbers of wife and husband petitioners were roughly equal between about 1937 and 1950.

Another important factor was the introduction of legal aid, which first became available in 1950[5] and became increasingly accessible through the 1960s. It improved poorer petitioners' access to divorce, disproportionately assisting wives who wished to divorce. Around the time of the advent of legal aid, the proportion of divorces granted to wives grew slowly from around 50 to 60 per cent, right up to just before the implementation of the 1969 Divorce Reform Act.

One important feature to note from Figure 2.1 is that the annual number of divorces was already increasing rapidly *before* 1971, as were the corresponding rates of divorce, so the subsequent increase cannot realistically be ascribed to the implementation of the Act. Indeed, the rate of increase appears to be sustained, rather than modified, throughout the period, although, as will be seen, part of the increase can be attributed to the release of a pent-up demand by husbands and wives who were able, for the first time, to petition and be granted divorce, thanks to the liberalisation effected by the 1969 Act. As the next section will show, there were both significant changes and equally important continuities in practice after 1971.

III. The Change in the Pattern of Divorce between 1965 and 1973: The Early Effects of the 1969 Act

Although the Divorce Reform Act 1969 was radical in that it allowed divorce to be obtained on the basis of separation, without establishing fault,[6] the subsequent pattern of usage by fact proven was not so fundamentally altered as might have been expected, largely due to the retention of the former fault grounds of adultery and desertion (and, also, it may be argued, cruelty, whose approximate equivalent was renamed less dramatically as 'behaviour' with which the petitioner 'cannot reasonably be expected to live'[7]).

[4] Enacted largely as a result of the efforts of AP Herbert, who had written a farcical novel, *Holy Deadlock*, with the serious purpose of canvassing for reform to remedy this impasse.

[5] As a result of the Legal Aid and Advice Act 1949.

[6] Strictly, the additional ground of incurable insanity in the 1937 Act was the first no-fault ground.

[7] Behaviour need not include fault: involuntary acts can constitute 'behaviour' under the 1969 Act. In *Thurlow v Thurlow* [1976] Fam 32 the involuntary behaviour stemmed from the respondent's chronic illness and indefinite hospitalisation. See Hall (1975) and see Miles, ch 8 of this volume.

Figure 2.2 plots the number of single-fact divorces granted to wives and to husbands by fact proven.[8] Divorces granted under the previous legislation up to 1971 are also shown. Similar line types have been used where the fact proven is the

Figure 2.2 Annual number of divorces granted to wives and husbands by the ground for divorce/fact proven, 1965–78, England and Wales

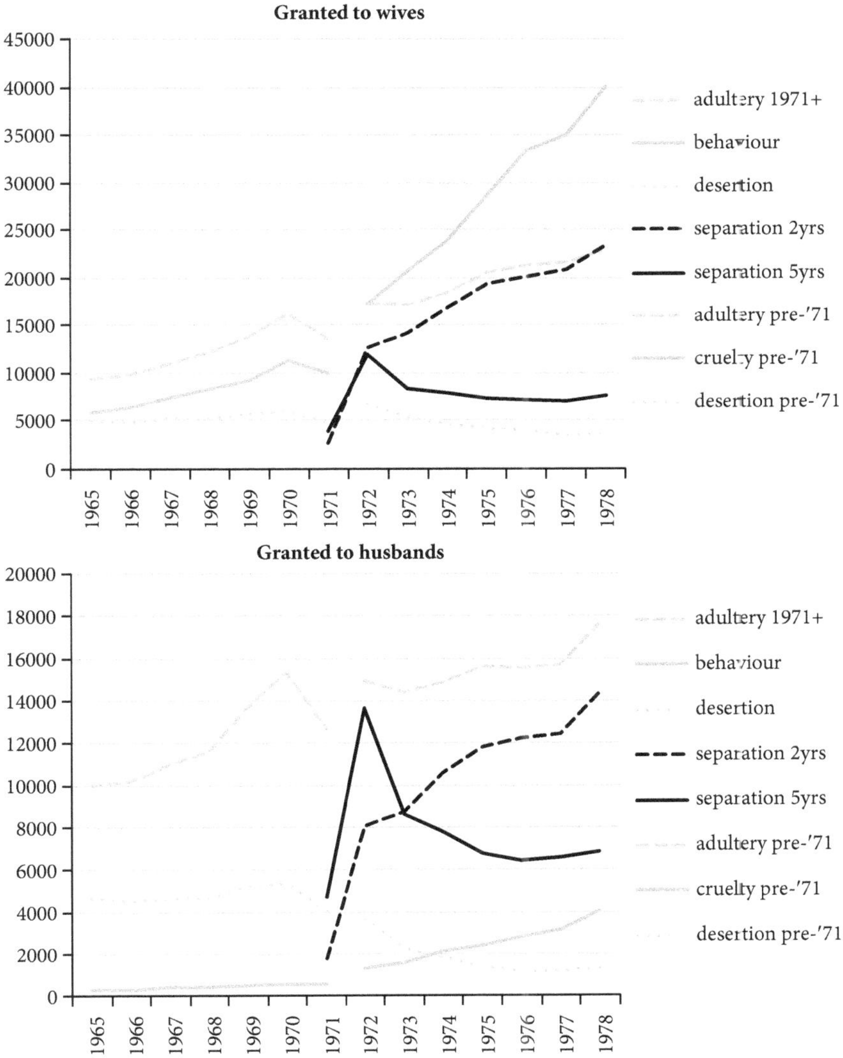

[8] Divorces on several facts – about 4% of all divorces in 1973 – have therefore been excluded, as also have divorces granted to both parties – representing 0.2% of all divorces in 1973.

same as, or roughly equivalent to, the divorce ground before 1971. Hence cruelty and 'behaviour' are both shown as a continuous grey line. Of course, divorces sought before 1971 and made absolute in or after 1971 have not been included as they were on the former grounds, not facts, and, in any case, their numbers rapidly dwindled, forming 65 per cent of all divorces in 1971, 6 per cent in 1972 and just 1.5 per cent in 1973.

There was an immediate jump in the number of wives divorcing on both separation facts between 1971 and 1972, with roughly equal numbers obtaining divorce on each separation fact. There was a corresponding surge in the number of divorces granted to husbands; five years' separation was almost the most common fact proven by husbands in 1972, well exceeding the number for two years' separation, which was, nevertheless, the third most common fact relied upon. During debates on what became the 1969 Act, there had been considerable concern that the introduction of divorce without consent would prove a 'Casanova's charter'.[9] Certainly, husbands used five years' separation more than wives in the early years 1971, 1972 and 1973, but not by a great margin, and from 1974 onwards, more wives than husbands used this fact. Wives were therefore equal beneficiaries of this aspect of the Act. Furthermore, an estimation of the numbers of extra remarriages of divorced husbands and wives (discussed further below) after 1971 suggests the former exceeded the latter, but not by a great margin, consistent with the usual differential in remarriage rates of divorced men and women.

The story for divorces based on two years' separation with consent is, however, quite different. The numbers of divorces awarded to husbands and to wives on two years' separation with consent rose steadily from the start, becoming the second largest category of divorce for men throughout the 1970s and for women towards the end of the 1970s. The annual number of these divorces awarded to wives was some 50 per cent larger than those awarded to husbands, and this differential applied in every year of the 1970s. However, these relative numbers might be expected: overall, around 60 per cent of divorces were granted to wives and 40 per cent to husbands, that is to say, overall 50 per cent more divorces were granted to wives than to husbands. Unlike the divorces granted to either spouse on five years' separation, which fell back and plateaued after 1972, those based on two years' separation continued to climb. It may be deduced that the former experienced a 'backlog' effect, whereas there was probably no such (or very much less) effect for the latter.

Nonetheless, immediately after the implementation of the Act, the most frequent fact used by wives and husbands continued to be a 'conduct' fact:[10]

[9] See Thompson, ch 6 of this volume.

[10] As Lady Hale notes in *Owens v Owens* [2018] UKSC 41, it is more accurate to describe adultery, behaviour and desertion as 'conduct-based' rather than fault-based.

'behaviour' for wives, and adultery for husbands. Furthermore, the use of those facts was set to increase, leaving only one 'no-fault' fact – two years' separation – to show a sustained rise.

Overall, the number of divorces rose steeply during the mid-1960s and the 1970s, with those based on behaviour, adultery and two years' separation increasing considerably before levelling off between 1976 and 1977.[11] The 1970s was a period of profound social change that the 'permissive' 1960s had catalysed. There had been a decisive change in attitudes to living arrangements and to sexual relationships in particular. The pattern of divorce by fact proven had shown the start of some remarkable trends, not unexpectedly given the pace of social change. In the late 1960s, abortion had been legalised and contraception made available to all women, so that having sex and having children had become decoupled. Pre-marital cohabitation had begun to increase from a very low level, and was more prevalent before second marriages.[12] With greater emphasis on individualism, there were, no doubt, higher expectations of the quality of married life. The general perception was that divorce had become easier, so that a less than fulfilling marriage could be terminated and a better relationship achieved with a new partner. Rates of remarriage fell dramatically,[13] and divorced men and women increasingly cohabited. One-parent families grew in numbers, with divorced lone mothers the largest group. All these changes occurred by the end of the 1970s, but the liberalised attitudes and diversity of lifestyles continued.

The same set of data as shown in Figure 2.2 may be considered in another, complementary way – shown in Figure 2.3 – in the form of percentage *profiles* by fact proven of the total number of single-fact divorces each year. Figure 2.3 shows the trends in the *proportion* of divorces by each fact, and so reveals their *relative* use, irrespective of the peaks and troughs in the associated numbers. The percentage profiles for 1971 and successive years are for single-fact divorces that were sought under the provisions of the 1969 Act. As already mentioned, some divorces granted in 1971 (or later) had been sought under the previous legislation,[14] but for clarity they have been omitted from Figure 2.3. Of all the divorce decrees made absolute in 1971, only 35 per cent were sought under the new legislation, whereas the corresponding proportion was 94 per cent in 1972. Hence the pattern of divorces by fact proven really only began properly in 1972.

[11] 1977 was the year in which the 'special procedure', originally introduced for couples without children petitioning on two years' separation with consent, was extended to all undefended divorces. It is difficult to discern any repercussions of this shift, although there was a very slight levelling off of the number of divorces granted on the 'conduct' facts.

[12] Haskey (2001).

[13] Haskey (1983).

[14] Matrimonial Causes Act 1965.

Figure 2.3 Percentage of divorces by ground/fact proven, by party granted divorce, 1965–78, England and Wales

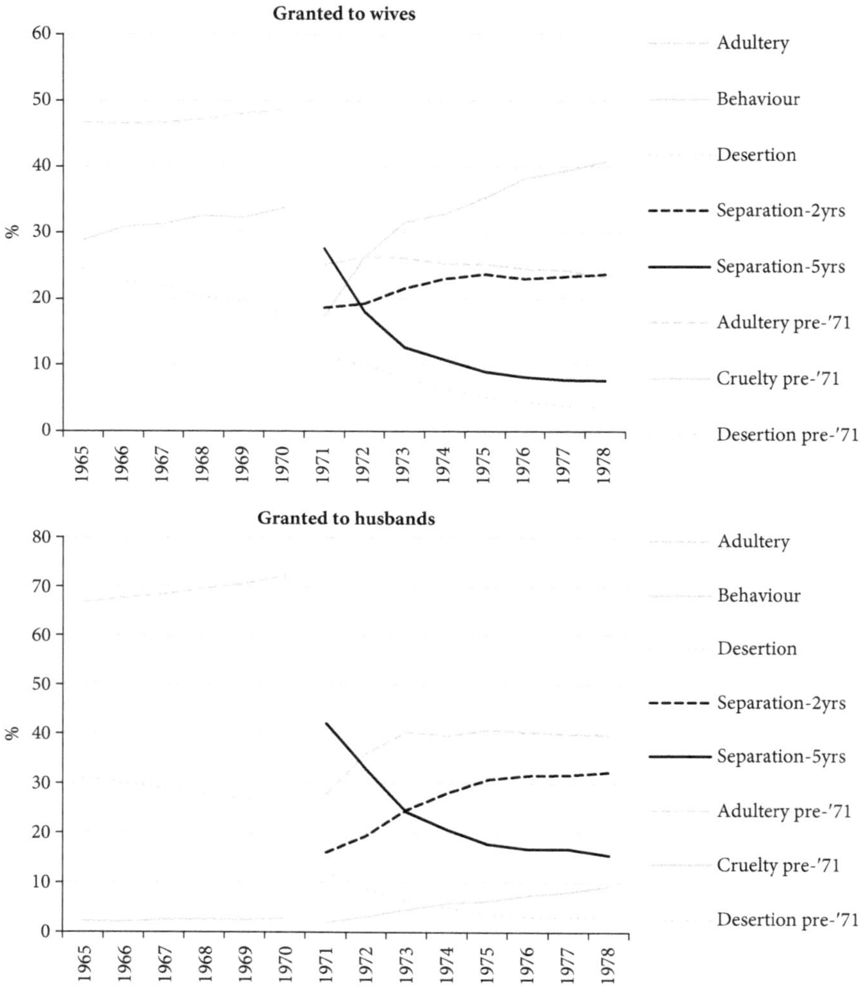

It may be seen that five years' separation dominated all other facts in 1971 for both husbands and wives (although only just for the latter). Of course, the number who were able to petition for, and be granted, divorce in the same year was inevitably limited, as petitions would have to be made early in 1971 for the decrees to be made absolute before the end of 1971. For this reason, the numbers of divorces in 1971 on two and five years' separation were between about one-fifth and one-third, respectively, of those of the following year. Whilst divorces on five years' separation declined fairly steeply as a proportion of all divorces after 1971, divorces on two years' separation increased, and, by around 1978, reached their peak: about one-third of all divorces granted to husbands and one-quarter of all divorces granted to wives. Nevertheless, one or other 'conduct' fact was the most frequently used by both husbands and wives in 1972 and subsequent years.

A somewhat surprising result from Figure 2.3 is the decided increase in the proportion of divorces granted to wives on the fact of behaviour. During the 1970s, divorcing wives who were granted divorce on behaviour tended to have the largest number of dependent children.[15] At the end of the 1970s, there was a steep social class gradient in the proportion of divorces granted to wives on behaviour, with relatively fewer being awarded to wives in the higher social classes, and relatively larger numbers to those in the lower social classes.[16] This same pattern had been reported earlier[17] for divorces on the grounds of cruelty, suggesting that, for this offence, social class patterns of petitioning had not changed substantially over the decade.[18]

Unlike the trend for all other facts, the proportions of divorces granted to both husbands and wives on the adultery of their spouses stayed fairly constant through the 1970s, albeit at a level roughly half that before 1971. At the turn of the 1980s, adultery was cited relatively more often among couples in the higher social classes than in the manual occupation social classes (the reverse of the situation for behaviour).[19] These patterns fit in with the popular view of the typical kinds of marital misbehaviour in the higher and lower social classes, and may reflect different social class attitudes as to what constitutes an 'acceptable' basis on which to petition.

Desertion, meanwhile, was declining as a proportion of all divorces for both husbands and wives before 1971, and continued falling afterwards. Part of the reason for its continued decline probably lies in the Act's stipulation that the respondent must have 'deserted the petitioner for a continuous period of at least two years immediately preceding the presentation of the petition'. This is exactly the same length of time as for the fact of two years' separation with the respondent's consent. Consequently, in this respect, desertion and two years' separation may be regarded as 'fault' and 'no-fault' equivalent facts. Possibly some who would otherwise have petitioned on desertion did so on either two years' or five years' separation. More attractively, though, for those who wanted a speedy divorce, petitioning on behaviour guaranteed a divorce with no such required wait, provided the case would be undefended.

One of the main concerns and criticisms of the 1969 Act was that it would allow petitioners to obtain a divorce without their spouse's agreement, and in particular that husbands, particularly middle-aged husbands, could 'exchange' their wives, remarrying younger women. Figure 2.4 investigates, showing the numbers of divorced men and women in each age group who remarried in the years after 1971.

[15] Haskey (1986a).
[16] Haskey (1986a).
[17] Chester and Streather (1972).
[18] See also Law Commission (1990) para 2.12 on the inaccessibility of the separation facts to spouses unable to secure a second property.
[19] Haskey (1986a).

Figure 2.4 Annual number of remarriages after divorce, by age at remarriage and sex, 1960–78, England and Wales

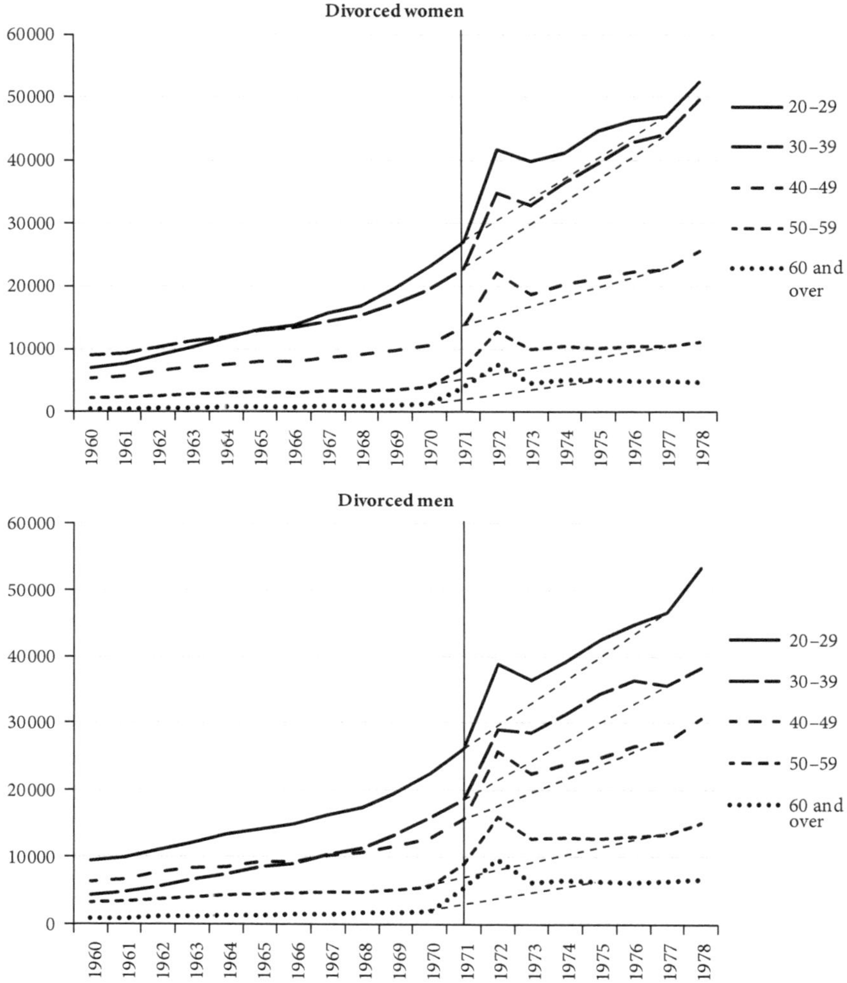

It is evident that there was a 'backlog effect' for both men and women, in which increased numbers remarried in 1972 and some subsequent years. Unexpectedly, there was an increase in every age group, although, proportionately, the increase was largest amongst the older age groups. The possible 'extra' remarriages are indicated by the heights above the light dashed lines, which have been added as a purely subjective (and necessarily tentative) judgement of how the numbers would have developed had the 1969 Act not been enacted. More importantly, because the relevant data are unavailable, it is not known what proportion of these extra remarriages were to divorced men and women who had obtained their divorce on a separation fact.[20] However, as was seen in Figure 2.3, roughly half of all divorces granted to husbands, and one-third of those granted to wives, in 1971 were on these 'no-fault' facts.

The older the age group, the greater the tendency for the first of the extra remarriages to take place during 1971. Whilst some of those so remarrying might, of course, have divorced under the previous legislation, it is likely that others obtained their divorce under the new Act and remarried promptly the same year. The increase in remarriages and the implementation of the Act seem unlikely to be a coincidence. Also, it appears that newly divorced women and men in every age group used the opportunity to remarry, and did so to a similar extent. The backlog 'extra' number of remarriages took place over more years for the younger divorced men and women, typically 1972–77. By contrast, for the older age groups, the surge in remarriages occurred only from 1971 to 1973, but subsequently stabilised on a higher level, more than triple that for 1970. As speculative estimates, overall some 90,000 extra divorced men and 83,000 extra divorced women may have remarried between 1971 and 1977, with larger proportions of younger petitioners using two years' rather than five years' separation, and vice versa for older petitioners.

IV. Developments Since the 1970s: The Longer-term Effects of the 1969 Act

The growth in the proportion of wives awarded divorce on the basis of behaviour continued for some two decades after 1971, and the corresponding proportion of husbands awarded divorce on behaviour has increased continuously for over four decades up to the most recent time. Figure 2.5 illustrates the proportions for the different facts over this entire post-implementation period to 2017. It may be seen that, roughly speaking, the pattern of divorce by fact proven had settled down by about 1978, although some steadier, long-term trends had emerged. Several features observed in 1971 and 1972 persisted during the following decade. A study showed that those who divorced in 1981 on five years' separation tended to be the oldest, and had been married for the longest time, while, perhaps more unexpectedly, those who petitioned on two years' separation were the youngest of all divorcing couples, and had been married for the shortest time.[21] The interval between petitioning and obtaining the divorce was generally shortest for divorces on the separation facts, and these couples were more likely to have no dependent children[22] and so fewer ancillary matters to settle.

[20] But based on a sample of couples who divorced on five years' separation in 1979, 50% of divorced husbands who were granted divorce, and 42% of divorced wives who were granted divorces, had remarried within 2½ years of their divorce (ibid).

[21] ibid.

[22] ibid.

Figure 2.5 Percentage of divorces granted by fact proven, by party granted divorce, 1971–2017, England and Wales

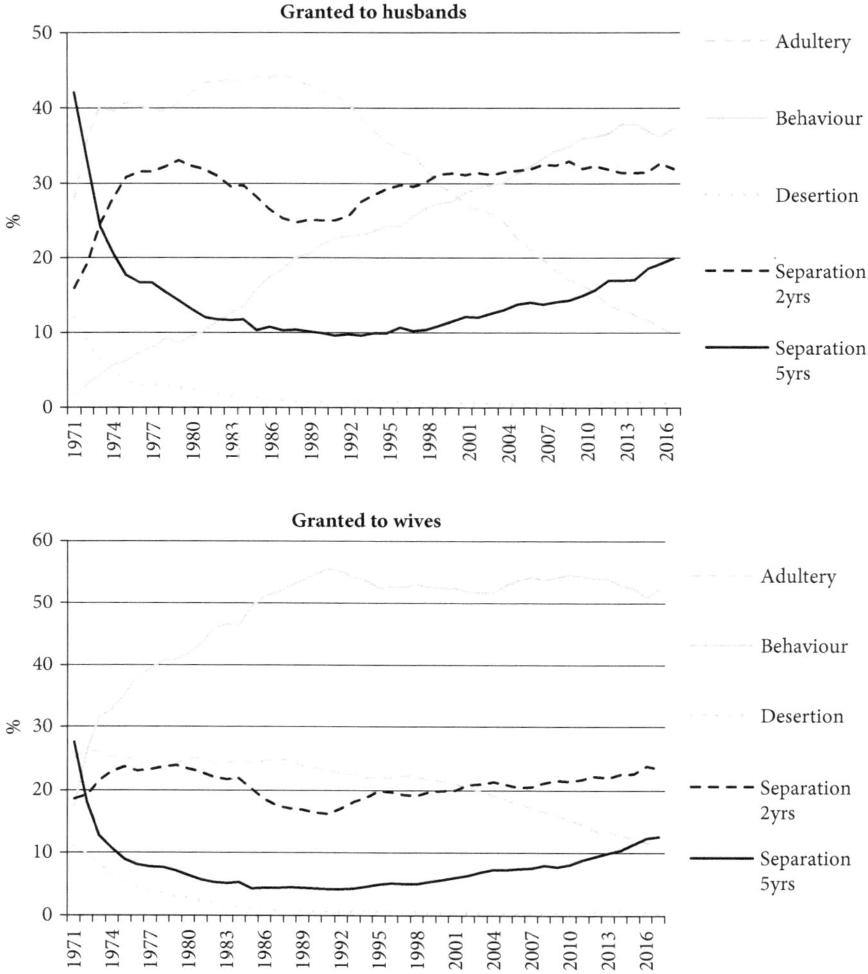

From late 1984, couples were able to petition for divorce after having been married for only one year, instead of three.[23] There followed a temporary minor surge in divorces: Figure 2.1 suggests that the effect of the Act was to bring forward some divorces into 1985 and 1986, which would otherwise have taken place later.[24]

[23] Matrimonial and Family Proceedings Act 1984

[24] Haskey (1986b).

Whilst two years' separation with consent has accounted for a fairly steady proportion of divorces for both husbands and wives – about 30 per cent of the former and 20 per cent of the latter – there has been much more variation in the proportion of divorces awarded on five years' separation. The 'backlog' effect appears to have persisted until around 1978 and then been succeeded by a gentler trend. However, from about 1986 or 1987, both separation facts constituted a fairly constant proportion of all divorces, and then, following 1991, both witnessed a modest but continuous growth in relative importance. The year 1991 seems to have marked a turnabout change for both divorcing husbands and wives for most of the facts proven. Also at this time, in 1992, the proportion of divorces granted to wives peaked at 72 per cent, the highest it has ever been, and in the following year, 1993, the number of divorces peaked, too.

Figure 2.6 uses the percentages shown in Figure 2.5 to measure the relative use of each fact by husbands compared with wives. In interpreting these ratios, it should be borne in mind that the number of divorces granted to wives exceeded that to husbands by around 3:2 in both 1971 and 2016 (and by a larger ratio in the intervening years) – as shown in Figure 2.1. So even though the relative use of a particular fact by husbands might be *larger* than that of wives, the actual number of divorces to husbands on that fact could be *smaller* than the corresponding number of divorces to wives.

Figure 2.6 For a given fact proven, the ratio of the % of that fact amongst all single fact divorces granted to husbands to the corresponding % of that fact amongst all single fact divorces granted to wives, 1971–2017, England and Wales

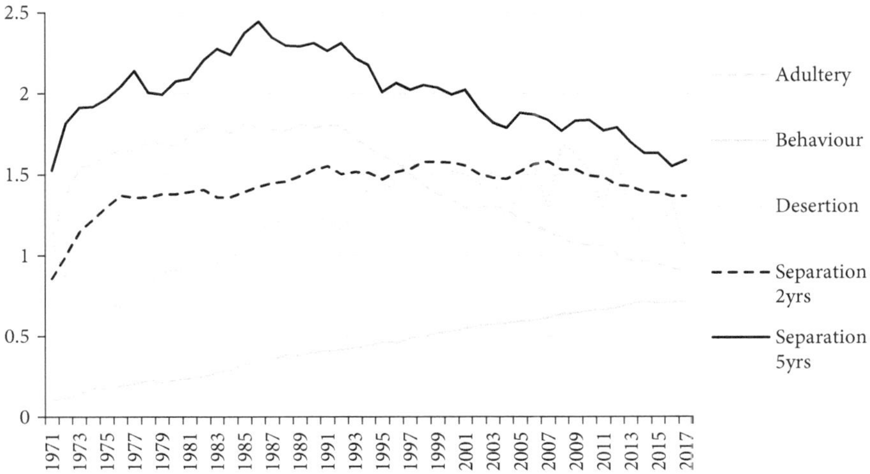

It may be seen that both separation facts were consistently used relatively more by husbands than wives. This relatively larger use continued up to the late 1980s. Thereafter the trends differed; the relative use of five years' separation by husbands compared with wives consistently fell after 1986 (but continued to exceed it, by a factor of between 2.5 and 1.5 times that of wives), whilst the relative use of two years' separation remained fairly constant, at around 1.5 times. Nevertheless, the important finding is that husbands have used both separation facts relatively more than wives throughout the entire period since the 1969 Act was implemented.

In contrast, although use of the behaviour fact has risen linearly throughout the whole period of just under 50 years, the relative measure of its use has been consistently less than one, indicating that husbands have been awarded divorce on this fact relatively less frequently than wives. Its value in 2017 was 0.7: the ratio of 37 per cent for husbands and 51 per cent for wives (37/52=0.7). Before 1971, cruelty was used predominantly by wives; very few husbands cited the ground, even though it was progressively interpreted as not requiring physical violence. When it was effectively replaced by behaviour, husbands began to use it and increasingly so, as Figure 2.5 demonstrates. It is also notable that it was only for desertion that there was a change from smaller relative use to larger relative use by husbands, and only for adultery that the change was the other way round. Adultery was used relatively more frequently by husbands than wives until around 2010 (when it accounted for about 15 per cent of divorces granted to both husbands and wives). Since 2010, wives have cited adultery slightly more (relatively) frequently than husbands.

Perhaps the most intriguing observation from Figure 2.6 is the apparent widening of the relative use of the different facts up to the mid- to late 1980s, followed in the early 1990s by a decided convergence. As mentioned previously, at this time the annual number of divorces started its long decline, as did the proportion of divorces granted to wives (Figure 2.1).

Investigating this convergence further, Figure 2.7 depicts the trends in the proportion of divorces according to whether the divorce was granted on the basis of 'fault' (desertion, behaviour and adultery, more accurately described as 'conduct') or 'no-fault' (the two separation facts). There is a very clear pattern of 'conduct' facts being increasingly used from just after the implementation of the 1969 Act up to 1991. After 1991, 'no-fault' facts formed a steadily growing proportion of all divorces. Most recently, the proportion of divorces granted to husbands on 'no-fault' facts has been roughly one half, whilst the corresponding proportion for wives has been just over one-third. Indeed, all four proportions of divorces on 'fault' and 'no-fault' facts have recently returned, somewhat uncannily, to almost exactly the same as those observed in 1973 – just after the implementation of the 1969 Act.

Figure 2.7 Percentage of divorces granted on a 'fault' or 'non-fault' fact, for single fact divorces, by party to whom granted, and year of divorce, 1971–2017, England and Wales

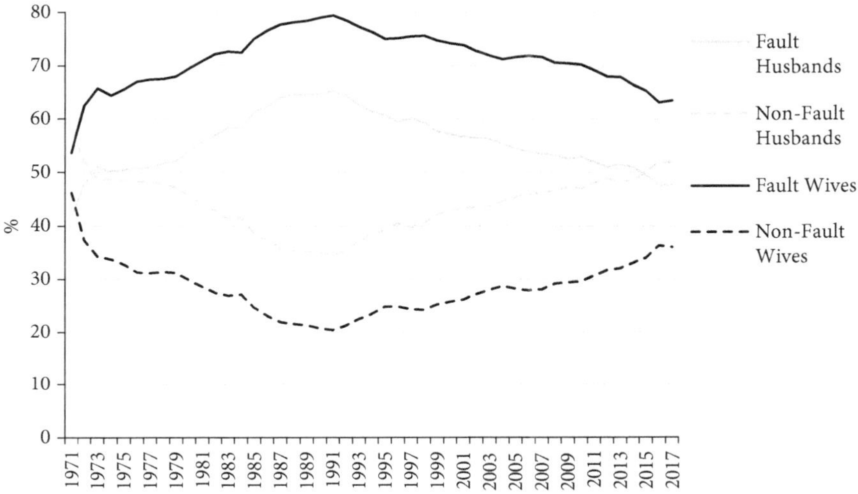

V. The Path to Reform

Since 1971, largely as a result of government cost-cutting, the divorce process has become much more streamlined and administrative, and less judicial. As an incidental rather than a planned result, it has become even closer to providing divorce on demand. If the petitioner has supplied all the required information, and the petition is undefended, the divorce is essentially rubber-stamped. While the courts are able to reject a petition if they are not satisfied that the marriage has irretrievably broken down, the petitioner's claim that the marriage has broken down – when undefended – is rarely questioned, and the veracity of statements of fact by the petitioner is not checked or challenged.

Divorcing couples have become pragmatic in using the provisions and proceedings of the existing divorce law. Petitioners have either learnt, or been advised, that petitioning on a 'fault' fact ensures a faster divorce than on a separation fact, with behaviour providing the fastest and easiest route of all (if undefended). That it is more urgent for divorcing wives to obtain financial provision[25] might well explain the differential between wives and husbands in using 'fault' facts, and the

[25] Eekelaar (1982).

weakening of this differential may be related to a fall in this urgency. Crucially, the role of the fact has not necessarily been to establish *the* cause (or even *a* cause) of the marital breakdown (as popularly believed); it has been to provide the *evidence* that the marriage has irretrievably broken down. Perhaps the most fundamental misapprehension is that the court will investigate and conclude whether the respondent has wronged the petitioner.

Furthermore, the required detail and strength of evidence in the statement of fact has become weaker over the decades, and for behaviour has, until recently, been relatively nominal, although there is an understandable tendency for petitioners to exaggerate the severity of the alleged fault.[26] On the other hand, though, petitioners (or rather their legal advisers) may have learnt not to do so, so as not to alienate the respondent and jeopardise cooperation. Were that to happen, the reaction of the respondent would be predictable: a wish to rebut the allegations; feelings of grievance; and a sense of injustice. But in practice there is usually little the respondent can do, since the petitioner's statement is accepted without scrutiny (and defending the divorce, which would allow the statement to be challenged, is not a practical option for the majority). This reality is part of a wider picture in which there has been a steady shift from the courts appearing to hold an inquest into the breakdown of the marriage to legal advisers adopting a supportive role in enabling divorce when it is applied for, in order to minimise bitterness and conflict.

Trinder's report indicated that only 65 per cent of petitioners alleging a 'fault' fact claimed it closely equated to the reason for the breakdown; unsurprisingly, the corresponding proportion of respondents was even smaller at 29 per cent.[27] This apparent dishonesty, together with the frustration and anger that it generates, was one of the reasons why there was pressure to reform the law.

VI. The Future, Possible Continuities and Changes, and Some Basic Indicators to Measure Them

With the implementation of the 2020 Act, the necessity to prove a specific 'fact' will disappear. Its loss for insight will not be greatly mourned, since, although it was indicative of how the law was used, it scarcely reflected the true situation of marital breakdown. There will, in any case, be other indicators of how the 2020 Act is working in practice.

One particularly interesting aspect of the new legislation is the innovatory option allowing spouses to *jointly* declare that their marriage has irretrievably

[26] The advice of the Law Society (Family Law Protocol) has been to encourage petitioners on behaviour 'only to include brief details in the statement of case, sufficient to satisfy the court'. Since *Owens v Owens*, however, petitioners are likely still to be brief, but to add 'beef'; see Trinder et al (2017).

[27] Trinder et al (2017) 39.

broken down. Joint notification can be taken as a measure of whether there is agreement between the spouses as to whether their marriage has broken down, and a willingness to cooperate in obtaining a divorce. Given the importance attached to the reduction of conflict by the architects of the new Act, the proportion of joint notifications will be a key measure of its success.[28]

Another indicator that can usefully be monitored is the split between husbands and wives notifying the irretrievable breakdown of their marriage individually. It may be predicted that the proportion of wives granted divorce is likely still be larger than that of husbands, continuing the trend under the 1969 Act. However, the proportion of wives initiating divorces has been declining ever since the peak of 72 per cent in 1992, being currently around 60 per cent, and may fall further. How the proportions for husbands and wives change will depend critically upon the effect of not having to allege blame or to separate. The split between husbands and wives under the 2020 Act is likely to be a better indicator of which spouse wished to end the marriage.

Up to this point all references have been to divorces of married *opposite-sex* couples. Both the current and new divorce law will apply equally to opposite-sex and same-sex married couples. With divorces of same-sex couples there will only be a distinction between single and joint notifiers of irretrievable breakdown, but the ratio of the numbers of men/men divorces to those of women/women can of course be monitored; the limited data so far available indicate that the proportion of women/women couples divorcing exceeds that of men/men.

For both opposite- and same-sex couples, the characteristics of the 'initiator' spouse can be compared with those of the respondent spouse, using the basic demographic factors, such as age, previous marital status, etc that are likely to be routinely recorded, so giving an appreciation of the differential features of the 'initiator'. The characteristics of the 'initiator' may be compared with those of the respondent to understand the dynamics and determinants of divorce.

Another feature to be considered is the ratio between the number of notifications and the number of final divorces. The direct equivalents under the 1969 Act are petitions filed and decrees absolute, and currently between approximately 80 and 90 per cent of the former translate into the latter. It will be interesting to see whether the equivalent proportion changes. An increase might signify would-be notifiers as being more likely to complete the divorce process and not be deterred by it, as might have happened to some petitioners under the 1969 Act, who dropped out for some reason before obtaining a decree absolute.

Overall, all the other measures and indicators mentioned can be analysed in relation to the basic demographic factors and other items of information routinely collected, to give clearer insights into how the 2020 Act is operating in practice.

[28] The obvious comparison is with two years' separation with consent, and the high hopes that this 'no-fault' fact would become the majority 'fact' on which to petition. However, *joint* petitioning, even with two years' separation with consent, is not possible.

Changes in the law, as well as the computerisation of forms and processes, provide rare opportunities to review and revise the routine collection of data for policy, planning and analytic purposes, but routine data can be supplemented by special ad-hoc surveys to discover how the new law works in practice, and in comparison with the 1969 Act.

The annual number of divorces is informative in its own right, insofar as increases and decreases can often be attributed to special circumstances (such as the pandemic), administrative changes, and regulatory and government initiatives. As an example, the Government, concerned over a recent increase in divorce, has arranged for the Ministry of Justice to provide tax-free vouchers to separating couples for mediation to resolve their differences amicably. Whilst the eventual total number of divorces might not thereby be changed, the timing of them might cause these divorces to reach the final stage more quickly and be reflected as a minor increase. However, another reason there will probably be a surge in the number of divorces will be due to the change in divorce law itself;[29] the increase arising from a number of couples suddenly being able to divorce under the new legislation, whereas under the 1969 Act they would have had to wait longer. Furthermore, after the surge there will probably be a fall back in numbers so that, overall, the total number of divorces over several years will not necessarily be larger than had the new legislation not been enacted.

VII. Conclusions

Early on in the lifetime of the 1969 law, the trends revealed the continued dominance of divorce on the 'conduct' facts against the expectation that reliance on those facts would decline and be replaced by use of the separation facts. Desertion virtually disappeared as a means of divorce soon after the implementation of the 1969 Act; the introduction of the fact of two years' separation, which required the same waiting-time as desertion, meant that a blame-free and stigma-free fact could be used instead with the same delay. The different patterns of petitioning on cruelty/behaviour by husbands before and after the implementation of the 1969 Act also suggested that perceptions of stigma played a role in selecting a ground for divorce.[30]

From 1972 to the present time, the annual change in the number of divorces, expressed as a percentage of those in the earlier year, has generally ranged between −10 per cent and +10 per cent. This annual variation is, for the most part, much smaller than the corresponding annual percentage change for all the years before 1972, suggesting that the 1969 Act may have had the effect of steadying the divorce trend.

[29] Haskey (2019).
[30] Haskey (1986c).

Nonetheless, the proportions petitioning on the different facts have varied considerably over the period since 1971, the pattern and trends in divorce by fact proven probably reflecting a host of influencing factors, including: the (relative) speed of obtaining divorce; the availability of financial provision; general social attitudes to divorce; expectations of marital satisfaction; and the growth of individualism. Nevertheless, the statistical information on such aspects as the party to whom divorce is granted, and the trends in the numbers and profiles of divorce, has thrown some light on how the law is used in practice.

Previous analyses[31] of divorce have indicated that the social and demographic characteristics of the groups obtaining divorce on the different facts are significantly different – but in understandable, interpretable ways, based on their particular social and economic circumstances. Further, these analyses reveal which groups resort to which provisions, or, perhaps more importantly, which provisions are not – or cannot be – used by certain groups, reflecting unequal access to the law. Such differences of access usually result from implementing general principles that can lead to some unintended, or at least unexpected, consequences. An example is the lesser use of two years' separation with consent by each of the following groups: husbands in unskilled occupations; wives in unskilled occupations; unemployed husbands; and housewives,[32] presumably because none of these groups can afford two residences. Similarly, wives with dependent children tended to petition on the fact of behaviour, largely it is believed because they could thereby obtain divorce quickly,[33] important if they were suffering domestic abuse, or needing immediate financial support.

Routine statistics, other than those derived from special surveys, certainly have their limitations; they do not, and cannot, illuminate many important aspects of divorce. They cannot measure the extent to which the process is adversarial and stressful, and certainly not the extent to which it is *needlessly* adversarial. They cannot assess the disincentive effect of a longer waiting-time for divorce, or only by the crudest comparisons between facts with different time provisions. They cannot detect whether the opportunities for reconciliation are inadvertently limited or discouraged, or whether sufficient time and conducive circumstances are made available for post-divorce arrangements to be agreed and put into place. All these aspects, their causes and potential remedies, are best investigated and identified by appropriate survey research,[34] and can usefully be supplemented by the experience of family law practitioners who guide divorcing couples through the entire process, and therefore are in closest touch with all the practical details. Perhaps, at best, the patterns in statistical background information can prompt questions that can be further investigated at a more detailed level by in-depth surveys.

[31] Haskey (1986a).
[32] ibid.
[33] Eekelaar (2018).
[34] See eg Davis and Murch (1988); Trinder et al (2017).

A general conclusion is that past experience shows that some predictions do not materialise, whilst other outcomes are unexpected. Examples since 1971 have ranged from the fear that introducing the fact of separation without consent would lead to husbands' swapping wives for younger women, to a belief that separation would become the most popular fact on which to petition.

References

Archbishop of Canterbury's Group on the Divorce Law (1966), *Putting asunder. A divorce law for contemporary society. The report of a group appointed by the Archbishop of Canterbury in January 1964* (London, SPCK).

Chester, R and Streather, J (1972) 'Cruelty in English divorce: some empirical findings' 34 *Journal of Marriage and Family* 706.

Cretney, S (2003) *Family Law in the Twentieth Century: a History* (Oxford, Oxford University Press).

Davis, G and Murch, M (1988) *Grounds for Divorce* (Oxford, Clarendon Press).

Eekelaar, J (1982) 'Law Commission Reports on the Financial Consequences of Divorce' 45 *Modern Law Review* 420.

—— (2013) 'Then and now – family law's direction of travel' 34 *Journal of Social Welfare and Family Law* 415.

—— (2018) 'Children in divorce: some further data' 48 *Family Law* 1006.

Gibson, C (1993) *Dissolving Wedlock* (London, Taylor & Francis).

Hall, J (1975) 'Illness as Behaviour' 34 *Cambridge Law Journal* 207.

Haskey, J (1983) 'Remarriage of the divorced in England and Wales – a contemporary phenomenon' 15 *Journal of Biosocial Science* 253.

—— (1986a) 'Grounds for divorce in England and Wales – a social and demographic analysis' 18 *Journal of Biosocial Science* 127.

—— (1986b) 'Recent trends in divorce in England and Wales: the effects of legislative changes' 44 *Population Trends* 9.

—— (1986c) 'Secular changes in divorce in England and Wales by class of decree – a socio-legal analysis' 3 *Biology and Society* 62.

—— (2001) 'Cohabitation in Great Britain: past, present and future trends and attitudes' 103 *Population Trends* 4.

—— (2019) 'Some scenarios ion the numerical implications of the proposed new divorce reform legislation for England and Wales' 49 *Family Law* 1040.

Herbert, AP (1934) *Holy Deadlock* (London, Methuen).

Law Commission (1990) *The Ground for Divorce*, Law Commission No 192 (London, HMSO).

Miller, J (1984) 'The Reform of the Law Relating to Financial Provision and Matrimonial Property' 15 *Cambrian Law Review* 73.

Ministry of Justice (2019) *Reducing Family Conflict: Government response to the consultation on reform of the legal requirements for divorce* at https://assets.publishing.service.gov.uk/government/uploads/system/uploads/attachment_data/file/793642/reducing-family-conflict-consult-response.pdf (last accessed 8 July 2021).

Trinder, L, Braybrook, D, Bryson, C, Coleman, L, Houlston, C and Sefton, M (2017) *Finding Fault? Divorce Law and Practice in England and Wales* (London, Nuffield Foundation).

PART TWO

Background

3

Dynamic Impasse: Divorce and British Film in the Mid-Twentieth Century

JAMES BROWN

This chapter addresses the relationship between divorce in Britain in the mid-twentieth century (c 1930–55) and a selection of British films. Many of the films can be construed as contributions to a debate about divorce and the nature of marriage. However, the relation between the substance of divorce – its incidence, its meaning, its social salience – and the debate surrounding it, especially regarding legal arrangements, is surprisingly opaque. Considered merely as contributions to that debate, the films would be of limited significance. However, a lot of them are at their most telling when doing something other than advancing an argument. There are at least two main reasons for this.

First, British film was censored. The British Board of Film Censorship (BBFC) (as it was from 1912 to 1984) imposed political and moral censorship. As Jeffrey Richards has argued, what lay behind moral censorship was often political conservatism and a desire to uphold established authorities so that, for instance, representing 'Medical Men' in an unfavourable light was frowned upon (something to bear in mind in relation to *Brief Encounter*).[1] Within a year of the BBFC's establishment, it extended its remit to uphold marriage. Sexual activity implied in any other context was likely to be banned. When the President of the BBFC, TP O'Connor, published a list in 1917 of 43 problematic things, it included '[s]ituations accentuating delicate marital relations',[2] and most of the items on O'Connor's list persisted and were added to as BBFC's work continued between the wars.[3] So where films queried the permanence of marriage they often did this obliquely, though one can find exceptions, often in costume drama, such as *Lady Hamilton* (dir Alexander Korda, 1941).

Second, story-telling or -enacting is not usually the most efficient way of arguing a case. A film that served merely as an example to illustrate an argument would risk alienating its audience by having too obvious a design upon them.

[1] Richards (1983) 15.
[2] Tighe (2005) 55–56.
[3] Robertson (1985) 7–8.

But cinema proved in some ways better placed than explicit argument to engage with the complexity of marriage and divorce, because it could engage both with its contested legal forms and with its cultural substance without having to reach a conclusion.

As explained elsewhere in this volume,[4] throughout the mid-twentieth century, legal arrangements for divorce in England and Wales were stable. They derived from nineteenth-century reforms, which had created a procedure for divorce that necessitated a trial in which one spouse had to prove the other guilty of a matrimonial offence, of which adultery was the leading example. Indeed, between 1923 and 1937 adultery was the sole criterion for divorce.[5] But if legal arrangements scarcely changed, other aspects of divorce changed a great deal. Starting from a low base, numbers rose during both World Wars, with a surge immediately after each War, after which a new, higher 'normal' rate emerged. Where divorces had been reckoned in their hundreds before the First World War, between the Wars they were reckoned in thousands, and after the Second World War in their tens of thousands. Some of these increases were the result of failed marriages being more likely to result in divorce than in other kinds of separation, but, especially from 1937 onwards, the rate at which marriages failed also increased.[6] Numbers peaked in 1947, and then diminished for a few years, only to rise again though in the 1960s in the run-up to the 1969 Divorce Reform Act. Thus the stability of the legal form of divorce in the mid-twentieth century was accompanied by transformations of its incidence and culture. Hence the title of this chapter. Those transformations can be charted by dividing the period into three phases: before the Second World War; the war and its immediate aftermath (c 1939–47); and post-war from c 1948 until divorces start to increase again c 1960.

I. Before the War

One More River (dir James Whale, 1934), made in the United States by Universal, is based on John Galsworthy's final novel, *Over the River* (1933). The story is a plea for legal reform. It portrays divorce prior to the Matrimonial Causes Act 1937. Galsworthy's interest was personal. He had fallen in love with the wife of a cousin, and she had had to secure a divorce to marry Galsworthy. With a British writer, a British director and a mostly British cast, it is an honorary British film.

James Whale had to be discreet in showing why the well-born Clare Corven (Diana Wynyard) is fleeing her marriage to colonial administrator Sir Gerald Corven (Colin Clive), who is a sadist. Whale is good at setting one speculating about what Corven is capable of. When he catches up with Clare at her uncle's London house, she retreats behind an armchair, and twice within a short discussion

[4] See especially Haskey, ch 2 of this volume.
[5] See Cretney (2005) ch 6.
[6] Stone (1990) 397.

he attempts to use force to bend her to his will. When he later finds her alone in her London home, we are left to guess what happens. In the trial, he insists that conjugal relations resumed; she denies it. It seems likely that, judged by today's norms, he raped her,[7] though under English law rape within marriage was not recognised until a ruling by the Law Lords in 1991.[8] Whale is now best known for his horror films; here, it is the 'respectable' male heterosexual who is monstrous.

Clare Corven is rich and well-connected. The film thus has no occasion to address the economic obstacles to divorce for women, who were usually financially dependent on their husbands. In other respects, the film reflects the divorce law of the time, which made infidelity the sole basis for divorce. This emphasis on sex kept many private detectives in employment. Whale has a relay of men in assorted hats and stick-on moustaches tail Clare and her friend 'Tony' Croom (Frank Newton). From the opening of the film, it is clear Tony is in love with Clare. However, Clare insists that their relationship remain platonic. On a drive, at some distance from the nearest town, the lights of their car fail, so they sleep chastely in the vehicle until dawn. This is witnessed by one of the snoopers.

Galsworthy can be interpreted as contriving a test case to demonstrate the fallibility of a law that depends on circumstantial evidence. When getting Clare back proves impossible, Corven seeks divorce on his own terms, alleging her infidelity, and the detective's evidence of their night in Tony's car proves decisive. Clare tells the truth and is disbelieved. Meanwhile her husband is shielded from awkward questions by the judge. Cruelty would not become grounds for divorce until the 1937 Act came into force in 1938. However, if speculation about Corven's sadism is barred, speculation about Clare and Tony's non-existent sex life is legally obligatory.

Figure 3.1 Diana Wynyard as Clare Corven in *One More River*, dir James Whale, © Universal Pictures (1934)

[7] Asimow (2000) 241.
[8] *Regina v R* [1992] 1 AC 599.

However, the fact that Tony and Clare were cultivating a relationship that was ready to become a sexual relationship the moment circumstances permitted, points to ways in which Galsworthy's test case was not merely challenging the law but had also absorbed something of its preoccupation with sex. Clare's reticence about her private life, even her ghastly sex life with Corven, the court's determination to shield Corven, the reticence imposed by censorship,[9] and even a certain self-imposed restraint on the part of the writer and of the film combine to create a wall of silence behind which Clare is trapped. To the extent that this silence makes any sense, it tacitly acknowledges the force of certain taboos.

Corven is granted his divorce, though he is denied the £2,000 in damages he had sought from Tony. Then the film gets to more interesting, less easily construed material. The trial leaves Clare in an ambiguous position: she is free of Corven, but she has been found guilty. Tony goes to Clare's London home. To his surprise, she welcomes him in: she has arranged a cold supper for them. An ungainly artificial flower hangs below her cleavage on a dress that leaves her back exposed and breasts unconstrained. It advertises her availability to him. It is an understandable reaction to the insistently prurient atmosphere of the court, as is Tony's fleeing in disgust. This is the moment (only briefly sustained, since he returns the following morning and they forgive each other) at which the distorting effects of narrowly sexual criteria for divorce on the substance of marriage and sexual love are most evident. The novel makes the rift between them longer-lived and motivates it differently: there Tony is disgusted at the thought of Clare's offering sex as a loveless payment. The film includes a line in which Clare insists, from a suggestively semi-recumbent posture, that she pays her debts. However, in the film there is arguably a stronger sense of the prurience of the trial infecting them both, muddying an intimacy that up this point we have trusted.

II. The Second World War and Its Aftermath

During the Second World War increased demand for divorce led The Law Society to set up a salaried divorce department as a temporary measure, and divorce became eligible for legal aid under the 1949 Legal Aid and Advice Act.[10]

Reflecting this formal acknowledgement of reality, several films released during and soon after the war represented marital breakdown and divorce as symptoms of difficult times. In *Waterloo Road* (dir Sidney Gilliat, 1945), for example, Tillie Colter (Joy Shelton), the wife of a conscripted soldier, has to contend with the advances of the local spiv, Ted Purvis (Stewart Granger), and Tillie's husband, Jim (John Mills), goes AWOL to save his marriage. The impact of war on middle-class marriages is touched on in *The Halfway House* (dir Basil Dearden, 1944). Damaged

[9] Asimow (2000) 241.
[10] Brooke (2017) 5.

lives and relationships are healed at a Welsh inn, where the guests are served by a landlord and his daughter (Mervyn and Glynis Johns), who had been killed by enemy action the previous year. It is a benign ghost story. One of the couples starts the film planning their divorce, to the dismay of their teenage daughter (Sally Ann Howes).

Dearden returned to the War's impact on romantic life with *The Captive Heart* (1946), which is a version of the Martin Guerre story. Celia Mitchell (Rachel Kempson) is married to a ghastly husband, who is killed in combat. A Czech officer, Karel Hašek (Michael Redgrave), assumes Mitchell's identity to save himself. The letters he has to write in Mitchell's name cause Celia to fall in love with him. Celia is unshakably true to her marriage vows (hers is the captive heart), but her story reveals the need for a way of dealing with impossible husbands other than waiting for them to be killed. A prisoner of war where Hašek is interned jokes about romance, notices the anguish of a fellow prisoner, who fears his fiancée has abandoned him, and remarks, 'I'm sorry old chap. I was forgetting you're a one-woman man.' The film implicitly accepts that some are cut out for permanent monogamy and some are not.

Where films sought acceptance of serial monogamy and the abolition of the stigma of divorce, they seldom did so explicitly. *The Way to the Stars* (1945) was mostly written by Terrence Rattigan and directed by Anthony Asquith. It is about relations between British and American airmen on an RAF base in the War, and their loves and friendships in the nearby town of Shepley. There is a dance near the end, the theme of which is partner-swapping. A 16-year-old Jean Simmons sings of letting a lover go because she has found 'a far more nicer boy'. The dance shows some people can happily engage in such swapping, but not all. Immediately afterwards, the platonic relationship between the married American pilot, Johnny Hollis (Douglass Montgomery), and the widowed manageress of the hotel, Toddy (Rosamund John), comes close to becoming romantic. The following day, Johnny backs out of going home to train new pilots, and then goes on what will be his final mission. He dies a martyr's death, seeking to land his damaged Flying Fortress with a bomb wedged in the bomb-bay, sooner than baling out and risking its crashing on Shepley. His motives for staying become impossible to disentangle: he is staying to risk his life for others, but Toddy has become the most compelling embodiment for him of those others, and he is also staying for her. Maybe, had he lived, their relationship would have continued to be friendship with an undertow of unrealised yearning. But film conventions dispose us, as spectators, to want to see them come together as a couple. Marriages in danger of breaking down because of the war also figure in *We Dive At Dawn* (dir Asquith, 1943), *While the Sun Shines* (dir Asquith, 1947) and *Carrington VC* (dir Asquith, 1955).

No director made more of the theme of marriage and divorce than David Lean. He was brought up a Quaker in suburban Croydon. In 1923, when Lean was 15, his father left his mother for another woman. This broke up the family home and caused his parents to resign from the Society of Friends, though their sons remained enrolled. The stigma of divorce had to be concealed. Of the two boys, Lean was closest to his mother, bound to her by tears that he nevertheless resented.[11] His mother never remarried. Lean himself would get divorced five times, the first of these divorces occurring in 1936. His marriages mostly broke down because of his affairs. His Quaker family was so dismayed by the first divorce that they refused to attend his second marriage. His marriage to Ann Todd, his third wife, who had previously been married to his cousin, caused further family ructions.[12] There is something unresolved in the way Lean remained close to his mother, even though he kept re-enacting his father's departure.

Some of his earliest films touch upon divorce. *This Happy Breed* (1944) is Lean's account of a lower middle-class family between the Wars, based on a play by Noel Coward. Young Queenie Gibbons (Kay Walsh – Lean's then wife) takes up with a married man, trusting to his promise to get a divorce and marry her. But since he is the guilty spouse, divorce is not in his gift but in his wife's, and she refuses to give it him – or so he says. Queenie finds herself cast adrift and shamed, until rescued by her longstanding sweetheart, Billy from next door, now a Petty Officer (John Mills). Prior to that her mother, Elsie (Celia Johnson), had refused to have anything to do with her disgraced daughter. Having learnt her lesson, Queenie settles for motherhood and wifely respectability.

A completely different kind of Coward play furnished the script for *Blithe Spirit* (1945). Charles Condomine (Rex Harrison) is entitled to marry his second wife, Ruth (Constance Cummings) after his first wife's death. But why put 'Condom' in his name if his story is really about the supernatural? But for one (and eventually three) of the principal characters being a ghost, *Blithe Spirit* would be a sex farce. In fact, Condomine was sexually tempted long before the death of his first wife, Elvira (Kay Hammond): on their honeymoon, Condomine and Elvira were already eyeing up other possible sexual partners. The film ends with Condomine, Elvira and Ruth as ghosts, and therefore presumably locked into an uneasy *ménage à trois* forever. This is Lean's most significant change to Coward's play (in the play Condomine simply leaves). Coward berated him for it. Silver and Ursini suggest the change might have been required to anticipate the censor's concerns by punishing irregular morals.[13] But it could also owe something to Lean's conflicted feelings about marriage.

If this moment reveals Lean's ambivalent relation to religious teaching, which he defied and yet deferred to, it was in some degree widely shared. In the mid-twentieth century, Anglican clergy took the lead in insisting on marriage's permanence and in thwarting reform of the divorce law, changing their minds only in 1966 with the report *Putting Asunder*, which helped to clear the way for the 1969 Act.

[11] Brownlow (1996) 21–25.
[12] ibid 264.
[13] Silver and Ursini (1974) 27.

Prior to that, for orthodox Anglicans the kind of partner-swapping that *Blithe Spirit* guys was meant to be regarded with holy dread.

It is surprising that *Brief Encounter* (1945), which is the last of the Coward/Lean collaborations, should so powerfully have evoked this dread. It is the story of how the happily married Laura Jesson (Celia Johnson) falls in love with Alec Harvey (Trevor Howard) and finally decides *not* to pursue their affair. It is based on Coward's *Still Life*, one of a cycle of short plays called *Tonight at 8:30* (1936). In its original form, the story never leaves a railway waiting room, and takes place over months rather than the film's six or seven weeks. So far from breaking off their affair, leaving it unconsummated, Alec and Laura in the play have an affair that ends because it runs its course. *Brief Encounter* is nominally set, like *Still Life*, before the War. Yet it evinces indirect awareness of it. For example, Laura sports quasi-military hats, which, notwithstanding Lean's comment about her hats having been chosen to locate her in the 1930s and indicate her dowdiness,[14] in 1945 would have evoked women's uniforms. The hats contribute to a sense of ambiguous temporality.[15] The film arguably reworks its pre-war source to reflect sexual anxieties of the war years. Being made and released when it was, it is tempting to see it in relation to what Elizabeth Bowen spoke of as a feeling of 'unmarriedness' that descended on people in wartime London.[16]

Brief Encounter has become a byword for superseded sexual mores, but it is complex and ambiguous. Plenty of people today are as opposed to 'cheating' as Laura was.[17] Nor does the film deny that people sometimes change their partners. Myrtle (Joyce Carey), the proprietrix of the café, explains that she walked out on her husband, telling him, 'There are just as good fish in the sea as ever came out of it,' and she is now being courted by the station master. The film takes this in its stride. However, what *does* now seem passé is the way it shows sexual mores being shaped by a preoccupation with respectability. That concern also informed the phenomenon of the 'open secret', such as the open secret of Coward's sexuality, which may now appear hypocritical but which was arguably intrinsic to his pursuit of life on his own terms in spite of prejudice and the law. Laura as reimagined for the film cannot assert that kind of freedom for herself. Viewers are often hard put to decide whether the frustration of the affair with Alec and the continuation of Laura's marriage with Fred (Cyril Raymond) constitute a happy ending. The last few moments can be seen in different ways, depending on how much one reckons Fred understands about what Laura has been silently confessing in voiceover. His 'Thank you for coming back to me' might merely mean 'it's just as well you snapped out of your unhappy daydream', and thus that their life will continue unchanged; but it could also indicate that he understands

[14] Silverman (1998) 64.
[15] Cook (2005) 102; Lant (1991) 159.
[16] Bowen (1998) 94.
[17] See also Jeffrey Richards, quoted in Silverman (1998) 64.

how close she came to leaving him, which might imply a renewed understanding between them.

The affair unfolds in flashbacks over seven Thursdays, Thursday being Laura's day for visiting Milford. It starts with a chance meeting when Alec, a doctor, is able to remove a piece of grit from Laura's eye at the railway station. This is a reminder of a Biblical warning: 'Thou hypocrite, first cast out the beam out of thine own eye; and then shalt thou see clearly to cast out the mote out of thy brother's eye'.[18] This implicit invitation to the audience to suspend judgement on Laura defines the artistic policy of the film. Laura is a sympathetic everywoman, rather than the kind of *outré* portrayal of an errant wife that Bette Davis had pulled off the previous year in *Mr Skeffington* (dir Vincent Sherman, 1944).

Figure 3.2 Laura in her armchair at home watches herself with Alec at the railway station in a flashback that she narrates in *Brief Encounter*, dir David Lean, © Carlton Film Distributors Ltd (1945)

If *Brief Encounter* refuses to invite the audience to pass judgement, Laura judges herself severely, anticipating the judgement that spectators might otherwise have passed on her (though her delays also exposed the film to the impatience of a spectator in Rochester, where Lean tried the film out, who got a big laugh when he urged Laura and Alec to get on with it).[19] The suspension of judgement is accomplished partly by noir-ish elements of narrative and imagery, which Lean, writing in 1947, ascribed to the influence of *Citizen Kane*.[20] Laura's double role as judge and judged is expressed and amplified in her much remarked double role as both character and confessor/narrator,[21] and this doubling of her is then

[18] Matthew 7:5.
[19] Silverman (1998) 64.
[20] Lean (1947) 30.
[21] Phillips (2006) 87; Dyer (1993) 16–24.

rendered visible in several complicated shots, sometimes involving the image of Laura and of her reflection, as in a moment when, sitting at her dressing table, she lies to her husband for the first time, or in images of herself and her reflection in the window of a railway compartment, with fantasised versions of Alec and herself projected into the darkness beyond her reflection. One of the most telling of these double images of Laura is a process shot, in which she sits in staid domestic comfort in an armchair, contemplating Alex and herself in the railway underpass, a space associated with turbulence, transience and desire. It's an image that encapsulates the way the film plays domesticity and probity off against passion.

The film's even-handedness makes Laura's wish to pursue an affair that might lead to divorce look like something that might befall anyone. This is all the more striking, because there is no excuse for it. The worst that can be said of Fred is that he is sometimes more interested in his crossword than in his wife.

Laura judges not only herself, but also many of the people around her. She sniggers with Alec at the cellist (Irene Handl) in the Kardomah, and again when she turns up playing the cinema organ. She privately dismisses Dolly Messiter (Everley Gregg) as a gossiping acquaintance 'I've known for years and never particularly cared for', and goes so far as to wish Dolly were dead. Then she judges herself, since the remark was 'silly and unkind'. When Mary Norton (Marjorie Mars) and her cousin happen upon Laura at her champagne lunch with Alec, the itch to pass judgement keeps pace with her fear of being judged. She speaks contemptuously of 'that rich over-made-up cousin of hers'.

Laura's fear of being judged by others is pervasive. As Richard Dyer notes, she quails before male authority figures: a clergyman in her compartment, the policeman who asks whether she is all right when she is smoking a cigarette by the war memorial, and doctors – both the unseen doctor who treats Bobby and Stephen Lynn (Valentine Dyall), from whom she flees so quickly she never sees him, so perhaps his withering disdain for the assignation he interrupts is imagined by Laura.[22] Thus *Brief Encounter* both invokes and challenges a judgemental impulse. In effect, it holds up for critical inspection the processes by which the taboo on divorce was maintained, and reveals the psychological cost people pay in sustaining it.

After the war, Lean extended his treatment of sexual restlessness in two further films: *The Passionate Friends* (1949) and *Summertime* (1955). The former invites comparison with *Brief Encounter*, not least in casting Trevor Howard as Steven Stratton, a professor of biology and possible lover of Mary Justin (Ann Todd, with whom Lean began an affair while making the film, and whom he married a few months after its release). However, it is really quite a different story, even though Mary ends up staying with her wealthy banker husband, Howard Justin (Claude Raines), just as Laura had stayed with Fred. Howard thwarts one attempt by the

[22] Dyer (1993) 25–31.

lovers to betray him. Then by chance Steven and Mary find themselves booked into adjacent rooms in a Swiss hotel. Howard misreads this circumstantial evidence and starts divorce proceedings.

That is as close as the film comes to an explicit point about divorce. But the film is also drawn to less explicitly argued possibilities to do with redefining what romance and marriage might mean. Lean attenuates the philosophical discussion in HG Wells' source novel, but something of its air of pursuing experiments in living persists in Mary's rebuke to Steven's insistence that their mutual love, in which each belongs inevitably to the other, must trump her cooler (if better resourced) partnership with her husband: her response is that she wants to belong to herself. The film examines the interplay of self-possession and desire. She realises that she wants a marriage that grants her love without possessiveness.

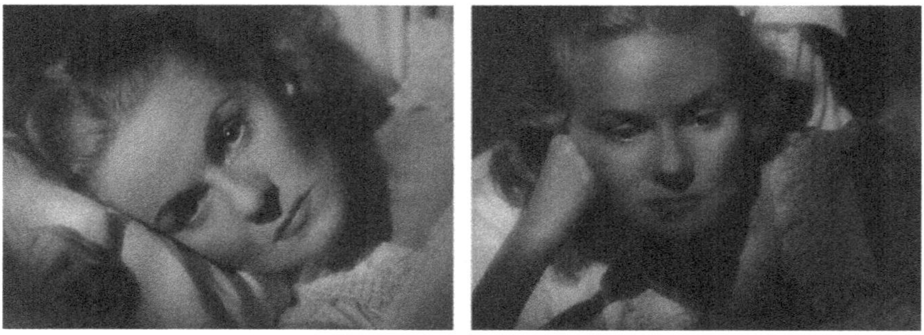

Figure 3.3 Two images of Ann Todd from within the same shot in *The Passionate Friends*, dir David Lean, © Carlton Film Distributors Ltd (1949)

Though Howard surprises himself by falling in love with his wife, having started their marriage expecting no more than loyalty and companionship, and she finds, to her surprise, that her tepid marriage has become the most important relationship in her life, the film really turns on Lean's complicated feelings about Todd. Lean has a way of shooting and lighting Todd so that, though her fair hair and pale skin glow, the eyes at times are like black holes. The emotional pitch of the film can be plotted in a series of shots of Todd's eyes, which are by turns agleam and expressive, and then remote and inaccessible. This is the normal currency of movie-photography, but Lean makes a great deal of this interplay. Under the film's ostensible debate about arrangements for sexual relationships (something more fully realised in Wells' novel), there is a meditation on the ways in which another can remain elusive, no matter how intimately one thinks one knows them, in ways that both spur desire and defeat it. Something remains unresolved in a film that, nevertheless, significantly extends Lean's treatment of desire and convention, and which in the process (though this is only a small part of what the film has to say) implicitly criticises the legal form of divorce.

Summertime (1955), which was based on Arthur Laurents' play *Time of the Cuckoo*, developed Lean's case. It's the story of Jane Hudson, an American spinster (Katharine Hepburn), who goes to Venice, has an affair with Renato (Rossano Brazzi), who is married, and then goes home having enjoyed this episode of passion. Though the Production Code Administration in the United States demanded changes before it would approve the film for release, the Catholic (aka National) Legion of Decency still deemed it to be 'morally objectionable in part'.[23] The adultery that was an insuperable obstacle in *Brief Encounter* now scarcely matters. Jane's objections to an affair with a married man are briskly disposed of by his remarking that she is like a child who is hungry and turns her nose up at ravioli because she wants beefsteak.

The real question within the film is less whether the affair will take place, but how to *finish* it gracefully, given that the film presents romantic life as a series of affairs. Though one might expect Renato to leave her, she chooses to end the affair so she can remember it as she wishes to. The ideas of conducting an affair and taking holiday photographs (as Jane does constantly) relate to each other: they are both about preserving an image of a brief and cherished experience. In this respect Jane Hudson, with her cine-camera and her craving for sexual passion, is akin to the director, even if Renato is the film's *raisonneur*.

Even so, someone watching the film now is likely to be struck by something else: Renato may indulge in passion on the side, while his unseen wife keeps an eye on their children; but it is doubtful whether the film would have been made had the roles been vice versa. However undeceived an account of romantic desire the film might *appear* to give, it is structured around the sexual double-standard: it implies that a married man may take his pleasure as he will, while only a permanent spinster, unlikely to be a candidate for marriage or motherhood, can be allowed such freedom.

Within the mainstream Anglophone cinema of c 1940–55, *Summertime* is about as far as one could go in making a case in a film with a modern setting for a sceptical reappraisal of marriage. By the time it appeared, films had been released on the other side of question, upholding the permanence of marriage and challenging moves to make divorce easier.

III. Reaction: The 1950s

No Place for Jennifer (dir Hanry Cass, 1950) is one of a handful of films to examine the consequences of divorce for the children involved.[24] In *No Place for Jennifer*, the 12-year-old Jennifer is caught between her warring parents, and the film

[23] National Legion of Decency (1959) 229 and viii.
[24] Elliot (2020).

culminates in her fleeing from the law court in which her parents are fighting for custody, and having a nightmarish time of it on London's streets before she is able to catch a train to friends with whom it is implied she will spend the rest of her childhood.

Unlike *Brief Encounter*, this film has no willingness to suspend judgement. It reflects the prevailing form of divorce in creating a story in which the audience is invited to find one party to blame: Jennifer's mother, Paula (Beatrice Campbell). She gave her husband, architect William (Leo Genn), cause to divorce her, and her behaviour continues to be shabby. William has been awarded custody, though Jennifer (Janette Scott) yearns for her parents to be together again. William arranges for Jennifer to stay with Paula. Paula then pretends that Jennifer is ill so she can keep her indefinitely. When that does not work, she tries to kidnap her and take her to Paris. William appears comparatively blameless. In the end, however, both parents are punished by their daughter's turning away from both of them.

The plot is less interesting than the imagery. The key word in the title is 'Place'. The film is set in contemporary Britain (that is, c 1950), yet it starts with a scene of carolling and a snowball fight that looks Dickensian. This sense of temporal dislocation might be related to Carol Smart's observation that, as divorce was legitimised in the late twentieth century, children were increasingly 'in a kind of Victorian time-warp in which they were constituted still as mere property'.[25] Janet Fink notes that the film fuses documentary and melodrama,[26] and it can be added that occasional scenes evoke specifically *period* melodrama. The snowball fight takes place just outside the home of Jennifer's friends, the Marshalls – a large family, presided over by a nurturing mother (Megs Jenkins) and a father with a childlike sense of fun (Philip Ray). The strangest thing about them is their home: a labyrinth of gothicky stairs and chambers, in which, under the eaves, Jennifer's particular friend, Martin Marshall (Brian Smith) has a room to himself for scientific experiments, model making and other boyish pursuits. This becomes Jennifer's safe place.

Her father's profession is significant. When we first encounter Jennifer, she is living with her father and her aunt (Jean Cadell) in a spacious though (for her) temporary home, in which nevertheless her room has been equipped and decorated with care, which implies that someone is doing their best to make her feel at home – her father, probably. By contrast, her aunt appears well-meaning but non-maternal. With nasty talk at school about her divorcing parents, Jennifer cannot wait to be gone. Thus the judgemental gossip that *Brief Encounter* had represented but declined to endorse appears here to be inseparable from divorce.

[25] Smart (2000) 374.
[26] Fink (2014) 154.

Figure 3.4 A dream of wish-fulfilment turns into a nightmare in *No Place for Jennifer*, dir Henry Cass, © Studiocanal Films Ltd (1950)

The film includes a *noir*-ish nightmare, in which a harsh piano teacher, cruel school friends, the telephone on which Jennifer had hoped to speak to her mother and (oddly) her own birthday cake, swirl about her. The sequence includes elements of wish-fulfilment (her parents together helping her cut the cake) and horror. As Fink notes, the plunging of the knife into the cake hints at something demonically destructive that threatens Jennifer's sense of self,[27] especially given the way the knife appears poised over her, and the way her image is split between the figure in the dream and superimposed head of the dreamer. This dream precipitates her move with her father to a large thatched cottage, which at first she finds idyllic ('the loveliest room I've ever been in' is her verdict on the main reception room), but all changes when her father re-marries. She sees the impending arrival of a baby as threatening to displace her.

The film uses sense of place to intimate Jennifer's sense not merely of being or not being at home somewhere, but of having no secure sense of being as such. Being largely visual, it sidesteps the film's itch to know the 'right' answer to divorce, which gives rise to an unresolved tension: the implication of the film is that one should avoid divorce, and yet it is hard to see any grounds on which Paula and William could or should be reconciled.

Background (dir Daniel Birt, 1953) is based on Warren Chetham-Strode's play of 1950. The previous year Birt had made *Circumstantial Evidence*, which warned of the danger of attaching too much weight to circumstantial evidence, and did so in a plot that (albeit implicitly) *favoured* easier divorce. However, *Background* adopts quite a different position.

[27] Fink (2014) 159–60.

Janet Fink notes that the voiceover that comes early in the film, just after a dinner party in which the barrister, John Lomax (Philip Friend), snipes at his wife, Barbie (Valerie Hobson), gestures towards documentary rather than fiction.[28] It is surprising, then, that its content is somewhat fanciful:

> When two people behave like that in public, it would seem here is the beginning of the end.... It is so simple – so terrifyingly simple – to end something. It is so convenient to be able to end quarrels and jealousies with one quick legal cut. It is so much more difficult to keep on with a promise you have made. Why go on with what has become an obligation? The law – comfortably manmade for man's uncomfortable conscience – can offer a convenient end. The law will, of course, apportion guilt and arrange sums of money. It will decide who may see the children and when. It is a clean, tidy operation, breaking up a home, for, legally, a home is merely a residence. It is sentimental to suggest that home is where the heart is. The law has no place for sentiment. Children have. Children go uncomfortably to the heart of the matter. Where will be our home?

This draws on the kind of arguments against making divorce easier that were being aired in the debate occasioned by the Morton Commission (1951–55). Where divorcing couples colluded, something like the *substance* of no-fault divorce was already coming into existence, in spite of a legal form that precluded it. But this was not because the law made divorce easy (*pace* the voiceover), but because the norms and taboos that had once sustained the legal regimen were changing.[29]

The voiceover reveals its position in its final sentence: it seeks to ventriloquise on behalf of children affected by divorce. In that, it follows the example of *No Place for Jennifer* (and Janette Scott, who had played Jennifer, plays Jess Lomax, the older of the divorcing couple's two daughters in *Background*). But the idea that it is 'simple – terrifyingly simple' to get divorced refers not to the prescribed legal procedure for securing a divorce but to the illegal way in which colluding couples could game the system.

A trial scene early in the film for which there is no corresponding scene in the play ironically confirms that the film is not primarily interested in legal procedures and definitions. Lomax is appearing in a case for the restitution of conjugal rights. When the scene begins, Lomax, defending the action, is cross-examining Mrs Young, who has brought the action. Lomax defends the action by, in effect, making a case for divorce: he argues that one would not wish to maintain a friendship that had deteriorated as badly as Mrs Young's marriage appears to have deteriorated. However, given the current law it would have been rational for Mrs Young to sue for restitution of conjugal rights to secure economic support. The film establishes her as being of a lower social class than Lomax and then draws a veil over the economic implications of divorce by ensuring that not only are the

[28] Fink (2014) 154.
[29] See Gibson (1994) 101–02.

Lomaxes comfortably off, but also the man whom Mrs Lomax aims to marry, Bill (Norman Wooland), is sufficiently wealthy to have a second home in the country, and to curry favour with Jess Lomax by buying her a pony. This skirting of the economic implications of divorce by making its protagonists wealthy shifts its discussion entirely onto grounds of moral principle.[30]

The film's main point is that people who get divorced are not paying attention to the moral or emotional implications of their choice. Friend and Hobson are affecting in the underplayed poignancy of moments when they realise, seemingly too late, what divorce entails. However, the emotional implications of their putative divorce are most keenly felt by their children. They are a slightly odd bunch. The two older children – Adrian (Jeremy Spencer, who would later play Renato's son in *Summertime*) and Jess – are monomaniacal and stereotypical: Adrian is into guns and dogs (he has his own rifle), and Jess is obsessed by horses. Each also conforms to other gender stereotypes: Adrian has a keen sense of responsibility for his youngest sister, Linda, and when his father declines to fight to stop Bill from taking 'what's his' (ie his wife), Adrian resolves to give combat on his behalf, and goes absent without leave en route back to school (the children board) with his rifle so he can shoot Bill. Jess sets about manipulating Bill and her father into getting things she wants: a horse from one and a bicycle from the other. Though she is criticised almost as much as her parents, she is also presented as the victim of adult neglect and mistaken attentions, which contribute to her being 'spoilt'.

When the Lomaxes, having decided to divorce, stop bickering and behave 'properly', they still lack emotional awareness. Having just broken the news of their impending divorce to their stunned children, they go out for a meal. Jess expresses delight at the prospect of going to live on Bill's farm, which boasts several horses. This infuriates Adrian, who starts a fight with her. There is a hint that certain of her mother's romantic feelings for Bill have rubbed off on Jess: she has demanded a portrait photograph of Bill. Adrian is intent on destroying Jess's photo, as he will later try to destroy Bill himself. Even more disturbing is the reaction of Linda (played by Mandy Miller, then famous for her role as the deaf-mute child Mandy in the previous year's film of the same name). She has been working on a story in which divorce figures. It is implied that, though she is the youngest, she has been the first to intuit that something is wrong between her parents. While Jess and Adrian fight, she stands quietly by the fire, tearing up the pages of her story and throwing them into the flames.

Cut to the parents, obliviously settling down to their meal. Lomax announces, 'I think they took it reasonably well, don't you? Children forget very quickly.' This cues us to look at them critically. In agreeing with each other how to effect their divorce (with Barbie, unusually, offering to be made the guilty party for the sake

[30] See Auchmuty, ch 4 of this volume, and Thompson, ch 6 of this volume, for accounts of how women campaigners countered this.

of Lomax's career) they are breaking the law. Notwithstanding Lomax's insistence that he does not want to hear further details of Barbie and Bill's arrangements, he has already heard too much to remain innocent of collusion. It is their willingness to collude that causes their divorce to appear to be, as the opening narration insists, too easy. The law itself, if 'manmade', was hardly '*comfortably* manmade': it was meant to set divorcing spouses at loggerheads. Until 1963, spouses shown to have colluded were automatically denied a divorce.[31]

The play on which the film was based was set entirely in the nursery, thus, implicitly, presenting everything from a child's point of view. As adapted for the screen, the story takes place in other locations too. This reveals that the adults lead lives almost entirely apart from their children. The children have supper in the nursery; their parents, even when they have no guests, dine separately in the dining room. For the greater part of each year the children are at boarding school. Reading the film against the grain, one might conclude that it is criticising a code of polite upper-middle-class behaviour that so effectively conceals emotion as to incur self-alienation. It is also one of several works at this time to examine the inner life of the child, though it does not, unlike *No Place for Jennifer*, imply that psycho-therapeutic expertise should be entrusted with articulating that inner life. Its message is that the children will be fine, provided their parents are together. At the end of the film, as soon as their parents explain that they have decided *not* to get divorced, the children, full of high spirits, rush into the garden to play, leaving their flabbergasted parents laughing hysterically. With 'normality' restored, the children do indeed give the impression of being likely to 'forget very quickly'. It is an odd thing to imply, given what the film has shown us of Linda.

The film's casting raises questions about its purported meaning. The sexual and marital ethics of people in show business, while not necessarily at loggerheads with those of society at large, *could* conform to what was virtually a separate culture of marriage and divorce. This was partly because, in an era in which marriage and professional life were often assumed to be incompatible for women, actresses did not face a marriage bar in their profession, and some enjoyed financial independence from their husbands.

The year before *Background* was released, Valerie Hobson, who plays Barbie, and her then husband, the film producer Anthony Havelock-Allan (producer of *Brief Encounter*, among other films), had divorced. In 1954, the year after *Background*, she married John (later 5th Baron) Profumo. Nine years later, in the year in which, according to Larkin's poem *Annus Mirabilis*, sexual intercourse began, she would become known as the woman who chose *not* to divorce her errant husband, and who maintained a dignified silence regarding her husband's notorious affair for the rest of her life. The Profumo affair impinged on perceptions of sexuality and the 1960s. A supposed pillar of the Establishment turned

[31] Gibson (1994) 204.

out to be more phallic than believers in respectable restraint and deference had supposed. Yet, curiously (or – who knows? – maybe predictably), the aftermath of the Profumo scandal was played out by certain of its key figures according to a decidedly old-fashioned script. Lady Profumo chose to stay with her husband, and became a model of wifely loyalty. Her husband embarked on decades of penance, toiling in Toynbee Hall in the East End, and was eventually rewarded with secular salvation in the shape of a CBE and an invitation to Margaret Thatcher's 70th birthday party, where he sat next to the Queen.

In the seeming contradictoriness of his position, Profumo cuts an interesting figure, especially at the turning point of his life early in the 1960s. Plenty of other politicians had committed adultery and even what were then defined as sexual crimes without seeming to feel much regret or any guilt. Profumo's simultaneous seeking of sexual excitement while also (it transpired) continuing to believe in a conservative code of sexual ethics in some respects mirrors the way his wife, having been a show-business divorcée, became a byword for wifely loyalty. In show business, divorce carried little of the stigma that attended it in other walks of life. For those in public life, however, divorce could be a problem. For example, the politician 'Chips' Channon survived his own homosexual infidelities relatively unscathed, partly because he was able to divorce his wife, thus emerging as, officially, the 'innocent' party. That is the significance of the offer that Barbie makes to Lomax, to allow him to divorce her: he will be officially innocent and (since she plans to stage the requisite adultery in remote Exmouth), with any luck, her 'guilt' will be relegated to the inside pages of a local newspaper far from town.

Film directors and actors, by contrast, could, if they wished, live by a different ethic. In show business, for men especially, there was seldom a *professional* price to pay for being the guilty party in a divorce, because within their profession no particular stigma attached to divorce as such (or even, notwithstanding its illegality, in some degree to male homosexuality – and it is coincidentally notable how often homosexual directors and writers extended sympathetic understanding to the plight of heterosexual people negotiating marriage and divorce). Show business thus presents something like a *culture* of no-fault divorce before its legal realisation. That explains the spirit in which David Lean's second wife, Kay Walsh, acceded to his request for a divorce so that he could marry Ann Todd. In doing so, legally she was alleging that he was guilty of a matrimonial offence. In reality, she was honouring an informal agreement she had previously made with him, and doing him a favour by giving him his freedom.[32] Such an arrangement speaks of a different culture of divorce from any that the law acknowledged; and the way in which law and culture could divide gives *Background* its curious doubleness.

[32] Brownlow (1996) 263–64.

IV. Conclusion

In thinking about the representation of divorce on film, one needs to bear in mind that film is not merely a mirror of society, but a part of it, and in some ways an idiosyncratic part. Arguably what occurs in the ways in which the film world interacts with divorce, especially prior to the 1950s, is that several films not only *represent* divorce, but they also implicitly present an *alternative* to the culture of divorce to challenge its stigma. This was partly to do with the way the stories were crafted, but also to do with what was known of the off-screen lives of some actors and directors. Anyone watching *Background* knowing that Valerie Hobson had got divorced the previous year could have taken a mixed message from a film that appears to set its face firmly against divorce. Similarly, in *Brief Encounter*, Laura's dread of scandal and fear of punishment by providence should she violate her marriage vows, while possibly expressing something of what Lean might have felt as a some-time Quaker, are cast in an ironic light if one happened to know on seeing the film in 1945 that Lean had been divorced.

Looking back on the debate about divorce in mid-twentieth-century Britain, it is striking in retrospect how clear the direction of travel has been, and yet how little was resolved by that debate. In retrospect, the general trend in divorce from the First World War until the mid-1990s was clearly upwards. But participants in the mid-century debate about divorce reform were unable to agree a way forward, even as society went ahead and collectively redefined the substance and meanings of marriage and divorce in spite of the law,[33] especially by abandoning key taboos. The situation as a whole might be described as a paradoxically dynamic impasse.

The films highlighted here can all be construed as having something to say in a continuing debate about marriage and divorce, and up to a point one can pigeonhole them according to the positions they adopt: pro serial monogamy, anti no-fault divorce, etc. But their most striking and durable features have less to do with the ways in which they can be construed as staking out positions in an argument than with their insights into moments where a certain complexity, even a contradictoriness, stands revealed.

One might think here, especially, of the way *One More River*, instead of ending with a seemingly unproblematic final reel clinch and the formation of the heterosexual couple as a straightforward resolution, shows Clare and Tony dealing with emotional damage as well as finally acting on desire. Or of Laura in *Brief Encounter*, deeply committed not just to the idea of monogamous marriage but to the marriage she actually has, yet powerfully drawn to Alec. Even where a film adopts an explicit point of view, as do *Background* and *No Place for Jennifer*, the

[33] Langhamer (2006).

moments of greatest resonance are less those that supposedly 'prove' the case they are arguing than those that communicate the pressure of experience. In that regard, these films of the 1950s, while clearly of their time, in directing our attention to the bewildering, powerful and formative experience of children are arguably still doing something of value.

If what this limited account reveals is a 'dynamic impasse' in the period reviewed here the impasse is mostly on the legal side of the question, and it would finally come unblocked with reforms at the end of the 1960s. By contrast, the films partly reflect that stymied debate, but they also point to factors driving forward the transformation of divorce, willy-nilly. Indeed, in some degree, the films themselves arguably *were* one such factor.

References

Texts

Asimow, M (2000) 'Divorce in the Movies from the Hays Code to Kramer vs Kramer' 24 *Legal Studies Forum* 221.

Bowen, E (1998) *The Heat of the Day* (1948), intr Roy Foster (London, Vintage Classics).

Brooke, H (2017) 'The History of Legal Aid 1945–2010', *Bach Commission on Access to Justice*, appendix 6 at www.fabians.org.uk/wp-content/uploads/2017/09/Bach-Commission-Appendix-6-F-1.pdf (last accessed 8 July 2021).

Brownlow, K (1996) *David Lean: A biography* (London, Faber & Faber).

Chetham-Strode, W (1951) *Background* (London, Samuel French).

Cook, P (2005) *Screening the Past: memory and nostalgia in cinema* (Abingdon, Routledge).

Coward, N (1979) *Tonight at 8:30* (1936) in *Coward Plays: Three*, eds R Mander and J Mitchenson (London, Eyre Methuen).

Cretney, S (2005) *Family Law in the Twentieth Century: a history* (Oxford, Oxford University Press).

Dyer, R (1993) *Brief Encounter* (London, British Film Institute).

Elliot, R (2020) 'Suffer the Children? Divorce and Child Welfare in Postwar Britain', *Journal of Family History* at https://journals.sagepub.com/doi/full/10.1177/0363199020945746 (last accessed 8 July 2021).

Fink, J (2014) '"They don't really care what happens to me": divorce, family life and children's emotional worlds in 1950s British cinema' in VB Cvetkovic and DC Olson (eds), *Portrayals of Children in Popular Culture: Fleeting Images* (New York, Lexington Books).

Galsworthy, J (1933) *Over the River*, *The Forsyte Chronicles*, pt 9, at http://gutenberg.net.au/ebooks03/0300241.txt (last accessed 8 July 2021).

Gibson, C (1994) *Wedlock Dissolved* (London, Routledge).

Langhamer, C (2006) 'Adultery in Post-war England' 62 *History Workshop Journal* 86.

Lant, A (1991) *Blackout: reinventing women for wartime British cinema* (Princeton, NJ, Princeton University Press).

Lean, D (1947) '*Brief Encounter*' 4 *The Penguin Film Review* 27.

National Legion of Decency (1959) *Motion Pictures Classified by National Legion of Decency, February, 1936–October, 1959* (New York, National Legion of Decency).

Phillips, GD (2006) *Beyond the Epic: The Life and Films of David Lean* (Lexington, KA, University Press of Kentucky).

Putting Asunder: A divorce law for contemporary society (1966), The report of a group appointed by the Archbishop of Canterbury in January 1964 (London, SPCK).
Richards, J (1983) 'Controlling the Screen: the British Cinema in the 1930s' 33 *History Today* 11.
Robertson, JC (1985) *The British Board of Film Censors: film censorship in Britain, 1896–1950* (London, Croom Helm).
Silver, A and Ursini, J (1974) *David Lean and His Films* (London, Leslie Frewin).
Silverman, SM (1998) *David Lean* (1989), intr Katharine Hepburn, rev edn (London, André Deutsch).
Smart, C (2000) 'Divorce in England 1950–2000: A Moral Tale' in SN Katz, J Eekelaar and M MacLean (eds), *Cross Currents: Family Law and Policy in the US and England* (Oxford, Oxford University Press)
Stone, L (1990) *Road to Divorce: England 1530–1987* (Oxford, Oxford University Press).
Tighe, M (2005) *Writing and Responsibility* (London, Routledge).
Wells, HG (1913) *The Passionate Friends* (New York, AL Burt).

Films

Background (1953) dir Daniel Birt (UK, Act Films).
Blithe Spirit (1945) dir David Lean (UK, Two Cities / Noel Coward – Cineguild).
Brief Encounter (1945) dir David Lean (UK, Cineguild).
The Captive Heart (1946) dir Basil Dearden (UK, Ealing Studios).
Carrington V C (1955) dir Anthony Asquith (UK, Romulus Films).
Circumstantial Evidence (1952) dir Daniel Birt (UK, Group 3 Films).
The Divorce of Lady X (1938) dir Tim Whelan (UK, London Films).
The Halfway House (1944) dir Basil Dearden (UK, Ealing Studios).
In Name Only (1939) dir John Cromwell (USA, RKO Radio Pictures).
Lady Hamilton (1941) dir Alexander Korda (USA, Alexander Korda Films).
Mandy (1952) dir Alexander Mackendrick (UK, Ealing Studios).
Mr Skeffington (1944) dir Vincent Sherman (USA, Warner Brothers).
No Place for Jennifer (1950) dir Henry Cass (UK, ABPC).
One More River (1934) dir James Whale (USA, Universal).
The Passionate Friends (1949) dir David Lean (UK, Cineguild).
Summertime (1955) dir. David Lean (UK/USA, United Artists).
This Happy Breed (1944) dir David Lean (UK, Two Cities/Noel Coward – Cineguild).
Waterloo Road (1945) dir Sidney Gilliat (UK, Gainsborough Pictures).
The Way to the Stars (1945) dir Anthony Asquith (UK, Two Cities Films).
We Dive At Dawn (1943) dir Anthony Asquith (UK, Gaumont British Picture Corp/Gainsborough Pictures).
While the Sun Shines (1947) dir Anthony Asquith (UK, ABPC).

4

Feminism, Property and Divorce Law Reform in the 1960s

ROSEMARY AUCHMUTY

I. Introduction

The coming into force of the Divorce Reform Act (DRA) 1969 was delayed until 1 January 1971 to permit the simultaneous implementation of the Matrimonial Proceedings and Property Act (MPPA) 1970, dealing with the financial arrangements connected with divorce. Earlier proposals, such as Eirene White's Matrimonial Causes Bill of 1951, would have postponed discussion of the financial impact of divorce on women in favour of immediate liberalisation of the divorce law, and there can be no doubt that the simultaneous timing, indeed the very existence, of the new financial arrangements alongside the DRA 1969 was due to lobbying of feminists inside and outside Parliament on behalf of the soon-to-be ex-wives.[1] Yet reading the parliamentary debates leading up to the DRA, one is struck by the lack of consensus among feminist MPs in their approach to the problem and, at times, their puzzling absence from the discussions.

The aim of this chapter is to analyse the feminist voices in the parliamentary debates on divorce law reform in the decade leading up to but not including the DRA and the MPPA, focusing on discussions of the financial consequences for women. Until the reforms introduced by the MPPA, disputes over shares in the family home concerned married couples, as cohabitation was still rare. But most legal accounts of these decades present only the property law perspective *or* the family law perspective; they are rarely treated together. Moreover, most histories of divorce law reform focus on those who successfully campaigned for reform. It follows that men tend to dominate these narratives (it has generally been men who call for easier divorce), while those who disagree and hinder, often women, are cast as reactionary trouble-makers standing in the way of progress. Lawrence Stone, for example, lumps together the Married Women's Association (MWA) and the Mothers' Union as 'conservative bodies',[2] even though the MWA opposed easier

[1] Stetson (1982) 207; see Thompson, ch 6 of this volume.
[2] Stone (1990) 408.

divorce for good feminist reasons and the Mothers' Union because they believed divorce to be morally wrong. In these accounts, negative consequences for women are often ignored or the victims dismissed as unfortunate casualties of a largely successful regime.[3] Left unanswered are the questions a feminist would ask: Was easier divorce *really* positive for women? Was it something that feminists actively sought, supported or welcomed, or was it positive only because it provided a catalyst for efforts to dismantle women's dependence? As this chapter will show, the desire for married women's property reform came out of the recognition – by women's organisations, individual women and their male supporters – that divorce often brought a catastrophic loss of economic security, not to speak of social status, to women who had been brought up (with no realistic alternatives) to be dependent housewives.

Non-legal historians are often better at confronting these sorts of issues, but their work has its own weaknesses. No scholar working in this area can overlook the brilliant study by American political scientist Dorothy M Stetson, *A Woman's Issue: The Politics of Family Law Reform in England*,[4] which traces the influence of feminist pressure groups on family law reform from the 1850s to the 1970s. But most of the otherwise excellent social and feminist histories of women during this period are weak on legal detail. Paul Addison's account of the DRA, for instance, contains the statement 'A closely allied measure, the Matrimonial Property Act of 1970, aimed to ensure that in the event of a divorce, each partner received half of the resources of the marriage'.[5] Here he seems to be conflating the feminist-inspired Matrimonial Property *Bill* of 1969 with the statute eventually enacted, the MPPA 1970, which certainly did not give divorcing partners half-shares in the household assets. Such accounts also tend to present legislation enacted as marking the satisfactory end of the matter, when in truth it often falls short and leads to further problems. 'Recognition was accorded this particular problem [the financial consequences of separation on women] in legislation passed during the 1960s, which improved the right of wives to stay in the matrimonial home,' writes Jane Lewis, without further discussion of the actual terms and many limitations of the Matrimonial Homes Act 1967.[6]

The 'feminism' of my title requires some explanation. Given that some feminists supported easier divorce, some opposed it and some ignored the issue altogether, can they all be encompassed within the label 'feminist'? The feminisms of the 1960s (a decade in which it used to be thought there was no feminism at all!)[7] had their roots in feminist approaches of previous eras: there were 'equal-rights' feminists and 'difference' or 'protectionist' feminists, both of whom were

[3] Rackley and Auchmuty (2020).
[4] Stetson (1982).
[5] Addison (2010) 209.
[6] Lewis (1992) 63.
[7] Wilson (1980) 2; Spender (1983).

motivated by the first-wave (nineteenth-century) feminists' wish to curb men's exploitation of women, even in the context of the acceptance (by some) of 'separate spheres' for men and women. In tactics, too, there were similarities and continuities. However suspicious one might be of some Victorian feminists' expressed belief that women were inferior to men,[8] there can be no doubt that conceding the point was tactically beneficial. In the 1960s, we still see appeals for justice for women couched in socially conservative terms, forcing us to ask ourselves whether those who expressed them *really* believed that marriage was women's best career,[9] or were simply arguing for justice for those women – the majority – who lived out the ideology. But once one accepts that strategies are often most effective when formulated within the accepted norms of the time, it becomes possible to include within the term 'feminist' a range of positions that do not require too great an interrogation into an individual's commitment to conservative ideas and institutions, nor prompt the critical dismissal by second-wave (1970s) feminists of their predecessors' failings. Anne Logan's use of 'feminist' to apply to 'people (not necessarily women) whose words or actions indicate that they perceived gendered inequalities in social relationships and access to power'[10] provides a useful lens for examining the range of arguments advanced in the parliamentary debates on divorce law reform, where the inequality of access of power was exemplified, as always on divorce, by the financial consequences for women.

The chapter is structured around the key divorce reform Bills of the 1960s leading up to (but not including) the final DRA. Section II describes the Hansard debates on the Matrimonial Causes and Reconciliation Bill 1963. It fills in the context (social, legal and feminist) for the debates, and summarises important legal developments in the following years. Sections III and IV consider the debates in the later Bills: the simultaneously debated Divorce Reform Bill 1968 and Matrimonial Property Bill 1969. Section V offers a discussion and conclusions.

II. Matrimonial Causes and Reconciliation Bill 1963

On 8 February 1963, Leo Abse (Labour, Pontypool) moved the Second Reading of his Matrimonial Causes and Reconciliation Bill (MCRB).[11] Notwithstanding the several clauses devoted to reconciliation (it was nicknamed the 'Kiss and Make Up' Bill),[12] its central aim was to permit divorce when the parties had lived apart for seven years. Easier divorce was presented as a means of strengthening rather than weakening marriage: the Bill, Abse explained, would enable thousands of couples,

[8] For example Caroline Norton and Emily Davies; see Auchmuty (2008) 26.
[9] A clue may lie in the fact that feminist activists rarely made a career of marriage themselves.
[10] Logan (2008) 4.
[11] *Hansard*, HC Deb 3 February 1963, vol 671, cols 806–84.
[12] Stetson (1982) 170.

currently living together as husband and wife but unable to marry because they could not divorce their first spouse, to do so.

Twelve years had passed since Eirene White's unsuccessful Divorce Reform Bill of 1951, in which, though conscious of the potential financial and social impact of easier divorce on women, she had urged the acceptance of the principle before facing 'any economic consequences'.[13] The concern expressed in the debates at this cavalier dismissal of women's situation was amplified in the consultations of the Royal Commission on Marriage and Divorce (1951–55), set up in response to the Bill. Individuals and women's groups from every angle gave testimony, forcing the Commission to give serious consideration to ways of ensuring that married women had better access to money and property. In their Report[14] the Commissioners made some recommendations but failed to agree even on the grounds of any proposed divorce reform, let alone ancillary matters.

Abse, while long associated with progressive causes such as homosexual law reform, could fairly be described as misogynist in his approach to women's issues. While recognising that he could not take White's 'divorce reform now, women's property rights later' position, he found another way to side-step the issue by proposing that a respondent could object to being divorced on the basis of separation and that, in such cases, a petitioner would only succeed if he could show that her objection was unreasonable. The implication was that refusal would be reasonable if indeed she would lose out financially. But how a court would interpret 'unreasonable' was open to doubt.

The Bill had strong support from Labour men and from the two women who spoke in the House of Commons debate. One, Eirene White (Labour, Flint), was an Oxbridge-educated journalist, married to another journalist and committed to equal rights for women: in 1947 she had persuaded the Labour Party conference to accept the principle of equal pay. The other, Joan Vickers (Liberal, Plymouth Devonport), was very different. Educated privately and in Paris, trained as a Norland nurse, presented at Court, she even rode to hounds; but her extensive experience in local government and on the wider political stage as UK delegate to the UN Status of Women Commission had given her insight into the situation of women who did not have her advantages. She too was committed to equality, requesting that 'spouse' be substituted for 'husband' in Abse's Bill, so that either party could rebut the presumption that they had condoned a matrimonial offence.[15] This shifted the normative understanding that it was always the husband who offended and the wife who chose to put up with it. Later, in answer to the question as to whether a woman's insistence on a child's being brought up in a particular faith would constitute 'unreasonable behaviour', she pointed out that the wife could not so insist, 'because she does not have equal guardianship with the father'.[16]

[13] *Hansard*, HC Deb 9 March 1951, vol 485, cols 926–1021, 931.

[14] HMSO, 1956.

[15] *Hansard*, HC Deb 3 February 1963, vol 671, col 826.

[16] ibid col 853; not won until the Guardianship Act 1973.

While individual clauses were debated at length, every speaker in the Commons offered qualified or unqualified support to Abse's proposals. The concern about the financial consequences for ex-wives that had been so evident in the debate on the 1951 Bill and in the representations to the Royal Commission was absent, with MPs such as Nicholas Ridley (Conservative, Cirencester and Tewkesbury) emphasising the emotional impact of not being able to obtain a divorce rather than the financial impact of being divorced.

It was quite different in the House of Lords.[17] By the time the Bill arrived there on 22 May 1963, the clause relating to divorce after seven years had disappeared, having been so substantially amended at Committee stage that it was withdrawn. In the intervening months, it had attracted considerable opposition outside Parliament.[18] Nonetheless, the risk of its being reintroduced led Baroness Summerskill to set out the case against it:

> I regarded the original Bill with the compulsion clause as a husband's Bill, drafted by a man who doubtless means well but who has failed to recognise that marriage has different values for a man and a woman, values which are determined by the fundamental difference in sex. The same different considerations influence their attitude to a break-up of marriage. I am not concerned with the theological approach or the doctrinal pronouncements of the Church; I am concerned with protecting the little earthly paradise, the home, the source of most women's greatest happiness, which she has created for her children.[19]

This passage is characteristic of Summerskill's rhetorical method. First, she used the term 'compulsion', much disliked by advocates of the Bill. Second, by noting that the clause was framed by a *man* (albeit one who 'means well') for the benefit of other *men*, she suggests that men are unable to to see beyond their own desires. Third, she adopted an essentialist view of the sexes, noting the different meanings attached to marriage and divorce and emphasising that they were entirely *social*, based on men's and women's gendered roles – what society expected of them. In shamelessly romanticising the home, Summerskill played up to her largely elderly, conservative, married male audience, who fully agreed that women's place was in the home. But such rhetoric ignored the fact that it was unhappy marriages that were under discussion, where the home was not a paradise for women but rather a place of misery and perhaps danger.

While most of the House, including Lord Denning, preferred to defer discussion of the controversial financial issues until 'a later stage',[20] in an unusually controversial maiden speech Lord Hodson, a Law Lord, drew on his experience in the divorce court to support Summerskill's position. Why should a woman dependent on her husband's pension be called 'vindictive' if she refused to divorce

[17] *Hansard*, HL Deb 22 May 1963, vol 250, cols 389–416.
[18] Stone (1963) 94.
[19] *Hansard*, HL Deb 22 May 1963, vol 250, col 397.
[20] ibid col 407.

him, Hodson asked.[21] There was one law for the rich and one for the poor. The poor man would never be able to satisfy a court that he could support an ex-wife, whereas, 'husband and wife being taxed together as one',[22] a well-to-do man could 'have half a dozen wives all living at the same time, deduct all allowances for surtax purposes and go on happily as before'.[23]

Meanwhile, the pro-divorce lobby continued to focus on emotions. Lord Silkin (a solicitor, former Labour MP for Peckham) stated that the goal of divorce law was, first, to safeguard the institution of marriage and, second, to 'safeguard the happiness of the individuals concerned'.[24] The emphasis on *happiness*, in stark contrast to Summerskill's and Hodson's focus on *money*, demonstrates the shift in how marriage was viewed. Of course people had long married for love, but also to fulfil a social obligation to create stable units in which to raise the next generation. The new prioritisation of (usually only one spouse's) happiness over the maintenance of these units meant that the consequences for the other spouse must necessarily be subordinated.

The 'compulsion' clause did re-appear at committee stage, but the Bill failed to progress. All that was left was the reconciliation principles, which, as Summerskill observed, were 'entirely innocuous' and which eventually constituted the Matrimonial Causes Act 1963.

A. Context

i. Society

The debates on divorce in the 1960s can best be understood in the context of the social and legal situation of women and men in the period leading up to them. There is a tendency to think of the 1950s as the high point of the domestic ideal in Britain, when marriage was every girl's goal (almost to the exclusion of any other) and heterosexuality the only permissible sexuality; when almost all women were housewives, most of them full-time, and men were breadwinners, contributing very little to housework or childcare. The 1960s are recalled rather differently, as the era of the 'sexual revolution' and 'swinging London', flower power, civil rights, the pill, the Beatles and the shift in sexual mores that led, in a single decade, to the liberalisation of laws concerning contraception, abortion and homosexuality.[25] The fact that divorce law reform was won at the end of this decade lends credence to its location in a classic Whig narrative of increasing modernisation.

[21] ibid col 402.

[22] Separate taxation for married couples was only introduced in the Finance Act 1988, s 32.

[23] *Hansard*, HL Deb 22 May 1963, vol 250, col 404.

[24] ibid, col 410.

[25] National Health Service (Family Planning) Act 1967; Abortion Act 1967; Sexual Offences Act 1967.

In fact, the 1950s and 1960s were not polar opposites but periods of parallel and conflicting ideologies and practices. It is true that marriage was very popular in the 1950s, but the rate was highest in the 1960s.[26] By 1966, 87 per cent of women aged 25–29 were already married, and the mean age for women to marry was the youngest ever, at 22.[27] At the same time, increasing numbers of married women were entering the paid workforce. With an expanding post-war economy and a labour shortage, governments found themselves having to draw on the hitherto economically inactive and ideologically untouchable married woman. Where in 1931 only one married woman in 10 had a job outside the home, by 1951 it was one in four and by 1961, one in three. In the period 1951–71 the proportion of married women in paid employment almost doubled, to form two-thirds of the female workforce in 1971.[28]

The decline in the numbers of young women willing to go into domestic service, now that more attractive options existed in offices, shops and factories, gave impetus to the speedy invention and production of 'labour-saving devices' such as twin-tub washing machines and refrigerators, which had never been a priority when human labour was cheap and plentiful.[29] These devices took a good deal of the burden off housewives in terms of both physical effort and time (no need to shop daily if you had a fridge), so working-class women who had completed their families (now smaller thanks to the wider availability of contraception) had a strong incentive to get a job in order to afford them, and to pay for less essential but more desirable luxuries such as television sets and family holidays.[30]

But the same transition that helped to liberate working-class women from drudgery had the opposite effect on middle-class wives, for whom domestic assistance – cook, housekeeper, nanny – had hitherto been the norm, and who now found themselves lumbered with the housework and childcare. This 'proletization' of middle-class women, as Elizabeth Wilson memorably calls it,[31] was accomplished almost without notice, for potential complaints were disqualified even before they could be articulated when the dominant message was of the huge improvement in women's lives with these labour-saving devices that took all the work out of housework.[32]

In the 1950s, in reaction to women's unprecedented freedom of action during the war, the full-time domestic role was elevated still further by an emphasis on the absolute necessity for children to have full-time attention from mothers, lest

[26] Harrison (2009) 298; Addison (2010) 197.
[27] Oakley (1976) 72.
[28] ibid; Harrison (2009) 32, 251.
[29] Dyhouse (1989) 107–11.
[30] Kynaston (2014) 203.
[31] Wilson (1980) 13, 55.
[32] Of course, anyone who remembers those twin-tub washing machines with their separate wringer knows only too well that they did not take all the work out of housework and that, even with a fridge, meals still needed to be planned, shopped for, prepared, served and cleared up afterwards.

they grow up 'maladjusted' or delinquent,[33] and for husbands to have total support in their careers (the advancement of which became their wives' career too), as well as domestic and sexual servicing lest they stray. In the debate on the Royal Commission on Divorce, Lord Silkin even suggested that middle-class women's lack of housekeeping skills was an indirect cause of divorce. He warned:

> I have known many young women enter into marriage who were not in a position to employ domestic assistance at the outset, even if they could have found it, yet who had no idea how to cook a meal. I should have thought that that was the worst possible beginning for a marriage.[34]

Women's magazines, at their peak in the 1950s, by focusing almost exclusively on domestic life reinforced the message that married women's mission in life was to keep a spotless home and contented husband and family, while their advertisements, and TV commercials from 1955, idealised both the products and those who used them. The consequence was that standards became ever higher and harder for women to reach.

By a clever sleight of hand, women's enhanced domestic role was then reconceived, developing the Victorian idea of separate spheres, as a symmetrical partnership, with different but essentially equal roles.[35] By the 1950s, this was firmly embedded in society as ideal and norm; as Sir Alfred Denning (later Lord Denning) put it in *The Changing Law*:

> The modern idea [is] that husband and wife are partners in all affairs which are their common concern. He goes out to work so as to earn money for the partnership. She stays at home so as to run the family side of the business.[36]

Domestic violence was played down as a private matter, possibly a ground for divorce, but not for police protection or prosecution.[37]

It was not surprising that many women who accepted the ideal were disappointed with the reality. In 1960, a letter to *The Guardian* from housewife Maureen Nicol, suggesting that 'perhaps housebound wives with liberal interests and a desire to remain individuals could form a national register so that whenever one moves one can contact like-minded friends', led to the formation of the National Housewives Register, an early form of consciousness-raising group for bored housewives.[38] And where in the United States Betty Friedan was able to give voice in *The Feminine Mystique* (in 1963) to women's lack of fulfilment in their appointed role, in the United Kingdom it was the title of Hannah Gavron's *The Captive Wife* of 1966 (based on her doctoral thesis) that encapsulated the hitherto

[33] Bowlby (1953); Winnicott (1957).
[34] *Hansard*, HL Deb 24 October 1956, vol 199, cols 972–89.
[35] Willmott and Young (1973).
[36] Denning (1953) 90.
[37] See Miles, ch 8 of this volume.
[38] National Housewives Register records.

unspeakable malaise of the full-time housewife. Married, with two small children, Gavron killed herself before the book was published.

Part of the explanation for the difficulty of voicing dissatisfaction was that it was so widely accepted that women had achieved full equality with men.[39] 'Equality' was now narrowly understood as the achievement of civil rights, entry to the professions and public office, and (more or less) equal treatment under the law. Already in 1952, Marghanita Laski (born 1915) had proclaimed that 'Older and nobler women struggled that I should be free, and did their work so well that I've never felt bound. Rights for me, so far as my generation is concerned, is a dead issue.'[40] Such a comment is typical of 'next' generations, who do indeed profit from the formal advances won by their predecessors but often fail to foresee the pitfalls of assimilation on men's terms and the persistence of discrimination through informal means. Feminism, which had enjoyed some respectability in earlier decades, became a pejorative term, associated with unattractive elderly spinsters, often objects of ridicule. As Wilson explains, most women accepted their lot because 'To be the equal companion of a man was almost to be a man, was better by far than to be a spinster, condemned to the narrow life of companionship only with her own kind.'[41]

In 1951, only 7 per cent of marriages ended in divorce, and even fewer during the ensuing decade, which helps to explain the absence of further divorce Bills or the implementation of any of the Royal Commission's proposals. But in the 1960s the rate rose sharply, reaching 24 per cent in 1966.[42] Autobiographical accounts remind us that, though increasingly common, divorce remained a matter of shame;[43] the Mothers' Union, for example, excluded divorced members. Single-parent families were rare, and unmarried mothers were expected to give up their babies for adoption. But the stigma of illegitimacy, which loomed large in some MPs' minds,[44] was probably not as strong as they imagined; most people were unaware of the marital status of their parents, especially as women tended to take their partner's surname whether they were married or not.

ii. Law

Coverture survived in the swathes of English law (employment, tax, social security, even criminal law) premised on a woman's dependence on a husband.

[39] This is a common backlash ploy after any advance for women, designed to hold back any further demands for change.

[40] Brittain (1953) 77 (quoting a 1952 article on 'Women'). Vera Brittain (born 1893), one of those 'older and nobler' equal-rights feminists, immediately castigated Laski for imagining that the battle was over.

[41] Wilson (1980) 166.

[42] Harrison (2009) 295.

[43] Juliet Gardiner's mother-in-law was 'mortified that she had lost her status as a wife': Gardiner (2017) 158.

[44] Jenkinson (2012) 212.

The entire apparatus of the welfare state was built on the wife's receiving her benefits through her relationship to her husband.[45] Take that husband away – worse, allow him to abandon a first wife to take on another – and the system could work only if the ex-husband had plenty of money or the woman married again, preferably a man without a first family. Divorce courts could, and did, order husbands to pay maintenance to their ex-wives and for their children, but such payments depended on the man's ability to pay. Capital awards or transfers were unknown; lump sums were only allowed after 1963.[46]

Where the law was gender-neutral, ideological and social expectations reinforced the old relationships: the Law of Property Act 1925, for example, allowed for co-ownership of property by husband and wife, with separate rights, but homes were still routinely conveyed to men, who held the property in their sole name. But the rising tide of property law disputes when couples separated gave impetus to Denning's project of invigorating the equitable jurisdiction. Appointed to the Probate, Divorce and Admiralty Division (precursor of the Family Division) in 1944 to help clear the backlog of matrimonial cases, and elevated to the Court of Appeal in 1948, Denning developed two important doctrines to assist wives who, on the breakdown of a relationship, claimed a right of occupation, or a share, in the family home legally held by the husband. The *deserted wife's equity* enabled women to remain in the family home even after separation,[47] while the *family assets* analysis allowed those who had contributed financially to the property to receive half of the proceeds of sale, on the basis that each made an equal contribution to the home, whatever the respective financial contributions.[48]

Two other legal developments are important. Equal pay was phased into the civil service, local government and teaching between 1954 and 1961.[49] The Life Peerages Act 1958 enabled women to sit in the House of Lords for the first time, giving feminists like Edith Summerskill a forum for powerful interventions in divorce law reform.[50]

iii. Feminism

Two strands of feminist thought and strategy emerged after the First World War. The first, emboldened by the successes of the campaigns for votes for women and entry to the professions,[51] aimed for further equality with men: equal grounds

[45] Atkins and Hoggett (1984) ch 6.

[46] Matrimonial Causes Act 1963, s 5.

[47] *H v H* [1947] 62 TLR 645.

[48] *Rimmer v Rimmer* [1953] 1 QB 63; *Fribance v Fribance* [1957] 1 WLR 384.

[49] Addison (2010) 86.

[50] Hereditary peeresses, few in number due to male primogeniture, continued to be excluded until the Peerage Act 1963.

[51] Representation of the People Act 1918; Sex Disqualification (Removal) Act 1919.

for divorce, equal guardianship of children, equal pay.[52] The 6-Point Group, founded in 1921 by Lady Rhondda to push for equal rights for women through legal reform, represented this approach. The second focused on women's special and particular role in marriage as homemakers, a role accorded appreciation and praise yet hardly valued in any material sense, and one that, though almost obligatory, left women over-burdened and vulnerable. It argued for protective legislation and material security for wives, best exemplified by Eleanor Rathbone's campaign for Family Allowances to be paid directly to mothers.[53]

These two strands of feminism responded very differently to divorce law reform. Protectionist feminists were both spurred to act by, and found it easier to operate within, the reinvigorated domestic ideology, adopting two strategies that built on rather than challenged women's appropriate role. First, they campaigned to get domestic work on to an equal footing with other professional work: hence the extension of 'home *economics*' and 'domestic *science*' into even academic girls' schools[54] and, briefly, at university level.[55] Second, they strove to improve women's financial position within marriage, for the call for easier divorce exposed wives' vulnerability in a social situation where the best or, indeed, *only* career option for women was premised on lifelong financial dependence on a husband. Following White's proposed divorce reform, Summerskill took forward some of the MWA's long-held goals in two Private Members' Bills[56] that aimed to provide married women with limited financial rights within marriage and a right to occupy the family home. The women she had in mind were those who had married before the war, when there was no expectation of paid work (indeed, when marriage bars were often in operation). These women had cared for large families with little money and few labour-saving appliances. They were without employment skills or experience, their health had probably suffered and they were no longer young enough to be obvious candidates for re-marriage. Despite strong support from MPs of both sexes, neither Bill progressed.

Equal-rights feminists, on the other hand, sought equality not in difference but in women's similarity to men. This explains their relative absence from the divorce reform debates up to the mid-1960s and their focus, rather, on issues like equal pay. Their rejection of special treatment explains the support of women like White for divorce law reform without safeguards for impoverished ex-wives. But their arguments foundered on the common understanding that women were already equal.

[52] Matrimonial Causes Act 1923; Guardianship of Infants Act 1925 (equal guardianship for separated parents). Equal pay did not come until 1970.

[53] Family Allowances Act 1944.

[54] Feeding into the conservative push by experts like John Newsom (1963).

[55] The work in Household and Social Science begun by Kings College for Women before the First World War was elevated by its successor, Queen Elizabeth College, London, into a degree course after the Second. See Attar (1990).

[56] Women's Disabilities Bills 1952 and 1953.

As the 1950s progressed, the Government's problem of reconciling the rhetoric of separate spheres with the growing industrial need provided equal-rights feminists with an opportunity to capitalise on (some) women's desire for a wider role. The challenge was cannily resolved by invoking the concept of 'women's two roles', a term not then used in the sense of 'double burden' it acquired in later years but here signifying a new 'bi-lineal' model for women's lives. Henceforth women would be allowed or expected to work until the birth of the first child (previously, until marriage) and then, after a period as full-time housewives while their children were small, to return to paid employment (instead of remaining full-time housewives for the rest of their lives).

In 1956, Alva Myrdal and Viola Klein[57] proposed ways in which domestic responsibilities and paid work could be combined, including the provision of part-time and shift work opportunities and nurseries, ideas that were taken up fairly enthusiastically in factories but not in professions monopolised by resistant men. While these authors stressed the national interest, Judith Hubback's *Wives Who Went to College* (of 1957) was more concerned with women's happiness and fulfilment. She acknowledged that many women found full-time homemaking stultifying, but cautioned that a supportive husband was a prerequisite and his approval necessary before a wife could act in her own interest. It was never suggested that husbands should take equal responsibility for the housework and childcare. Male commentators writing enthusiastically of the rise of the 'companionate' marriage[58] noted instances of men helping in the home and pushing prams, but that help (surveys showed) was minuscule.[59] Thus the association, indeed equation, of married women with housework remained as fixed as it had been before the war. Even those who had some financial independence thanks to work outside the home tended to be clustered in sex-segregated jobs with earnings only a little over half of men's, so remained financially dependent on breadwinner husbands. The consequence was that this radical shift in the way married women's lives were understood and lived failed in the end (as second-wave feminists were to recognise) to liberate them from patriarchal power structures.

B. What Came Next

The year 1964 saw the enactment of the short but significant Married Women's Property Act, which, after a long campaign by the MWA, allowed married woman to keep half the housekeeping savings. For some women, this was the first time

[57] Myrdal and Klein (1956). See also Klein (1965), which was more critical of married women's double burden.

[58] eg Fletcher (1962). For critique of the idea of 'companionate marriage', see Fisher (2013).

[59] A 1961 survey showed that where women did 440 minutes of housework per day, men did 19: Addison (2010) 86.

they had money of their own.[60] Less happily, 1965 saw the end of the 'deserted wife's equity' remedy, with the House of Lords holding that a married woman's occupation of the matrimonial home was not a right recognised in English land law, for (not being a *proprietary* interest and not capable of registration) it could not bind third parties.[61] Parliament responded by enacting the Matrimonial Homes Act 1967, introduced by Summerskill, which allowed spouses to register a right of occupation effective against third parties. But its usefulness was limited: as Olive Stone pointed out, even if they knew such protection existed, wives were unlikely to imagine they needed it.[62] Denning's other creation, the 'family assets' doctrine, lasted little longer than his deserted wives' equity: landmark House of Lords decisions in *Pettitt v Pettitt*[63] and *Gissing v Gissing*[64] established that the constructive trust, based on intention and contributions, would thenceforth determine shares in the family home.

The appointment of the first women to hold regular judicial office in England and Wales – Rose Heilbron (as a Recorder) in 1964 and Elizabeth Lane (to the High Court) in 1965 – marked the start of a very slow process of dismantling the masculine bias of the higher judiciary; both brought a feminine sensibility to their work, derived from their life experiences as women, and both supported and encouraged other women in law, but neither called herself a feminist.[65] The movement for equal pay was advanced beyond middle-class interests when women workers at the Ford car plant in Dagenham went on strike in 1968, an action ultimately leading to the Equal Pay Act 1970.

Through all these developments, divorce law reform was never off the agenda. In 1964, John Parker (Labour, Dagenham) introduced a Private Member's Bill proposing divorce after a five-year separation. The Matrimonial Causes Act 1965 was a consolidating measure. In 1966 and again in 1967, Leo Abse tried and failed to get a Second Reading for divorce Bills on the simple ground of five years' separation. In February 1968, another Bill introduced by William Wilson (Labour, Coventry South) passed its Second Reading but, after committee discussion, ran out of time.

III. Divorce Reform Bill 1968

When Alec Jones (Labour, Rhondda West) moved the Second Reading of the Divorce Reform Bill 1968[66] on 6 December, he still faced opposition to the

[60] Thompson (2019) 263.
[61] *National Provincial Bank v Ainsworth* [1965] AC 1175.
[62] Stone (1968).
[63] *Pettit v Pettit* [1969] UKHL 5.
[64] *Gissing v Gissing* [1970] UKHL 3.
[65] Heilbron (2012) vii; Lane (1985) 60–62.
[66] *Hansard*, HC Deb 6 December 1968, vol 774, cols 2033–56.

'irretrievable breakdown' principle. Bruce Campbell (Conservative, Oldham West), who had practised at the divorce Bar since the war, threatened the 'steady disintegration of family life' if the Bill were passed. But in describing the man who 'grows tired of his wife, [when] she ceases to be attractive to him', so that he 'goes off with a younger woman' and forces 'his completely innocent wife into a divorce',[67] he roused two women MPs to protest against the old stereotypes. Women leave their husbands too, Joan Lestor (Labour, Eton and Windsor) reminded him.[68] There is never a totally innocent and a totally guilty party, insisted Lena Jeger (Labour, Holborn and St Pancras). Most divorces were of younger people; only 10 per cent involved women over 50. 'It is middle-aged men who get fat and bald and unattractive', Jeger added mischievously. But, more seriously, 'We really cannot allow this important matter to be argued in terms of the age cycles of men and women.'[69]

Jeger was an MP in the Eirene White mould – educated in the state system and at Birkbeck College, a civil servant (during the war she had worked in the Ministry of Information) and journalist; her husband had been a GP and MP, and she had been elected to his seat on his death in 1953. With her intervention we see the most developed expression of equal-rights feminism in the parliamentary debates on divorce law reform in the 1960s. 'We have to break away from the concept of total domesticity and total dependency when we are trying to do something to put the marriage laws on a fairer basis,' she said.[70] 'It is because our society insists on continuing to regard women as the appendages of their husbands that we get into this muddle.'[71] What married women needed was not provisions to compensate for their dependence and vulnerability in marriage, which (she omitted to say) also acted as inducements to accept (or even choose) this status, but the *removal* of that vulnerability through independent access to paid work, benefits and property. 'We must be campaigning for a more independent economic status for married women and for them to have individual National Insurance rights.'[72] She quoted a constituent who told her she never wanted a penny from her husband: rather, 'I want a day nursery where I can leave my child, so that I can go to work. I want to work'. 'This,' Jeger concluded, 'is increasingly the pattern of the future.'[73] For this reason, as White had done in a very different social and demographic context, she argued that the principle of divorce law reform should be separated from the issue of fair shares for women in property and pensions – which, as she also pointed out from her own experience, affected widows as much as divorcees.

It comes as no surprise to see Vickers, now Dame Joan, endorsing Jeger's observations. Most divorces were undefended, she pointed out; most were to young

[67] ibid col 2045.
[68] ibid col 2046.
[69] Ibid col 2053.
[70] ibid col 2055.
[71] ibid col 2052.
[72] ibid.
[73] ibid col 2055.

people; most divorcees remarried. But the statement that brought home most clearly that equal-rights and separate-spheres feminists had come to an agreement about divorce law reform, so long as women's property rights were simultaneously addressed, was this:

> I am chairman of a committee which co-ordinates 23 women's organisations.[74] If there had been the sort of outcry from them which has been suggested, they might have removed me from my chairmanship. They have had plenty of time now to take this matter into account and I have not noticed any such strong opposition.[75]

The main reason the Bill was acceptable to all was the almost simultaneous introduction of a Bill (one of several put forward by interested organisations) dealing with married women's property, drafted by a committee of practising lawyers and legal academics including Olive Stone, Reader in Law at the London School of Economics.[76]

IV. Matrimonial Property Bill 1969

Introduced by Edward Bishop (Labour, Newark), the Matrimonial Property Bill 1969[77] proposed the 'equal division of family property' in the form of 'community of gains',[78] a regime favoured by the MWA. Under this arrangement, all items acquired during a couple's marriage would belong to them jointly, but not those owned separately prior to marriage. Gifts and inheritances to individuals would remain separate property, but any increase in their value would be jointly held.[79] This meant that women with little property of their own could share in profit built up in part thanks to their unpaid labour.

Those in favour of the Bill drew attention to the injustice of a situation where a woman who had made valuable contributions to the household was left with nothing at the end of the relationship if everything was held in her husband's name. In contrast to earlier representations, the women described here included those who had made a financial contribution – wives of publicans and farmers, or in jobs outside the home – as well as full-time housewives. Almost everyone in the House said that they approved the principle of modernising the law to recognise married women's entitlements. But all, except for the proposers, were unsparing in their attacks on the *form* of the proposals. Arguments included that the Bill was unworkable,[80] ignored widows[81] and was premature: Parliament should wait for a

[74] The Status of Women Committee, which Vickers founded in 1960.
[75] *Hansard*, HC Deb 17 December 1968, vol 775, col 1080.
[76] Auchmuty (2021) 449–50.
[77] *Hansard*, HC Deb 24 January 1969, vol 776, cols 801–95.
[78] ibid col 801.
[79] ibid col 810.
[80] ibid col 813.
[81] ibid col 821.

government Bill.[82] The language used by these (exclusively male) critics was sufficiently immoderate to suggest real anxiety that the Bill might pass. One described the proposal as 'ridiculous',[83] while Abse, cross because his Divorce Reform Bill had been held up thanks to this concern for married women's property, dwelt on 'the obvious and overwhelming deficiencies of drafting' committed by academic lawyers who had made 'enormous gaffes', and suggested that it was outrageous that the 'faithless woman, the incorrigible scold' should get half. Moreover, he contended, this Bill was unnecessary, since *his* Bill would have allowed property settlements of any amount, as well as lump sums and maintenance for life.[84]

Only two women spoke in favour of the Bill (none against). Both were Conservatives. The contribution of Jill Knight (Birmingham, Edgbaston) began in similar rhetorical style to Summerskill's, with sweeping statements about tradition, law and nature.[85] She then proceeded to explain (*again*) why so many housewives had no property of their own because of their responsibility for childcare. She noted that married women were increasingly going out to work, but that this only meant they did a double job, since they were still solely responsible for housework, and that the money they earned tended to go towards things for the family, like clothes and holidays, rather than into the value of the home. She emphasised that neither their unpaid labour nor their financial contributions to anything other than the home counted in law as a contribution to the property:

> It is not until a man is left with young children to look after that he begins to realise the great benefit of his wife to him in economic terms. It is not until he has to get a housekeeper or to make arrangements for his children or house to be looked after that it is recognised that the job which his wife was doing was of considerable value.[86]

Those who remember Knight's later support of Section 28 of the Local Government Act 1988 (which forbade the 'promotion' of homosexuality) and her opposition to same-sex marriage may find it hard to think of her as a feminist. Yet there is much that is feminist in this speech. Knight, whose parents had divorced when she was a child, and who had served in France in the WAAF during the war, presented a clearly gendered analysis of marriage, and her concerns paradoxically formed the basis of socialist feminist activism in the 1970s.

The other female sponsor of the Bill was Joan Vickers, who briskly countered the Attorney-General's assessment of the 'impossible burden' on judges, pointed out that '[t]hey manage perfectly well in other countries', dismissed her male colleagues' fear that men would lose out ('Hon Members who fear that the Bill would improve only the position of women need not worry') and took on

[82] ibid col 808.
[83] ibid col 818.
[84] ibid cols 820–21, 824.
[85] ibid col 826.
[86] ibid col 827.

the drafting critics by reminding the Solicitor-General that the Government had accepted no fewer than 700 amendments to its own Transport Bill.[87]

Alexander Lyon (Labour, York) added that such divisions of property were already routine in divorce courts,[88] and William Wilson made a wise intervention from his experience as a lawyer:

> Whenever the bride-to-be asks me whether the house should be in their joint names, I say that there is no doubt that it should be. I always add that if the husband-to-be has any question about it, that is the first indication that the bride is marrying the wrong man, because the very element of matrimonial property should be that it is joint.[89]

But the (Labour) Government was fiercely opposed. The Solicitor-General's[90] language ('defective', 'unworkable', placing an 'impossible burden' on judges) shows how important it thought it was to persuade the House to reject the Bill.[91] It emerged that the Lord Chancellor (Gerald Gardiner) had issued a three-line Whip against it for Ministers and a two-line Whip for non-Ministers, which were withdrawn after Prime Minister Wilson's intervention the night before the debate.[92] The Conservatives were rightly accusatory: 'they have chosen to give time to divorce reform,' observed Mark Carlisle (Runcorn), 'but are not prepared to give time to consideration of the great difficulties involved with the disposition of property on the breakdown of a marriage'.[93] He did not say, but we might think, to consideration of women's issues.

This official disapproval must explain the silence of the three Labour women present at the debate, Jennie Lee (Cannock), Joyce Butler (Wood Green) and Joan Lestor, all of whom nevertheless voted in favour of a Second Reading. The Ayes won the vote, but the Bill never saw the light of day. A cross-party group of sponsors came to an agreement with the Government that, if they withdrew the Bill, the Government would introduce its own Bill after the Law Commission had completed its report on matrimonial property relief.[94]

V. Discussion

What do we learn from the divorce reform debates prior to the DRA? We learn that concern for women's position was cross-party, with Labour and Conservative supporters of both sexes. We learn, moreover, that a 'feminist' approach cannot

[87] ibid cols 845–46, 849.
[88] ibid col 852.
[89] ibid col 859.
[90] Sir Arthur Irvine (Labour, Liverpool Edge Hill).
[91] *Hansard*, 24 January 1969, HC Deb vol 776, cols 832, 834.
[92] Stetson (1982) 195.
[93] *Hansard*, 24 January 1969, HC Deb vol 776, col 877.
[94] Stetson (1982) 199; Law Commission (1969).

simply be attributed to women, since many men put forward feminist analyses and proposals, while many women avoided the issue because they were not feminists and/or were not interested (Margaret Thatcher, elected in 1959, is a case in point). That said, not a single woman MP who spoke in these debates ignored the disproportionate effect of divorce on women, even if, as did White and Jeger, they preferred to treat the two issues separately. Many men, on the other hand, *did* ignore it. This is because, as Jeger once noted, women MPs were often expected to represent their sex as well as their particular constituents.[95] Moreover, women MPs had personal experience of the expectations imposed on girls growing up, and of the sexism, discrimination and misogyny routinely directed at women,[96] and they had no masculine rights and privileges to defend.

The debates are revealing of the techniques used by men (and only men) to try to block or limit reforms that benefited women at men's expense, and of the feminists' irritated responses. Both types of feminist challenged the sexist depictions of divorced women that focused on their looks and likelihood of finding another husband: 'even to-day a judge in the courts will look at a woman and say to himself, "She is not bad looking; therefore another man will come along",' Summerskill reminded the House of Lords; 'a woman is still treated as though she were in the cattle market'.[97] Nor were they afraid to challenge male self-interest. That their tactics were effective is clear from many men's outraged and defensive reactions, which included personal attacks on feminists, Summerskill in particular.[98]

The debates expose the slippery reasoning employed by advocates of divorce law reform when they portrayed it as a means of strengthening marriage. It was not. Divorce rates rose, marriage rates fell and marriage has never recovered its 1960s popularity.[99] Many speakers in the debates commented that marital breakdown had increased because marriage had become too easy – too many people entered into it too lightly. But few dared to suggest that the real problem was marriage itself.[100] One exception was Bruce Campbell, Tory arch-opponent of divorce law reform, who declared (presumably ironically, but actually presciently) 'The time must surely soon come … when we must ask ourselves whether the institution of marriage is worth bothering about any more'.[101]

To return to the question posed in the introduction: Was easier divorce *really* positive for women? Leaving aside the obvious benefit of enabling more women to get out of unhappy marriages and the obvious disadvantage of the poverty and ostracism that often resulted, what really proved positive in the long run was that

[95] In her Foreword to Margaret Torrie, *My Years With Cruse* [a charity supporting widows], Jeger quoted a typical letter she received: 'It's no use writing to my MP because he is a man and he will not understand' (Cruse House, 1987) xi.

[96] Williams (2009) 150–52.

[97] Divorce Reform Bill 1969, HL Deb 15 July 1969, vol 304, cols 140–240, 148–49.

[98] eg Abse (1973) 175.

[99] Deech (1990).

[100] As did second-wave feminists, eg Smart (1984).

[101] Divorce Reform Bill 1968, HC Deb 6 December 1968, vol 774, cols 2033–56, 2044.

divorce reform brought into the parliamentary spotlight, and gave legitimacy to, the longstanding concern of both groups of feminists about women's financial vulnerability in marriage, hitherto largely ignored. This, in the context of married women's evolving role in the 1960s, galvanised both protectionist and equal-rights feminists to formulate legislative strategies to improve their position, either through bestowing property rights in marriage and on divorce or through independent access to resources.

It was the protectionist strategy that won the short-term goal, ensuring that divorce law reform could not come about without improved financial provisions for divorced wives, although the actual provisions of the MPPA 1970 were a disappointment.[102] As far as long-term strategy is concerned, however, history has been on the side of the equal-rights feminists, who focused on challenging women's dependence *on marriage* rather than *in marriage*.[103] They were keenly aware that rights only obtainable through a relationship to a husband depended on, first, the existence of that husband – useless to unmarried women, then – and, second, the dependability and durability of that relationship. Breadwinners might earn a 'family wage' but did the family always get their share? And what if he left? Aided by an expanding economy, equal-rights feminists achieved a number of measures to enable women to enjoy an economic status independently of men. Barbara Castle (Labour, Blackburn) oversaw the passage of the Equal Pay Act 1970 and, as Secretary of State for Health, abolished the married women's stamp in 1977.[104]

Equal-rights feminists strove to keep the debate gender-neutral and looked to a world in which men and women would have equal access to financial resources through paid work, property ownership and benefits in their own name But they did not really address the conundrum of who would keep house and care for children; the assumption was perhaps that women with money could pay for other women to do this, though Castle's biographer tells us that she did all her own housework and cooking,[105] and left-wing Jeger anticipated the Women's Liberation Movement's 1970 demand for state-provided nurseries.

Equal-rights feminists foresaw that once women had money of their own, they would not necessarily want to share it with their husbands. Not all of them supported community of property. They were as alert to the lazy, improvident working man who drank or gambled away the matrimonial assets as they were to

[102] Though the Act permitted the court to make both capital and real property transfers, on the basis of factors that included the contribution of the parties to the welfare of the family, there was no community of property, no pension-sharing, no guaranteed household income and no automatic rights in marriage or on divorce.

[103] As first-wave feminists had done, by opening educational and employment opportunities to Victorian women as an alternative to marriage.

[104] Castle (1993) 135. The 'married women's stamp' was the reduced rate of National Insurance that married women could choose to pay, on the assumption that they would have lifelong support from their husbands. This meant that the pensions these women received on retirement were not enough to live on without that support from a husband.

[105] Martineau (2011) 185.

the male gold-digger who married a propertied woman for her money. Perhaps this reaction was a recognition that there were many such men in a society that so entitled the male sex. But it may also indicate that, under capitalism, people do want to hang on to the fruit of their labours; and women, given men's advantages, will behave just like men.

VI. Conclusion

Second-wave feminists have been hard on 1960s feminists. On the rare occasions where they have even acknowledged their existence, they have criticised them for not challenging the fundamental gender divisions in society and not really confronting male power.[106] Anne Logan suggests that all groups were limited by operating within the context of liberal feminism.[107] It is true that, as with their first-wave predecessors, 1960s feminists often couched their analysis in liberal (even conservative) terms, but this was usually a tactical decision to mask the fact that it was actually an *attack* on liberal reform. This strategy brought protectionists into uneasy alliance with other opponents of reform who held quite reactionary views of women, and led to their being tarred with the same brush – something that happens to feminists all the time when they criticise liberal approaches to reforms, for example same-sex marriage or the regulation of prostitution. The irony is that these radical critics are then perceived as obstructive and *illiberal* (or worse).

What the feminists in the divorce reform debates actually did was to expose the injustice of persuading (virtually forcing) women to embrace a challenging role that worked in the interests of men but which gave women status, security and a measure of power and fulfilment, and then changing the rules so that all of this could be whipped away and divorced women abandoned resourceless in a judgemental world. In other words, 1960s feminists challenged the exploitation by a class of men, aided by a patriarchal state, of a class of women – which looks like a radical feminist analysis to me.

Divorce reform in the 1960s offers a paradigm example of feminist legal history: the struggle to get women on the agenda at all; the fierce opposition to the removal of some of men's privileges (the Englishmen's ability to own his own property was one of the really significant privileges that many men were reluctant to share, and another was the ability to keep 'his' woman in dependence and service); and, finally, the fact that the measure achieved fell short of what feminists had wanted, even if it was better than what had gone before. These features are common to almost all legal landmarks for women.[108] Thus, insofar as legal feminism is always about politics as well as theory and methodology, these 1960s debates exemplify

[106] Lewis (1990) 184; Bruley (1999) 145.
[107] Logan (2007) 7.
[108] Rackley and Auchmuty (2019).

the truism of feminist legal history that it is often the paths not taken, the battles fought but not won, or not completely, that constitute the most important lessons for strategists for future reform.

References

Abse, L (1973) *Private Member* (London, MacDonald).
Addison, P (2010) *No Turning Back: The Peacetime Revolutions of Postwar Britain* (Oxford, Oxford University Press).
Atkins, S and Hoggett, B (1984) *Women and the* Law (Oxford, Basil Blackwell).
Attar, D (1990) *Wasting Girls' Time: The History and Politics of Home Economics* (London, Virago).
Auchmuty, R (2008) 'The Married Women's Property Acts: Equality Was Not the Issue' in R Hunter (ed), *Rethinking Equality Projects in Law: Feminist Challenges* (Oxford, Hart Publishing).
—— (2021) 'The Road to Olive Stone' in U Schultz, G Shaw, M Thornton and R Auchmuty (eds), *Gender and Careers in the Legal Academy* (Oxford, Hart Publishing).
Bowlby, J (1953) *Child Care and the Growth of Love* (WHO).
Brittain, V (1953) *Lady Into Woman: A History of Women from Victoria to Elizabeth II* (London, Dakers).
Bruley, S (1999) *Women in Britain Since 1900* (Basingstoke, Macmillan).
Castle, B (1993) *Fighting all the* Way (Basingstoke, Macmillan).
Deech, R (1990) 'Divorce Law and Empirical Studies' 106 *Law Quarterly Review* 229.
Denning, A (1953) *The Changing Law* (London, Stevens).
Dyhouse, C (1989) *Feminism and the Family in England 1880-1939* (Oxford, Basil Blackwell).
Fisher, K (2013) 'Marriage and Companionate Ideals Since 1750' in S Toulalan and K Fisher (eds), *The Routledge History of Sex and the Body* (London, Routledge).
Fletcher, R (1962) *The Family and Marriage in England Today* (Harmondsworth, Pelican).
Friedan, B (1963) *The Feminine Mystique* (London, Gollancz).
Gardiner, J (2017) *Joining the Dots: A Woman in her Time* (London, Collins).
Gavron, H (1966) *The Captive Wife* (Harmondsworth, Pelican).
Harrison, B (2009) *Seeking a Role: The United Kingdom 1951–1970* (Oxford, Clarendon).
Heilbron, H (2012) *Rose Heilbron: The Story of England's First Woman Queen's Counsel and Judge* (Oxford, Hart Publishing).
Jenkinson, S (2012) 'The Co-Respondent's Role in Divorce Reform After 1923' in R Probert and C Barton (eds), *Fifty Years in Family Law: Essays for Stephen Cretney* (Cambridge, Intersentia).
Kahn-Freund, O (1953) 'Inconsistencies and Injustices in the Law of Husband and Wife' 16 *Modern Law Review* 148.
—— (1955) 'Matrimonial 'Matrimonial Property Law in England' in W Friedmann (ed), *Matrimonial Property Law* (London, Stevens).
Klein, V (1965) *Britain's Married Women Workers* (London, Routledge & Kegan Paul).
Kynaston, D (2014) *Modernity Britain: A Shake of the Dice, 1959–62* (London, Bloomsbury).
Lane, E (1985) *Hear the Other Side: Audi Alterem Partem, the Autobiography of England's First Woman Judge* (London, Butterworth).

Law Commission (1969) *Family Law: Report on Financial Provision in Matrimonial Proceedings*, Law Com No 25 (HMSO).
—— (1978) *Third Report on Family Property: The Matrimonial Home (Co-ownership and Occupation Rights) and Household Goods*, Law Com No 86 (HMSO).
Lewis, J (1992) *Women in Britain Since 1945* (Oxford, Blackwell).
—— (1990) 'Myrdal, Klein, *Women's Two Roles* and Postwar Feminism 1945–1960' in H Smith (ed), *British Feminism in the Twentieth Century* (Aldershot, Edward Elgar).
Logan, A (2008) *Feminism and Criminal Justice: A historical perspective* (Basingstoke, Palgrave Macmillan).
Martineau, L (2011) *Politics and Power: Barbara Castle*, 2nd edm (London, Andre Deutsch).
Myrdal, A and Klein, V (1956) *Women's Two Roles* (London, Routledge & Kegan Paul).
National Housewives' Register, Records (Women's Library, LSE) at https://discovery.nationalarchives.gov.uk/details/r/96f6b758-596c-451e-9f58-b0e4f5063cca (last accessed 25 May 2021).
Newsom, J (1963) *Half Our Future* (London, HMSO).
Oakley, A (1976) *Housewife* (Harmondsworth, Pelican).
Rackley, E, and Auchmuty, R (2019) (eds), *Women's Legal Landmarks: Celebrating the History of Women and Law in the UK and Ireland* (Oxford, Hart Publishing).
—— (2020) 'The Case for Feminist Legal History' 40 *Oxford Journal of Legal Studies* 878.
Royal Commission on Marriage and Divorce Report 1951–1955 (1956) (London, HMSO).
Smart, C (1984) *The Ties That Bind* (London, Routledge & Kegan Paul).
Spender, D (1983) *There's Always Been a Women's Movement This Century* (London, Pandora).
Stetson, DM (1982) *A Woman's Issue: The Politics of Family Law Reform in England* (Westport, CT, Greenwood).
Thompson, S (2019) 'Married Women's Property Act 1964' in E Rackley and R Auchmuty (eds), *Women's Legal Landmarks: Celebrating the History of Women and Law in the UK and Ireland* (Oxford, Hart Publishing).
Stone, L (1990) *Road to Divorce: England 1530–1987* (Oxford, Clarendon).
Stone, OM (1963) 'The Matrimonial Causes and Reconciliation Bill 1963' 3 *Journal of Family Law* 87.
—— (1968) 'The Matrimonial Homes Act 1967' 31 *Modern Law Review* 308.
Torrie, M (1987) *My Years With Cruse* (Cruse House).
Williams, S (2009) *Climbing the Bookshelves* (London, Virago).
Wilson, E (1980) *Only Halfway to Paradise: Women in Postwar Britain 1945–68* (London, Tavistock).
Willmott, P and Young, M (1973) *The Symmetrical Family* (London, Routledge & Kegan Paul).
Winnicott, D (1957) *The Child and the Family* (London, Tavistock).

5

Putting Asunder – Reappraised

ROSIE SINCLAIR

I. Introduction

This chapter re-examines the influence of the Church of England on the Divorce Reform Act 1969.[1] A major part of this reappraisal involves scrutinising the role of the group set up in 1964 by the then Archbishop of Canterbury, Michael Ramsey, to consider divorce reform. Its report, published in 1966,[2] proposed both substantive and procedural changes: first, that the principle of 'irretrievable breakdown' should replace the old matrimonial offences; and, second, that there should be an 'inquest' to determine whether any given marriage had indeed broken down irretrievably. The group's subsequent negotiations with the newly created Law Commission were crucial in influencing the design of the Divorce Reform Bill and the eventual Act.[3]

The Church of England's role in family law policy is not a new subject. As the Established Church, its involvement with family law has been a long one, and the dynamic between Church and State has been commented on by theologians, historians and lawyers.[4] Studying family law reforms from 1909 to 1937, for example, Cordelia Moyse concluded that the Church of England's input into a range of family law legislation was based on a Christian understanding of marriage as a lifelong commitment.[5] By contrast, Stephen Cretney, analysing the influence of *Putting Asunder* on the Divorce Reform Bill, traces the steps of a previously conservative Church of England in the 1950s, opposing divorce reform, to one endorsing divorce based on irretrievable breakdown of marriage.[6]

[1] This chapter is based on the author's MPhil study: Sinclair (2017).
[2] *Putting Asunder: A Divorce Law for Contemporary Society* (London, SPCK, 1966) (hereinafter '*Putting Asunder*').
[3] These negotiations are documented in the papers of Gordon Dunstan, a member of the *Putting Asunder* group: London, Lambeth Palace Library, Papers of Gordon Reginald Dunstan, MS 4503.
[4] See eg Atkinson (1979) 36–69; Bennett (1994); Cretney (2003); Holmes (2017).
[5] Moyse (1996).
[6] Cretney (1998) 33–72.

Yet despite this previous work, there is still room for a reappraisal of the group's influence owing to its critical importance in shaping the Divorce Reform Act. This study develops previous work in three ways. First, it provides a more detailed analysis of the background of the group's members by looking at biographical materials and their published writings to gain a greater understanding of why their decision to support the concept of irretrievable breakdown was made so quickly, in just their third meeting. Second, it draws on previously little-used source material, the Dunstan papers, to provide more insight into the negotiations between the *Putting Asunder* group and the Law Commission, and to show how the settlement between them, hereinafter referred to as the *Consensus*, was reached. The key issue here is to understand why the group conceded some of their major proposals so quickly, primarily the insistence in their report on an inquest into the breakdown of marriage. Third, it examines the process of the Bill's passage through Parliament to assess the Christian input of Christian MPs in the House of Commons and of the bishops and archbishops in the House of Lords, and it shows how *Putting Asunder* and the *Consensus* were strategically used to support the Bill.

II. The *Putting Asunder* Group, its Deliberations and Conclusions

In order to determine how the *Putting Asunder* group came to conclude that divorce should be based on the irretrievable breakdown of marriage, it is necessary to consider how the group came into being, assess its members' backgrounds and appraise their views as expressed in their other writings.

While Ramsey was not a member of the group he had commissioned, he had an influence behind the scenes: the group was well aware of his position. In the previous decade, when Ramsey had been Archbishop of York, he was already anticipating the evils that might occur if divorce by matrimonial offence was abandoned and replaced by a divorce law based on breakdown as established by a period of separation, either with or without the other party's consent. In his view, the first amounted to marrying with a break clause and would destroy the Christian idea of lifelong marriage, as the parties could end the marriage just because they had become tired of each other; while, in the second instance, a person who was guilty of, say, adultery could divorce the other party. In a 1957 article he quoted an earlier comment by Bishop Mortimer to emphasise his point:

> Those who contract a marriage under such a system of law can only with the greatest difficulty be said to be contracting a lifelong and exclusive union, for they would then be contracting a union which could be terminated by the will of either or both of them …[7]

[7] Ramsey (1957) 3.

However, by 1963,[8] when opposing a Bill for divorce reform presented by Leo Abse MP, Ramsey publicly[9] indicated his openness to the idea of divorce based on breakdown of marriage, and indicated that he might convene a group to consider this:

> If it were possible to find a principle at law of breakdown of marriage which was free from any idea of consent … then I would wish to consider it. Indeed, I am asking some of my fellow churchmen to see whether it is possible to work at this idea, sociologically as well as doctrinally, to discover if anything can be produced.[10]

In a subsequent letter inviting Reverend Canon Bentley to be part of such a group, he wrote:

> The C of E upholds the meaning of marriage as a life-long union, and attaches the utmost importance to the fact that, both in a church marriage and in a registry office marriage, the parties enter upon a life-long covenant.[11]

Thus, the challenge for the group was to find a form of divorce that met the Archbishop's desire not to allow divorce by consent if breakdown of marriage became the central principle in divorce law.[12] Given the hierarchical nature of the Church of England, the Archbishop's view was important.

The original group consisted of Robert Mortimer, Norman Anderson, GB Bentley, Mark Colville, Patrick Devlin, GR Dunstan, Quentin Edwards, Donald MacRae, Helen Oppenheimer, Henry Phillimore, DA Pond, Joan Rubenstein and EW Short.[13] It was primarily a mixture of churchmen, academics and lawyers.[14] Cretney raises the question whether the group should be seen as representing the views of the Church of England or as more of an unrepresentative, eclectic, broadly Christian group, being a result of a trawl of 'the great and the good' as advised by the Lord Chancellor and Home Office.[15] However, he also notes that the Home Office only appointed two members of the group, Colville[16] and Short, and the second of these, the Labour MP for Newcastle-upon-Tyne Central, resigned in November 1964 after being appointed as Labour Chief Whip so only attended two meetings.[17] It was Anderson, himself a leading evangelical Christian,[18] who

[8] *Hansard*, HL Deb 21 June 1963, vol 250, col 1547.

[9] Prior to this, private discussions about the Church of England's involvement had been going on with government officials, and the concept of divorce based solely on irretrievable breakdown of marriage had emerged: Cretney (2003) 355.

[10] *Hansard*, HL Deb 21 June 1963, vol 250, col 1547.

[11] *Minutes of the Archbishop's Group on the Reform of the Law of Divorce*, Lambeth Palace Library.

[12] This was the conclusion of Lewis and Wallis (2000).

[13] *Putting Asunder* (1966) 1–2.

[14] ibid 1. In addition to those discussed below, Rubenstein was a partner in a London firm of solicitors, Phillimore was a High Court judge and Devlin was a Law Lord. Pond was a consultant psychiatrist at University College Hospital and Maudsley Hospital.

[15] Cretney (2003) 356; Cretney (1998) 48–50.

[16] Viscount Colville of Culross, Barrister-at-law, President of the National Council for the Unmarried Mother and her Child.

[17] *Putting Asunder* (1966) 2. His replacement, Mr AJ Irvine, QC and MP, only attended after the decision in favour of adopting the principle of irretrievable breakdown had been made, and also resigned.

[18] Cretney (1998) 49, fnn 112–16.

had suggested most of the names. Moreover, examination of the workings of the group reveals that the leading influences were high-profile individuals within the Church, both clergy and lay, and it was they who shaped events.

Mortimer chaired the group, and also the theological sub-committee. His status as one of the senior Diocesan bishops, along with his academic credentials, made him an obvious choice. He had been Regius Professor of Moral and Pastoral Theology at Oxford prior to becoming Bishop of Exeter, and was the most senior Anglican academic on the subject of ethics. He had published on Christian ethics and been involved in Church discussions on other public policy issues.[19] He had also substantially revised and updated Lacey's *Marriage in Church and State* in 1947.[20] This had argued that all marriages, and not only Christian marriages, are indissoluble according to natural law, that is divinely ordained,[21] and concluded that while the Church does not deny the State's authority to allow divorce for 'the hardness of men's heart',[22] Christians should encourage, through example and word, 'a healthier public opinion' of marriage, which would ultimately lead to the state's divorce law being redundant.[23] However, thinking on the Christian attitude to public policy had since changed, and while Mortimer's view of marriage and divorce for members of the Church remained the same, his position had moved as regards legislating for the general public.[24] For Ramsey to appoint Mortimer and for Mortimer to advocate breakdown as the way forward suggests that Ramsey knew Mortimer's stance on divorce reform and that it agreed with his own.

The other dominant voices in the group were also high-profile members of the Church of England. Oppenheimer was an Oxford graduate and taught Christian ethics at Cuddeston College, with which several other members of the group, including the Archbishop and Dunstan, had associations. Dunstan, who chaired the 'social' sub-committee that looked at such matters as reconciliation, arrangements for the children and division of finances, was ordained, serving as a Minor Canon of Westminster Abbey, and a top-ranking academic, being the first holder of the FD Maurice Chair of Moral and Social Theology at King's College, London. As Secretary of the Church of England's Council for Social Work, he had a central role in formulating the Church's response on ethical issues; a traditional Anglican, but as an academic open to new ideas.[25] Bentley, the Canon of Windsor, drafter of the report, was a distinguished scholar and more cautious about reform.

[19] Such as the issues of decriminalising suicide and homosexuality: Skinner (1979) 130–32.

[20] Lacey (1947).

[21] ibid 23. Atkinson (1979) 25 describes this as the 'rigorist view'.

[22] Lacey (1947) 212.

[23] ibid 213.

[24] As late as 1962, Oppenheimer refers to Mortimer as an indissolubilist ((1962) 68), but she was basing this on his book *Christian Ethics*, published in 1950. That his position had moved from this strict position is obvious from his being prepared to chair a Group whose task was to consider a new divorce law and his speech in Parliament supporting the Divorce Reform Bill (see *Hansard*, HL Deb 30 June 1969, vol 303 col 375.

[25] Holtman (2008).

Their other writings on marriage are illuminating. Dunstan's *The Family is not Broken* – written in answer to the Mothers' Union's assertion that the family was disintegrating – took the view that 'the marriages of the post-war generation may well prove to be more stable'[26] and did not consider that the high divorce rate following the Second World War would necessarily continue. This suggests that he was less likely to be anxious that divorce reform would increase the divorce rate. Oppenheimer's *Law and Love*[27] made a plea that marriages should be relationships of quality, not just duty, and argued that Christian faith and morals cannot be reduced to a set of rules. In her later work *The Marriage Bond*,[28] she advocated a better way than either rigorism[29] or liberalism, and she defended the view that, notwithstanding the idea – based on a metaphysical understanding – that marriages can never break down, in reality they can, and advocated that people be allowed to remarry in church in certain circumstances where the marriage bond had broken irretrievably. She justified the theology of *Putting Asunder* that a secular divorce law was needed to accommodate people's 'hardness of heart', and was adamant that its 'recommendation was not a capitulation to secular pressure'.[30]

The third sub-committee, which focused on legal issues, was also chaired by a churchman – Edwards was an evangelical, a circuit judge and a legal adviser to the General Synod. By contrast, some of the non-Anglican members of the group had less influence than might have been expected. Lord Devlin attended only one meeting, and after reading the draft report, felt unable to endorse the procedural changes required.[31] Similarly, MacRae, who was Professor of Sociology at the University of London, attended only four meetings owing to illness, and his report into sociological considerations was inconclusive and not completed in time to be formally adopted by the group, though it was published as part of the report (Appendix F).[32]

One of the strengths of the group, and perhaps one of the reasons its report was given so much weight, was that its membership was drawn from across the Church of England traditions, including two evangelicals. Post-war evangelicals had largely concentrated on issues of doctrine, but this was changing in the 1960s, and Anderson, who became Mortimer's right-hand man in the negotiations with the Law Commission, had held multi-disciplinary discussions on social policy at the Institute of Advanced Legal Studies, of which he was director. Some of the people he met through these meetings became members of the *Putting Asunder* group.[33] He was also a lay reader at the major Anglican evangelical church in London, All

[26] Dunstan (1962) 70.

[27] Oppenheimer (1962).

[28] Oppenheimer (1976).

[29] The rigorist approach would not allow remarriage in church after divorce in any circumstances.

[30] Oppenheimer (1976) 76. For a more detailed analysis of the works of Dunstan and Oppenheimer see Holmes (2017) 100–102.

[31] *Putting Asunder* (1966) 63.

[32] ibid 2, 167. Some of its content was discussed at the 17th meeting of the group.

[33] Anderson (1985) 181.

Souls Langham Place,[34] where he worked alongside the leading evangelical theologian Reverend Dr John Stott. Anderson's 1968 publication *Into the World, the Needs and Limits of Christian Involvement* recognised that a Christian in politics 'must necessarily settle for the best legislation which public opinion will accept' as politics is 'the pursuit of the possible rather than the attainment of the ideal'.[35]

The Group met 18 times over a period of two years, with eight of the meetings lasting two days. They heard oral evidence from 19 witnesses. Of these, five were judges, including Sir Jocelyn Simon P, six were lawyers specialising in family law, and the remainder were probation officers, marriage counsellors, a psychiatrist and a professor of law from Freiburg University. There was written evidence from five organisations, the Lawyers' Christian Fellowship being the only explicitly Christian one.[36] They also received letters from individuals. There was no input from theologians, presumably because the theology was already decided, or because it was considered that the group itself contained the leading moral theologians of the day.

Given that it was a working group established by the Archbishop of Canterbury, it might seem surprising that theology was not its primary focus. The first clue is in the terms of reference, which had been agreed with government officials: these were to review the law of England concerning divorce and,

> recognizing that there is a difference in the attitudes of the Church and State towards the further marriage of a divorced person whose former partner is living, to consider whether the inclusion of any new principle or procedure in the law of the State would be likely to operate
>
> (1) More justly and with greater assistance to the stability of marriage and the happiness of all concerned including children than at present; and
> (2) In such a way as to do nothing to undermine the approach of couples to marriage as a lifelong covenant.[37]

This emphasised that there was a difference between the Church's own discipline (which would, for example, deal with the questions of whether divorcees could be admitted to communion or remarry in church) and the secular law of divorce and remarriage, and that the group was only tasked with examining the latter. It was emphasised that this should be underlined in 'the reddest of red inks':[38]

> How the doctrine of Christ concerning marriage should be interpreted and applied within the Christian Church is one question: what the Church ought to say and do about secular laws of marriage and divorce is another question altogether. This can hardly be repeated too often.[39]

[34] Cretney (1998) 49, fn 114.
[35] Anderson (1968) 52.
[36] These written submissions appear to have been lost and are not available at the Lambeth Palace Library.
[37] *Putting Asunder* (1966) ix.
[38] ibid 3.
[39] ibid 3–4.

This allowed the Group to examine divorce law without recourse to biblical principles established in the creation story[40] and alluded to by Jesus in the Gospel of Matthew.[41] Jesus, when questioned about divorce, referred back to the Creation and the fact of the lifelong union of husband and wife from the beginning being the intention in creation for all mankind. However, the report's theology places great emphasis on Jesus' reference to Moses, in The Old Testament, allowing a law of divorce because of the hardness of heart of the people.[42] Hardness of heart, the report pointed out,[43] could be interpreted as 'unteachable' rather than its more natural meaning of 'sinful'. So in a society where it was no longer obvious to most people that divorce was not right, either because they did not give credence to the teaching in the Bible or because it was not apparent to them by the law of nature, the State is permitted to legislate for divorce. Furthermore, the Church was entitled to accept such a law for the purposes of the secular sphere. In fact, it would be unjust to impose a Christian model on the world:

> Any advice that the Church tenders to the State must rest, not upon doctrines that only Christians accept, but upon premises that enjoy wide acknowledgement in the nation as a whole. No one should think, therefore, that advice from the Church in this matter is bound to represent an ecclesiastical attempt to obtain legal enforcement of specifically Christian tenets.[44]

Thus, it is not as surprising as it might first seem that the group accepted a strong prima facie case for accepting irretrievable breakdown as the basis for divorce by only its third meeting. Ramsey's views, expressed in his letter of invitation to potential group members and reinforced by Mortimer at the first meeting, along with the background and associations of the group members and their emerging views, made it likely that this would be the case. Moreover, given the dominance of Anglicans within the discussions, it was more of a Church of England group than the original appointments might suggest or for which Cretney gave it credit. And the perception that it articulated the view of the Church of England was to prove influential in subsequent debates.

III. How was *Putting Asunder* used by the Law Commission?

In 1966 a new law advisory body, known as the Law Commission, came into being as a result of the Law Commission Act 1965. Its first chairman was Lord

[40] See Genesis 1 and 2.
[41] Matthew 19: 3–9.
[42] *Putting Asunder* (1966) 8, 9 and 12.
[43] ibid 9.
[44] ibid 12.

Justice Scarman, who had previously been President of the Probate, Divorce and Admiralty Division, and one of the first tasks it undertook was a review of divorce law.[45] The interaction and dynamic between the Law Commission and the *Putting Asunder* group, which developed into the *Consensus* and a draft Bill by the Law Commission, was highly significant in how the law was shaped. Members of the two groups met during 1966 and early in 1967. The *Putting Asunder* group responded to the early meetings by making some changes to their report to firm up their own position.[46] However, the Law Commission had the considerable advantage of being able to read and respond to *Putting Asunder* before finalising their own report.[47]

In a meeting of the group on 29 January 1966, Anderson gave an account of his meeting with Scarman and Professor Gower, one of the Commissioners, in which *Putting Asunder* had been discussed.[48] He quoted Scarman as stating that he considered the report to be an 'admirable document'.[49] However, Anderson had formed the impression that the Law Commission might use it for its own purposes rather than in the way intended by the group. He feared that the Law Commission might adopt the group's support for the concept of irretrievable breakdown but merely add that ground to a list of matrimonial offences. Indeed, Scarman gave a talk two months later in which he advocated just this.[50]

In response to this, it was decided that the *Putting Asunder* group would strengthen its arguments against this formulation, in particular by reference to Lord Walker's position in the Morton Report.[51] The group believed that adding breakdown as an additional ground was just a pragmatic response to 'hardship cases' and did not get to the root of the problem with the law. Its reasoning is not set out in detail, but it is evident from the report that this was the group's thinking.[52] If irretrievable breakdown was just added as an additional ground, the court would continue to look at superficial reasons for the divorce and would not enquire more fully into whether a marriage was saveable.[53] In addition, using irretrievable breakdown as an additional ground would tend to increase divorce, as parties who could not prove an offence could try for divorce on this ground.

[45] Law Commission (1966).

[46] *Minutes of Putting Asunder Group*, 29 January 1966, MS 3460, 149.

[47] Cretney (1998) 58.

[48] *Minutes of the Archbishop's Group*, 29 January 1966, MS 3460, 149.

[49] ibid.

[50] Paulsen (1966) 93.

[51] *Putting Asunder* (1966) 94, gives a summary of Lord Walker's minority report from the Morton Report (Cmnd 9678, 341) in which he advocated that the matrimonial offence doctrine should be abandoned and be replaced by the doctrine that a marriage is indissoluble unless the couple have lived apart for at least three years and the marriage is found to be broken down.

[52] *Putting Asunder* (1996) 59.

[53] ibid 57. The perception that divorces were based on 'superficial' grounds owed much to the group's acceptance of the theory of 'depth' psychology, the implication of which is that divorce cannot be understood in terms of one party's misdemeanour but by a complex web of considerations going back to childhood.

By contrast, the group believed that divorce would be made more difficult to prove under a principle of irretrievable breakdown as established by a judge through an inquest. On this model, the finding of a matrimonial fault would not of itself be sufficient to show that a marriage was at an end: the judge would have to be satisfied, in addition, that, notwithstanding an incident of, say, adultery, the marriage was not saveable owing to that incident. The group's members thus appeared to believe that a move to the principle of irretrievable breakdown would not necessarily increase the number of divorces, since some divorces that would have been granted on the basis of fault would not be granted on the basis of breakdown. It was also suggested that the increasingly liberal interpretation of the grounds of 'cruelty' and 'insanity' meant that the matrimonial offence principle was becoming more and more insubstantial.[54]

In just a few weeks,[55] the *Putting Asunder* group and the Law Commission had reached a compromise known as *The Consensus*[56] and the Church had conceded its key safeguard of requiring a full inquest to ascertain the breakdown of the marriage. Instead, it agreed that breakdown could be presumed from one of five facts. It did so because Mortimer had become convinced that the provisions that allowed for a rebuttal of the presumption of breakdown would be effective.[57] He also convinced himself that he was not conceding divorce by consent, describing the Archbishop's concern that this was the case as 'facile' in a letter to Scarman the following year.[58]

The group could have pulled out of the negotiations. It would have been justified in doing so, given that it was asked to concede its key recommendation.[59] It had, after all, previously stated emphatically that if an inquest were not possible then the law should remain based on the matrimonial offence.[60] That it did not choose to pull out can be explained by several reasons. As a matter of principle, the new concept avoided laying blame on either party and examined the substance of a marriage, not just its form.[61] As it noted, 'the principle of breakdown might make secular divorce in some respects less offensive to Christian sentiment than it is now'.[62] This was coupled with Mortimer's growing belief that the present law was so bad that anything was better,[63] and a fear that a divorce law could emerge that was far more offensive to the Church than the one proposed and agreed to.

[54] See the discussions in *Putting Asunder* (1966) 57–59.

[55] Based on the discussions between the group and the Law Commission as recorded by the Dunstan papers from early December 1966 to mid-March 1967. A joint meeting was held on 17 February (Dunstan Papers, 229). The Consensus itself was dated 2 June 1967.

[56] *Reform of Grounds of Divorce: Result of Discussions between Archbishop's Group on Divorce and Law Commission*, Lambeth Palace Library, Ramsey Papers, vol 117, 328–36.

[57] See eg the letter from Mortimer to Scarman, dated 30 January 1967 (Dunstan Papers, 225) and that from Scarman to Mortimer, 1 March 1967 (Dunstan Papers, 230).

[58] National Archives, BC3/378, Letter from Mortimer to Scarman, 20 January 1968.

[59] *Putting Asunder* (1966) 67.

[60] ibid 67.

[61] ibid 60.

[62] ibid 61.

[63] The *Daily Mirror* (2 February 1968) quoted Mortimer as saying, 'I dislike the existing marriage laws so much that I think almost anything would be an improvement'.

IV. Use of the *Putting Asunder* Report and the *Consensus* in Parliament

The *Consensus*, with some minor but significant amendments,[64] became the basis of what eventually emerged as the Divorce Reform Act 1969. This chapter does not seek to give a general account of the passage of the Act[65] but focuses on the use that was made during the debates of both *Putting Asunder* and the amended proposals in the *Consensus*.

As noted in Section II, *Putting Asunder* was considered as representing the view of the Church of England. This, of course, hugely over-simplified the range of views within the Church. The Church of England did not speak with one voice, and the debates should be set against the background of theological differences and innovations within the Church. The term 'Two Christianities' has been used to describe the split in the Church of England between the radicals proposing a 'new theology'[66] and 'new morality', and those who remained conservative.[67] Elsewhere, the categories of conservative, liberal and pragmatist have been used to illustrate the different approaches to public policy by members of the Church.[68] Neither approach sufficiently describes the complexities of the different views and strategies of members of the Church. What can be said is that the emergence of this 'new theology' occurred at the same time as a move towards an acceptance of a pluralist society.[69] From this stemmed a growing body in the Church that, whilst adhering to traditional morality on marriage for its own members, took the view that it was not possible to achieve this morality in the secular law and that a more humanist, pragmatic approach should be taken towards public policy.

On the specific issue of divorce law reform, there was no official Church of England party line as such, even though the Church Assembly had accepted the principle of irretrievable breakdown in 1967.[70] The varied opinions within the

[64] There were two main changes. The first was that the *Consensus* referred to 'intolerable conduct', which the petitioner could not reasonably be expected to live with, rather than just 'behaviour'. This did not appear in the draft Bill and so was presumably dropped by the draftsman. Its significance is that it appears to reduce the level of behaviour required. The second was that the *Consensus* contained a general prohibition on the court's granting a divorce if, due to the conduct of the parties and interests of the parties and children, it would be wrong to dissolve the marriage. In the Bill this defence became one of grave or financial hardship, and in the Divorce Reform Act 1969 its scope was limited to the five-year separation fact.

[65] For an excellent account, see Lee (1974).

[66] This new theology has been identified with Robinson (1963).

[67] Norman (1976) 417.

[68] McLeod (2007) 215–39.

[69] Norman (1976) 417.

[70] The Church Assembly was the Church's equivalent of a parliament and a predecessor of the General Synod. In 1967 it passed one motion welcoming the conclusions of *Putting Asunder* and another asking the Convocations of Canterbury and York to reconsider whether divorcees could remarry in church. In some respects, a divorce law based on irretrievable breakdown would give the Church greater flexibility in deciding who might qualify to remarry in church, as the court would no longer categorise divorcees as innocent or guilty.

Church were reflected in the contributions made in the debates, both by MPs who happened to be members of the Church of England and by bishops in the House of Lords. However, the power of dissenting voices was diminished because of the input of the *Putting Asunder* group into the *Consensus*.

A. The Debates in the House of Commons

Lee's work analysing the parliamentary debates is useful in identifying MPs of faith, though he rightly points out that it is always difficult to tell how deep that conviction goes and that the religion (if any) of 133 members was unknown.[71] Christian MPs were clearly divided on their view of the Bill. Alec Jones, the Bill's sponsor, was an active member of the Church of Wales,[72] whilst Bruce Campbell, its main opponent, was a Baptist. Daniel Awdry, Conservative MP for Chippenham and an active member of the Church of England,[73] in turn opposed Mr Campbell's arguments. Of the eight Conservatives and six Labour MPs who spoke against the Bill, the majority were Catholics,[74] although only one MP specifically referred to his Catholic faith, and even he indicated that he was not speaking from a faith perspective.[75] Overall, Lee's analysis[76] reveals that Roman Catholic MPs were largely opposed to the Bill, while Free Church Christians were mostly for it. Anglicans, including those belonging to the Church of Scotland and the Church in Wales, were more equally divided, with 21 per cent voting for the Second Reading of Bill and 25 per cent against, and the remainder either not attending or abstaining. By contrast, 66 per cent of known atheists and agnostics were for the Bill. However, the biggest factor in determining how an MP would vote was not religion but political party and age: Labour Party MPs (though there was no party whip as this was a moral issue on which MPs had a free vote) and younger MPs were more likely to vote in favour.

The Church of England's influence was more evident in the reference made to *Putting Asunder*. Marcus Worsley, a prominent Anglican, opposed the Bill on the basis that, unlike *Putting Asunder*, it continued to rely on the matrimonial offence principle.[77] While the report was in his view 'brilliant, stimulating and well-written', the inquest proposal was wholly impractical;[78] on the other hand, simply adding two new separation facts alongside the existing matrimonial offences made the concept of irretrievable breakdown meaningless.

[71] Lee (1974) 137.
[72] ibid, 113.
[73] ibid, 128.
[74] ibid, 132, table 1.
[75] *Hansard*, HC Deb 17 December 1968, vol 775, col 1088.
[76] Based on Richards (1970).
[77] *Hansard*, HC Deb 17 December 1968, vol 775, col 1060.
[78] ibid, col 1061.

He was, however, the only speaker to pick up on the difference between *Putting Asunder* and the Bill based on the *Consensus*. Those promoting the Bill used the group's subsequent agreement with the Law Commission to draw support for the Bill from *Putting Asunder* itself. For example, in moving for its Second Reading, Alec Jones had referred to the *Putting Asunder* report as giving an 'objective criticism'[79] of the current law, and quoted its conclusion verbatim:

> That the law as it stands is unsatisfactory, all the judges and lawyers who gave evidence agreed, however much they differed concerning the remedies to be applied. We are far from being convinced that the present provisions of the law witness to the sanctity of marriage or uphold its public repute in any observable way, or that they are irreplaceable as buttresses of morality either in the narrower field of matrimonial and sexual relationships or in the wider field which includes considerations of truth, the sacredness of oaths and the integrity of professional practice: as a piece of social mechanism, the present system has not only cut loose from its moral and judicial foundations it is quite simply inept.

He added:

> Those are not my words but the words of Putting Asunder.[80]

In his summing up, he referred to it as a 'consensus Bill', formulated after long discussions:

> [I]t is unashamedly a consensus Bill, it is supported by Members on both sides. Its structure and fine balance are the result of long discussions between churchmen, lawyers and politicians.[81]

This hardly reflected the speed with which the agreement between the *Putting Asunder* group and the Law Commission had been reached.[82]

Leo Abse is the clearest example of a non-Christian MP using *Putting Asunder* to support the Bill. He emphasised that all those who gave evidence to the group found the law 'unsatisfactory',[83] which ignored the fact that some did not think the new principle was entirely satisfactory either.[84] Similarly, Daniel Awdry, responding to Bruce Campbell's criticism of the Bill, claimed that such criticism

> ignores the fact that many distinguished lawyers and leaders of the Church also want to see a major reform made in the divorce law. It ignores the Church's report, 'Putting Asunder.' It ignores the report of the Law Commissioners. The people who helped to

[79] *Hansard*, HC Deb 6 December 1968, vol 774, col 2036.
[80] ibid.
[81] ibid, col 2043.
[82] Mortimer met with the Law Commission in December, there was a meeting of representatives of both groups on 17 February and a Consensus was reached on 2 June. See the Dunstan papers, Lambeth Palace Library MS 4503.
[83] *Hansard*, HC Deb 17 December 1968, vol 775, col 1124.
[84] See, for instance, the evidence of Sir Jocelyn Simon and Sir Geoffrey Lawrence QC: *Minutes of the Archbishop's Group on the Reform of the Law of Divorce*, Lambeth Palace Library, MS 3460, 29–37 and 77–78.

> write those reports are not guilty people. They were sensible, humane people who realise that the present divorce laws are neither fair nor just.[85]

The Bill passed its Second Reading with a clear majority of 77. *Putting Asunder* was cleverly used by the main promoters to dismiss the concept of the matrimonial offence and embrace the principle of irretrievable breakdown, whilst minimising the report's other conclusion that the principle of irretrievable breakdown should only be adopted if a full inquest procedure were to be accepted. *The Consensus* made it impossible for the report to be used in its original form. The Bill's promoters could refer to the principle of irretrievable breakdown as having official Church of England support. This may explain why none of the Bill's opponents, except Marcus Worsley, referred to *Putting Asunder* at all.

B. The Debates in the House of Lords

It was in the Lords that reformers could expect more opposition to the Bill, given the presence of the Church of England Bishops and its generally more conservative nature. Certainly, the Bill's promoters were anxious to get the Bishops on board.[86] While some of the Bishops did oppose reform, their authority was diminished by the fact that they were not arguing from a common position and because attention was diverted from their individual speeches to *Putting Asunder* and the *Consensus*.

Lord Stow Hill, who introduced the Bill, made the House laugh at the suggestion that the Church of England would agree with a Casanova's charter, a label some opponents had put on the Bill because it allowed divorce on the basis of five years' separation against an 'innocent' spouse's will.[87] He also used the *Putting Asunder* group's support for the concept of irretrievable breakdown of marriage to reassure the House that 'If this change is in principle right, the rest of the Bill follows from it.'[88] In further discussion, he commented that 'I always think how wise the Archbishop's Group was in advising us to travel away from 1857 to 1969 and to dump the matrimonial offence and all the antiquated junk that goes with it beneath the waves for ever.'[89]

The theological differences in the Church of England are most clearly reflected in the speeches of the three Bishops who spoke in the Second Reading debate in the Lords. Whilst all three upheld a Christian doctrine of lifelong marriage for the Church of England's own members, they differed in their opinions on

[85] *Hansard*, HC Deb 17 December 1968, vol 775, col 1091.

[86] The Bishop of London reported to Robert Beloe that he had talked to Stow Hill, who took the involvement of the Bishops very seriously: 'Stow Hill was very anxious to do anything he could to make it possible for the Bishops to support the Bill – short, of course, of altering it!' (Ramsey Papers, vol 162, 60).

[87] *Hansard*, HL Deb 30 June 1969, vol 303, cols 296–97; Lee (1974) 172. See further Thompson, ch 6 of this volume.

[88] ibid col 298.

[89] ibid col 303.

the secular law. They were able to speak according to their conscience in this regard, and did not necessarily adhere to the conclusions of the *Putting Asunder* group in either their original or negotiated form, despite the group's having been appointed by the Archbishop.

This was made most obvious because the Archbishop himself, whilst upholding the conclusions of *Putting Asunder*, expressed doubts about the *Consensus*.[90] Ramsey thought that in general terms, the principle of irretrievable breakdown of marriage was not incompatible with lifelong marriage if the 'blemishes' in the Bill could be dealt with.[91] When the time came to vote, he abstained.

Mortimer, by contrast, voted for the Bill. He admitted that he had changed his stance from being an indissolubilist, believing that marriages *could* not come to an end, to believing in lifelong marriage which *should* not end but in reality sometimes did. He expressed puzzlement that he had reached this position: 'I still believe, if not in the metaphysical doctrine of the indissolubility of marriage, at least that the obligations of a marriage, duly contracted, are lifelong.'[92]

He put much reliance on the courts' ability to rebut the presumption of breakdown by an inquiry into the facts, having conceded the need for an inquest in the negotiations with the Law Commission:

> [T]he courts must take seriously their duty to inquire into all the facts alleged and be quite sure that they are satisfied that the marriage has irretrievably broken down. In other words, the evidence of the matrimonial offence as proof of irretrievable breakdown of the marriage must be treated as rebuttable, and not as conclusive, evidence.[93]

The Bishop of Leicester, conversely voted against the Bill. He argued not only against *Putting Asunder*'s support for the principle of irretrievable breakdown, but also against the Bill, largely on the basis of the law's educative effect and his concern that lack of any matrimonial offence meant lack of a matrimonial standard: 'Houses of Parliament convey in a subtle way to the people, that, after all, marriage is not so very permanent and indissoluble.'[94]

The debate went on for over seven hours with 28 speakers. About half of these referred to the Church of England's stance, with most of these citing *Putting Asunder* as supporting the demise of the matrimonial offence and a few regarding it as supporting the principle of irretrievable breakdown. Twice as many spoke

[90] *Sunday Times* (5 February 1968); Ramsey Papers, vol 117, 113.

[91] *Hansard*, HL Deb 30 June 1969, vol 303, col 338. These three blemishes related, first, to the presumption of breakdown based on a two-year period of separation rather than three where there was consent (though this Bill could not be criticised as introducing consent any more than was operating under the old law); second, the financial safeguards in the case of unilateral divorce after five-year separation, as only needing to be the 'best that can be made in the circumstances' and not necessarily needing to be 'reasonable and fair'; and, third, the seeming weakness of the wording of the public interest/interests of justice defence where one party had behaved so badly that it would be inequitable to grant them a divorce.

[92] ibid col 375.

[93] ibid col 379.

[94] ibid col 406.

for the Bill as spoke against it, even though some supporters had some reservations and made some criticisms. However, there was an overwhelming sense that if the principle of irretrievable breakdown were agreed, the detail of the Bill could be dealt with in committee. Despite the Archbishop's abstention, he was seen as supporting the abolition of the matrimonial offence and upholding the central new principle of irretrievable breakdown.

No one, not even the Archbishop, argued from the point of view of *Putting Asunder* that an *inquest* was the only real way of determining whether a marriage had in fact broken down. Therefore, whilst other Christian views were expressed, particularly that this change in principle would erode moral standards in marriage, Lee is correct in stating that 'ever since the Church of England had accepted the principles laid down by *Putting Asunder*, a systematic opposition against the Bill had been lacking'.[95] The vote in favour of the Bill was overwhelming – contents 122 and non-contents 34. Five Bishops voted in favour of the Bill and three against. Whilst the Bishops who did not attend the vote could be criticised for their absence when such a major social change was being discussed, it would have made little difference to the final result.

Analysis of the amendments at Committee and Report Stages and the Third Reading debate indicates that there seems to have been general support for the *Consensus* position among the Bishops, but at times a push back in favour of the original position in *Putting Asunder* where this seemed achievable. This demonstrates their anxiety that the law should really have the principle of irretrievable breakdown at its centre and not be a cloak for the old law of matrimonial offence. It is, however, difficult to see an entirely consistent pattern of involvement and voting by the Bishops, especially given that not all were present at the same sittings. The Archbishop, it should be noted, took no part in these proceedings, and there is no evidence to indicate what advice, if any, he gave to other Bishops who were involved.

The most interesting amendments were those that centred on how irretrievable breakdown of marriage should be proved. Lord Ilford, for example, proposed that the five facts (from which irretrievable breakdown of marriage was to be presumed) should be scrapped in favour of an investigation of irretrievable breakdown in each individual case. His amendment was really a re-run of the earlier negotiations between the *Putting Asunder* group and the Law Commission, and an attempt to reintroduce the inquest-style investigation into breakdown. While all the speakers could see the inconsistency in the Bill of the ground for divorce being the irretrievable breakdown of the marriage but this only being provable by one of five facts, it was felt that this must be accepted in order to avoid 'endless expense, endless delay and inquiries into intimate human behaviour that … it is [not] appropriate or right to inquire into'.[96] None of those who attended defended

[95] Lee (1974) 117.

[96] Lord Goodman, *Hansard*, HL Deb 10 July 1969, vol 303, col 1217.

the original *Putting Asunder* position, putting an end to any hopes that its recommendations, rather than the negotiated *Consensus*, would be adopted.

Other amendments suggested some desire to move back to the original *Putting Asunder* report. Viscount Hodson, for example, proposed an amendment to make it a positive requirement for the petitioner to show that the marriage had irretrievably broken down in addition to proving one of the five facts, rather than irretrievable breakdown's being presumed from proof of a fact.[97] All six Bishops present voted for this amendment.[98] Similarly, all five Bishops present voted for Viscount Dilhorne's proposed amendment, which would have the effect of removing the possibility of establishing irretrievable breakdown on the basis of the adultery fact. Mortimer himself spoke in favour of the amendment.[99] Strange as some other members of the House found this,[100] this position was consistent with *Putting Asunder*'s principle of irretrievable breakdown with as much enquiry by the court into the facts as possible, as it envisaged that such cases would come under the 'behaviour' fact. It would also be consistent with the *Putting Asunder* group's desire to move away from using a fact that smacked of the old matrimonial offence doctrine. Despite the Bishops' support, none of these proposed amendments were accepted. Mortimer's attempt to bring back a more general public interest defence also failed.[101]

In the final analysis, it was agreeing to the *Consensus* that, for better or worse, was the decisive point. Most of the clauses in the *Consensus* emerged in a very similar form in the final Act and during the debates, particularly in the Lords, those speaking on behalf of the Church of England repeatedly described the *Consensus* as the Church of England's position. *Putting Asunder* was relevant only insofar as it had informed the *Consensus*, and the conditions on which it had endorsed the principle of irretrievable breakdown were overlooked or ignored.

V. Conclusion

The Church of England's influence on the Divorce Reform Act 1969 came primarily, though not exclusively, through the influence of *Putting Asunder*. This chapter builds on Cretney's observation that the group was an unrepresentative collection of the 'great and the good' who reached a presumption in favour of the principle of

[97] Amendment 14, *Hansard*, HL Deb 11 July 1969, vol 303, col 1314.
[98] ibid.
[99] Amendment 3, *Hansard*, HL Deb 10 July 1969, vol 303, col 1229.
[100] Lord Goodman pointed out to the Bishops that marital fidelity was at the heart of marriage and that divorce law should emphatically declare this by retaining adultery as evidence of breakdown. Baroness Summerskill was also amazed that the Bishops should suggest 'that we should dispense with the guidelines for adultery'.
[101] For a more detailed analysis of the passage of the Bill through Parliament, including the tabled amendments, see Sinclair (2017).

'irretrievable breakdown of marriage' by their third meeting. A closer look at the background of the members and the workings of the group reveals that behind the scenes, many of the members had been seriously considering this concept before the meetings began and knew that the Archbishop who authorised the group was of that mind. Whilst Ramsey was not opposed to having members from other disciplines involved, believing the Church could learn from this,[102] their influence should not be overstated. The membership of the group represented a range of Anglican churchmanship, including those from an evangelical background, and could therefore justifiably be regarded as incorporating the opinion of much of the Church of England.

The group's pragmatic approach to parliamentary strategy resulted in the *Consensus*. However, the compromise made with the Law Commission – whereby the group's idea of an inquest to establish breakdown was replaced with a presumption of breakdown based on one of five facts' having been established – meant the Church of England lost the freedom to argue from the original report's position. Having endorsed the principle of irretrievable breakdown, the Church was not later able to dictate the conditions or parameters surrounding that principle. In addition, MPs of all backgrounds, faiths, and philosophical and political beliefs referred to the fact that there was agreement between the *Putting Asunder* group and the Law Commission to support and justify their reforming stance. It is unsurprising that those without church allegiance were able to recommend the Church of England position because of its appeal to the humanist approach.

In 1990, Helen Oppenheimer reflected on the law 19 years on and realised that many of the Church of England's aspirations had not been realised.[103] In particular, she noted that the law effectively allowed divorce by consent, which was what the Church had most tried to avoid. She noted how procedural changes for undefended cases had made it difficult for any of the facts from which breakdown was presumed to be challenged, the lack of opportunities for reconciliation and how defences intended to safeguard respondents' financial position had been narrowly interpreted by the courts. She suggested that in contemplating further law reform, the law should return to an 'irretrievable breakdown of marriage plus', which would take seriously the need to consider the reasons for the breakdown and attempts at reconciliation.

However, the Church of England has never argued or had the opportunity to argue for 'irretrievable breakdown of marriage plus' in Parliament. In the 1990s, the Bishops in the House of Lords spoke in favour of abandoning the five facts from which breakdown was presumed, and moving to a complete no-fault divorce, as they believed divorce over time with an emphasis on reconciliation and mediation was preferable to the mixed approach of the Matrimonial Causes Act and

[102] Ramsey (1965) esp 59–71.
[103] Oppenheimer (1990) ch 8.

the speed of the special procedure for uncontested divorce.[104] In 2020 a different group of Bishops opposed complete no-fault divorce as proposed in the Divorce, Dissolution and Separation Bill 2020, arguing that 'unilateral, no reason divorce'[105] made marriage meaningless and that the Bill provided no opportunity for reflection or reconciliation in the way the Family Law Act 1996 had.[106]

The *Putting Asunder* group would be dismayed that its recommendation of irretrievable breakdown of marriage had led to what the group would believe was divorce by consent, divorce without consent and a divorce incompatible with lifelong marriage.

References

Atkinson, D (1979) *To Have and To Hold: The Marriage Covenant and the Discipline of Divorce* (London, Collins).

Anderson, N (1968) *Into the World: The Needs and Limits of Christian Involvement* (London, Falcon Books).

—— (1985) *An Adopted Son: The Story of My Life* (Leicester, Inter Varsity Press).

Bennett, BS (1994) 'The Church of England and the Law of Divorce since 1857: Marriage Discipline, Ecclesiastical Law and Establishment' 45 *Journal of Ecclesiastical History* 625.

Cretney, S (1998), *Law, Law Reform and the Family* (Oxford, Oxford University Press).

—— (2003) *Family Law in the Twentieth Century: A History* (Oxford, Oxford University Press).

Dunstan, GR (1962) *The Family is not Broken* (London, SCM Press).

Holmes, AS (2017) *The Church of England and Divorce in the Twentieth Century: Legalism and Grace* (Oxford, Routledge).

Holtman, N (2008) 'Dunstan, Gordon Reginald (1917–2004): Church of England clergyman, theologian, and writer on medical ethics' *Oxford Dictionary of National Biography*.

Lacey, TA (revised by RC Mortimer) (1947) *Marriage in Church and State* (London, SPCK).

Law Commission (1966) *First Annual Report 1965-6* (London, HMSO).

Lee, BH (1974) *Divorce Law Reform in England* (London, Peter Owen).

Lewis, J and Wallis, P (2000) 'Fault, Breakdown, and the Church of England's Involvement in the 1996 Divorce Reform' 11 *Twentieth Century British History* 308.

McLeod, H (2007) *The Religious Crisis of the 1960s* (New York, Oxford University Press).

Moyse, CA (1996) 'Marriage and Divorce Reform in England and Wales 1909–1937' (unpublished doctoral thesis, Cambridge University).

Norman, ER (1976) *Church and Society in England 1770–1970: A Historical Study* (Oxford, Clarendon Press).

Oppenheimer, H (1962) *Law and Love* (Leighton Buzzard, The Faith Press).

[104] The Bishops of Worcester, Oxford and Birmingham all spoke in the Second Reading in favour of the Bill: *Hansard*, HL Deb 30 November 1995, vol 567 cols 715–17, 734–36 and 752–54.

[105] Speech of Bishop of Carlisle, *Hansard*, HL Deb 5 February 2020, vol 801, col 1815.

[106] The Bishop of Carlisle, the Bishop of Portsmouth and the retired Bishop of Oxford spoke in the debate, ibid cols 1814–15, 1824–25, 1835–39.

—— (1976) *The Marriage Bond* (Leighton Buzzard, The Faith Press).
—— (1990) *Marriage* (London, Mowbray).
Paulsen, MG (1966) 'Divorce: Canterbury Style' 1 *Valparaiso University Law Review* 93.
Ramsey, M (1957) 'Marriage, Divorce and the Royal Commission' February 1957, *York Quarterly* 3.
—— (1965) *Sacred and Secular* (London, Longmans).
Richards, PG (1970) *Parliament and Conscience* (London, George Allen & Unwin).
Robinson, J (1963) *Honest to God* (London, SCM).
Sinclair, R (2017) 'The Church of England's Influence on the Divorce Reform Act' (MPhil dissertation, University of Chester).
Skinner, BG (1979) *Robert Exon: A Biography of Dr RC Mortimer, Bishop of Exeter from 1949–1973* (Bognor Regis, New Horizon).

6

Behind Casanova's Charter: Edith Summerskill, Divorce and the Deserted Wife

SHARON THOMPSON

I. Introduction

The Divorce Reform Act 1969 is a landmark in legal history because for the first time in English law, it enabled spouses to divorce on the basis of irretrievable breakdown instead of requiring a matrimonial offence.[1] Yet in 1973, Leo Abse MP wrote in his memoirs that it was a 'real wonder … that the Divorce Bill ever reached the statute book'[2] at all, because of the grievances levied against it by Edith Summerskill, who at that time was a life peer in the House of Lords. As a leading advocate of the Act, Abse's frustration in his memoirs is palpable: 'No one was more successful in delaying its passage, and in arousing hostility to its objectives, than … Summerskill,' he said.[3]

Abse's frustration is arguably misplaced. The two-year delay in the Act's coming into effect was of critical importance because it meant that the financial consequences of divorce could be reformed too. However, in the story of the Divorce Reform Act 1969, Edith Summerskill is not remembered as the militant feminist pioneer who won a hard-fought battle for impoverished deserted wives. Instead, she is best known as designating the 1969 Act a 'Casanova's Charter' for husbands wishing to divorce their middle-aged wives and marry younger women.[4] Her opposition on this basis is considered 'illogical' in some accounts,[5] with her feminism challenged for being 'contradictory',[6] given that other feminists were in support of

[1] Pursuant to s 1 of the consolidating Matrimonial Causes Act 1973, this is based on the sole ground of irretrievable breakdown of a marriage.

[2] Abse (1973) 180.

[3] ibid.

[4] *Hansard*, HL (series 5) 8 November 1967, vol 286, col 428.

[5] Abse (1973) 180.

[6] Smart (1984) 70.

an easier divorce process that would allow women to be liberated from unhappy marriages.[7] In this chapter, these characterisations of Summerskill's view are challenged and this history is revisited, using new and previously unexplored sources. In short, this chapter argues that dismissing Edith Summerskill's view as anti-divorce per se would be a mistake. She did more than simply condemn Casanovas; she gave voice to deserted wives by fighting for their financial protection.

The chapter first presents the 'textbook' account of the Divorce Reform Act and its delay so that additional legislation dealing with the financial consequences of divorce could be introduced. Against this backdrop, the chapter then explores Edith Summerskill's intervention in this debate. Detailed examination of what motivated her view is presented, challenging received understandings of the story of the Divorce Reform Act 1969. Her claim that the reform represented a Casanova's Charter is dissected into five arguments. As well as her words in Parliament, this is supported by a range of sources, including new interview data, data from interviews between Summerskill's son and Summerskill's contemporaries, and other previously unexplored archival material.

As feminism is not a monolith, there was not one unified feminist response to the Divorce Reform Act, and so Summerskill's feminism was not 'odd'[8] for failing to align with that of other women's rights advocates at the time. By homing in on Summerskill's role in divorce reform, this chapter does not try to fit her into established narratives and templates of feminist thinking, but instead investigates the spaces between dominant discourses surrounding the 1969 Act. This in turn uncovers the richness and variety of ways in which competing ideas and beliefs about divorce, women and feminism are negotiated.[9] It also illuminates the delicate balance of advocating for protection for married women without reinforcing gendered stereotypes of vulnerable housewives. While this chapter does not show that Summerskill managed this balancing act effectively, it does uncover the importance of her role in advocating for deserted wives, which became a catalyst for the core tenets of financial provision to be reassessed.

II. Background

As the Divorce Reform Bill was moving through Parliament it had widespread support. Even Conservative MPs, for whom the sanctity of marriage was core to their conservative ideology, were not expected by their party to oppose the Divorce Reform Bill.[10] From this perspective, it seemed almost inevitable that the Divorce Bill would get Royal Assent. But there was one stumbling block in particular that

[7] Stetson (1982).
[8] Abse (1973) 181.
[9] Green (2004).
[10] Gilbert (2018); Cretney (2003) 354.

almost prevented the Bill from becoming law – the financial consequences of divorce for women.

A major threat to the passage of the Divorce Reform Bill was the concern that it could be economically disastrous for a woman to be divorced by her husband without her consent after a period of five years' separation (which was one of the routes to establishing irretrievable breakdown pursuant to the Divorce Reform Act 1969 and Section 1(2)(e) of the consolidating Matrimonial Causes Act 1973). This reform could be seen as radical when compared to the previous law, and was the only basis upon which an 'innocent' spouse wishing to stay married could be divorced. Edith Summerskill is frequently positioned as the antagonist of those who supported this provision, because she referred to it as the 'Casanova's Charter' – a 'crude but effective caricature'[11] coined to describe her apprehension that husbands would be empowered by Section 1(2)(e) to leave their wives, marry younger women and financially support their new family instead of their old one. Put simply, the institutional account explains the Casanova's Charter view as opposition to divorce without consent, a view dismissed by some at the time who retorted 'Casanovas do not bother with charters',[12] because an individual's decision to desert their spouse for another woman was not thought to be based on law.

It is interesting to note that the Casanova's Charter opposition was the most powerful impediment to the Divorce Reform Act (and indeed the Act nearly foundered because of it), yet those pushing for reform were not apathetic about the financial consequences of divorce for the non-moneyed spouse either.[13] Indeed, proponents of the Bill argued that the hardship of the existing law for wives made reform of divorce all the more urgent, with the Law Commission and Archbishop of Canterbury's group both emphasising the harsh consequences of the law for the more economically vulnerable spouse.[14] This concern filtered into Section 5 of the Matrimonial Causes Act 1973, preventing divorce based on five years' separation in the event of 'grave financial or other hardship to [the respondent] and that it would in all the circumstances be wrong to dissolve the marriage', and Section 10 (which applied to both separation facts), facilitating postponement of the decree absolute (the legal end of the marriage) so that financial provision for the non-moneyed respondent spouse could be arranged.

In addition, the introduction of the Divorce Reform Act 1969 was delayed until the Law Commission had fully investigated the financial consequences of divorce. The recommendations in the Law Commission's report[15] sought to ameliorate the concerns of those opposed to divorce because of the potential consequences for married women. These were enshrined in the Matrimonial

[11] Cretney (2003) 373.
[12] *Hansard*, HL (series 5) 30 June 1969, vol 303, col 296.
[13] Smart (1984) 70.
[14] Law Commission (1966); Church of England (1966).
[15] Law Commission (1969).

Proceedings and Property Act 1970, and subsequently consolidated in the Matrimonial Causes Act 1973. The effect of the Act was transformative, in that where the court previously made maintenance and lump sum orders on a discretionary basis that operated to penalise the spouse 'at fault',[16] the new legislation gave the court wide- ranging discretionary powers to make financial orders regardless of fault, which included redistribution of property.[17] This redistributive power was a turning point in family law, because it marked a shift in emphasis away from making the wife dependent on maintenance towards helping her become economically independent by providing her with property and therefore 'purchasing power'.[18]

Institutional accounts of the passage of the 1969 and 1970 Acts along these lines represent the dominant narrative and the accepted 'textbook' version of events. These accounts acknowledge the myriad reasons why the Divorce Reform Act 1969 was introduced, including changes in family structure, shifts in religious and public opinion, various alliances of judges, politicians and activists, and reports published by special bodies.[19] A similarly complex institutional narrative underpins the delay of the 1969 Act and the introduction of the Matrimonial Property and Proceedings Act 1970, which overhauled the financial consequences of relationship breakdown and married women's property rights. But within these accounts, an often overlooked force behind this reform was the work of Edith Summerskill. Though her opposition is important within the dominant narrative, this does not properly examine what shaped her views, leading to assumptions that she was inherently anti-divorce and even puritanical. As this chapter will argue, examining Summerskill's campaign against divorce reform is an important part of family law history.

III. Unpacking Summerskill's View

The rest of this chapter draws on new data from semi-structured interviews with Edith Summerskill's grandson, Ben Summerskill, and daughter-in-law, Maryly Lafollette,[20] as well as archival interviews between Summerskill's son, Michael, and her contemporaries.[21] By adopting this biographical approach and comparing

[16] There was no rationale for such orders and there was a clear lack of consistency in case law, see Douglas (2018) 118.

[17] Also introduced the minimal loss principle, considered further in Section IV.D.

[18] As noted by Douglas (2018) 118, and in *Trippas v Trippas* [1973] Fam 134, CA; *O'D v O'D* [1976] Fam 83, CA.

[19] Law Commission (1966); Church of England (1966): see Sinclair, ch 5 of this volume.

[20] Undertaken by the author on 28 June 2019 and 26 July 2018 respectively. Summerskill's grandson, Ben, would have been 18 years old when Summerskill died but recalls spending long periods of time with his grandmother. He later became Chief Executive of Stonewall. Summerskill's daughter-in-law, Maryly Lafollette, is stepmother to Ben Summerskill and is a retired family lawyer (formerly a partner at Charles Russell Solicitors).

[21] Records of the Women's Library, SUMMERSKILL/1/46.

Summerskill's personality with her words recorded in *Hansard*, a more nuanced and detailed understanding of her views is garnered.

Edith Summerskill, often referred to in the press as 'Dr Edith', was a Labour MP from 1938 until she became one of the earliest female life peers in 1961, when she was promoted to the House of Lords. By this time, there had been only three other female Ministers of State, and the only woman to have been an MP longer than Summerskill was Nancy Astor (who had never held a ministerial position).[22] When in the House of Lords, Summerskill continued actively to promote the legal rights of women inside and outside the home, heightening her political authority through her status as a doctor and mother.[23] Her grandson, Ben Summerskill, told me that 'as far as [he is] aware, she was the first woman politician who happily called herself a feminist'.[24]

Much of Summerskill's career was devoted to improving women's rights in law. She worked for decades to secure the introduction of the Married Women's Property Act 1964, which gave wives a one-half share of housekeeping savings.[25] She was a driving force behind the Matrimonial Homes Act 1967, which gave deserted wives the right to occupy the matrimonial home. Her Casanova's Charter campaign to oppose divorce reform and fight for new financial provision law in the 1960s and early 1970s was perhaps her most prominent stand in Parliament. Underpinning her activism was a belief that the institution of marriage could be strengthened by improving the economic and legal status of married women, as seen through her prominent roles in pressure groups such as the Married Women's Association, which sought to reform the financial consequences of marriage so that women's work inside the home could be valued equally to men's work outside it. Her views did not always align with those of other feminists, who decried her talk of housework as women's work.[26] In Summerskill's son's interviews with other politicians and contemporaries of hers, she is described as pragmatic, with a touch of arrogance and shyness, and unwavering,[27] all of which appeared to set her apart from other members of the House. As Labour MP Barbara Castle saw it, she was 'a bit of a loner'.[28]

Understanding these aspects of her personality, and in particular her reputation as an outsider, is important when investigating what her views on divorce were and why they are commonly misrepresented or even dismissed by others.

[22] Summerfield (2005).

[23] ibid 136.

[24] Interview by author with Ben Summerskill, 28 June 2019.

[25] Summerskill had fought for this reform since the 1940s, and first introduced legislation to reform the issue of housekeeping savings in the Women's Disabilities Bill 1952.

[26] *Manchester Guardian* (18 February 1950) 17.

[27] Interviews by Michael Summerskill with Michael Stewart, Lord Denning and Suzanne Knowles, Records of the Women's Library file, SUMMERSKILL/1/46.

[28] Interview by Michael Summerskill with Barbara Castle, Records of the Women's Library, SUMMERSKILL 1/46.

IV. Behind Casanova's Charter: Five Reasons Why

A logical starting point when analysing Summerskill's view of the Divorce Reform Act is the passage from *Hansard* in which she first labelled the Divorce Reform Act a 'Casanova's Charter' in Parliament.[29] Though she repeated this term in press reports and speeches, this particular passage is analysed, as five major arguments are made in the speech[30] that explain and rationalise her view of the Divorce Reform Bill as a Casanova's Charter: that the innocent spouse would be compelled to divorce without consent; the Divorce Reform Act is a law made by men; marriage means more to women than to men; husbands cannot provide for two households; and women's unpaid labour must be recognised in economic terms. In the rest of this section, each of these five reasons is examined in turn as they appeared in Summerskill's speech, alongside other source material.

A. Reason 1: Innocent Spouse Compelled to Divorce without Consent

> I beg the Government not to be precipitate but to give the most careful consideration to the proposition that matrimonial offences should be replaced by the breakdown of marriage as the ground for divorce, and that an innocent spouse should be compelled to accept divorce after a few years of separation …[31]

It is unsurprising that Summerskill first criticised the fact that the Divorce Reform Bill would allow the 'innocent spouse' to be 'compelled to accept divorce' after five years of separation.[32] Divorce without consent was a powerful and memorable refrain that featured in several of Summerskill's appeals to the media and talks to women's rights groups.[33] Her expression of 'grave concern' at the innocent man or woman's being divorced against their will 'for the first time in our social history' was reported by the press.[34] Support for her view even featured in Catholic newsletters;[35] ironic given not only Summerskill's atheism, but also her antagonistic history with the Catholic Church, which had successfully thwarted one of her early election campaigns because of her support for birth control.[36] Though some of

[29] This is not the first time Summerskill is recorded as using the expression 'Casanova's Charter'. She is thought to have coined this term in a speech to the Married Women's Association: Records of the Women's Library, SUMMERSKILL/7.

[30] *Hansard*, HL (series 5) 8 November 1967, vol 286, cols 421–28.

[31] *Hansard*, HL (series 5) 8 November 1967, vol 286, col 421.

[32] Just over a decade earlier the Royal Commission on Marriage and Divorce opposed this (1956, Cmd 9678).

[33] For example, in 1968 she delivered a talk entitled 'Divorce Without Consent' to the Married Women's Association, Records of the Women's Library, SUMMERSKILL/1/99.

[34] Records of the Women's Library, SUMMERSKILL/1/99.

[35] *The Catholic Transcript* (27 June 1969) 11.

[36] This story is recounted in her memoirs: Summerskill (1967).

her views were shared by the Catholic Church, her point of view was not at all influenced by religion. Instead, to Summerskill, removing the requirement of a matrimonial offence meant punishing a party who was 'innocent' of causing the breakdown of the marriage. In her son Michael's writings, he surmised 'Perhaps Edith's wish to adhere to the concept of a matrimonial offence reflected her view of women as wronged.' He went on to say that this sense of injustice came from Summerskill's frustration at centuries of 'men's use and abuse of their physical and economic superiority'.[37]

On the other hand, it is difficult to understand how maintaining the matrimonial offence and making divorce inaccessible to spouses when their marriage had broken down irretrievably would help the middle-aged women for whom Summmerskill advocated. The Law Commission's report found a pressing need to dissolve empty shell marriages that benefitted neither party.[38]

Still, Summerskill was eminently pragmatic and would not accept the view propounded by others that divorce reform was generally emancipatory for deserted middle-aged wives:

> It is no good sitting here pretending to ourselves that all the women of the country are emancipated; that all of them have higher education; that all of them are skilled, and that all of them can earn their own living. The fact is that the great majority of married women in this country have worked well for their families … [I]f I had been assured that these women, after years of work, would have some financial provision, I should not have objected so very much …[39]

It would therefore be a mistake to depict the Casanova's Charter opposition as an attempt only to preserve the sanctity of marriage. This would unfairly historicise Summerskill's view in a conservative and puritanical way, when from another perspective Summerskill was espousing, as Gillian Douglas put it, 'the modern view that a wife is *entitled* to a *share* in the family assets, rather than the traditional stance that she is a dependant seeking the husband's largesse'.[40] This is supported by her son's comment that 'it was not a kind of moral statement that marriage must be indissoluble – it was more a practical one that she said [the wife] would never get the right financial support'.[41]

This makes sense when reflecting on Summerskill's background and personality. She had been the first President of the Married Women's Association, a pressure group that shared her lifelong cause of economic equality between spouses. Her work was more consistent with concepts of fairness and financial security than with preserving marriage for the sake of it. Overlooking this broader biographical

[37] Records of the Women's Library, SUMMERSKILL/7.
[38] Law Commission (1966).
[39] *Hansard*, HL (series 5) 8 November 1967, vol 286, cols 1294–96.
[40] Douglas (2018) 116 (original emphasis).
[41] Interview by Michael Summerskill with Lord Denning, Records of the Women's Library, SUMMERSKILL 1/46.

context means missing the most important aspect of Summerskill's opposition to divorce reform – the unresolved issue of married women's property.

B. Reason 2: The Divorce Reform Act is a Law Made by Men

> My noble and learned friend (the Lord Chancellor) has told us to-day that … there is a consensus of opinion. He mentioned the Church of England, the Methodist Church … and the Law Reform Committee. But these are organisations composed almost entirely of men …[42]

Summerskill's next point of contention was that though the Lord Chancellor, Gerald Gardiner, noted a consensus in favour of reform among the Church of England, the Methodist Church and the Law Commission, these bodies consisted almost entirely of men. This was problematic because, as Summerskill had repeatedly argued, the proposed reform would be disproportionately harmful to middle-aged and older women, whose experiences were not being heard or understood. As Summerskill put it, divorce without consent (pursuant to Section 1(2)(e)) was 'opposed by every women's organisation in the country, and they, as we know, are not represented in this House in great numbers'.[43]

From Summerskill's perspective, therefore, predominantly male law-makers would make a divorce law that suited men, and she was not convinced this would address the plight of the women for whom she advocated. Her point is significant for legal historians because it reinforces the importance of assessing legal history from a gendered perspective, makes us question how women's position was accounted for in divorce reform, and reassesses the 'neutrality' of law[44] that, in Summerskill's view, marginalised the lives and experiences of deserted wives. Yet Summerskill's gendered critique of law reform and law reformers features nowhere in institutional historical accounts of the Divorce Reform Act.

C. Reason 3: Marriage Means More to Women than to Men

> Marriage means much more to a woman than to a man. Marriage means to a woman an arrangement whereby a man and a woman live together in order that they may have children, an arrangement which will protect those children as long as possible …[45]

Examining Summerskill's words on divorce reform not only helps bring the gendered dimensions of this history to the fore, but also affords better insight into what she thought about marriage, women and men. Summerskill argued that

[42] *Hansard*, HL (series 5) 8 November 1967, vol 286, col 422.
[43] *Hansard*, HL (series 5) 10 July 1969, vol 303, col 1296.
[44] See Lacey (1995).
[45] *Hansard*, HL (series 5) 8 November 1967, vol 286, col 422.

marriage means more to women than to men in terms of commitment, because easier divorce, she said, would encourage husbands to leave their wives when they would otherwise have made do. Summerskill repeated this in Parliament, arguing further that the corollary of easier divorce was that more children would be born out of wedlock, and this would disproportionately affect women. This was paradoxical according to those in favour of reform, like Abse, who argued that there were greater numbers of 'illegitimate' children because of the existing law,[46] as inaccessible divorce did not prevent new unions outside marriage but *did* prevent remarriage. The concern on both sides of the debate over the now dated (and virtually redundant) notions of illegitimacy and living in sin indicates that, in making these arguments, Summerskill and Abse were conservative but were also reflecting the deep-set social norms of the day, albeit from antipodal standpoints.

Still, given Summerskill's liberal and resolute stance in favour of birth control, abortion and women in the armed forces, her son Michael noted 'It was surprising to find Edith in opposition to a measure designed to avoid the dishonesty occasioned by existing laws and to free people tied to an empty marriage.'[47] In trying to understand his mother's perspective, he considered that her reasoning 'reflect[ed] her respect for the institution of marriage as a protection for women'. He went on to say that despite being atheist, his mother's

> sentiment [about children] could well have come from a Christian marriage service. Edith did not explain why marriage meant more to a woman. Was she referring to a woman's economic needs or to her emotional needs? If the one, the statement was one of fact; if the other, perhaps she was claiming that women had a deeper level of emotional response. I believe that she was speaking of women's greater responsibility and maturity. The implication was that men were usually less responsive, sensitive and mature.[48]

If Michael Summerskill is correct about what Edith Summerskill meant here, it is understandable why some feminists have been critical of her perception of marriage. While many feminists have located marriage as a site of oppression for women,[49] Summerskill believed in the institution of marriage. She fought for economic equality within marriage, but did so without acknowledging that marriage as an *institution* was part of the problem as other feminists did. For Summerskill, inequality between spouses could be dealt with practically and constructively, such as through law reform ensuring women's entitlement to a share in the family assets (as reasons 4 and 5 detail further in Sections IV.D and IV.E). This corroborates what others said about Summerskill too. Her daughter-in-law and grandson saw her as being a pragmatist, obstinate in trying to achieve practical antidotes to the

[46] Abse (1973) 180.
[47] Records of the Women's Library, SUMMERSKILL/7.
[48] ibid.
[49] Auchmuty (2012).

poverty and vulnerability experienced by women Summerskill encountered in her work as a doctor, politician and feminist activist.[50]

In addition to Summerskill's defence of marriage as an institution, some feminists have also castigated her essentialising of women and men. It is easy to see why. In *Letters to my Daughter*, she suggests that having children is women's true desire[51] and that there are certain roles that men are better equipped to do.[52] Smart argues that Summerskill's failure to recognise the problem not only of marriage, but also of women's traditional role within it meant that Summerskill's view reinforced the idea of women as a class of dependants 'who then could hardly survive outside marriage'.[53] Others of Summerskill's contemporary feminists recognised this too; as Barbara Castle noted, she 'had some curious blind spots, did Edith'.[54] Yet it would be unfair to assume that such essentialism meant that her opposition to the Divorce Reform Act was immaterial, or that she believed women's place was in the home and men's place was outside it. First, she was adamant that women's emancipation depended upon men's taking up historically gendered roles like cleaning, and indeed her *own* marriage was an example of one in which her husband was responsible for more childcare than she was. Her former secretary, Suzanne Knowles, recalled that in a confrontation with an aggressive man at a Labour Party meeting, Summerskill's retort was 'Why don't you go home and help your wife with the washing up?'[55] And so she asserted that husbands should support their wives' professional success in the public sphere through taking on some of the domestic labour, arguing that this was essential for women's success outside the home.[56]

Second, it is important to remember that, as Summerfield has put it:

> In spite of her essentialist view that women were motivated above all by the desire to have children, Summerskill … was unusual among feminists of the 1930s and 40s for fighting simultaneously for both sets of goals: welfare and equality.[57]

In other words, she campaigned both for the removal of barriers to equality[58] and for women's welfare and protection in recognition of their *in*equality. This again underscores her pragmatism and undermines the characterisation of Summerskill as someone who tended to philosophise about the innate qualities of men and women.

[50] Based on interviews by the author on 28 June 2019 and 26 July 2018 respectively.

[51] However, when it came to her daughter Shirley Summerskill's future, Summerskill's daughter-in-law told me, 'there was certainly no question that Shirley was going to have an education and have a profession'. Interview by author with Maryly Lafollette, 26 July 2018.

[52] Summerskill (1957).

[53] Smart (1984) 71.

[54] Interview by Michael Summerskill with Barbara Castle, Records of the Women's Library, SUMMERSKILL 1/46.

[55] Interview by Michael Summerskill with Suzanne Knowles, Records of the Women's Library, SUMMERSKILL 1/46.

[56] Summerskill (1967).

[57] Summerfield (2005) 141.

[58] For example, she was a prominent figure in equal pay campaigns in the 1950s.

Indeed, she wrote in her memoirs that she had little interest in theory or philosophy,[59] but instead was focused on the realities and experiences of others. Perhaps, then, by appealing against divorce without the consent of the deserted wife, she was arguing that the Government had not properly acknowledged the different experiences of husbands and wives.[60] That the experience of spouses *was* gendered in the 1960s is clear. Letters to Summerskill corroborate the very different ways in which men and women were affected, with the problem in every letter identified as being financial: 'Middle-aged wives should be given proper financial consideration. It is disgraceful to talk about them having to go to public authorities for money,' writes one woman.[61] Another woman wrote informing Summerskill[62] that she had written to *The Times* and Leo Abse to say 'it's about time the wife's point of view was listened to'[63] and 'when this Bill is Law and my husband divorces me, my little girl and I will probably end up like "Cathy come home"[64] with nowhere to live'.[65] This shows that in many ways Summerskill was correct, as many of the women writing to Summerskill *did* appear to be impacted by marriage and divorce differently from their husbands.

D. Reason 4: Husbands Cannot Maintain Two Households

> Surely few men can keep two families … If a law is not enforceable it is a bad law, and if a law is so framed that only wealthy men can take advantage of it is a bad law.[66]

All of Summerskill's reasons for opposing the Divorce Reform Act are inextricably linked to her concern for the financial position of the first wife, whom she believed had inadequate protection under the law. In this fourth reason, Summerskill argued that a man with obligations towards a second family would not be able to support those from his first marriage, and that the law could not provide proper protection to the wife and children left behind. As noted in Section II, the Government included a safeguard in the Divorce Reform Act (Section 5 of the consolidating Matrimonial Causes Act 1973), stipulating that if one spouse petitioned for divorce based on five years' separation, the respondent could defend the petition if they could prove it would cause 'grave financial hardship' and that it would be wrong in all the circumstances to dissolve the marriage.

[59] Summerskill (1967).
[60] Gilligan (1993).
[61] Records of the Women's Library, SUMMERSKILL/1/101.
[62] 18 December 1968, Records of the Women's Library, SUMMERSKILL/1/101.
[63] Copy of letter to *The Times* (18 December 1968), Records of the Women's Library, SUMMERSKILL/1/101.
[64] Referring to the 1966 BBC television play, *Cathy Come Home* directed by Ken Loach, which depicted a young woman's homelessness.
[65] Copy of letter to Leo Abse (18 December 1968), Records of the Women's Library, SUMMERSKILL/1/101.
[66] *Hansard*, HL (series 5) 8 November 1967, vol 286, col 427.

For Summerskill, this protection was insufficient:

> This woman has to plead that she is suffering very grave hardship. How can she prove to a judge that she is suffering very grave hardship? Hardship is not going to be enough; it has to be grave hardship.[67]

Summerskill had a point. Since it was introduced, Section 5 has been successful in only a small number of cases,[68] indicating courts' unwillingness to apply it. Even before it came into effect, the Law Commission recognised that the provision would apply only in exceptional circumstances:

> [I]t is much to be hoped that resort to it could be infrequent: it is offensive to decency and derogatory to respect for family ties to preserve the legal shell of a dead marriage for purely monetary consideration. Moreover, a rich husband can easily make satisfactory financial provision for his wife and get his divorce; a poor man cannot, and it will be argued that it would be discriminatory for the law to refuse him a divorce on that account.[69]

Put simply, a husband should be able to divorce his wife regardless of whether he can provide adequate financial relief. This did not mean the Law Commission viewed wives' poverty as irrelevant, but it did make it clear that divorce should not be means-tested and dependent upon a husband's being able to maintain two households. Instead, the Law Commission looked outside the Divorce Reform Act to develop a separate law on financial remedies. This meant the issue of divorce was separate from but connected to financial provision, making divorce possible without the financial aspects necessarily being finalised.[70] However, the non-moneyed spouse would not be made destitute if her ex-spouse had the means to support her, because as Section II of this chapter explained, the courts were given wide-ranging discretionary powers to make financial provision and adjust property rights.[71] When that Act was first introduced, consolidating both the Divorce Reform Act 1969 and the Matrimonial Proceedings and Property Act 1970, it required the courts to

> place the parties, so far as it is practicable and, having regard to their conduct, just to do so, in the financial position in which they would have been if the marriage had not broken down and each had properly discharged his or her financial obligations and responsibilities towards the other.[72]

[67] *Hansard*, HL (series 5) 10 July 1969, vol 303, col 1295.

[68] In *Reiterbund v Reiterund* [1974] 1 WLR 788, Ormrod LJ (at [110]) reasoned that even if the hardship were grave, it would 'be quite ridiculous' to refuse to dissolve the marriage, pursuant to the second limb of the test. See also *K v K (Financial Provision)* [1996] 3 FCR 158.

[69] Law Commission (1966) para 40.

[70] It is standard practice for financial remedies to be resolved before the divorce is finalised by the decree absolute; but in some cases, financial redistribution has taken place decades after the divorce (see eg *Wyatt v Vince* [2015] UKSC 14).

[71] Pursuant to the Matrimonial Causes Act 1973, s 23 and s 25.

[72] Matrimonial Proceedings and Property Act 1970, s 5, consolidated in s 25 of the Matrimonial Causes Act 1973.

This objective, known as the minimal loss principle,[73] placed the onus on the moneyed spouse (usually the husband) to continue to provide for his former spouse financially, unless she remarried. The minimal loss principle was removed in 1984,[74] four years after Summerskill's death, but it could be argued that its existence had endorsed what Summerskill had fought for, in that it directed the court to protect the ex-wife who continued to be dependent on her ex-husband. As Douglas notes, it stemmed from the concept of financial provision as 'repudiation of the marriage tie', whereby the first husband must 'pay for his freedom'.[75]

One would have thought that this sweeping reform of financial provision, ostensibly placing the financially vulnerable ex-wife at the centre of proceedings, was a huge victory for Summerskill and her Casanova's Charter campaign. But for Summerskill, this was not good enough. In one of her personal letters, she wrote that she was 'losing faith' in the Law Commission.[76] This is because at the forefront of Summerskill's and her supporters' concerns was the issue of pension provision for wives, which the Law Commission had not properly addressed. Furthermore, the financial and property consequences of divorce had been reformed, but property rights *during* marriage had not. At this time, Summerskill was receiving many letters from women who were worried about being divorced without their consent and losing any share in their husband's pension at an age when retraining and employment were unlikely, with the result that they would be spending old age in destitution without a pension of their own. These were legitimate and serious anxieties, yet even though the 1970 Act significantly improved the financial impact of divorce for women, the issue of pension sharing was not dealt with comprehensively until 1999.[77]

Summerskill therefore remained ambivalent about divorce reform. She predicted that husbands could not financially support two households, even if legislation said that they should. An unenforceable law is a bad law, she said. In many ways, Summerskill was correct. The minimal loss principle arguably *was* 'bad law' because, according to members of the judiciary,[78] the majority of husbands could *not* support two households, and research published in 1977 indicated that the principle had been virtually abandoned in practice.[79] By 1984, it had been replaced by the 'clean break' principle, and ever since then research has consistently indicated that women take longer to recover financially from divorce than men do.[80]

[73] Gillian Douglas notes that John Eekelaar coined this term: (2018) 117, citing Eekelaar (1984) 109.

[74] Pursuant to the Matrimonial and Family Proceedings Act 1984.

[75] Douglas (2018) 117.

[76] Records of the Women's Library, SUMMERSKILL 1/99.

[77] Pursuant to the Welfare Reform and Pensions Act 1999. But even now, lack of pension sharing on divorce has been one of the greatest causes of financial inequality on divorce. See Woodward and Sefton (2014); Buckley and Price (2021).

[78] See Ormrod J in *Wachtel v Wachtel* [1973] Fam 72, 77.

[79] Barrington Baker (1977), cited in Douglas (2018) 118.

[80] See Fisher and Low (2016).

On the other hand, Summerskill's argument could be countered by asking *why* a husband should have to maintain two households when the first marriage has been dissolved. It is arguably unfair to the husband, does not enable the parties to move on properly and suggests that the wife is necessarily a needy supplicant. Indeed, Summerskill has been criticised by some feminist scholars for insisting on protection for the housewife, as in their view the only way women could achieve full citizenship was to be emancipated from the home.[81] Summerskill's strategy was different: instead of arguing that women should be released from housework and childcare, she contended that this work should be recognised in economic terms. She believed this would help level the financial playing-field outside the home too, where women also lacked equal opportunity. The women in employment writing to Summerskill were mainly employed in low-paid or part-time work, but also undertook all the domestic labour.[82] Ever the pragmatist, Summerskill acknowledged this reality and the fact that domestic and caregiving roles were gendered, maintaining that these roles should be valued economically. She had fought for this throughout her career, consistently being met with opposition in Parliament from those who felt her suggestions were outlandish and would lead to a bad atmosphere at the breakfast table.[83]

As a result, closer inspection of Summerskill's words reveals that while her argument for protection of the first wife could be seen as reinforcing vulnerabilities, dependencies and inequalities stemming from traditional marriage, it would be a mistake to dismiss her views on this basis, because she was – importantly – arguing that women's caregiving and domestic work should be valued economically. This is clear when analysing the fifth and final reason why Summerskill viewed divorce reform as being a Casanova's Charter.

E. Reason 5: Women's Unpaid Labour Must be Recognised in Economic Terms

> There is a tendency in many quarters to disregard the fact that men can earn their income and accumulate capital only by virtue of the division of labour between themselves and their wives … Sir Jocelyn Simon, President of the Divorce Court … [has] said: 'The cock bird can feather his nest precisely because he is not required to spend time sitting on it'. This being so, a separation of goods between married people cannot be said to do justice to the wife …
>
> My purpose to-day is simply to try to persuade the Government, before they embark – or before a Private Member embarks – on legislation calculated to undermine the

[81] See discussion in Section IV.C.

[82] See Scott and Dex (2009). For the impact of the Covid-19 pandemic on women in the home, see Gulland (2020).

[83] As suggested when the Women's Disabilities Bill 1952 was debated: *Hansard*, HC (series 5) 25 April 1952, vol 499, col 97.

> institution of marriage as we understand it in Britain, to change the policy. However, if they find that a Private Member is persuaded to draft a Casanova's Charter, then they must incorporate … a matrimonial property law which includes community of goods, in order to protect the discarded wife.[84]

Here, Summerskill was not just demanding a new matrimonial property law; she wanted women's unpaid labour to be recognised in economic terms, and for spouses to share the financial fruits of the marriage both during the relationship and when it dissolved. This argument sits at the heart of Summerskill's opposition to divorce reform and was the central theme of the letters she had been receiving at this time. In these letters, women described a range of personal and individual experiences, but the fundamental problem in each of them was financial. As one letter objecting to divorce reform put it, 'The money question is SERIOUS – for a woman with children to bring up alone … this Bill will create a new poor in our welfare state.'[85] For this reason, the significance of the delay of the Divorce Reform Act 1969 to facilitate sweeping reform of financial remedies pursuant to the Matrimonial Property and Proceedings Act 1970 should not be underestimated.

There are several interesting points revealed in this final extract from Summerskill's speech. First, although she uses the 'Casanova's Charter' sound-bite in the same breath as calling for financial reform, her specific demands for economic spousal equality are commonly overlooked. Summerskill's rationale for financial provision mirrors the modern rationale underpinning the redistribution of assets on divorce, which is not just about protection but also about entitlement generated by financial *and* non-financial contributions. Law Lord Jocelyn Simon's cock bird metaphor (referred to in the above extract from Summerskill's speech) perfectly encapsulated Summerskill's own assertion that it is the 'fundamental division of labour between husband and wife which frees the husband for the acquisition of goods'.[86]

The gendered division of labour in the marriage meant that the wife, as Summerskill put it, 'must be able to count on her share of the goods accumulated through the marriage'.[87] She went on to explain that the wife earned this share by bearing and rearing the children and in tending the home, leaving the husband free for his economic activities. This language of entitlement is important, as it denotes a broader context in which Summerskill had been fighting for property rights for married women since the late 1930s. Her son discovered, when interviewing Lord Denning, that when Summerskill was pushing for wives' right not to be evicted under the Matrimonial Homes Act 1967, it was a real struggle to achieve reform where 'the wives' interest would be a fetter on property'.[88] She therefore must have

[84] *Hansard*, HL (series 5) 8 November 1967, vol 286, cols 427–28.

[85] Records of the Women's Library, SUMMERSKILL/1/101 (original emphasis).

[86] *Hansard*, HL (series 5) 8 November 1967, vol 286, col 427.

[87] ibid, col 426.

[88] Lord Wilberforce and Lord Upjohn were very worried about this according to Lord Denning: Interview by Michael Summerskill with Lord Denning, Records of the Women's Library, SUMMERSKILL 1/46.

known that arguing for financial relief far beyond maintenance and lump sum orders was controversial. But as former Conservative politician and editor of the *Daily Telegraph* Bill Deeds noted, 'I don't think she was a lady who was very easily pushed off her point of view. She stuck to it.'[89] So, instead of framing wives' property rights in terms of need, in the context of divorce reform Summerskill argued instead for recognition of wives' *entitlement*. Family lawyers will be familiar with this terminology from the House of Lords case *White v White*[90] in 2000, and therefore it is interesting to see Summerskill framing financial provision in a similar way more than 30 years previously.

For Summerskill at this time, the most radical and straightforward way to reflect the equal importance of financial and non-financial roles in marriage was 'community of goods' or community of property; a matrimonial property regime whereby spouses' assets and debts automatically go into a pot that is divided in half on divorce.[91] Though property in marriage has been owned by spouses separately in England and Wales since the Married Women's Property Act 1882, the Royal Commission on Marriage and Divorce in 1956 and the Law Commission in 1988 *did* consider the community of property, deciding against introducing this matrimonial property regime because it would be too complex.[92]

Correspondence with Edward Bishop MP reveals that Summerskill had been involved in efforts to introduce community of property, provided for in Bishop's Matrimonial Property Bill in 1969. But he agreed not to pursue it so that the Law Commission's recommendations for financial provision reform could be introduced by the Government. He reflected on this deal in a letter to Summerskill in May 1970: 'We had no alternative but to co-operate to get the [Matrimonial Proceedings and Property Act 1970] through, and we should have been very worried had it not done so.'[93] It should be noted that Summerskill had not campaigned throughout her life for community of property. Rather, she had argued as part of the Married Women's Association for equal partnership in marriage, which included co-ownership of income and the matrimonial home but did not go as far as community of property. It could be argued, therefore, that Summerskill's demand for 'community of goods' at this time was opportunistic, as this was what Edward Bishop's Bill was seeking to introduce at the time to slow the progress of the divorce reform.[94]

[89] Interview by Michael Summerskill with Bill Deeds, Records of the Women's Library, SUMMERSKILL 1/46.

[90] [2000] UKHL 42.

[91] It is not clear what form of community she preferred, though the Bishop Bill she supported (see below) was based on deferred community, or equal division of property acquired during the marriage at the point of divorce.

[92] Royal Commission on Marriage and Divorce (1956); Law Commission (1988). See also Cooke et al (2006).

[93] Records of the Women's Library, SUMMERSKILL/1/101.

[94] Cretney (2003) 134.

In spite of these failed attempts, it could be argued that Summerskill's hopes for equal partnership in marriage were eventually realised in part, even if her desire for reform of property ownership *during* marriage was not. This evolution in common law was only possible because of the broad discretion accorded to the judiciary by the 1970 reforms consolidated in the Matrimonial Causes Act 1973. As already explained, this discretion – and the property orders that could be made pursuant to it – transformed financial provision for women because it opened up the possibility for divorcing women to become economically independent through property rights instead of indefinitely dependent on maintenance. Delaying the Divorce Reform Act 1969 enabled this legislation to be introduced. And looking behind the catchphrase 'Casanova's Charter' makes evident the importance of Summerskill's intervention in this delay.

V. Conclusion

The term 'Casanova's Charter' is typically explained in institutional accounts as encapsulating Edith Summerskill's opposition to divorce reform because she wanted to prevent husbands from being able to leave their middle-aged wives for younger women too easily. This superficial outline of her argument meant that Summerskill was criticised for her 'odd brand of feminism',[95] for behaving unrealistically in opposing the legal end of an already broken marriage, and for reinforcing the infantilising and gendered norm of the wife as needy supplicant. After all, women are statistically much more likely to petition for divorce than men,[96] and during the 1970s the number of wives petitioning increased significantly.[97] The reform introduced by the Divorce Reform Act 1969 enabled the dissolution of thousands of unhappy marriages, which has been considered a positive development by many feminist commentators. It is therefore unsurprising that, for many, 'Casanova's Charter' has seemed an inappropriate or even strange label for legislation used more by wives. Indeed, as Jonathan Herring noted in his *Family Law* textbook, 'with a five-year wait between marriages, a Casanova would require patience!'[98]

Therefore, while the Casanova's Charter soundbite was a useful tool that captured the attention of the press and public, it arguably misrepresents the importance of Summerskill's role in the Divorce Reform Act 1969. A closer and more comprehensive assessment of Summerskill's argument reveals she was doing

[95] Abse (1973) 180.

[96] Though statistics suggest women and men equally rely upon the five-year separation fact: see Haskey, ch 2 of this volume.

[97] Office for National Statistics (2017).

[98] Herring (2019) 155.

more than simply opposing divorce. Rather, she was demanding recognition of wives' work in the home. She was arguing that divorce without the consent of one of the parties would be problematic if financial matters had not been resolved. And, perhaps most importantly, she was making the struggle and frequent destitution of married women visible in Parliament. As Leo Abse (somewhat resentfully) recalled, 'it is to her credit, or discredit, that she succeeded in delaying' the Divorce Reform Act 1969.[99] Although he believed that 'certainly in the divorce reform battle [he] was her victim'[100] and her opposition constituted 'alarmist clarion calls',[101] the alternative analysis of Summerskill presented in this chapter instead reveals her pragmatism and unblinking focus on women's realities and experiences, as evidenced in her speeches and in interviews with those who knew her. There are lessons to be learned from Summerskill's realism and persistence. Reform that ostensibly furthers equality might not do so in practice for women who have no financial stability. In other words, reform that ignores economic dependency will only exacerbate inequality on gender lines. Summerskill's work also demonstrates that reformers should look to the experiences of those not necessarily being heard in Parliament when evaluating policy.

Summerskill's lessons continue to resonate today, as 2020 saw the passing of the landmark Divorce, Dissolution and Separation Act, and financial provision law is once again under parliamentary scrutiny.[102] The backdrop is different, but legislators face issues similar to those raised by Summerskill, as the gap between men and women's economic recovery rates on divorce persists.[103] As a result, writing Summerskill's contribution back into history means recognising, for example, that Law Commission recommendations alone cannot adequately explicate the origins of our current law of financial provision on divorce. This story is much more complex and includes not only the fact of Summerskill's intervention in debates surrounding the Divorce Reform Act 1969, but also *why* she intervened: as a result of her many years of feminist activism and experience of married women's poverty. This is one of the many reasons why it is important not only to adopt a feminist approach to legal history but also to recognise the broad spectrum of perspectives feminism encapsulates when taking a historical approach. It ensures that women like Summerskill do not simply make a 'cameo appearance',[104] as they often do in institutional accounts. Instead, it challenges institutional accounts by looking behind formal procedures of reform, to focus on why change was demanded and by whom, from the ground up.

[99] Abse (1973) 180.
[100] ibid.
[101] ibid.
[102] Divorce (Financial Provision) Bill 2019–2021.
[103] See Miles and Hitchings (2018).
[104] Auchmuty (2011) 229.

References

Abse, L (1973) *Private Member* (London, Macdonald).
Anon (1969) 'British House Okays Bill Making Divorce by Consent Legal' *The Catholic Transcript*, 27 June.
Auchmuty, R (2011) 'Whatever Happened to Miss Bebb? *Bebb v The Law Society* and Women's Legal History' 31 *Legal Studies* 199.
—— (2012) 'Law and the Power of Feminism: How Marriage Lost its Power to Oppress Women' 20 *Feminist Legal Studies* 71.
Barrington Baker, W (1977) *The Matrimonial Jurisdiction of Registrars* (SSRC Centre for Socio-Legal Studies, Wolfson College Oxford).
Buckley, J and Price, D (2021) 'Pensions on divorce: where now, what next?' 33 *Child and Family Law Quarterly* 1.
Church of England (1966) *Putting Asunder: A Divorce Law for Contemporary Society* (SPCK).
Cooke, E, Barlow, A and Callus, T (2006) *Community of Property: A Regime for England and Wales?* (London, Nuffield Foundation).
Cretney, S (2003) *Family Law in the Twentieth Century* (Oxford, Oxford University Press).
Douglas, G (2018) *Obligation and Commitment in Family Law* (Oxford, Hart Publishing).
Eekelaar, J (1984) *Family Law and Social Policy*, 2nd edn (London, Weidenfeld & Nicolson).
Fisher, H and Low, H (2016) 'Recovery from Divorce: Comparing High and Low Income Couples' 30 *International Journal of Law, Policy and the Family* 338.
Gilbert, A (2018) *British Conservatism and the Regulation of Intimate Adult Relationships* (Oxford, Hart Publishing).
Gilligan, C (1993) *In a Different Voice* (Cambridge and London, Harvard University Press).
Green, A (2004) 'Individual remembering and "collective memory": Theoretical presuppositions and contemporary debates' 32 *Oral History* 35.
Gulland, J (2020) 'Households, bubbles and hugging grandparents: Caring and lockdown rules during COVID-19' 28 *Feminist Legal Studies* 329.
Herring, J (2019) *Family Law*, 9th edn (London, Pearson).
Lacey, N (1995) 'Feminist Legal Theory Beyond Neutrality' 48 *Current Legal Problems* 1.
Law Commission (1966) *Reform of the Grounds of Divorce: The Field of Choice* (Cmnd 3123).
—— (1969) *Financial Provision in Matrimonial Proceedings* (Law Com No 25).
—— (1988) *Family Law: Matrimonial Property* (Law Com No 178).
Miles, J and Hitchings, E (2018) 'Financial remedy outcomes on divorce in England and Wales: Not a "meal ticket for life"' 31 *Australian Journal of Family Law* 43.
Morton, F (1956) *Report of the Royal Commission on Marriage and Divorce 1951–1955* (Cmd 9678).
Office for National Statistics (2017) *Dataset: Divorces in England and Wales.*
Scott, J and Dex, S (2009) 'Paid and Unpaid Work: Can Policy Improve Gender Inequalities?' in J Miles and R Probert (eds), *Sharing Lives, Dividing Assets: An Inter-Disciplinary Study* (Oxford, Hart Publishing).
Smart, C (1984) *The Ties that Bind* (London, Routledge).
Stetson, D (1982) *A Woman's Issue: The Politics of Family Law Reform in England* (Oxford, Oxford University Press).
Summerfield, P (2005) '"Our Amazonian Colleague": Edith Summerskill's Problematic Reputation' in R Toye and J Gottlieb (eds), *Making Reputations: Power, Persuasion and the Individual in Modern British Politics* (London, IB Tauris).

Summerskill, E (1957) *Letters to my Daughter* (London, Heinemann).
—— (1967) *A Woman's World* (London, Heinemann).
Woodward, H and Sefton, M (2014) *Pensions on Divorce: An Empirical Study*.

Archival Material

Records of the Women's Library, London, LSE:
SUMMERSKILL/7.
SUMMERSKILL/1/33.
'Woman's Work: Dr Summerskill Differs from Early Feminists' *Manchester Guardian* (18 February 1950) 17.
SUMMERSKILL 1/46.
Interview by Michael Summerskill with Barbara Castle
Interview by Michael Summerskill with Bill Deeds
Interview by Michael Summerskill with Lord Denning
Interview by Michael Summerskill with Suzanne Knowles
Interview by Michael Summerskill with Michael Stewart
SUMMERSKILL 1/99.
SUMMERSKILL/1/101.
Copy of letter to *The Times* (18 December 1968).
Copy of letter to Leo Abse (18 December 1968).

PART THREE

Telling Stories about Divorce and Marriage

7

Divorced from Reality? Literary Depictions of the Legal Process for Ending a Marriage, 1971–2021

REBECCA PROBERT

I. Introduction

Unhappy marriages, and the difficulties facing those who wanted to extricate themselves from the legal tie, have provided the mainspring of many novels over the years, particularly when divorce required a private Act of Parliament or could only be granted upon proof of the other spouse's adultery. Novelists vividly depicted the plight of those trapped in unhappy marriages without recourse to a legal divorce because they were unable to satisfy the limited grounds laid down by the law. For those writing after the advent of judicial divorce in 1857, the tensions of the divorce court also provided fertile ground, with novelists often highlighting the artificiality of the law as well as its limitations and complexities.[1]

But what happens when it is well known that a divorce will be available sooner or later should either of the parties to the marriage wish to end it, regardless of whether anything can be alleged against the other? How do novelists engage with and depict the legal process of ending a marriage when there is no uncertainty as to whether their characters will be able to do so, and no courtroom scenes to add drama to the narrative? This chapter draws on over 50 novels and collections of short stories published since the Divorce Reform Act came into force in 1971, to explore how the story told about the law has shifted since 'irretrievable breakdown' became the sole ground for divorce, albeit one that had to be evidenced by demonstrating one of five facts. It shows that while a distinct shift in emphasis can be seen from previous depictions of divorce law in several respects, the overarching story being told about the law both before and after reform is how far it is divorced from reality.

[1] For discussion of the way in which divorce was depicted in earlier novels, against which the post-1971 shifts are assessed, see Probert (2008) and (2019).

The first and most striking change within the post-reform literature is the normalisation of divorce, as reflected not only in the frequency with which divorces feature in these novels but also in how they are discussed. The second is the way in which individuals are depicted as engaging with the law. From the 1970s onward, the courtroom scene disappeared from fictional depictions of divorce to the same extent as it did from the law, that is to say, almost completely; lawyers still featured as sources of advice, but the way in which they were portrayed suggested a certain ambivalence about their role, and there was a growing emphasis on the importance of resolving matters amicably. This brings us on to the common thread running through fictional depictions of the law before and after 1971: their focus on the law's artificiality. The facts that had to be established under the Divorce Reform Act 1969 may have been easier to satisfy than the grounds required under the previous law, but characters still found themselves baffled by what the law regarded as sufficient to justify the ending of a marriage. Alongside this continuity, however, was a shift in focus in the literature from the spouse who wanted the divorce to the spouse who did not, and to the way in which divorce plots were resolved.

These four themes will be considered in turn. Before doing so, however, I should say something about the corpus of novels and stories on which I draw. Some were chosen specifically because they had 'divorce' in the title or otherwise alluded to multiple marriages.[2] The titles are themselves significant, as is the fact that they are concentrated in the past 20 years: the decision to allude to divorce in the title of these particular novels could be seen as a ploy to tap into a particular market, reflecting the authors' perceptions of just how common divorce has become.[3] Others were not selected specifically for the purposes of this study, but upon being read for other reasons turned out to be relevant to it. Overall, works by 38 authors were considered; of these, 29 were women, reflecting the fact that most of the novels with titles alluding to divorce or marriage were by female writers. Where more than one book by a particular author was chosen, it was because they were from different decades and so had the potential to show how depictions of divorce might change over time even within the work of a single author: thus the sample included works by David Lodge and Margaret Drabble from the 1970s through to the 1990s, by Fay Weldon from the 1970s to the 2000s, and by Penelope Lively for all five decades. While the sample represents only a tiny fraction of novels from the period and is of necessity selective, examining how the law of divorce is depicted in popular literature can tell us a lot about how it is understood – and misunderstood. As we shall see in each of the four themes, while novels may portray the law as divorced from reality, they do not always reflect the reality of the law.

[2] See eg Trollope (2000); Matthews (2000); Clementis (2004); Tucker (2005); Parks (2005); Coleridge (2006); Buchan (2006); Dowling (2006); Fallon (2007); Pasternak (2007); Stimson (2007); Odone (2009); Cox (2009); Strachan (2009); Moggach (2013); Prowse (2016).

[3] Some – such as *The Good Divorce Guide* (Odone (2009)) or *How to Lose a Husband and Gain a Life* (Strachan (2009)) – even sound more like self-help books than novels.

II. The Normalisation of Divorce

Erica Jong was exaggerating somewhat when she claimed in 1973 that 'In nineteenth-century novels, they get married. In twentieth-century novels, they get divorced'.[4] There are plenty of nineteenth-century novels featuring marital breakdown, and equally plenty of twentieth-century (and twenty-first century) ones featuring lifelong marriages. Nonetheless, there is certainly a shift towards the normalisation of divorce. This manifests itself in a number of different ways: in the frequency of references to divorce, the matter-of-fact way in which it is depicted, and the way in which a number of novels begin with the divorce, or even relegate it to the back story of the characters. What is also noticeable, however, is that some novelists exaggerate the extent to which divorce has become the norm, especially when citing statistics.

The novels and collections of short stories were, of course, all selected because they included some reference to divorce. The increasing *frequency* of references to divorce can, however, be illustrated by looking at collections of short stories and at the occasional novel that presents multiple possible versions of the lives of the characters. Divorce is a key theme in four of the 11 short stories in Fay Weldon's 1981 collection *Watching Me, Watching You*. In a similar vein, Margaret Drabble's 2011 collection of short stories published from the early 1970s quickly moves from depicting women in unhappy marriages ('The Gifts of War' (1970) and 'A Day in the Life of a Smiling Woman' (1973)) to women who have extricated themselves from such marriages (the divorced friend in 'Homework' (1975), the narrator of 'The Dower House at Kellynch: A Somerset Romance' (1993) who is 'giddy with relief' at having left her 'cad of a husband'[5]) to those who have accumulated more than one spouse ('The Caves of God' (1999), the second husband having been 'a mistake made on the rebound'[6]). And in Laura Barnett's *The Versions of Us* – which presents three versions of the story of Eva and Jim – divorce seems to be an almost inevitable part of the life course. In version one, they marry, but divorce when he has an affair with a younger woman (who leaves him in turn); in version two, she marries David, he leaves her for a younger woman and they divorce; she then marries Ted, and only after his death does she finally get together with Jim; in version three, she marries David, but he proves unfaithful and she has an affair with Jim and they marry after the divorce.[7]

The normalisation of divorce is also reflected in changes in the way in which spouses are depicted as reacting to the revelation of an affair. In novels from the earlier part of the period, divorce is often not even considered. In Barbara Pym's *An Academic Question* – written in 1971, although not published until later – Caro

[4] Jong (1973) 277.
[5] Drabble (2011) 165.
[6] ibid 190.
[7] Barnett (2015).

is asked by a friend whether she is thinking of divorcing her unfaithful husband, and notes that she 'must have looked startled, for the idea of divorce had never entered my mind'.[8] The cuckolded husband in Penelope Lively's 1977 novel *The Road to Lichfield* simply makes her aware that he has known of her adultery for months, and, tucking into his dinner, coldly comments 'I assume it isn't going to become a habit'.[9] And when Philip Swallow confesses his adultery to his wife Hilary, his anxious query 'I hope you aren't thinking of divorce, or anything silly like that?' brings not only her reassurance that she is not, but also her view that even asking the question was 'a remarkably panicky reaction'.[10] In later novels, by contrast, an affair is more likely to be depicted as a catalyst for a divorce, if not necessarily as the reason for the breakdown of the marriage.[11]

Divorce is also normalised by the matter-of-fact way in which characters refer to it. As Fay Weldon drily noted in one short story from 1976, 'it had been a good marriage, as marriages go. And as marriages go, it went'.[12] Ian McEwan's *Solar* begins with a professor musing on the disintegration of his fifth marriage; he thinks of his marriages as 'tidal', with 'one rolling out just before another rolled in'.[13] Characters are often reassured that divorce is nothing unusual: the mother in *the last year of being married* is reassured by the staff at her son's nursery that 'divorce and separation are becoming the norm, not the exception'.[14] Others are implicitly reproached for not accepting the breakdown of their marriage: the 61-year-old wife in Joanna Trollope's *Marrying the Mistress*, whose husband has left her for a woman 30 years her junior, is depicted as being unreasonable, obstinate and demanding, and her son tells her that 'things just happened in life, some good, more bad, and that you had to just accept them without screwing yourself up apportioning blame and finding reasons'.[15] In a similar vein, the wife who is devastated by her husband's departure in *My Husband's Wife* is briskly told by her best friend that '[i]t feels terrible right now because it is terrible, but these things happen and you will move on'.[16]

While some novelists focus on the slow and often painful unravelling of a marriage,[17] the removal of any kind of dramatic tension as to whether a divorce will be obtained makes it understandable that many of the novels that take divorce

[8] Pym (1986) 129.
[9] Lively (1977) 215.
[10] Lodge (1975) 147, 149. See also Read (1979), in which the husband has no intention of ending his marriage when embarking on an affair.
[11] Odone (2009); Prowse (2016).
[12] 'Alopecia' (1976) in Weldon (1981) 44. Contrast her 1971 novel *Down Among the Women*, which begins some 20 years earlier with one of the characters preparing for the Thursday meeting of Divorcees Anonymous – '[t]his being 1950, a group such as this is a rarity, and its lady members the more amazed at their fate': Weldon (1971) 8.
[13] McEwan (2011) 3.
[14] Tucker (2005).
[15] Trollope (2000) 68.
[16] Prowse (2016).
[17] Trollope (1989); Prowse (2016).

as their theme begin rather than end with the breakdown of the marriage. Nina Bawden's *Familiar Passions*, Margaret Drabble's *The Radiant Way* and David Nicholls's *Us* all begin with one spouse announcing that the marriage is at an end.[18] Cristina Odone's *The Good Divorce Guide* and Penelope Lively's *How It All Began* both open with a wife discovering that her husband is having an affair; while Bernadette Strachan's *How to Lose a Husband and Gain a Life* begins with the husband's arrest for money laundering, which is the prompt for the wife to seek to extricate herself from the marriage. And in the very first line of Francesca Clementis' *A Perfect Divorce*, the narrator explains that it took 20 years for her and her partner to decide to get married, 'and less than ten months to decide we were getting a divorce'.[19]

The normalisation of divorce is also reflected in the way that, in many novels, divorce has moved out of the narrative altogether and simply forms part of the backstory of a character – but not, as might have been the case in earlier generations, to convey any sense of stigma.[20] Carole Matthews' *For Better, For Worse* opens with a conversation between the soon-to-be divorced spouses: the split and the resulting sadness are in the past and the wife is ready to move on.[21] Anna Pasternak's *Daisy Dooley Does Divorce* begins with the PDD – the 'post-divorce date' – while Josephine Cox's *Divorced and Deadly* focuses on its main character's life as a single man after divorce.[22] Lucy Diamond's *On A Beautiful Day* similarly briefly introduces the divorce of one of the central characters within the first few pages, primarily as a means of illustrating the supportive network of female friends of which she is part and setting up the context for her new relationship.[23] Even novels whose primary focus is the beginning, rather than the ending, of a marriage will often feature a divorce sub-plot along with one or more weddings.[24]

Indeed, for many novelists, an earlier divorce is mentioned solely because of the challenges that it poses to an existing relationship. Ex-spouses may need to be skirted cautiously in the early stages of a relationship (as in Penelope Lively's *Family Album*) or remain a source of tension throughout its duration (as in Elizabeth Buchan's *The Second Wife*).[25] The children of new partners also regularly feature as a plot device: Joanna Trollope depicted the challenges posed by blended families in *Other People's Children*, and the daughter of a divorced dad is the focus of one of the sub-plots in *On A Beautiful Day*.[26] Again, however, the narrative about such families generally

[18] Bawden (1979); Drabble (1987); Nicholls (2014).

[19] Clementis (2004) 1.

[20] See eg Lively (1983) (number of characters have earlier marriages that have ended in divorce) and (1991) (central character is divorced); James (2004) (divorce eight years earlier); Barnes (2011) (earlier marriage and divorce sketched out in a few lines); Forster (2013) (short-lived marriage as explanation for character's attitude to both men and property).

[21] Matthews (2000).

[22] Pasternak (2007); Cox (2009).

[23] Diamond (2018).

[24] Ashley (2009); Matthews (2016); Johnson (2019).

[25] Lively (2009); Buchan (2006).

[26] Trollope (1998); Diamond (2018).

focuses on how they are nothing out of the ordinary. One character in Jane Fallon's *Getting Rid of Matthew* muses that 'this was real twenty-first century dysfunctional happy families – a separated couple, stepchild, half-brother and sister'.[27] Similarly, the children of the divorced father in Alice Adams's *Invincible Summer* see the divorce as normal and nothing that needs to be discussed: 'Loads of kids at school have divorced parents, and step-parents too.'[28] Such pragmatic responses are an implicit response to an earlier narrative regarding the guilt felt by parents who divorced about the effect it might have on their children.[29]

This normalisation of divorce to some extent reflects the very real increase in divorce in the wake of the reforms coming into effect in 1971. The number of divorces jumped from 58,239 in 1970 to 74,437 in 1971 and 119,025 in 1972, and thereafter climbed more or less steadily throughout the 1980s and early 1990s, peaking at 165,018 in 1993.[30] But it should also be noted that there is a divergence between perceptions of just how common divorce is, as revealed by discussions between characters in the literature, and its extent in reality. When characters comment on how common divorce is, they frequently overstate its extent. In Marian Keyes' *Sushi for Beginners*, for example, the couple getting divorced seek to reassure themselves that it is in fact the majority of marriages – two out of three, they claim – that end in divorce.[31] It might be that this was deliberate, and that Keyes wanted to illustrate the self-delusion of her characters, but this assumes that she knew, and knew her readers would know, that it was still only a minority of marriages that ended in divorce.[32]

Where the comments on the extent of divorce are made by a character who might be expected to have an accurate grasp of the statistics, the author must have intended them to be taken seriously. In *The Adultery Club*, Tess Stimson made one of her central characters, Nicholas, a divorce lawyer; musing on how lucky he is to have a happy marriage, he notes that he is 'only too aware how rare it is these days to attain your fifth wedding anniversary, never mind your tenth'.[33] This considerably overstates the extent of divorce. Ben Wilson and Steve Smallwood calculated that in 2005, fewer than 10 per cent of marriages ended in divorce before the couple had reached their fifth wedding anniversary, and a little over 20 per cent before their tenth; moreover, after the tenth anniversary, the likelihood of divorce fell, with fewer than 15 per cent of couples who had been married for more than 20 years divorcing, and 10 per cent surviving to celebrate their diamond wedding anniversary.[34] While divorce has become normalised, it is not the experience of the majority who marry.

[27] Fallon (2007) 310.
[28] Adams (2016) 290.
[29] Drabble (1972).
[30] ONS (2020) table 1.
[31] Keyes (2000).
[32] Haskey (1996) put the figure at around two in five.
[33] Stimson (2007) 16.
[34] Wilson and Smallwood (2008).

III. Engaging with the Law

A second key feature of the post-reform literature is the way in which characters are depicted as engaging with the law, and with lawyers. There is a shift from the courtroom to the lawyer's office, and from there to dispensing with formal legal advice altogether. Again, while much of this reflects the changed reality of obtaining a divorce, many novelists' depictions of lawyers bear little resemblance to the (presumably less fiction-worthy) 'helpful professional' observed in empirical research[35] and instead perpetuate certain stereotypes about how lawyers themselves engage with the law.

Novels depicting any kind of courtroom battle over whether a divorce should be granted simply fizzled out. *The Needle's Eye*, published in 1972, is a relatively late example of a novel featuring a defended divorce, and even then does so indirectly, as the divorce has already happened by the time the novel opens; it had, moreover, been granted under the pre-1969 law. By the time of Fay Weldon's short story 'Christmas Tree', set in 1975, the battle has moved out of the court, with the wife countering her husband's allegations of adultery 'by solicitor's letter'.[36] In later novels, even the sense of a contest fades away, with characters simply sending back the paperwork with little drama. The husband in *The Chymical Wedding* accepts his wife's wish for a divorce, telling her to 'Get a solicitor to serve me some papers or whatever they do. I'll sign.'[37] In *For Better, For Worse* the divorce is all but completed by the time the novel opens, with the central character simply reporting that she has 'recently sent the papers back'.[38] And in *Husbands*, the first husband's immediate assumption upon meeting his wife and her new husband is that there must have been a letter that he has missed: 'I move around a lot, post doesn't always find me.'[39]

This reflected the changed reality of divorce and in particular the introduction of the 'special procedure' in the 1970s. Limited first to undefended divorces based on two years' separation with consent, but quickly extended to all undefended divorces, the special procedure enabled the decision as to whether the grounds for divorce were satisfied to be made on the basis of written evidence rather than oral testimony in court. With all but a tiny number of divorces being undefended, divorcing couples would have no reason to attend court, at least not in relation to the grant of the divorce itself.

Linked to this is the virtual disappearance in many novels of any discussion of the basis on which a divorce is or was granted. This may, of course, simply reflect novelists' own lack of engagement with the law. Nicholas Coleridge's

[35] See eg Eekelaar, Maclean and Beinart (2000); Maclean and Eekelaar (2016).
[36] 'Christmas Tree' in Weldon (1981).
[37] Clarke (1989) 413.
[38] Matthews (2000) 21.
[39] Parks (2005) 160.

A Much-married Man contains just a brief description of the first divorce of the central character, noting that the couple had been separated for two and a half years, and the wife 'agreed to admit to abandoning her husband and child for another man';[40] from this, the reader might be baffled as to whether this was intended to denote adultery, desertion or separation. In Julian Fellowes' *Snobs*, the characters readily confess their ignorance of whether any facts have to be alleged in order to obtain a divorce: 'If he were to divorce you now it would have to be for a reason, or has that finished? I'm not too sure.'[41] *How to Lose a Husband and Gain a Life* is one of the few novels to depict any glitch with the process of obtaining a divorce, and even here the challenges faced by the wife are procedural rather than substantive, the husband having failed to return an acknowledgement of service. Her lawyer, however, reassures her that she will 'get her freedom', even if '[t]he word *eventually* had hung in the air'.[42]

The value of solicitors in protecting the interests of the vulnerable is made particularly clear in one of the early short stories in the sample. Fay Weldon's short story 'Alopecia', published in 1976, features a woman who has left her violent husband; her solicitor efficiently 'collects evidence and affidavits from doctors and hospitals all over London', obtains a 'restraining order' against the violent husband, ensures that the wife and her daughter can return to the family home, and not only 'starts and completes divorce proceedings' but also gets generous maintenance, all within six months.[43] The timing of the story fits with both the greater awareness of domestic abuse and a number of initiatives designed to help those in need of public legal assistance.[44] Tellingly, the husband's perception of events is a very different one, accusing his wife's friend of 'egging her on' to leave her marriage: 'It was you who made her go to law, and once things get into lawyers' hands they escalate, as who better than I should know? The law has nothing to do with natural justice'.[45] His reaction provides a reminder of how more powerful individuals may object to lawyers precisely because the law takes away the advantage that their wealth, strength and violence otherwise confers.

This particular solicitor, it should be noted, is a free one, reflecting the availability of legal aid to deal with such disputes. In other novels, a more negative portrayal of lawyers is linked to their cost. Within the same collection, Weldon features another failed marriage, which leaves the husband 'with a sense of tragedy behind him, and solicitors' letters and bills still falling through the letter box'.[46] Lawyers themselves are depicted as highly conscious of the costs that their clients are incurring. The husband seeking legal advice in David Lodge's *Therapy* notices

[40] Coleridge (2006) 95.
[41] Fellowes (2004) 278.
[42] Strachan (2009) 152.
[43] 'Alopecia' (1976) in Weldon (1981) 58.
[44] For discussion, see Maclean and Eekelaar (2019) 9.
[45] 'Alopecia' in Weldon (1981) 58–59.
[46] 'Holy Stones' (1979) in Weldon (1981) 91.

that his lawyer's desk had 'a digital clock, subtly angled towards the client's chair like a taxi-meter, so you can see how much his advice is costing you'.[47] The lawyer in *the last year of being married* is even more direct, advising her client to '[t]ry not to waste too much time crying in this hour as it's expensive'.[48]

Many of the novels in the sample also depicted lawyers as both partisan and pugnacious. The husband seeking a divorce in *The Adultery Club*, himself a divorce lawyer, notes that once the papers have been served on his wife, '[o]ur legal mercenaries will enter the ring on our behalf to do battle'.[49] Penelope Lively implicitly acknowledged that there were divorce lawyers 'whose first move is to urge some counselling, a visit to Relate, a cooling-off period', but the lawyer in *How It All Began*, is 'not one of those … He is an old hand and he is in this business for a living.'[50] At the end of the novel, it is noted that his bill was 'impressive'.[51] The wife's divorce lawyer in *The Good Divorce Guide* is similarly confrontational in his approach, to the extent that her husband asks her to consider mediation on the basis that with this particular lawyer, 'things are bound to escalate'.[52] As the wife later ruefully ponders, her lawyer 'did manage to extract a tidy sum' from her.[53]

The cost of lawyers, their adversarial nature and their potential to inflame tensions between separating spouses have all been key themes in policy debates in recent decades. But the reality of this depiction should be measured against the large body of empirical work into the work of solicitors dealing with divorce. In one recent investigation, Mavis Maclean and John Eekelaar observed family law solicitors at work and found 'no indication of an aggressive approach, or of any reluctance to cooperate with other forms of dispute resolution', even among those working with high net-worth clients.[54] It may be that an adversarial lawyer is the next best thing to a courtroom drama for these novelists in terms of driving the plot (and providing someone to blame), but it is not a realistic depiction of how most operate.

For the characters depicted in these novels, the alternative to consulting a solicitor is generally not some form of alternative dispute resolution or mediation but an entirely DIY divorce. The title of *A Perfect Divorce* is telling: the couple in question were determined to have an amicable divorce and agreed that they would not need to consult lawyers:

> Instead we bought a £9.99 Handle Your Own Divorce kit from the newsagent/down the road. It even came with a free CD-ROM. Now you don't get one of them from a lawyer …[55]

[47] Lodge (1995) 219.
[48] Tucker (2005) 75.
[49] Stimson (2007) 373.
[50] Lively (2011) 53.
[51] ibid 244.
[52] Odone (2009) 156.
[53] ibid, 362.
[54] Maclean and Eekelaar (2016) 54.
[55] Clementis (2004) 7–8.

Such depictions are in line with what has become the 'dominant discourse', the idea that 'ex-partners should be able to self-manage their own relationship breakdown'.[56] But for many of those negotiating the end of their marriage without access to legal advice, the reality may be rather less than perfect. Resolving disputes outside court may result in unfair bargains being struck, whether because of inequality of bargaining power as between the parties or their lack of knowledge of their legal entitlements.[57]

Of course, the focus on parties resolving matters for themselves is in the context of the consequences of divorce, not the process of obtaining a divorce. That process by its very nature requires at least some engagement with the law. But as the next section will discuss, the law governing that process is seen as highly artificial.

IV. The Artificiality of the Law

There are a number of different ways in which novelists depict the law as being artificial: first, in relation to its language; second, in the way in which events are analysed through a legal lens; and, third, in the necessity of establishing particular facts in order to obtain a divorce, even if these have nothing to do with why the marriage has broken down. Again, however, in stressing how far the law is divorced from reality, some novelists rather exaggerate its requirements.

The law is depicted as having its own language. In *The Adultery Club*, the husband seeking a divorce, being a divorce lawyer himself, is conscious of the difference in register, reflecting how once his wife has been served with the divorce papers, their 'tentative cordiality … will disappear under a storm of disclosures and Form Es and *our client believes* and *Without Prejudice*'.[58] Those who are less familiar with the language of the law are portrayed as struggling to understand its meaning. In *Sushi for Beginners*, the wife is initially confident that she can manage without a solicitor; later, receiving the divorce petition, she realises 'how badly she needed a lawyer', the language being 'pompous and impenetrable'.[59] Those with lawyers to advise them do not necessarily fare much better: *The Good Divorce Guide* depicts one wife trying to navigate the process of getting divorced, but when talking to her lawyer she is sunk in gloom by the 'legal jargon'[60] and relies on the guide that a friend offers her to see her 'through the legalese'.[61]

The way in which events are analysed through a legal lens is used to highlight the disjunction between what the law regards as relevant and what individuals

[56] Hitchings (2017); see also Reece (2003); Mant and Wallbank (2017).
[57] Barlow et al (2017).
[58] Stimson (2007) 372.
[59] Keyes (2000) 472.
[60] Odone (2009) 111.
[61] ibid, 159.

themselves feel to be important. Rose, the central character in *The Needle's Eye*, makes this explicit when she comments to her barrister that what the law takes seriously is 'a kind of code … for what really goes on'.[62] The divorcing wife in AS Byatt's *Babel Tower* similarly identifies the 'discrepancy between what caused her pain and what must be adduced as evidence' in order to bring the marriage to an end legally.[63] More crudely, the solicitor advising the wife in *the last year of being married* sees material that will be useful for the case as 'good stuff', while her barrister advises that it is a 'game'.[64]

The law is also seen as artificial in requiring specific facts to be established to prove irretrievable breakdown. Given how few novels feature any discussion of the basis for divorce, this particular theme emerges in only three of the novels in the sample – Keyes' *Sushi for Beginners*, Parks' *Husbands* and Stimson's *The Adultery Club*.[65] The first two both feature a husband and wife sitting down together to discuss how they will bring their marriage to an end, and reviewing the various facts from which irretrievable breakdown will be inferred. There is a clear sense of the authors displaying their legal knowledge – the couples work through the possible options as assiduously as a student faced with a problem question in an examination, even reviewing the possibility of relying on desertion despite the unlikelihood of its being cited.[66] Nonetheless, in all three novels the reader is left with the clear impression that the law is absurd, and potentially harmful.

The perceived absurdity of the law is underlined by a number of sarcastic exchanges between the wife and her first husband in Parks' *Husbands* – the plural here illustrating the central issue that Belinda, or Bella as she has become known, has acquired two husbands, and needs to negotiate with the first over how a divorce can be obtained so that she can (re)marry the second legally. His response to her telling him that the courts 'will recognise an eight-year separation as "irretrievable breakdown"', is a dry 'Who said the law was an ass?'[67] He similarly makes fun of her suggestion that he could divorce her on the basis of desertion:

> 'We only needed to be apart for two years for the courts to be convinced that I …' She trails off.
>
> 'Definitely wanted to desert me and hadn't just popped out for a pint of milk and forgotten where we lived.'
>
> 'Yes,' she says, flushing to crimson. 'We just have to prove that I haven't been in touch.'
>
> 'Not tricky.'[68]

In the end, he relents and they divorce on the basis of two years' separation and consent.

[62] Drabble (1972) 72.
[63] Byatt (1997) 323.
[64] Tucker (2005) 124, 148.
[65] Keyes (2000); Parks (2005); Stimson (2007).
[66] On the rarity with which desertion is cited today, see Trinder et al (2017).
[67] Parks (2005) 222.
[68] ibid, 222–23.

By contrast, it is the hurt that can be generated by the citation of fault even when the divorce itself is consensual that comes out particularly strongly in Keyes' novel. The couple at its heart, Lisa and Oliver, agree that they want to end their marriage. Since they want a divorce as quickly as possible, and neither has committed adultery (or at least not what they would define as adultery), there is only one choice, 'unreasonable behaviour'.[69] As Oliver notes, either one of them could bring the petition: it is 'only a formality … it's not about allocating blame'.[70] Lisa duly receives the petition for divorce with the five examples that Oliver told her were required:

> Working nine weekends in a row. Missing his parents' thirtieth wedding anniversary due to work commitments. Cancelling their holiday in St Lucia at the last minute because she had to work. Pretending she wanted to get pregnant. Owning too many clothes. Each instance cut through her like a knife. Apart from the owning-too-many-clothes one. She presumed that by example five he'd run out of real complaints.[71]

There are clear parallels between this and the findings of the Nuffield-funded research into the operation of divorce law led by Liz Trinder over a decade and a half later.[72] As this found, petitioners' decisions as to which fact to choose was driven by a combination of circumstantial factors (the urgency of the case and whether they had the cooperation of their spouse), their awareness and understanding of the law, and the importance they attached to harm-minimisation versus formally recording the reason and responsibility for relationship breakdown. Oliver's commitment to harm-minimisation in Keyes' novel is demonstrated by the fact that he rings her to apologise for putting these things on the petition: 'I don't mean to bad-mouth you, you know that, right? … But they're the rules … we have to give some reason to the court.'[73] The examples given would almost certainly satisfy the low threshold: as Trinder et al noted, 'even citing the mildest action or inaction that could be attributable to the respondent, would be very likely be accepted'.[74] Yet Lisa's emotions upon reading the petition underline how, even when the divorce is agreed, 'the inherent hurtfulness of allegations'[75] made by one spouse against the other may make the divorce more bitter than it needs to be.

Stimson's *The Adultery Club*, by contrast, features a wife who is distraught upon discovering her husband's affair and outraged when he petitions for divorce on the basis of her behaviour:

> I can't believe he's done this. Actually gone to a solicitor, sat in an office and regurgitated the story of our marriage to a virtual stranger, sifted through the dirty laundry of our

[69] On the misleading message sent by this familiar contraction of MCA 1973, s 1(2)(b), see Miles, ch 8 of this volume.
[70] Keyes (2000) 358.
[71] ibid, 473.
[72] Trinder et al (2017).
[73] Keyes (2000) 476.
[74] Trinder et al (2017) 79.
[75] ibid, 113.

> lives together for something to fling at me, to make this outrageous charge of *unreasonable behaviour* stick … I bury my head on my arms, the ugly legal papers scattered over the table in front of me.[76]

The tendency for fault-based divorce to generate conflict was again echoed in the *Finding Fault* study, in which 78 per cent of those who had been respondents to a fault-based divorce agreed that citing fault made the divorce process more bitter than it needs to be. As the authors noted, the particulars of behaviour could exacerbate existing tensions, especially where 'fault was being used pragmatically by a petitioner who it was agreed was in fact responsible for the separation'.[77]

While none of these three novels included any real uncertainty as to whether a divorce would be obtained, they, along with others in the sample, did reveal interesting assumptions about the interpretation of different facts. Discussions of adultery, for example, indicated quite a disjunction between what the characters regard as being unfaithful and the legal concept of adultery as sex with one person while married to another. In Fay Weldon's 1979 short story 'Holy Stones', Adam's first wife divorces him on the basis of adultery, which he unsuccessfully defends on the basis that 'he had not … started going with other women until he had been driven to it' by sexual frustration.[78] Twenty years later, in *Sushi for Beginners*, Lisa more successfully resisted the idea that Oliver might divorce her on the basis of adultery, on the basis that she had been 'totally faithful while they'd been together': her post-separation sexual relationships were not seen by her as adulterous.

There are also intriguing indications that basing a divorce on a spouse's adultery is seen as more complex than the alternatives. In *Husbands*, the (remarried) wife resists her first husband's suggestion that he cite adultery by reminding him that they wanted 'a quick no-mess divorce'.[79] In that case, the couple had already been separated for a long period of time, so relying on two years' separation with consent involved no delay. More oddly, in Julian Fellowes' *Snobs*, waiting for two years is seen as an easier option than relying on adultery; the latter, it is thought, 'means such a palaver'.[80] While this might seem to overstate the difficulty of obtaining a divorce on the basis of adultery, at least where the adultery is admitted, novelists do seem to be reflecting the contemporary shift in the likelihood of adultery's being cited. As a number of commentators have noted,[81] there has been a noticeable decline in the percentage of spouses citing adultery as evidence of irretrievable breakdown, from 24 per cent of wives and 41 per cent of husbands in 1979 to just under 10 per cent of wives and 9 per cent of husbands in 2019.[82]

[76] Stimson (2007) 358 (original emphasis).
[77] Trinder et al (2017) 104; and see Trinder, ch 9 of this volume.
[78] 'Holy Stones' (1979) in Weldon, *Watching Me, Watching You*, 98.
[79] Parks (2005) 223.
[80] Fellowes (2004) 249. They may of course simply be aping royals in favouring separation: see Monk, ch 10 of this volume.
[81] Haskey (2018).
[82] ONS (2020), table 5.

A similar emphasis on the artificiality of the law – combined with an exaggeration of its requirements – appears in David Lodge's *Therapy*, in which he derives some humour from the conditions under which couples have to live in order to satisfy the two-year separation fact if neither is able to move out and live elsewhere. A divorcing couple are portrayed as living separate lives under the same roof, with a rota for who uses which parts of the house at what times. This is in line with the case law on the meaning of separation, the court's having held in *Mouncer v Mouncer* that a couple who occupied separate bedrooms and had ceased to have sex but who both used the other rooms of the house, ate meals together and shared various household tasks between them, were not living apart for the purposes of the statute.[83] As the judge noted, the fact that the couple had done so 'from the wholly admirable motive of caring properly for their children' was simply immaterial.[84] Lodge's portrayal of the situation, however, pokes fun at both the law and his characters. He has one character comment that 'the British courts' are apparently 'very strict on laundry', and reporting the husband as saying that if his wife 'knowingly washed his socks it could screw up her petition'.[85] As that character adds, there is little risk of the couple's falling foul of this requirement, given that they 'don't even speak to each other when they meet on the stairs' but 'send each other notes, like North and South Korea'.[86]

Despite such occasional exaggerations for comic effect, there is a strong sense that the few novelists who specifically engage with the question of how a divorce may be obtained have done their research into the law, and their depictions of the ways in which their characters react are in line with the empirical research.

V. The Perspective of the Spouse Who Did Not Want the Divorce

The final shift in focus in the literature is from the spouse who wants the divorce to the spouse who does not. This is perhaps an inevitable concomitant of the shift from fault-based divorce to a system that is, in principle at least, no-fault: the stock character of the unhappily married spouse who cannot obtain a divorce because they cannot establish specific grounds disappears, but novelists find that just as much drama can be obtained from the character of the spouse who thought they *were* happily married, or at least happy enough.

A few characters articulate their unhappiness at the shift away from fault. In Fay Weldon's 1981 short story 'Watching Me, Watching You', the first wife notes

[83] *Mouncer v Mouncer* [1972] 1 WLR 321.
[84] ibid 323.
[85] Lodge (1995) 166.
[86] ibid.

the differences between her lifestyle and that of her former husband and his new wife:

> 'I live in penury, while she lives in style. He is Wendy's father; he has an obligation to support us. He was the guilty party, after all.'
>
> 'The law no longer says guilty or not guilty, in matters of divorce.'
>
> 'Well, it should!'

Almost two decades later, one of the characters in Odone's *The Good Divorce Guide* is similarly unreconciled to her divorce:

> The worst of it was, he could get away with murder because of this country's idiotic no-fault divorce. How can there be no fault when one partner cheats and lies, and the other gets hurt? What kind of justice is that? I'll tell you what kind: *man* justice.[87]

It is worth noting that both writers are women, and there are obvious echoes here of the arguments made by various feminist critics of the proposed reforms.[88]

These, however, were very much minority views within the sample. The freedom to end a marriage is generally valued. For the wife in *How to Lose a Husband and Gain a Life*, divorce enables her to free herself from a husband who is both violent and criminal. Moggach's *The Ex-Wives*, which culminates with the central character's being snowed in with his three former wives at a cottage, draws a parallel between their plight and that of those whose religious beliefs might bar them from obtaining a divorce: 'This is what Catholics must feel … When they want to get divorced. Permanently snowed in. For life.'[89]

Yet even if there is relatively little criticism of the basic premise of no-fault divorce, the fact that it is often the central character who finds out that their spouse is having an affair or wants a divorce, with the novel then focusing on their reactions and navigation of post-divorce life, provides a counter-balance to the normalisation narrative. These novelists are depicting divorce as a shock, as something unwanted. In *The Radiant Way*, one of the central characters only becomes aware that her husband is seeking a divorce at their New Year's Eve party to mark the start of the new decade. For her, divorce changes not merely the future but also the past: she 'had assumed … an abiding sense of the profound importance of their mutual self-knowledge and exploration … Had she now to learn to disbelieve the meaning, the very existence, of their mutual past?'[90] The wife in *Marrying the Mistress*, meanwhile, is pessimistic about the future, meeting the suggestion that a divorce offers her a chance to start again on her own terms with the tart rejoinder 'At sixty-one?'[91] And the central character in Fay Weldon's 2009 novel *Chalcot Cresent* was divorced in 1975, but the divorce is still a source of pain to her.

[87] Odone (2009) 140.
[88] See Auchmuty, ch 4 of this volume; and Thompson, ch 6 of this volume.
[89] Moggach (2013) 297.
[90] Drabble (1987) 142.
[91] Trollope (2000) 88.

Life post-divorce is depicted in bleak terms for men as well as for women. As Lindsay Clarke graphically puts it in *The Chymical Wedding*, 'Marriages vanish like disposable waste these days, and because they are not entirely biodegradable, their relics litter the land.'[92] The ex-husband in Moggach's *The Ex-Wives* describes himself in very similar terms: 'My ex-wife threw me out, you see. I ended up in this place. Blomfield Mansions is full of redundant husbands, a human scrap heap.'[93] The perennial understudy in David Nicholls' 2005 novel of that name – who specialises in playing cadavers – is divorced and living in a bedsit purchased 'during the insane booze and grief-blurred weeks after the end of his marriage'.[94] Similarly, the personal ad composed by Brian Marley in James Hawes's *Speak for England* quickly descends from the positive ('dvrcd (but flly rcvrd!))' to the bitter:

> I know we are all supposed to be oh-so-happy with our little flats … and our white grave-goods piling up on 0% credit but I've written this and you're reading it so we both know that's all lies …[95]

Despite this, most of the novels in the sample end more or less happily, with the left-behind spouse finding a new and usually happier relationship.[96] There is also the divorce novel that does not end in divorce – where the parties go through the process but ultimately reconcile. This is the case for the central characters in *A Perfect Divorce*, *My Fabulous Divorce*, *The Adultery Club* and *How It All Began*.[97] The fact of such reconciliation is not new to the post-reform literature, but these characters are not staying with each other because they cannot obtain a divorce, nor even because they are putting up with a less than perfect marriage,[98] but because they have fallen back in love with their spouse. The ultimate romance, it seems, is not finding Mr Right but realising one is already married to him: these novels can be seen as the reverse of the traditional rom-com, with the initial split replacing the meet-cute but with a similar trajectory of working through difficulties to be reunited at the end.

Yet it is in foregrounding reconciliation that these novels are most at odds with reality. The *Finding Fault* study did identify a handful of cases where the petitioners had changed their minds, with four not applying for a decree nisi and one reconciling with the respondent before it had been made absolute, but this was out of a sample of 300.[99] It also found little evidence that the existing reconciliation

[92] Clarke (1989) 111.
[93] Moggach (2013) 16.
[94] Nicholls (2005) 37.
[95] Hawes (2006) 82.
[96] See eg Matthews (2000); Prowse (2016).
[97] Clementis (2004); Dowling (2006); Stimson (2007); Lively (2011).
[98] Contrast some of the novels from the earlier part of the period, where the reconciliation is more pragmatic than romantic: Drabble (1972) (reconciling for the sake of the children); Lodge (1984) (settling for comfort).
[99] Trinder et al (2017) 59.

provisions were effective, in part because the decision to end the marriage had not been taken lightly in the first place.[100] Nonetheless, one of the arguments put forward by the Government to justify the move to a pure 'no-fault' system was that the existing law 'works against agreement and reconciliation', specifically noting that 'allegations about conduct' may make reconciliation less likely.[101] It will be interesting to see whether no-fault divorce does indeed encourage such reconciliations, or whether they remain more common in fiction than in real life.

VI. Conclusion

The impact of the Divorce Reform Act 1969 has been reflected in the way novelists have depicted the legal process for ending a marriage over the last 50 years: as a mundane paper exercise that has become nothing out of the ordinary. Even novels that took divorce as their focus have tended to spend little time on the basis for its being granted. Some have highlighted the artificiality of the law in requiring particular facts to be established, others have glossed over the basis for the divorce and focused on the financial consequences of divorce and the arrangements to be made for the children. But despite occasional exaggerations, most novels have been realistic in their depiction of the law and the legal process.

At the same time, novelists have also highlighted the pain of divorce in a way that the legal process no longer does. As one ex-husband mused, 'even when your marriage is categorically unsalvageable, it turns out that divorce is really, really painful'.[102] The move to pure no-fault divorce will no doubt be beneficial in removing the incentive for one spouse to make allegations about the other in order to obtain a divorce: some of these allegations are just as fictional as the novels in the sample, or at least are unlikely to reflect the reality of why the marriage broke down. The novelists of the future will be unable to portray the law as divorced from reality. But they will no doubt continue to chronicle the impact of divorce on the human heart.

References

Ashley, T (2009) *Wedding Tiers* (London, Avon).
Adams, A (2016) *Invincible Summer* (London, Picador).
Barlow, A, Hunter, R, Smithson, J and Ewing, J (2017) *Mapping Paths to Family Justice: Resolving Family Disputes in Neoliberal Times* (Basingstoke, Palgrave Macmillan).
Barnes, J (2011) *The Sense of an Ending* (London, Jonathan Cape).

[100] ibid 134.
[101] Ministry of Justice (2018) 20.
[102] Adams (2016) 269.

Barnett, L (2015) *The Versions of Us* (London, Weidenfeld & Nicolson).
Bawden, N (1979) *Familiar Passions* (2011 edn, London, Virago).
Buchan, E (2006) *The Second Wife* (London, Michael Joseph).
Byatt, AS (1997) *Babel Tower* (London, Vintage).
Clarke, L (1989) *The Chymical Wedding* (2010 edn, Richmond, Alma Books Ltd).
Clementis, F (2004) *A Perfect Divorce* (London, Piatkus Books).
Coleridge, N (2006) *A Much-married Man* (London, Orion Books).
Cox, J (2009) *Divorced and Deadly* (London, HarperCollins).
Diamond, L (2018) *On A Beautiful Day* (London, Macmillan).
Dowling, C (2006) *My Fabulous Divorce* (London, Headline Review).
Drabble, M (1972) *The Needle's Eye* (London, Weidenfeld & Nicholson).
—— (1987) *The Radiant Way* (1988 edn, London, Penguin).
—— (2011) *A Day in the Life of a Smiling Woman: The Collected Stories* (London, Penguin Classics).
Eekelaar, J, Maclean, M and Beinart, S (2000) *Family Lawyers: The Divorce Work of Solicitors* (Oxford, Hart Publishing).
Fallon, J (2007) *Getting Rid of Matthew* (London, Penguin).
Fellowes, J (2004) *Snobs* (2005 edn, London, Phoenix).
Forster, M (2013) *The Unknown Bridesmaid* (London, Chatto & Windus).
Haskey, J (1996) 'The proportion of married couples who divorce: past patterns and current prospects' 83 *Population Trends* 25.
—— (2018) 'Facts and figures: grounds for divorce since the 1969 Divorce Reform Act in England and Wales' 48 *Family Law* 1006.
Hawes, J (2006) *Speak for England* (London, Vintage).
Hitchings, E (2017) 'Official, operative and outsider justice: the ties that (may not) bind in family financial disputes' 29 *Child and Family Law Quarterly* 359.
James, E (2004) *Love and Devotion* (London, Orion).
Johnson, D (2019) *A Wedding at the Comfort Food Café* (London, HarperCollins Publishing).
Jong, E (1973) *Fear of Flying* (1974 edn, London, Grafton Books).
Keyes, M (2000) *Sushi for Beginners* (London, Michael Joseph).
Lively, P (1977) *The Road to Lichfield* (London, Heinemann).
—— (1983) *Perfect Happiness* (London, Penguin).
—— (1991) *City of the Mind* (London, Deutsch).
—— (2009) *Family Album* (2010 edn, London, Penguin)
—— (2011) *How It All Began* (2012 edn, London, Penguin).
Lodge, D (1975) *Changing Places* (1978 edn, London, Penguin).
—— (1984) *Small World* (1985 edn, London, Penguin).
—— (1995) *Therapy* (1996 edn, London, Penguin).
Maclean, M and Eekelaar, J (2016) *Lawyers and Mediators: The Brave New World of Services for Separating Families* (Oxford, Hart Publishing).
—— (2019) *After the Act: Access to Family Justice after LASPO* (Oxford, Hart Publishing).
Mant, J and Wallbank, J (2017) 'The Mysterious Case of Disappearing Family Law and the Shrinking Vulnerable Subject: The Shifting Sands of Family Law's Jurisdiction' 26 *Social and Legal Studies* 629.
Matthews, C (2000) *For Better, For Worse* (London, Headline Book Publishing).
—— (2016) *The Chocolate Lovers' Wedding* (London, Sphere).
McEwan, I (2011) *Solar* (London, Vintage).

Ministry of Justice (2018) *Reducing Family conflict: Reform of the legal requirements for divorce* (September 2018).
Moggach, D (2013) *The Ex-Wives* (London, Vintage Books).
Nicholls, D (2005) *Understudy* (London, Hodder & Stoughton).
—— (2014) *Us* (London, Hodder & Stoughton).
Odone, C (2009) *The Good Divorce Guide* (London, HarperPress).
Office for National Statistics (2020) 'Divorces in England and Wales: 2019' (November 2020).
Parks, A (2005) *Husbands* (London, Penguin).
Pasternak, A (2007) *Daisy Dooley Does Divorce* (London, Vermilion).
Probert, R (2008) 'Divorced from reality? An analysis of divorce in literature, 1800–2008', paper presented at Sussex Law School's conference on *Gender, Family Responsibility and Legal Change*, 10–12 July 2008.
—— (2019) 'Divorced from reality? Criminal conversation in Thackeray's *The Newcomes*', SLS conference, 4 September 2019.
Prowse, A (2016) *My Husband's Wife* (London, Head of Zeus).
Pym, B (1986) *An Academic Question* (2012 edn, London, Virago).
Read, PP (1979) *A Married Man* (London, Secker & Warburg).
Reece, H (2003) *Divorcing Responsibly* (Oxford, Hart Publishing).
Stimson, T (2007) *The Adultery Club* (London, Pan Books).
Strachan, B (2009) *How to Lose a Husband and Gain a Life* (2011 edn, London, Sphere).
Trinder, L, Braybrook, D, Bryson, C, Coleman, L, Houlston, C and Sefton, M (2017) *Finding Fault? Divorce Law and Practice in England and Wales* (London, Nuffield Foundation).
Trollope, J (1989) *A Village Affair* (London, Black Swan).
—— (1998) *Other People's Children* (London, Bloomsbury).
—— (2000) *Marrying the Mistress* (London, Bloomsbury).
Tucker, S (2005) *the last year of being married* (Richmond, MIRA Books).
Weldon, F (1971) *Down Among the Women* (1986 edn, London, Penguin).
—— (1981) *Watching Me, Watching You* (2003 edn, London, Flamingo).
—— (2009) *Chalcot Cresent* (London, Corvus).
Wilson, B and Smallwood, S (2008) 'The proportion of marriages ending in divorce' 131 *Population Trends* 28.

8

Judging Matrimonial Behaviour

JOANNA MILES

I. Introduction

> The court hearing a petition for divorce shall not hold the marriage to have broken down irretrievably unless the petitioner satisfies the court of one or more of the following facts, that is to say—
>
> ...
>
> (b) that the respondent has behaved in such a way that the petitioner cannot reasonably be expected to live with the respondent ...[1]

This chapter explores the history of the behaviour 'fact'– perhaps the most important of the facts on which the 1969 reform's ground of irretrievable breakdown of marriage could be established, viewed in terms of the numbers citing it. It also explores the judges' role in having to adjudicate on behavioural expectations of matrimony over the last 50 years, and the public discourse prompted by such cases.

To date,[2] divorce has never been available in England and Wales purely because one or both spouses no longer wish to be married.[3] In the leading eighteenth-century case[4] on the law of cruelty, *Evans v Evans*, Sir William Scott remarked:

> The humanity of the Court has been loudly and repeatedly invoked. Humanity is the second virtue of courts, but undoubtedly the first is justice. If it were a question of humanity simply, and of humanity which confined its views merely to the happiness of the present parties, it would be a question easily decided upon first impressions. Every body must feel a wish to sever those who wish to live separate from each other, who cannot live together with any degree of harmony, and consequently any degree of happiness; but my situation [as a judge] does not allow me to indulge the feelings, much less the first feelings of an individual. The law has said that married persons shall not be

[1] Originally Divorce Reform Act 1969, s 2(1)(b); from 1973–2022, Matrimonial Causes Act 1973, s 1(2)(b).

[2] Until the implementation of the Divorce, Dissolution and Separation Act 2020.

[3] *Buffery v Buffery* [1988] 2 FLR 365. The closest thing to mutual consent or unilateral no-fault divorce in the 1969 Act were the two separation facts.

[4] This case, pre-dating judicial divorce, involved an action for separation in the Ecclesiastical Court.

> legally separated upon the mere disinclination of one or both to cohabit together. The disinclination must be founded upon reasons which the law approves, and it is my duty to see whether those reasons exist in the present case.[5]

As the fate of Mrs Tini Owens nearly 230 years later made plain, this remained the case well into the twenty-first century, despite the adoption of 'irretrievable breakdown' of marriage as the sole ground for divorce.[6] Under the 1969 regime, if the pleaded 'fact' cannot be made out no divorce will be forthcoming, however plain and profound the breakdown.

Commonly misdescribed as the 'unreasonable behaviour' fact, even by high authority,[7] the behaviour fact was intended to serve as the effective replacement of the old 'cruelty' ground that had been introduced by the Matrimonial Causes Act 1937.[8] Just as the cruelty ground had become less demanding of petitioners over time, so too did the behaviour fact. Nevertheless, both involved the judges in a task quite different from that asked of them by the adultery ground/fact.[9] Writing about the cruelty ground, Sir Roger Ormrod (former Family Division judge and Lord Justice of Appeal, writing extra-judicially) remarked that it 'subtly changed' the judges' role:

> Deciding whether or not two people have committed adultery when they deny it is much the same as trying any other issue of fact: the evidence is confined in its scope both in time and place, and the decision does not depend, except as to credibility, on the character or personalities of the persons concerned. But defended cruelty cases … were different. The complaints often covered most of the period of the marriage and were set out in the pleadings at great length. Hearings lasted for many days. Both spouses spent hours in the witness box being examined and cross-examined. Many separate issues had to be decided, and the impact of the behaviour on each spouse had to be assessed. All this involved careful study of the personalities and the temperaments of the people involved, and demanded a great deal of human understanding. In other words, judges had to make very difficult value judgements in these cases.[10]

As discussed in Section II, the behaviour fact was intended to inherit all bar one of the features of the cruelty ground, but the advent of the 'special procedure' for uncontested cases did away with the vast majority of behaviour trials, leaving judges to make their value judgements about spousal interaction on the basis of paper evidence. But that judgement had still to be made and, on those rare

[5] (1790) 1 Hag Con 35, 36.

[6] *Owens v Owens* [2018] UKSC 41.

[7] See eg Lord Wilson's *mea culpa* in *Owens v Owens*, ibid [37].

[8] The ground had featured previously in the law – as a ground for judicial separation from 1857; an aggravating factor for wives' divorce petitions pre-1923; and an aspect of the magistrates' jurisdiction, on which see Savage (1999), Williamson (2011).

[9] The desertion ground/fact was also potentially less straightforward, requiring investigation of whether one spouse's alleged desertion was justified and so placed the remaining spouse in constructive desertion.

[10] Burgoyne, Ormrod and Richards (1987) 52–53.

occasions where divorce was defended, it potentially involved a painful, protracted exercise in court.

The value judgement entailed in determining whether the petitioner could 'reasonably be expected to live with the respondent',[11] given the latter's behaviour, necessarily took judges deep into the minutiae of everyday married life. Whilst the decision about whether the decree nisi could be granted under the 1969 Act was not – as a matter of law – a punitive one,[12] it would undoubtedly be perceived as such by many respondents, especially perhaps (though far from only) in some defended cases.[13] In exploring one reason why family law should abjure a 'punitive' approach based on moral evaluation, John Eekelaar has said that

> if people suffer punishment at the behest of others, even if those others hold judicial office, there must be reasonable confidence that those others are not themselves guilty of the offences for which they are imposing punishment … In most of the matters for which judges impose penalties, there can be reasonable confidence that they are not themselves contravenors. This most definitely cannot be said with regard to the matters which advocates of punitive family law would like to see reintroduced. The chances that judges would be acting with hypocrisy would be very high.[14]

Hence, pre-1969, Lord Chancellor, Viscount Kilmuir's requiring that a metropolitan magistrate who exercised matrimonial jurisdiction resign after his divorce, and Sir Robin Dunn's surprise at Sir John Arnold's appointment – in 1972 – as a Judge of the Family Division, the first divorced person to exercise that jurisdiction.[15] Sir John went on to become President of the Division, so his personal life was clearly no impediment, and may even have given him some of that 'human understanding' that Ormrod prescribed. Indeed, his obituary in *The Times* noted that he had 'the insight into human relationships that marks a good family lawyer'.[16] However, while the 1969 Act's move away from matrimonial fault made the risk of hypocrisy in the administration of the law less acute, there remained significant interest in (and some anxiety about) the judicial approach to the behaviour question. This interest – particularly on one striking occasion involving a Mr and Mrs Mason[17] – found its way into the press and extended into the judges' private lives.

[11] Matrimonial Causes Act 1973, s 1(2)(b), the oft-forgotten second limb of the behaviour fact, commonly garbled into the entirely misleading 'unreasonable behaviour' shorthand.

[12] A punitive analysis is precluded by the 1969 Act's replacement of matrimonial fault with irretrievable breakdown of marriage as the sole ground for divorce (see, eg, *Pheasant v Pheasant* [1972] Fam 202, 209), and the absence of any direct or indirect 'penalty' in the financial remedies for the 'guilty' party (save in the most egregious cases: *Wachtel v Wachtel* [1973] Fam 72). But Lord Pearce in *Williams v Williams* [1964] AC 698, 752–53 denied the presence of any punitive element even *pre*-1969.

[13] See eg Trinder et al (2017), ch 8; and Trinder and Sefton (2018).

[14] Eekelaar (2017) 121.

[15] Dunn (1993) 198. Sir John had remarried in 1963, so was divorced under the old law (on what ground unknown).

[16] *The Times* (9 December 2004) 73. See also Burgoyne et al (1987) 18 on parliamentarians' transparency regarding their own matrimonial biographies when debating changes to the law in 1984.

[17] (1980) 11 *Family Law* 143.

With this background in mind, this chapter first analyses the relationship between the behaviour fact and its 'cruel' precursor, and parliamentary and other anxieties about the shift to the behaviour fact and the judges' role administering it. It then moves on to consider some of the post-1969 case law and its reception, notably *Mason v Mason* and its sequelae. The judges' having been forced to adopt the mantle of 'arbiters of … the limits of acceptable marital behaviour',[18] what moral code did they articulate and how was it received?

II. From Cruelty to Behaviour

To ascertain what could constitute sufficient reason for divorce under the 1969 Act based on the other spouse's conduct (other than adultery or desertion), one must first examine the previous law of 'cruelty' in which the behaviour fact originates. The law had come a long way since *Evans* in 1790, particularly following two key House of Lords decisions – *Gollins*[19] and *Williams*[20] – handed down together in June 1964,[21] the last occasion on which substantive divorce law would reach the top court until *Owens* in 2018.[22] By 1969, the law of cruelty still required 'grave and weighty' behaviour by the respondent that caused either a present danger to the petitioner's life, limb or health, or reasonable apprehension of the same. It also remained the case that the mere fact of the petitioner's ill-health was insufficient; nor, given the logic of the fault-based law, would the ground be made out if the respondent were justified in his behaviour (for example, by provocation).[23] However, *Gollins* had established that the respondent needed neither to have *intended* to be cruel to the petitioner, nor to have *aimed* his conduct at her; and *Williams* that cruelty could be found even if the respondent were insane and so bore no responsibility for his actions. Those decisions, together with the inclusion from the late nineteenth century of danger to the petitioner's *mental* health,[24] meant that the cruelty ground had become more heavily focused on the impact of the respondent's conduct on the petitioner.[25] Proof of negative impact to health had over time became something of a formality,[26] some would – and did – say a 'farce'.[27] Moreover, the test was already in the objective/subjective

[18] Cretney (2010) 254.
[19] *Gollins v Gollins* [1964] AC 644.
[20] *Williams v Williams* [1964] AC 698.
[21] For an exhaustive statement of the law pre-1964, see Biggs (1962).
[22] *Owens v Owens* [2018] UKSC 41.
[23] On some mid-20th century magistrates' somewhat Victorian views of wives' 'failure' to uphold their end of the marital bargain here, see Williamson (2011) 244–46.
[24] *Russell v Russell* [1897] AC 395: see Sumner Holmes (1999) on the saga that continued for some years.
[25] On this, see Cretney (2010) 268 and generally in ch 7.
[26] *Hansard*, SC Deb (C) 24 April 1968, col 164.
[27] Notably Lord Reid, who had sat on *Gollins* and *Williams* and endorsed the drafting of the behaviour clause in the Bill, stated that the requirement of medical evidence 'was getting to be rather a farce': *Hansard*, HL Deb 30 June 1969, vol 303, col 350.

form that we recognise today from the modern case law: the question was whether *this petitioner* could reasonably be expected to tolerate the respondent's conduct.[28]

The reform recommendation that finally emerged from the Law Commission and Archbishop's Group,[29] the parliamentary debate on the Bills[30] that preceded the 1969 Act, and the editions of the practitioner and academic texts first following the Act's coming into force in January 1971,[31] all make clear how firmly rooted the new behaviour fact was in the old cruelty case law. As the Solicitor-General, Sir Arthur Irvine, had put it at Report Stage in the House of Commons:

> [T]he Bill seeks … to achieve something that is inherently desirable: namely, in effect to preserve the respondent's cruelty as one of the facts from which breakdown is to be inferred, but in doing so to avoid the use of the phrase 'matrimonial offence', with all its emotional overtones and implications … The formula employed in the Bill … has the effect … of preserving the law as declared by the House of Lords in [*Gollins* and *Williams*], and to do so with this single element of change that there is henceforward not to be a requirement of actual or apprehended injury to the petitioner's health. All the other criteria in the existing law would remain.[32]

So it was still necessary – just as in 1790 – to show something about the conduct of the respondent that justified the court's freeing the petitioner from the marriage, not the 'ordinary wear and tear of married life'[33] and certainly not 'mere disinclination' to remain married. This reflected the recommendation of the Morton Commission, which had in 1956 cautioned against removing safeguards that would 'lead to divorce on the ground of incompatibility of temperament' for fear of the implications of such a step for the institution of marriage.[34] So, as the Attorney-General Sir Elwyn Jones remarked at Committee stage:

> The present law, which … the Clause does not alter, is that the test is objective in the sense that it is for the court and not the petitioner to decide whether the respondent's behaviour is such that the petitioner cannot reasonably be expected to live with him. It is for the judge to decide that, otherwise … there could be divorce for the most trivial misbehaviour, such as some of the grounds under the American doctrine of incompatibility.[35]

[28] See, eg, *Gollins* [1964] AC 644, 672. Though, again, compare what was going on in some magistrates' courts: Williamson (2011) 250.

[29] Law Commission (1968), 31, note 3.

[30] For systematic overview, see Lee (1974).

[31] See, notably, *Rayden* (1971), Bromley (1971), Cretney (1974). Bromley, for one, continued to refer to cruelty case law well into the 1980s.

[32] *Hansard*, HC 12 June 1969, vol 784, cols 1909–10.

[33] *Gollins* [1964] AC 644, 659 per Lord Reid.

[34] Morton Commission (1956) [129]. See also Denning LJ's warning in *Kaslefsky v Kaslefsky* [1951] P 38, 48.

[35] *Hansard*, SC Deb (C) 24 April 1968, col 165. On contemporary US incompatibility divorce laws, see Kirkpatrick (1964).

III. Parliamentary and Public Worries about Judges Judging Spouses

The Attorney-General's commentary on the behaviour fact had attempted (with mixed success) to allay the worries of parliamentarians who had got very confused about the function of the reasonableness test, but who were also concerned about the power that it appeared to give (albeit not, in fact, for the first time) to judges. These concerns varied in nature. Some – whether for liberal or conservative reasons – objected to the reliance of the proposed simple statement of law on an open-ended 'reasonableness' test. Would this make the test too easy compared to the cruelty test? Was it too vague and uncertain,[36] even devoid of meaning?[37] Were there certain types of conduct (notably rape and sodomy) that should – like adultery and desertion – continue[38] without (much) more by themselves to constitute a 'fact', so as not to be subject to judicial evaluation?[39] Did it impose too great a burden on judges, requiring them to build up a new body of case law – case law that might start off 'on the wrong foot' producing a 'ridiculous' body of precedents?[40]

At least one parliamentarian feared that judges would be too conservative. Dr Hugo Gray MP was particularly vehement in his commentary, if indiscriminate and apparently oblivious to the substantial judicial softening of the (statute-made) cruelty laws that had occurred in the preceding decades:

> Judges are well known in our society to be hopelessly out of touch with current feeling. Indeed, they provide a brake on reform. We all know from the way in which laws have been interpreted by the courts that an extremely hard interpretation is always applied in accord with what has happened in the past, certainly not in accord with what is happening at present ... It seems to me that the Clause might make divorce intolerably difficult, which is why I oppose it. When I think of the values and viewpoints of aged judges and of many aged lawyers, it frightens me how difficult divorce might be to obtain if the Clause were passed.[41]

At the next session, Dr Gray invoked[42] as support for his position no less a legal giant than John Mortimer QC, better known as a playwright and the creator of the fictional Rumpole of the Bailey, the long-suffering husband of 'She Who Must Be Obeyed'. Mr Mortimer, whose focus had shifted to criminal law upon taking silk

[36] eg, Sir Lionel Heald MP, *Hansard*, SC Deb (C) 24 April 1968, various interventions, a topic that he revisits during debates on the second Bill in SC Deb (B) 29 January 1969, col 37.

[37] Mr Richard Wood MP, *Hansard*, SC Deb (C) 10 April 1968, cols 126–27.

[38] Under Matrimonial Causes Act 1857, s 27, rape, bestiality and sodomy had been grounds on which a wife could obtain a divorce, rather than simply aggravating factors that could accompany a wife's plea of adultery, and so survived the change in 1923 that relieved a wife from having to establish aggravating factors in addition to her husband's adultery.

[39] *Hansard*, SC Deb (C) 1 May 1968, col 206.

[40] Dame Irene Ward MP, ibid, 10 April 1968, cols 130–31.

[41] ibid, 10 April 1968, cols 121–22.

[42] ibid, 24 April 1968, col 143.

but who had just written a divorce comedy for the BBC, had been quoted in *The Times* that morning as fearing that divorce might be made more difficult by the Bill than it was under the present law, 'which he regards with affectionate tolerance' as having been converted from 'ecclesiastical hangover … by intelligent judges into a practical system', because it 'gives discretion to the judge'.[43] Quite why these same judges would now make divorce harder is not made clear, and another notable wordsmith and proponent of the Bill, the liberal lawyer Leo Abse MP, summarily dismissed Mortimer's musings: 'great as he may be as a playwright, [he] has not understood [the clause] as a lawyer'.[44] As it turns out, Mr Mortimer need personally have had no fears: his first wife, novelist Penelope Mortimer, clearly had no trouble divorcing *him* in December 1971, by reference to his adultery; indeed, the judge obligingly expedited the grant of the decree absolute so that he could marry his partner Miss Gollop (aged 22) with whom he was already living with their baby daughter, who had been born that October.[45]

But before this encouraging evidence of judicial humanity had been supplied, Dr Gray persisted – albeit more moderately – with his concerns, not unreasonably asking the Attorney-General:

> Will my right hon and learned Friend explain how the judge arrives at his own concept of reasonableness? What considerations does he take before he decides that something is reasonable or not? Legal authorities? Sociologists? Social philosophers? The thoughts of today, or yesterday or of tomorrow?
>
> My right hon and learned Friend has not done anything to remove my fear that the judge has been left with a personal discretion. We know that judges differ … Are people who petition for divorce still to be at the mercy of individual judges' values, or are the values of today to be codified in some way? Is it to be said how they have changed?[46]

IV. Examining Judges Judging Spouses

The task imposed on judges by the 1969/1973 Act – to examine marital behaviour and to make an evaluation about what spouses could reasonably expect in their marriages – would plainly take them deep into the parties' lives and characters. To use Leo Abse's vivid observation (of the cruelty case law), they would be acting as 'scavengers, having to scrape round for the worst obscenities they can find within a married life'.[47] The required evaluation would also, inevitably – though

[43] 'The Times Diary' *The Times* (24 April 1968) 10.

[44] *Hansard*, SC Deb (C) 24 April 1968, col 143.

[45] 'Divorce is speeded so QC can marry Penny, 22' *Daily Mail* (15 December 1971) 12. The newlyweds' marriage was to last until Mortimer's death in January 2009, the 1971 baby becoming actor Emily Mortimer.

[46] *Hansard*, SC Deb (C) 24 April 1968, cols 166–67.

[47] *Hansard*, HC Deb 17 December 1968, vol 775, col 1126.

not articulated expressly by them in these terms – take them into the territory of large social, cultural, political and ideological questions about marriage. But would Dr Gray's fears be realised? What values would the judges apply in making their judgements of what spouses could reasonably expect?

A. What the Judges had been Doing and Saying Pre-1969

Plainly, none of this was new: the law of cruelty had demanded a similar task. Nor is this, therefore, a novel subject of academic inquiry. In his fascinating study of Victorian and Edwardian cruelty cases,[48] James Hammerton describes the judges' finding themselves having to determine just how far husbands could reasonably be permitted to go within the framework of a patriarchal law of marriage, which necessarily gave the husband various rights and powers over his wife's conduct and person. Faced with a growing number of divorce petitions from middle-class wives complaining about their husbands' conduct,[49] the judges' decisions – argued Hammerton – refashioned the idea of what made a good husband within that patriarchal universe. Wives' complaints reflected their 'heightened expectations of conjugal behaviour',[50] and required judges to investigate domestic life more intrusively than before. The result – which would surprise Dr Gray MP – was the emergence from this instinctively conservative, elderly, male,[51] upper-class judiciary[52] of a more 'progressive construction' of what behaviour was expected of husbands, notably through the recognition of non-violent forms of cruelty that controlled husbands before the criminal law came to do so.[53] Importantly, while wives' non-violent resistance to what they considered husbands' unreasonable demands upon them was pleaded by husbands as provocation justifying their conduct, such defences rarely succeeded.[54] So even before *Jackson's* surprisingly controversial[55] declaration in 1891 that husbands no longer had the right to control and chastise their wives,[56] the evolving law of cruelty was giving wives more freedom within marriage by identifying in some detail the boundaries of

[48] Hammerton (1992)

[49] This was a key feature of case law pre-1923, when wives had to plead an aggravating factor (such as cruelty) alongside an allegation of adultery in order to secure divorce. Post-1923, cruelty claims dropped off: ibid 168.

[50] ibid 4.

[51] I have identified just two reported cases (of course, post-1969) involving female judges before Ladies Hale and Black's involvement in *Owens*, necessarily recent: *Cotterell v Cotterell* [1998] 3 FCR 199 and *Hadjimilitis (Tsavliris) v Hadjimilitis* [2003] 1 FLR 81.

[52] Hammerton (1992) 118. See also Savage (2009) 53–54 on the elite nature of the tiny corps of Divorce Court judges; contrast the vast lay magistracy's diverse and often less progressive approach to their cruelty jurisdiction: Savage (1999) 245.

[53] Savage (2009) 54.

[54] Hammerton (1992) 112.

[55] Frost (1999) 133 records the law journals' horror at the perception that the decision had been driven by the judges' personal preferences.

[56] *R v Jackson* [1891] 1 QB 671: see Frost (1999); Bibbings (2014) ch 5.

what constituted the *reasonable* exercise of husbands' powers.[57] As Gail Savage has put it (of the magistrates' jurisdiction, but equally apposite here), the law 'upheld the authority of some men over other men by defining some male behavior as unacceptable, thus further legitimating the authority of those men who conformed to acceptable standards of husbandly conduct'.[58] Hammerton concludes that although patriarchy was far from ejected from marriage by this process, it was at least 'civilised',[59] to protect the institution of patriarchal marriage from husbands whose excesses would bring it into disrepute.[60] And so emerged a particular (gender-unequal) conception of the 'companionate' marriage.[61]

The context in which the equivalent evaluations of marital conduct are made in the late twentieth to early twenty-first centuries is evidently worlds apart from the context of the eighteenth, nineteenth and even mid-twentieth centuries. But the basic endeavour remains the same. As the Supreme Court observed in *Owens*, while the basic *test* has not changed over time – cruelty case law was cited in behaviour cases well into the 1970s and beyond[62] – its *application* has changed in light of evolving social norms about the nature of relationship created by marriage and the roles of the spouses (until recently, exclusively, the potentially gendered roles of 'husband and wife'[63]) within it.[64] Thus, Lord Wilson's 2018 description of that relationship would be unrecognisable by Sir William Scott in 1790 and by Hammerton's Victorian and Edwardian judges. Sir William, in what might be called the marriage guidance counselling portion of his judgment after having denied the wife her decree, hoped that Mrs Evans nevertheless understood 'that the dignity of a wife cannot be violated by submission to a husband'.[65] Contrast, over two centuries later, Lord Wilson, remarking that:

> The relevant social norm which has changed most obviously during the last 40 years has … related to our society's insistence upon equality between the sexes; to its recognition that marriage is a partnership of equals; and, specifically, to its assessment of the

[57] Hammerton (1992) generally ch 4.

[58] Savage (1999) 240–41.

[59] Hammerton (1992) 72; see also Williamson (2011) 250 in the context of the magistrates' jurisdiction.

[60] Hammerton (1992) 133. Notably, this included limiting husbands' access to their wives for sexual intercourse: Savage (2009).

[61] Hammerton (1992) 6–7 and 169. On the problematic – because so fluid – concept of 'companionate' marriage, see Fisher (2013); Griffin et al (2009) 13; Szreter and Fisher (2009) 132–33.

[62] Albeit decreasingly and sometimes rejected outright: see Dunn J in *Livingstone-Stallard v Livingstone-Stallard* [1974] Fam 47, 54, preferring the 'very simple language' of the new law (to the consternation of Hall (1974)), and the UKSC's endorsement of the abandonment of the 'grave and weighty' test: *Owens* [2018] UKSC 41 [27]. So the law of behaviour slipped its moorings in the cruelty case law; but note the support drawn in *Owens* at [40] from *Jamieson v Jamieson* [1952] AC 525 on the cumulative impact of behaviour.

[63] See now Marriage (Same Sex Couples) Act 2013.

[64] Burgoyne et al (1987) 19; Biggs (1962) 59–60.

[65] *Evans v Evans* (1790) 1 Hag Con 34, 128. For further discussion of such 'homilies' to wives, see Hammerton (1992) 122ff.

> moment when a husband's behaviour, in the light of its effect on his wife, begins to make it unreasonable to expect her to continue to live with him. For a wife that moment now arrives earlier than it did before; it now arrives at the same time for both sexes in equivalent situations.[66]

And, to underscore his point, he condemned the view expressed by a judge in 1970 that it had been reasonable for a husband to seek to rectify the couple's sexual problems by force.[67]

B. What the Judges Did and Said Post-1969

So I turn now to the post-1969 Act case law. The discussion is based here on reported case law and then, in the next section, its reception in the media. It is important to acknowledge the limitations of both sources, not least that they only deal with the rare beasts – defended divorce petitions with reported decisions – and not the daily diet of the divorce court, which – from 1977 – would very largely have been handled on paper as uncontested cases. Statistical surveys and other empirical studies give insight into that day-to-day experience of most divorcing spouses. From these we know that the old cruelty law had been 'monopolised' by wife-petitioners,[68] whose resort to the cruelty ground (rather than adultery or desertion) gradually increased over time, presumably in line with the loosening of its requirements. And we know that wives continued to use the new behaviour fact far more than husbands, behaviour quickly coming to underlie the largest proportion of wives' petitions.[69] We know too that physical violence dominated cruelty petitions,[70] and that physical abuse – often serious – has remained a central feature of many behaviour petitions to the current time.[71] But it is what judges are reported to have said about behaviour cases that is more important in shaping legal and (when more widely reported) public attitudes towards marriage and divorce, and so that judicial discourse on behaviour in marriage is my focus here.

We know from early reported case law on the behaviour fact (at least before the Select Committee on Violence in Marriage in 1974–77[72]) that some judges' attitudes

[66] [2018] UKSC 41 [34].

[67] ibid, re *Priday v Priday* [1970] 3 All ER 554, 557. But note that such judicial views were not universal even in the 19th century: Savage (2009).

[68] Chester and Streather (1972) 706.

[69] See Haskey, ch 2 of this volume, for an analysis of patterns pre-and post-1969; for earlier data, see McGregor (1957) ch 2, pre-dating some important liberalisations in the cruelty case law; Williamson (2011), in the magistrates' court; Murch, cited in Burgoyne et al (1987) 33; and Hammerton (1992) table 4.2 for a less scientific but still striking finding about the weight of wives' cruelty allegations pre-1923 (in cases of divorce, as an aggravating feature of their adultery petition).

[70] Chester and Streather (1972).

[71] Trinder et al (2017); and Trinder, ch 9 of this this volume.

[72] See variously: 1974-75 HCP 229 and 553, 1975-76 HCP 260 and 666, 1976–77 HCP 329 and 431.

towards domestic abuse were far from progressive[73] and – continuing the pattern of many magistrates' decisions within their old cruelty jurisdiction[74] – apparently classist. The most infamous example is Bagnall J's declaration in *Ash v Ash* that 'a violent petitioner can reasonably be expected to live with a violent respondent' – though he did grant Mrs Ash's petition, despite her 'penchant for self-dramatisation to an extraordinary degree'.[75] Sadly, he was not alone, other judges being reported to have offered discriminatory observations regarding domestic abuse and alcohol consumption by reference to social class and geographical regions. For example, Dunn J was reported as having remarked in 1974 that northern wives would settle for being beaten but would not tolerate adultery, whereas southern wives took the opposite position: 'He withdrew his observations the next day, and apologised to the angry women of the North.'[76]

Otherwise, a significant strand of the post-1969 case law continued the judicial endeavour to civilise husbands.[77] But the exercise was now to be undertaken in a context where the structures of patriarchy had been very substantially removed from the face of the law,[78] ideas of 'companionate' marriage and what that might require of both spouses having therefore shifted significantly.[79] If anything, adjudicating on this question without any surrounding legal structure (save an implicit – yet not fully realised or articulated until much later – legal norm of equality in marriage) simply risked getting the judges into hotter water as they navigated ever-finer details of marital expectations,[80] and risked exposing parties to very near-the-knuckle judicial character assassinations. Thus, we see a string of unreconstructed husbands finding themselves on the receiving end of rather devastating judicial critique, going way beyond the usual fare required to assess witness credibility.[81]

[73] Though minimisation of domestic abuse allegations persists in some courts, particularly in child arrangements cases: see *Re H-N* [2021] EWCA Civ 448 and related discussion.

[74] Williamson (2011); Hammerton (1992) Pt I; Savage (1999) 243–45; Frost (1999) 112–13.

[75] [1972] Fam 135, 140.

[76] Obituary, *Daily Telegraph* (31 March 2014) 27. See also Hollings J's remarks on different social classes' supposed alcohol consumption and habits of life, *Shears v Shears* (1972) 117 *Solicitors Journal* 33.

[77] Other strands of case law address the impact of varying degrees of mental ill-health, notably *Thurlow v Thurlow* [1976] Fam 32; *Katz v Katz* [1972] 1 WLR 955; *Richards v Richards* [1972] 1 WLR 1073; and *Smith v Smith* (1973) 118 *Solicitors Journal* 184, 14 December 1973 (overruled in *Thurlow*). Another series of cases feature financial woes, including: *Ash v Ash* [1972] Fam 135; *Carter-Fea v Carter-Fea* (1987) 17 *Family Law* 131; and *Buffery v Buffery* [1988] 2 FLR 365.

[78] Marital rape immunity lingered, albeit in slightly attenuated form, until 1991: *R v R* [1992] 1 AC 599; but wives also remained unequal for some time post-1970 in other spheres, notably as regards income taxation and in the practices of financial lending institutions.

[79] See n 61 on 'companionate' marriage.

[80] Parliamentarians' musing on the question had canvassed various spousal activities, including the cracking of nuts with one's teeth, interminable tv-watching, hoarding, the moving in to the matrimonial home of the mother-in-law, the absence of husbands [*sic*] from home for regimental dinners (perhaps a rather niche concern) and – most worryingly for that sub-group – the protracted absence from home of MPs.

[81] See also, for example, *Carew-Hunt v Carew-Hunt* [1972] *The Times* 28 June and (1972) 2 *Family Law* 106; *Birch v Birch* [1992] 1 FLR 564; *Hadjimilitis (Tsavliris) v Hadjimilitis* [2003] 1 FLR 31, cf the husband's claims (not pursued, it appears, with evidence at trial) reported by Millar (2002).

Amongst the most pointed is Dunn J's evaluation of Mr Herbert Livingstone-Stallard. The Livingstone-Stallard saga was surely always destined to end badly: for a 56-year-old retired insurance broker of old-fashioned ideals who had already been divorced for cruelty[82] by one younger wife to marry a strong-minded (and even younger) woman of 24 in any era, never mind 1969, has to ring alarm bells. By November 1972, after a decidedly rocky engagement, honeymoon and short period of married life, Mrs Livingstone-Stallard (no 2), Brenda, had moved with baby Jason to her mother's flat in Cotswold Road, Westcliff-on-Sea, leaving Herbert in their co-owned home at Thorpe Bay.[83] Alongside his stream of petty criticism, Herbert was found guilty of name-calling, kicking Brenda out of bed in a temper, criticising her manner of washing her underclothes and her entertainment of 'tradesmen' (in fact, their wedding photographer) with sherry in his absence, and forcibly ejecting her from the home in a violent assault that left Brenda in 'a very nervous state for about six weeks' and in need of medication. Dunn J did not notably hold back in describing the husband as

> self-opinionated, didactic and critical … [his approach being] to educate the wife to conform entirely to his standards … [subjecting the wife] to a constant atmosphere of criticism, disapproval and boorish behaviour.[84]

But in his autobiography, Sir Robin (Dunn J) records that a Family Division colleague, Neville Faulks, 'after reading the judgment said "I don't know why you didn't just say that the man was a shit". I replied that I preferred to let the facts speak for themselves.'[85] Either way, one can only imagine Mr Livingstone-Stallard's reaction to this absolute drubbing by Dunn J, enthusiastic rider to hounds and holder of the Military Cross for his bravery in the Second World War, clearly a pukka good chap of the best British traditions. (Mr Livingstone-Stallard's own war record is not known.)

Meanwhile, Mr O'Neill, of Salterton Road, Exmouth, has gone down in the family law annals for inflicting wildly over-ambitious and socially embarrassing DIY projects on Mrs O'Neill and their children, Jane and Derek. But it seems Mr O'Neill's greater sin, in the eyes of the Court of Appeal, was his casting doubt in a letter to his wife's solicitors on Jane and Derek's paternity, with no evidence whatsoever to support the claim. Roskill LJ joined his colleagues in considering that that alone (like the DIY enterprise) would have satisfied the behaviour fact, saying that 'to describe it as wicked is an understatement' – 'a deliberate attempt to wound the wife, *in the most cruel way in which it is possible for a husband to*

[82] According to *The Daily Mail* (20 March 1974) 3, reporting 'The husband who was always nagging.'
[83] ibid.
[84] *Livingstone-Stallard v Livingstone-Stallard* [1974] Fam 47, 55.
[85] Dunn (1993) 201.

wound his wife, by accusing her of gross infidelity'.[86] Given the myriad of other ways in which a husband might literally wound his wife (and worse), Roskill LJ's striking remarks echo the sort of comments made by the Victorian and Edwardian judges in defending a particular model of the good wife and mother in her domestic sphere.[87]

So there remains a sense of quite conservative, traditionally-minded judges seeking to save the institution of marriage by expunging from it those 'cads' whose uncivilised behaviour gave the institution a bad name – just as Hammerton's Victorian and Edwardian judges had done in relation to 'cruelty'. Whilst some readers might deplore the intrusion into the private lives of the parties[88] and the thrust of the judicial character assassinations that some spouses had to endure, it is hard to blame the judges for *undertaking* the task: they were simply applying the test that Parliament had set down.

V. Public Judgements about Judges Judging Spouses (Especially Regarding Sex)

Hammerton highlighted the old cruelty case law's role – aided by the uninhibited press reporting of these cases (pre-1926[89]) – in stimulating public discourse across the full social spectrum about marriage, conjugal behaviour, gender relations, the place of women in society and legal reform. As a result, he concludes, 'behaviour to one's spouse gradually become a matter of more conscious reflection and social consequence, for both litigants and the public'.[90] The commentariat – composed of emerging new types of 'expert' (including psychologists and agony aunts) in place of the nineteenth-century clergymen[91] – accordingly 'tended to focus increasingly on the quality of the sexual relationship rather than on more

[86] *O'Neill v O'Neill* [1975] 1 WLR 1118, 1125 (emphasis added).

[87] Cf Hammerton's discussion ((1992) 114–16) of husbands' invading their wives' right to manage the household and denigrating them in front of the servants.

[88] The trial judge in *O'Neill* had had to engage with arguments about the relative cleanliness of the husband.

[89] The Judicial Proceedings (Regulation of Reports) Act 1926 – prompted by a second, unrelated, long-running Russell divorce saga during the 1920s that attracted the consternation of George V – proscribed some of the more colourful narrative detail hitherto reported, outlawing the publication of any 'indecent matter … the publication of which would be calculated to injure public morals' (s 1(a)) and anything beyond a brief account of the details of matrimonial cases (s 1(b)). See Savage (1998). As she discusses, the powers-that-be were concerned that press reporting of divorce cases to an increasingly literate working class was not serving its intended functions, but rather undermining both public morality and (in case of aristocratic protagonists) the governing class's authority.

[90] Hammerton (1992),103.

[91] Griffin et al (2009) 13–14.

general companionate ideals'.[92] Many couples born in the first decades of the twentieth century regarded such public discussion of sex within marriage and the growing market of sexual advice literature as an improper intrusion into marital privacy.[93] But, as the century wore on and the 1960s came and went, the interest of the tabloid (and even broadsheet) press of the later twentieth century was piqued by divorce cases that examined the (in)adequacy of spouses' sex lives.

Thus it was that the *Daily Mail* in 1978 reported Mrs Diane Dowden's disappointment in the Court of Appeal:[94] 'No divorce for the once-a-month wife', despite sexually 'cold and indifferent' Donald's acquiescence in a divorce and his having left the family home in Shinfield, Reading.[95] The *Daily Mirror*'s headline was more emphatic, proclaiming 'Once a month is NOT enough: bedtime blues of a wife who yearned for more.'[96] But its article concluded with poor Diane's 'coming in for a blasting from the Marriage Guidance Council',[97] not about her sexual complaints but about her chosen manner of divorcing: '"If she had wanted a divorce it could have been done painlessly [ie using the two-year separation fact]. Sex once a month is unusual – but then there are no set guidelines. Everyone is different".' Helen Reece's concept of 'divorcing responsibly' was clearly already in evidence.[98]

That coverage set the precedent for the headline-grabbing case two years later: *Mason v Mason*, decided by Sir Robin Dunn, now in the Court of Appeal, alongside Ormrod LJ and Arnold P on 4 December 1980. Like *Dowden*, *Mason* was legally reported only in *Family Law*.[99] But the decision attracted widespread public notice, featuring as the front-page headline story for *The Sun* newspaper the following day (see Figure 8.1), on page 3 of several of the other tabloids[100] and the *Telegraph*, and (more discreetly and briefly) on page 4 of *The Times* and *The Guardian*. And so it is that we know rather more than we might otherwise have done about moustachioed 30-year-old petitioner Mr David Mason, motor mechanic originally of Isleworth, and his respondent fair-haired wife Mrs Brenda Mason, also aged 30, mother of their two boys, who denied that the marriage had broken down irretrievably.

[92] Hammerton, 168. The lead example is Marie Stopes' book (1918), which Lord Russell (in the 1920s case) had sent to Lady Russell to try to encourage her in that department: Savage (1998) 524. Coincidentally, the Lord Russell of the 1897 case, together with his second wife, Mollie, is reported (by Wikipedia) to have been a strong supporter of Stopes.

[93] See Szreter and Fisher (2010) 349–52.

[94] *Dowden v Dowden* (1978) 8 *Family Law* 106. See also *Pheasant v Pheasant* [1972] Fam 202, where the argument also failed.

[95] *Daily Mail* (5 November 1977) 10.

[96] Greig (1977).

[97] Later to become Relate and whose President from 1949 was Lord Denning.

[98] Reece (2003); and see Burgoyne et al (1987) 17.

[99] (1980) 11 *Family Law* 143.

[100] Including *The Daily Mirror* and the *Daily Mail*.

Figure 8.1 'Sex Once a Week is Enough', *The Sun*, 5 December 1980 (*The Sun/News Licencing*)

THE Sun

12p

TODAY'S TV: PAGES 14 and 15

PREMIER AND HIS MISTRESS KILLED IN PLANE CRASH

See Page 11

SEX ONCE A WEEK IS ENOUGH

Three judges cancel divorce

By SUN REPORTER

SEX once a week is enough to keep a marriage together, three Appeal Court judges decided yesterday.

They overturned a ruling by a divorce court that it was unreasonable for a wife to ration sex to Saturday nights.

ANGRY

FEAR

BENN LEFT OUT IN THE COLD

12 posts. Mr Benn came 13th. Top of the poll was Roy Hattersley who now ranks No 3 after leader Michael Foot and Denis Healey.

See Page Two

CHARLES IN THE TEMPLE OF LOVE—Page 3

David's complaint was that Brenda would not permit sexual intercourse between them more than once a week, an event that customarily occurred on Saturdays.[101] In order to help ease Brenda's fears of further pregnancies, which had earlier in their marriage resulted in no sexual intercourse at all,

[101] *The Sun* (5 December 1980) 1.

David had had a vasectomy. He needed to have sex on at least 12 occasions over a three-month period (on average once a week) before going for a test that would ascertain whether the procedure had been effective. The Court of Appeal overturned the trial judge's decision on the behaviour fact, thereby depriving David of his divorce. The judge had overlooked both David's own evidence that the couple had indeed had the required amount of sex to permit testing of the procedure and David's failure to offer to use a 'sheath' to allay Brenda's fears further. So it was that Dunn LJ concluded, giving the lead judgment, that it was impossible to see on the evidence how the judge could possibly have concluded 'that sexual intercourse about once a week after the vasectomy was so unreasonable that it justified him in saying that the wife had behaved in such a way that her husband could not reasonably be expected to live with her'. He also noted the fact that David was, by then, embroiled in an affair with a married woman, identified in the newspaper coverage simply as 'pretty 29 year-old divorcee', Alison, for whom he had left Mrs Mason, setting up home together in Higher Union St, Torquay. As the newspapers reported, this early December bombshell had dashed David and Alison's Christmas or New Year wedding plans, though Alison was quoted as observing quite stoically that they had waited quite a while already, so could wait a bit longer.[102]

As Sir Robin remarks in his autobiography, he was

> careful to confine [his] remarks to the facts of the case and not to make any generalised comments. Roger [Ormerod LJ], however, had no such inhibitions. 'I have never', he thundered, 'heard such an absurd proposition that for a wife to limit sexual intercourse to once a week constitutes unreasonable behaviour [*sic*] towards her husband.'

He goes on to relate:

> The press reacted at once. That evening, before I returned home, Judy [his wife] had been rung up by a reporter and asked for her reaction to the judgment. Wisely she replied, 'No comment'. Next morning the story was all over the front pages and featured in the BBC news.[103]

It seems that Lady Dunn was not alone in the unwanted call from the press. Lord Hailsham mentioned the incident during parliamentary debates on the Contempt of Court Bill a month or so later:

> The headline in the press was 'Once a week is enough'. I do not know whether once a week is enough; I am too old to care. What I do know is that no fewer than three newspapers tried to interview the wives of the judges concerned.[104]

[102] ibid 2. Mr Mason would be able to get his divorce in three-and-a-half years under the five-year separation fact.

[103] Dunn (1993) 241. Compare the discretion of Lady Dunn and her judicial-wife friends here with the attendance of the wives of two judges in the *Jackson* case, who joined their husbands up on the bench: Bibbings (2014) 161.

[104] *Hansard*, HL Deb 20 January 1981, vol 416, col 409.

Whilst the press's attempts to obtain conjugal insights from the judges' wives failed, the papers nevertheless dug out what they could about the judges' personal, marital and fertility histories (though, interestingly, made nothing of the fact that 'twice-married' Sir John Arnold had been the first divorced person to be appointed as a Family Division judge). *The Sun*'s front page coverage featured a photo of Brenda Mason – '… still in love with her husband' – flanked at one side by mug shots of the judges and brief personal details, their ages prominent in larger bold font.[105]

The intended implication was, presumably, that these chaps, more than twice Mr Mason's age, were out of touch with the amount of sex that a vigorous young husband could reasonably expect to have – precisely the sort of fear that Dr Gray MP had harboured. Notably, all three judges were of the same generation as the participants (born between 1901–31) in Szreter and Fisher's study of marital sexual relations prior to 1963.[106] Those spouses did not regard the frequency of sex as an indicator of the quality of their sex lives; indeed, the authors report their participants' being 'baffled' by questions about the frequency of sexual intercourse in their marriages.[107] Since these couples also spurned any sort of public discussion of their sex lives (even with close friends) or advice literature, they were largely content in their ignorance of what 'normal' marital sex consisted of – unlike the *Cosmopolitan/Men's Health* generations.[108]

Meanwhile, the cartoonist Raymond Jackson, known as JAK, produced 'Is it Saturday already?' for *The Daily Express* (see Figure 8.2) This featured half a dozen bewigged and begowned, elderly, male judges dashing out of The Strand entrance to Royal Courts of Justice towards a Rolls Royce motor car, saluted by a police constable and observed by a pair of city gents holding their 'Once a week sex …' newspapers next to a newsstand displaying the headline 'Only on a Saturday'. Sir Robin Dunn records that his downstairs loo was adorned by the original, sent to him by JAK.[109]

So, the papers had their fun. But there was a serious side to the coverage as well, the judgment providing an opportunity for wider discussion about modern marriage that a 'No sex please, we're British'[110] readership might otherwise have avoided.[111] The spokesman for the National Marriage Guidance Council was quoted on page 2 of *The Sun* as saying:

> We know of couples who are very happily married who don't have sex at all. Others find they need sex more frequently than once a week, others less often. It is not the frequency of the sex that is important but the quality of the relationship.

[105] The *Daily Mail* was to adopt a similar composition for its front page featuring 'Enemies of the People': *Daily Mail* (4 November 2016) in response to *R (Miller and Dos Santos) v Secretary of State for Exiting the European Union and others* [2016] EWHC 2768 (Admin).

[106] Szreter and Fisher (2010).

[107] ibid 347.

[108] ibid 357–59; cf Tyler (2004).

[109] Dunn (1993) 241.

[110] This critically-panned but very popular farce hit the West End in 1971 and ran for 15 years.

[111] Cf the common fare of modern lifestyle magazines: Tyler (2004).

Figure 8.2 'Is it Saturday already?', *Daily Express*, 5 December 1980 (*Jak/Daily Express/Reach Licensing*)

Meanwhile, an unnamed doctor at the Institute of Psychiatry was quoted in several papers, including the *Daily Mail* under the disheartening (or perhaps, for some readers, reassuring) sub-heading 'Fading passion of newly-weds',[112] for his or her provision of the data that, whilst newly-weds made love five times a week on average in the first year, thereafter most couples made love twice a week on average. This happily corresponds with *The Joy of Sex*'s observation (in 1974) that two or three times a week was a 'common rate', whilst urging readers not to 'be compulsive about frequency … You aren't being scored.'[113] But the doctor quoted in the *Daily Mail* also said that it was quite common for one partner to want sex more often than the other, and that treatment involved trying to persuade a couple to agree on some sort of compromise.[114] And the *Daily Mirror*'s inimitable Marje Proops[115] took the opportunity to dole out some sage advice about couples' sexual compatibility and the need for frank discussion before marriage:

> Lord Justice Ormond [*sic*] is a brave man when he lays down the law on the frequency (or infrequency) of sexual intercourse. Couples have different sex drives, not only from each other but at different times in their lives. There are many well-worn jokes about the excuses wives make to avoid sex and lots of equally well-worn jokes about husbands who think of nothing else. The truth is that there is no 'normal' pattern. It's vital for a couple to discuss their sexual needs frankly before they marry. It's no use a man who needs sex every day thinking he's ever going to change a girl who is satisfied with it once

[112] 'Only on Saturdays!' *Daily Mail* (5 December 1980) 3.

[113] Comfort (1974) 65, 67.

[114] The latest data, collected since 1990 in the National Surveys of Sexual Attitudes and Lifestyles, show declining frequency of sex in marriage: Mercer et al (2013).

[115] Journalist Marjorie Proops OBE (1911–96), married mother of one son, was best known for her long-running agony aunt column in the *Daily Mirror*.

> a week – and not very keen on it at that … Since each individual is unique I don't see how any judge can put a time span on love.[116]

Whilst the rather 'proper' women's magazines of the time did not cover stories like that of the Masons,[117] the advice pages – notably Virginia Ironside's column in *Woman* magazine – gave readers insight into other women's marriages and advice about how to deal with various types of disappointment.

It is probably also not a coincidence that *The Sun* placed a strong editorial piece calling for tax justice for working wives immediately below its page 2 coverage of *Mason*, bemoaning the fact that 'for almost two centuries women have been treated by the tax authorities as second-class citizens', subsumed into their husbands' fiscal identities. Gender and family justice cut both ways, and there was still work to be done for wives to gain full legal equality.[118]

VI. Concluding Thoughts

The Masons' case and its coverage illustrate how the behaviour fact, like the cruelty fact before it, required the judges to articulate their views about the marital relationship and what parties' expectations of marriage should be – and in turn stimulated public debate about matters of concern to many couples. Importantly, whilst the 'teaser' effect of the headlines may have had a frivolous, naughty seaside postcard character,[119] the media took the opportunity to discuss the wider issues in a relatively light way, prompting their readers to reflect on their own situations. But the tabloid media can be excused their interest in the judges' personal lives; building on Eekelaar's argument set out in Section I, it is hardly unreasonable that the public should be interested in the 'credentials' of those adjudicating on their matrimonial troubles.

That the judges found themselves having to lay down the law in this area was, of course, not their fault. They had been consigned to that fate by Parliament, and trod a careful line ensuring that the 'facts' prescribed by the 1969 Act were not interpreted in such a way as to render them nugatory, given Parliament's clear intention not to allow divorce on grounds of mere incompatibility.[120] So the real question is whether the *law* should have anything to say about marital conduct at

[116] 'And Marje Proops Says …' *Daily Mirror* (5 December 1980) 3.

[117] I searched *Woman's Weekly* and *Woman* magazine around December/January 1980–81 for signs of *Mason* with no result, but found a lot of scary knitting patterns, Mills & Boon-style short stories and recipe suggestions.

[118] Though *The Sun*'s page 3 model feature, which will have appeared opposite this item, persisted until 2015.

[119] Exactly the sort of thing that the promoters of the 1926 Act feared: see n 89.

[120] See, for example, the meticulous care taken by the judges in cases such as *Pheasant v Pheasant* [1972] Fam 202 and *Santos v Santos* [1972] Fam 247 to interpret the behaviour and separation facts meaningfully.

all, beyond the law of domestic abuse (and related issues such as arrangements for children) and relevant criminal laws.

That question has now been answered in the negative by the Divorce, Dissolution and Separation Act 2020, bringing this centuries-long jurisprudential saga to a close and finally allowing – in effect – mere incompatibility to ground a divorce. Given the overwhelming response to Tini Owens' predicament in 2018, the withdrawal of the law from this arena will surely be welcomed by most, not least the judges who will now be spared this very occasional task. Indeed, I suspect that Sir William Scott – the human being, not the judge – would thoroughly approve.

References

Bibbings, L (2014) *Binding Men: Stories about violence and the law in late Victorian England* (London, Routledge).

Biggs, J (1962) *The Concept of Matrimonial Cruelty* (London, The Athlone Press).

Bromley, P (1971) *Family Law*, 4th edn (London, Butterworths).

Burgoyne, J, Ormrod, R and Richards, M (1987) *Divorce Matters* (London, Penguin).

Chester, R and Streather, J (1972) 'Cruelty in English Divorce: Some Empirical Findings' 34 Journal of Marriage and Family 706.

Comfort, A (1974) *The Joy of Sex: A Gourmet Guide to Lovemaking* (London, Quartet Books).

Cretney, S (1974) *Principles of Family Law*, 1st edn (London, Sweet & Maxwell).

—— (2010) *Family Law in the Twentieth Century: A History* (Oxford, Oxford University Press).

Dunn, R (1993) *Sword and Wig: Memoirs of a Lord Justice* (London, Quiller Press).

Eekelaar, J (2017) *Family Law and Personal Life*, 2nd edn (Oxford, Oxford University Press).

Fisher, L (2013) 'Marriage and Companionate Ideals Since 1750' in S Toulalan and K Fisher (eds), *The Routledge History of Sex and the Body, 1500 to the Present* (London, Routledge).

Frost, G (1999) 'A Shock to Marriage?: the Clitheroe Case and the Victorians' in G Robb and N Erber (eds), *Disorder in the Court: Trials and Sexual Conflict at the Turn of the Century* (London, Macmillan).

Greig, S (1977) 'Once a month is NOT enough: bedtime blues of a wife who yearned for more' *Daily Mirror* (5 November) 3.

Griffin, B, Delap, L and Wills, A (2009) 'Introduction: The Politics of Domestic Authority in Britain since 1800' in L Delap, B Griffin and A Wills (eds), *The Politics of Domestic Authority in Britain since 1800* (Basingstoke, Palgrave Macmillan).

Hall, J (1974) 'Family Law – Behaviour One is Not Expected to Endure' 33 *Cambridge Law Journal* 219.

Hammerton, AJ (1992) *Cruelty and Companionship: Conflict in Nineteenth-Century Married Life* (London, Routledge).

Kirkpatrick, G (1964) 'Incompatibility as a Ground for Divorce' 47 *Marquette Law Review* 453.

Law Commission (1968) *Third Annual Report 1967–68* (London, HMSO), Appendix 3: 'Reform of Grounds of Divorce'.

Lee, B (1974) *Divorce Law Reform in England* (London, Peter Owen Ltd).

McGregor, O (1957) *Divorce in England* (London, Heinemann).

Mercer, C, Tanton, C, Prah, P, Erens, B, Sonnenberg, P, Clifton, S, Macdowall, W, Lewis, R, Field, N, Datta, J, Copas, A, Phelps, A, Wellings, K and Johnson, A (2013) 'Changes in sexual attitudes and lifestyles in Britain through the lifecourse and over time: findings from the National Surveys of Sexual Attitudes and Lifestyles (Natsal)' 382 *Lancet* 1781.

Millar, C (2002) 'I feared wife spending my £50m' *The Standard* (26 June 2002) at www.standard.co.uk/hp/front/i-feared-wife-spending-my-ps50m-6327747.html.

Morton Commission (1956) *Royal Commission on Marriage and Divorce* (Cmnd 9678) (London, HMSO).

Rayden (1971) *Rayden's Law and Practice in Divorce and Family Matters in the High Court, County Courts and Magistrates' Courts*, 11th edn, ed-in-chief J Jackson (London, Butterworths).

Reece, H (2003) *Divorcing Responsibly* (Oxford, Hart Publishing).

Savage, G (1998) 'Erotic Stories and Public Decency: Newspaper Reporting of Divorce Proceedings in England' 41 *The Historical Journal* 511.

—— (1999) '"The Magistrates are Men": Working-Class Marital Conflict and Appeals from the Magistrates' Court to the Divorce Court after 1895' in G Robb and N Erber (eds), *Disorder in the Court: Trials and Sexual Conflict at the Turn of the Century* (London, Macmillan).

—— (2009) '"… the instrument of an animal function": Marital Rape and Sexual Cruelty in the Divorce Court, 1858–1908' in L Delap, B Griffin and A Wills (eds), *The Politics of Domestic Authority in Britain since 1800* (Basingstoke, Palgrave Macmillan).

Stopes, MC (1918) *Married Love or Love in Marriage* (London, Putnam).

Sumner Holmes, A (1999) '"Don't Frighten the Horses": the Russell Divorce Case' in G Robb and N Erber (eds), *Disorder in the Court: Trials and Sexual Conflict at the Turn of the Century* (London, Macmillan).

Szreter, S and Fisher, K (2009) 'Love and Authority in Mid-Twentieth-Century Marriages: Sharing and Caring' in L Delap, B Griffin and A Wills (eds), *The Politics of Domestic Authority in Britain since 1800* (Basingstoke, Palgrave Macmillan).

—— (2010) *Sex before the Sexual Revolution: Intimate Life in England 1918–1963* (Cambridge, Cambridge University Press).

Trinder, L, Braybrook, D, Bryson, C, Coleman, L, Houlston, C and Sefton, M (2017) *Finding Fault? Divorce Law and Practice in England and Wales* (London, Nuffield Foundation).

Trinder, L and Sefton, M (2018) *No Contest: Defended Divorce in England & Wales* (London, Nuffield Foundation).

Tyler, M (2004) 'Managing Between the Sheets: Lifestyle Magazines and the Management of Sexuality in Everyday Life' 7 *Sexualities* 81.

Williamson, M (2011) 'Fair Wear and Tear' 8 *Cultural and Social History* 233.

9

Telling Tales? Establishing Irretrievable Breakdown under the Matrimonial Causes Act 1973

LIZ TRINDER

I. Introduction

For a very long time, getting a divorce in England and Wales has involved being able to tell a persuasive story. Those stories have taken increasingly standardised formats, from the 'hotel divorces' of the inter-war years, to what became a routinised production line of oral hearings after the implementation of the Divorce Reform Act 1969. This chapter explores the final act in this drama, where written statements of case produced under the 'special procedure' in the mid-2010s resulted in divorce narratives in their most formulaic and ritualised form.

The analysis draws upon 300 statements of case from a nationally representative sample of undefended cases from 2014–15, collected for the *Finding Fault* study.[1] The analysis makes use of the 'narrative turn' in the social sciences over recent decades to explore how those stories are produced in, and for, a very particular legal context. Drawing on comparisons with both the literature on legal narratives and Riessman's sociological work on non-legal narratives of divorce,[2] it highlights the distinctiveness of these statements of case. The analysis also underlines the extent to which legal scrutiny of divorce in the mid-2010s had become an administrative routine, yet still framed within an inquisitorial process, set within an

[1] *Finding Fault* was a large, multi-method study conducted in 2015–17 to examine the operation of the divorce law in England and Wales. It included qualitative interviews with petitioners and respondents, focus groups and qualitative interviews with family lawyers, analysis of court files of 300 undefended and 150 defended cases, observation of 292 cases being scrutinised, and interviews with legal advisers and judges. The project was funded by the Nuffield Foundation, but the views expressed are those of the author and not necessarily the Foundation's. The project homepage, including a full methodological report is available at www.nuffieldfoundation.org/project/finding-fault-divorce-law-in-practice-in-england-and-wales.

[2] Riessman (1990).

adversarial family justice system. The chapter therefore gives some further insight into the extent to which law reform was required. It also contributes to the literature on legal narratives, which has hitherto largely focused on oral narratives in a courtroom context.

II. A History of Story-Telling in Divorce

Ritualised or formulaic story-telling to achieve a divorce in England and Wales is nothing new.[3] Petitioners, often in concert with respondents, have been engaging in ritualised story-telling for many decades. The most dramatic, or notorious, examples were the staged 'hotel adulteries' of the 1920s, where the respondent arranged to be seen in a hotel bed with a supposed female partner, but who had been paid to play the role.[4] The practice was fictionalised in another narrative – AP Herbert's book *Holy Deadlock*[5] – which was, in turn, a major influence on the reforming Matrimonial Causes Act 1937.

The 1937 Act extended the grounds of divorce, but also the range of stories that could be told: as Chester and Streather noted, 'whatever the client's reason for wanting divorce, the lawyer's function is to discover grounds'.[6]

The ritualised telling of divorce stories continued under the Divorce Reform Act 1969 (DRA), later consolidated into the Matrimonial Causes Act 1973 (MCA). The MCA does, in effect, invite petitioners to tell a story to 'satisfy the court' about the irretrievable breakdown of their marriage with reference to one of five facts.[7] The conduct-based or (as experienced by the vast majority of respondents in practice) fault facts, in particular, invite stories about what has happened – that the respondent has committed adultery,[8] that the respondent has behaved in such a way that the petitioner cannot reasonably be expected to live with the respondent,[9] or that the respondent has deserted the petitioner for two years.[10]

In the early years of the DRA/MCA, that story would be produced on paper in the divorce petition and then tested orally, with the court assigned an inquisitorial role 'to inquire, so far as it reasonably can, into the facts alleged by the petitioner and into any facts alleged by the respondent'.[11] In practice, by the mid-1970s, if not

[3] It is also not restricted to England and Wales. See, for example, Rheinstein (1972), especially ch 4, for a history of collusion, migratory divorce and annulment in the United States.

[4] See Stone (1990), Cretney (2003) and Probert (1999).

[5] Herbert (1934).

[6] Chester and Streather (1972) 712.

[7] DRA 1969, s 2, now MCA 1973, s 1. Three of the facts rely on conduct or fault: adultery, behaviour and desertion. Otherwise, the petitioner must rely on separation for two years with the consent of the respondent, otherwise separation for five years.

[8] MCA 1973, s 1(2)(a).

[9] ibid s 1(2)(b).

[10] ibid s 1(2)(c).

[11] ibid s 1(3).

earlier, the court had largely given up any pretence of effective inquiry. Instead, an observational study in the mid-1970s showed that oral hearings had become a production line, where lawyers took their clients through their well-rehearsed answers in under 10 minutes, and with minimal chance of the court refusing the decree.[12] As one petitioner commented to the researchers, 'you feel you're in some kind of play. You are learning a part. She (the barrister) says, "well, I will ask you the following questions and you will answer in the following way."'[13]

A spike in divorces following the introduction of the 1969 Act resulted in the introduction of a 'special procedure' in 1973 for childless two-year separation cases, whereby scrutiny relied solely on written submissions with no need for the parties to attend court. The 'special procedure' was extended to all undefended divorces in 1977.[14] With even less information available to the court, the Law Commission noted in 1990 that it was 'practically impossible to test the facts' in undefended cases, and that the 'present law pretends that the court is conducting an inquiry' but it can do no such thing.[15] In 1990, the Law Commission concluded, in quite strong terms, that the law was confusing and misleading, and that law and practice allowed, and even encouraged, parties to lie or (at least) exaggerate.[16]

Three decades on, the scrutiny process had become even more streamlined, primarily to reduce the financial costs to the family justice system. Assistant Justices Clerks (also known as Legal Advisers), rather than judges, were processing the majority of undefended decree nisi applications.[17]

The types of stories that can be told have also been reduced. Greater recognition of the harm that can be done by allegations of fault, contrary to the wider objectives of family policy, has led to a number of changes. These include revisions to the Family Procedure Rules that discourage the naming of the co-respondent in adultery cases.[18] They also include revisions to the Law Society *Family Law Protocol*[19] and the Resolution *Code of Practice*,[20] both of which emphasise the desirability of a constructive and non-confrontational approach to divorce, particularly in relation to behaviour petitions.

Taken with the introduction of the special procedure in the 1970s, substantial changes have been made to practice and procedure in lieu of substantive law reform. The *Finding Fault* study in 2017 established that the few minutes of scrutiny time per case were focused on checking that the identities of the parties were correctly established and the minimum ingredients of one of the five facts had

[12] Elston, Fuller and Murch (1975).
[13] ibid 614.
[14] It also applies to civil partnership dissolution under the Family Procedure Rules 2010, r 7.19.
[15] Law Commission (1990) para 2.11.
[16] ibid paras 2.7–2.21.
[17] The power was bestowed under the Crime and Courts Act 2013.
[18] Family Procedure Rules 2010, Practice Direction 7A – Procedure for Applications in Matrimonial and Civil Partnership Proceedings, para 2.1.
[19] First published in 2002, now in its 4th edn (2015).
[20] Available at https://resolution.org.uk/membership/our-code-of-practice/

been described, not whether the particulars were true, or even plausible.[21] As in the 1970s, the risk of refusal on substantive grounds (rather than technical paperwork or other deficiencies) was absolutely minimal.

The combined effect has been to reduce, or streamline, as far as possible the court's responsibility for processing undefended divorces. In doing so, it has meant a move even further from a judicial process and ever further towards a purely administrative process for undefended cases. In practice that means that the court focuses on whether a fact has been described, rather than testing the veracity of the story.

III. Narratives in Law and Lore

Although the routinised nature of scrutiny has been evident for decades, there has been no research to date on the narratives that are used to secure those divorces. What exactly, or more precisely how little, is needed to secure a divorce? And how do these narratives compare to those told in other legal contexts?

Over recent decades there has been an explosion of research interest in narratives as social scientists have recognised the pervasive nature of story-telling in human culture, including in legal contexts. As Peter Brooks puts it:

> Narrative appears to be one of our large, all-pervasive ways of organizing and speaking the world – the way we make sense of meanings that unfold in and through time. The law, focused on putting facts in the world into coherent form and presenting them persuasively – to make a 'case' – must always be intimately intertwined with rhetoric and narrative.[22]

What exactly counts as a narrative is open to debate, but Olson, writing in a legal context, suggests that the minimal ingredients of a narrative include 'agents with human-like subjectivity, involve changes or a description of human-like experience, and take place in some identifiable space and time'.[23] There is general agreement amongst narrative scholars, however, that narratives are contextual. They are not fixed stories to be told in the same way regardless of time, place or audience, but draw upon specific historical contexts and social norms and expectations.[24] This is relevant to any discussion of narratives in law. There is likely to be a difference between the form and content of narratives told to friends, family or therapists, to one's lawyer or in front of a jury.[25] There are also likely to be differences between narratives offered or elicited in adversarial, compared to inquisitorial, systems.[26]

[21] Trinder et al (2017).
[22] Brooks (1996) 14.
[23] Olson (2018) 23.
[24] Riessman (1990).
[25] Brooks (1996) 17–18.
[26] Olson (2018) 26.

Riessman emphasises that narratives are also purposive, not just 'innocent' stories. Narratives are a means for people to make sense of events in their own lives, but they are also a means to persuade others, often in making a moral claim. That purposive element is of clear importance in a legal context, where the goal is to persuade a decision maker.[27]

Given that narratives can alienate as well as persuade,[28] the task of analysts is therefore to try to understand what makes stories more or less persuasive, or credible, in any particular context.[29] The evidence to date is that narratives tend to be more emotionally resonant, and therefore persuasive, when they are particularised and unique, rather than being generic or over-standardised.[30]

At the same time, there is also evidence that narratives are more effective when they build upon familiar cultural beliefs and norms, or 'doxa'.[31] In a divorce context, Riessman has explored how narrators – the former spouses – draw upon a familiar cultural script of the failed dream of the companionate marriage to explain and justify their decision to divorce.[32] In a legal context, Gewirtz suggests that lawyers might be most successful if they can shape their narrative to fit specific cultural norms.[33] In rape cases, for example, this might draw upon shared beliefs about how women should behave in public spaces.[34]

There are also specific features of legal narratives and story-telling that are worth noting. A number of scholars have argued that the law, at least in courtroom contexts, generally seeks to control how narratives are told, in order to formalise accounts. Di Donato, for example, has explored how lawyers act as translators, turning a lay story into an appropriate, and more formal, legal narrative.[35] Similarly, Ewick and Silbey have traced how lawyers typically 'objectify' lay stories to orientate them towards the facts of who has done what, how, when, why and where.[36] In court, there is evidence that the story-telling preferences of lay parties may be disrupted by a turn-taking question-and-answer format.[37] This disjunction between lay story-telling and the rational and structured approach of the law may mean that some will be disadvantaged in their capacity to tell an institutionally relevant or competent story in specific legal contexts.[38] Litigants in person and women and religious minorities may be particularly affected.

[27] Gewirtz (1996) 5.
[28] Love (1998) 92.
[29] Gewirtz (1996) 6.
[30] Gewirtz (1996).
[31] ibid 8–9.
[32] Riessman (1990) 24.
[33] Gewirtz (1996).
[34] Brooks (2006) 9.
[35] Di Donato (2020).
[36] Ewick and Silbey (1998).
[37] See especially Brooks (1996) and Ehrlich (2015).
[38] Ehrlich (2015).

IV. Short Stories: Eliciting the Statements of Case

For those seeking a divorce in England and Wales, the context in which narratives are elicited is currently[39] the divorce petition or Form D8. On that form, petitioners are required to tick one box to confirm that their marriage has broken down irretrievably, and a second box to identify which fact they are relying upon as evidence of irretrievable breakdown. There is then a blank text box in which petitioners are required to set out the statement of case.

In stark contrast to a formal trial, the process of eliciting divorce narratives is therefore quite unstructured. The narrative has to be in written form, but there are few other constraints. It is left to petitioners to decide what details are relevant and how they wish to present them. Nor is there any real risk that the story will be disrupted or challenged by any counter-narrative from the respondent, as in a trial or most other legal processes. Unless a respondent is one of the few to take the legally and financially challenging route of defending the divorce, they are given no formal opportunity to comment on the petitioner's story about why their marriage has ended.[40]

The one message that the court does give on the petition form is that the statement should be short. The instructions preceding the text box – 'please state briefly any relevant details about the fact(s) on which you rely' – give a very clear direction that long accounts are not required. The message about brevity in the rubric is reinforced by the physical size of the text box for the statement of case. During the fieldwork, the non-expandable text box was the width of the page and just 5.5cm deep, limiting how much could be written without having to resort to additional sheets of paper.[41]

As mechanisms to elicit legal narratives, the divorce petition is therefore quite unusual in its very limited attempt to shape what is included, as well as the lack of opportunity to elicit counter-narratives. The only real attempt to influence narratives is in relation to length. What this appears to reflect is a reorientation of the role of the court in scrutinising divorce. Instead of the detailed inquisition of the nineteenth and early twentieth centuries, the court's expectations are minimal – just a couple of sentences will do to evidence irretrievable breakdown, rather than affidavits, inquiry agents, cross-examination and the like, however routinised. The forms themselves reflect the court's role as an administrator processing divorce claims, and an already busy administrator at that, not an inquisitor.

[39] At least until the implementation of the Divorce, Dissolution and Separation Act 2020.

[40] Some respondents did add comments in the margins of the paper Acknowledgement of Service. That limited opportunity was not available in the electronic version of that document.

[41] The software available to lawyers did permit the text box to be expandable.

V. The Statements of Case – The Routinisation of Narratives

Given the emphasis on brevity in the D8 petition form, it is not surprising that the statements of case were short. The median length was just 67 words, literally two or three sentences to tell the tale of why the marriage had ended.

There was some variation in the sample. Statements of case for represented parties were longer than those of litigants in person, at a median 126.5 words compared to 46 words. That said, there was considerable variation within each group, with very long statements from some litigants in person and some very short statements from represented parties.[42]

There were also significant differences in statement length according to which fact was used to evidence irretrievable breakdown. The three separation-related statements of case were typically the shortest, 36 words for two years with consent, 33 words for five years and 34 for desertion.[43] The median for adultery was not much higher, at 50 words. By far the longest statements, as might be expected, were those for the behaviour fact, at 193 words. That said, behaviour statements were the most variable of all the facts in their length.[44]

Aside from the brevity of the statements for the non-behaviour facts, what was striking was how standardised or formulaic almost all of them were. The great majority were simply restatements of the relevant fact, with minimal additional detail. Thus the formula for separation statements was to state that the parties had separated and to give a date of the separation, sometimes adding that the parties remained separated. A typical example was case M141: 'The P and R separated on [date] and have lived separate and apart since that date.' Two-year separation cases might also add that the respondent consented to the decree.

A typical adultery statement simply noted the fact of adultery, with no names and no details. Case L124, for example, simply stated that 'The respondent has formed an adulterous relationship with another woman and the relationship is continuing.' Slightly longer adultery statements might include more detail, such as frequency and general location of the adultery.

The non-behaviour cases, therefore, produced stories in their most reduced form. Human actors and events within a specific timeframe were referenced, but in the most minimal fashion to satisfy the legal requirements. Only rarely were there attempts to go beyond restating the very basic facts required. This stands, of

[42] This was reflected in high standard deviations of 117.551 for the litigant in person cases and 147.842 for represented cases.

[43] The brevity of the desertion petitions might seem surprising given that desertion is a 'fault' or conduct fact with a very long history as a matrimonial offence. However, it is now rarely used and then often by mistake by litigants in person.

[44] The standard deviation for behaviour petitions was 151.152, compared to 69.876 for adultery and less than 38 for all the separation facts.

course, in stark contrast to the elaborate processes required to secure divorce in the past, most notably the hotel divorces, but even for the production-line, pre-special procedure divorces of the early 1970s. That said, although the level of detail is very different between the pre- and post-special procedure divorces, the resulting narratives were equally formulaic.

In contrast, behaviour narratives were necessarily more varied in content than separation or adultery statements. The open-ended nature of the behaviour fact means that, in contrast to simply asserting the reality of separation or adultery, a petitioner has to set out the nature of the behaviour and its impact on the petitioner. However, most remained formulaic.

VI. Behaviour Statements as Habitual Narratives

Riessman's analysis of divorce narratives gathered for sociological research provides a very helpful point of contrast to understand the structure, content and purpose of the behaviour statements of case produced as part of the legal divorce. In Riessman's sample, most divorce narratives were in what she calls story form. Those story narratives are distinctive in that the teller creates a life world and then a change or transition is described, such as a problem overcome. Stories broadly follow a classic narrative structure, as set out by Labov,[45] starting with an abstract (the plot summary) and moving on to an orientation (to place, time, characters and situation), a statement of the events (complicating action), the attitude of the narrator towards them (evaluation) and resolution of the action, concluding with a coda (or ending) that returns the narrator to the present.

As Riessman argues, stories are told to make a point, typically a moral one. The evocation of the storyworld and the transition – for example, from victim of domestic abuse to survivor – is an effective means to engage the listener and to make the story compelling and persuasive.

But narratives are contextual. They are told in a particular context to achieve a specific purpose. Riessman argues that for her research sample, the teller's task was to convince both themselves and the listener (a researcher, not a lawyer or judge) that the marriage was seriously troubled and that the teller was justified in leaving it.[46] The primary task for petitioners is different: to persuade the court that they meet the legal requirements for divorce and that they have either been separated for a sufficient period or the respondent has engaged in relevant conduct. In contrast to Riessman's sample, the court is not a deeply fascinated researcher but rather a busy administrator, who has already signalled, via the format of the petition form, that it is not interested in long stories of what went wrong in someone's marriage.

[45] Labov (1972).

[46] The narratives in Riessman's sample were elicited simply by a question 'What were the main causes of your separation?' Riessman (1990) 223.

There were multiple examples of story narratives amongst our sample of behaviour petitions, but by far the most common narratives were what Riessman calls habitual narratives. These are narratives that capture the general course of something over time, such as a marriage.[47] Habitual narratives are still organised temporally, from the beginning of the marriage to the end, but describe recurring difficulties, rather than concrete or specific events. In contrast to the story form, Riessman argues that in an habitual narrative the listener does not live or experience the story with the narrator, but they will understand what has happened.

A classic example of an habitual statement of case, and indeed one that is typical of the whole data set, was given in this extract from case L126, involving two unrepresented parties:

- The respondent on numerous occasions has stated that she does not love the petitioner anymore, which has caused the petitioner distress
- The respondent has consistently shown little interest in socialising with the petitioner in private or public
- The respondent is often selfish in the way she behaves and has in recent times not prioritised the parties [sic] relationship in any way
- The respondent does not sleep in the same bed with petitioner since [date] causing petitioner distress
- The respondent has had a bad temper which she has lost on numerous occasions causing petitioner distress
- The respondent has never liked the petitioner's family despite the petitioner's best efforts and has never socialised with them as much as petitioner has requested causing the petitioner distress.[48]

The narrative draws entirely on familiar ideas about the failure of the dream of the companionate marriage, based on emotional intimacy, companionship and sexual fulfilment.[49] It is a description of a relationship that has drifted apart, evidenced by a loss of emotional investment in the couple relationship and pursuit of individual interests away from the partner and their world. In terms of content, the narrative is very similar to many of those of Riessman's informants, who also told stories about the failed dream of a companionate marriage.

Where the L126 narrative differs from most of Riessman's informants is in the adoption of the habitual narrative rather than story form. There is no chronology. The habitual narratives in the sample, like L126, instead used bullet points to itemise the respondent's behaviour. Each bullet was then typically used to describe a specific behaviour or examples of a general behaviour to establish a general pattern of events. In L126, like many others, each behaviour was then presented as recurring or repeated, rather than as a one-off. In L126, for example, acts of commission

[47] ibid 84.

[48] Any dates and/or identifying features have been omitted or changed in all the statements that are reproduced here. The use of bullet points is a common feature of the statements of case, particularly habitual narratives.

[49] Riessman (1990) 24, 37.

were described as occurring on 'numerous occasions', 'consistently' or 'often',[50] while acts of omission were described as 'not' or 'never' happening.[51]

Another common formula was to team the itemised behaviour with a description of the impact of that behaviour on the petitioner, reflecting the statutory test for the behaviour fact.[52] In four of the six bullets in L126, the listing of the behaviour was followed, rather unimaginatively and repetitively, by stating that the behaviour of the respondent had caused the petitioner distress.

Case L096, another habitual narrative from an unrepresented petitioner, followed a very similar formula to L126. The content again made the same reference to the failure of a companionate marriage – the lack of shared activities and mutual support, and retreat into individual interests. The format is also strikingly similar, with bullet points itemising behaviour and impact. The statement consisted of four bullet points, again with the behaviour and impact elements. But L096 was a slightly more sophisticated version of L126, adding in a time frame and an example, to produce a formula for each bullet point of *time period + respondent's generalised behaviour + example of behaviour + impact on the petitioner*, as shown here in the first two bullets:

- From [month year] and ongoing until separation [time period] the respondent never helped the petitioner with household chores despite the fact that the petitioner works full time [generalised behaviour]. By way of example, the respondent expected the petitioner to perform all household duties such as cleaning, washing, vacuuming, shopping and cooking [example]. This made the petitioner feel depressed and unsupported [impact].
- From [month year] and ongoing until separation [time period] the respondent displayed a hostile attitude towards the Petitioner's family and friends [generalised behaviour] which has made it difficult for the petitioner to maintain these relationships [impact]. By way of example whenever the petitioner has invited her family or friends to the former matrimonial home the respondent has behaved rudely and aggressively towards them [example] making them feel uncomfortable and unwelcome [impact].

The statement concluded with a mini coda at the end of bullet 4, 'as a result of the Respondent's unreasonable behaviour the petitioner and the respondent have lived entirely separate and apart'.

Case L018 is a third example of what will now be an extremely familiar habitual narrative in terms of both content and format:

- The Petitioner feels that since the marriage began they have spent ever decreasing time together as a couple. The Respondent preferred to spend time away from the home either working or pursuing his own activities such as [hobby], and leaving the

[50] Bullets 1, 2, 3 and 5.
[51] Bullets 3, 4 and 6.
[52] MCA s 1(2)(b), 'that the respondent has behaved in such a way that the petitioner cannot reasonably be expected to live with the respondent'.

Petitioner to spend more and more time alone. They now have very little common interests which the Petitioner finds upsetting.
- The Petitioner and the Respondent have no common social circle or friends. Since the marriage began their respective friendship circles did not merge and the Respondent made little effort to assist. This has caused the Petitioner to feel torn and isolated.
- The Respondent made many promises to the Petitioner about changing his behaviour but those promises never came to fruition, which has made the Petitioner feel let down.
- As a result of the above the Petitioner has formed the view that the marriage has fallen far below her reasonable expectations of a marriage and that it be dissolved.

Unlike L096 and L126, both parties in L018 were legally represented. The input of the lawyers is possibly detectable in the rather more imaginative descriptions of the impact of the respondent's behaviours and in the final flourish that rather loosely references the statutory definition of Section 1(2)(b) of the MCA. In practice, though, there is no real difference between the habitual narrative of L018 and the others, with the use of bullets and the behaviour + impact device designed to capture the quality of the marriage.

VII. What Explains the Dominance of Habitual Narratives amongst Behaviour Petitions?

Why do so many petitioners produce a habitual rather than a story narrative to describe the breakdown of their marriage? It is worth remembering that narratives are produced in a specific context. The petitioner narrator has not chosen to tell the story, but instead is required to produce an account within particular (if loose) legal parameters to achieve their objective of a legal divorce. The reader also has some specific requirements, however minimal. The petitioner has to reassure the court that there is a pattern of behaviour, or at least an instance of behaviour, that meets the legal threshold and can be used to show that the relationship is not salvageable.

At the same time, a petitioner may simply not have ammunition to use against the respondent other than prosaic everyday complaints, or they may be reluctant to use what ammunition they have to avoid damaging the relationship. Alternatively, the respondent may not allow the petitioner to use what material is available. Unlike Riessman's narratives, many of the statements of case will have had a complex authorship, with both petitioner and respondent, together with any lawyers, contributing to the final draft. Indeed best practice, according to the Law Society Protocol and Resolution Code of Practice, is that respondents should be given an opportunity to comment on a draft petition.[53]

[53] Law Society (2015); Resolution (undated).

An habitual narrative of commonplace or everyday complaints fits neatly into those constraints of potentially multiple objectives (achieving divorce but avoiding exacerbating conflict), multiple authors (petitioner, respondent, lawyers) and multiple audiences (the court, the parties and their friends and family). But whilst an habitual narrative is likely to be the most effective format to meet multiple objectives, certainly in contrast to a story narrative, the likelihood is that the material relied upon will be thin, or have to be stretched to achieve its legal and relational purpose. In that context, the use of bullet points makes more sense as a means to eke out limited material to achieve the legal standard. The multiple bullets give an impression of a range of behaviours – a full charge sheet – when in fact, the material amounts to little more than a drifting apart of the couple.[54]

The material in the three statements is also quite generalised. Case L126 provides no really specific examples of behaviour, whilst the example in L096 describes repeated behaviour but no specific instances. Whilst L018 does include a reference to a specific hobby,[55] the narrative otherwise refers to generalised behaviours that might apply to almost anyone at some point in a marriage. Habitual narratives are about capturing the general quality of something, rather than telling stories about specifics. In this context, the absence of detail may also reflect a lack of specific instances to recount or an unwillingness to have them included. Either way, it is noteworthy that the petitions, all of which were granted without question, included none of the concrete examples of a specific action or event that might be expected in other legal contexts, whether in an adversarial process or in a witness statement.

The language used also contributes to meeting potentially mixed objectives. The three examples in Section VI, and indeed most of the statements, were drafted using formal language, often peppered with legal terms and concepts, rather than everyday speech. That is to be expected where both parties were represented, as in L018, but it was also true where both parties were unrepresented, as in L126 and L096. There are multiple websites where litigants in person can find examples of draft petitions, or examples of conduct that might be copied or modified for a statement of case.

The use of formal language does, of course, give statements more weight and authority in a legal context and meets the goal of achieving the decree. It also, curiously, makes the narrative more impersonal and, perhaps, therefore less accusatory. This is reinforced by its being written in the third person and referring to the legal personas of 'petitioner' and 'respondent', rather than using personal names or the relationship roles of 'husband' and 'wife'. The formality adds gravitas, but also an element of detachment that de-personalises what is still highly emotive material.

[54] Of course, the reality of why the marriage failed may be entirely different, as the case law expressly accepts and allows: *Stevens v Stevens* [1979] 1 WLR 885.

[55] Omitted to protect anonymity. The hobby was a fairly common pastime.

In other statements, typically by represented petitioners, another distancing technique was to use the formulation 'the petitioner would say' followed by an example of behaviour such as 'the respondent spends too much time at work'. The 'would say' formulation again appears to soften the accusation by placing it in a conditional tense, rather than the more accusatory 'the petitioner says' active tense.

Another point to note is that these habitual stories focus on communicating facts to aid the reader's understanding, rather than attempting to engage the audience and getting them to empathise with the narrator's plight. The widespread use of the behaviour + effect on the petitioner device shows an awareness of the law and of the legal test that the petitioner must satisfy. By spelling out the two elements separately, it also means that the petitioner is not relying on the reader to fill in the gaps or work out the implications of behaviour. Instead, both behaviour and the impact on the petitioner are clearly and (often) repetitively spelt out for the reader, leaving nothing to chance. This is very different from the story narratives that were most prevalent in Riessman's non-legal sample.

The risk of relying on the habitual narrative is that the opportunity to engage the reader and win them over to your side is lost. However, as discussed in Section VIII, that is less relevant here as it is not an adversarial context, nor indeed is it really an inquisitorial one. The respondent is not given an opportunity to respond and the court does not take on the role of inquisitor. The narratives can therefore be boring, repetitive and self-evidently boiler-plate compositions or model answers.

On that final point, an additional pragmatic reason for litigants in person to utilise the habitual narrative format is that it made it much easier to draft statements of case without access to legal advice. As long as the petitioner had found some advice sites on the internet,[56] it would be possible to draft the statement using boilerplate text that is freely available, possibly adding their own examples and what additional details they wished. In contrast, drafting a free-form story would be far more challenging for most, both in terms of knowing what was required and the physical act of drafting.

VIII. Statements of Case as Legal Narratives

The prevalence of habitual rather than story narratives showed how the statements of case are different from divorce narratives elicited for sociological research. At

[56] The most detailed guide to drafting a statement of case, including a formula of date, action and impact for each bullet point, is available on Divorce Online at www.divorce-online.co.uk/blog/wording-unreasonable-behaviour-allegations/. Other examples are provided by Stowe Family Law at www.stowefamilylaw.co.uk/blog/2021/03/19/how-to-word-unreasonable-behaviour-allegations/ and the forums on https://divorce.wikivorce.com.

the same time, the statements of case are also markedly different from narratives produced in and for other legal contexts. As noted previously, the body of research on the persuasiveness of legal narratives has emphasised the importance of specificity and of internal coherence and consistency. It is very difficult to imagine the highly standardised boilerplate format of the statements of case, with limited personalisation and very limited specificity in relation to facts, being acceptable, yet alone persuasive, in any other legal context.

The reliance upon a single narrative, without being tested by a competing narrative or a neutral inquisitor, is also highly unusual in formal legal processes. Narrators do not usually get the opportunity to tell their story on their own terms, without interruption and without opposition. They have instead to work hard to produce a coherent and logical narrative, free from inconsistencies that an opponent or an inquisitor could exploit.

Whilst in almost all other contexts, legal narratives are expected to be internally consistent to be persuasive,[57] problems with the statements of case appeared to go unquestioned or even unnoticed. Whilst multiple statements of case so self-evidently followed a boilerplate template, there was no attempt in any of the *Finding Fault* cases to challenge or query them, or even to acknowledge their shortcomings. Indeed, even when the compositional cracks were shown, it went unremarked by the court.

Examples of those cracks included the mistaken submission of what were early drafts of a petition, highlighting the fact that narratives were not settled or authoritative accounts. There were also examples where the narrative switched back and forth from third to first person mid-text, again showing clear evidence of multiple drafts, probably by different authors.

Nor did the court seem unsettled when presented with an alternative narrative with a different set of facts. There were only a couple of behaviour petitions that were initially refused in the *Finding Fault* sample, always on the basis that the petition simply described a mutual separation rather than any behaviour that could be attributed to the respondent.

Two examples showed radically different responses to the initial rejection. In case M130, a very mild habitual narrative petition was minimally amended to add, in a classic behaviour + impact formulation, 'because the Respondent became emotionally distant from the Petitioner and refused to engage with her. The Respondent also refused to share a bedroom with the Petitioner which greatly saddened her.' The revision was accepted without comment by the court.

In contrast, in case M082, a gentle narrative about drifting apart was replaced by a dramatic story of drunken arguments, disappearances and the respondent's verbal abuse, with the swear words reproduced verbatim. The completely revised statement, with entirely different content and narrative form, was also accepted

[57] Brooks (1996).

without comment by the court. It is difficult to imagine any situation where such a volte-face could either be deployed or not be followed up within a formal legal process.

IX. Looking at the Bigger Picture

In the mid-1970s, Elston and colleagues expressed their dismay at the 'most ritualised' nature of oral hearings in divorce cases under the MCA.[58] They lamented that the adversarial process of oral hearings was ineffective in defended cases where there was no conflict over a justiciable issue. In their view, the adversarial procedure hampered the court's ability to conduct any proper investigation in what was, in effect, an inquisitorial process.[59]

The introduction of the special procedure did remove all trappings of an adversarial procedure, but the court did not embrace the opportunity to adopt an inquisitorial process. Instead, pressure of resources, changing social attitudes and judicial disinterest in policing marriage meant a further hollowing out of the process. By the time of the *Finding Fault* research, the scrutiny process had became no more than an administrative process, albeit still framed in statute as inquisitorial and still set within an adversarial justice system. The habitual narratives, so common in behaviour cases, encapsulate the extent to which the court had simply given up, with minimal expectations of narratives being met with boilerplate accounts of marriage breakdown that the court was, in turn, only too willing to accept.

What was surprising, if anything, was the extent to which the parties did still take the time and trouble to draft particulars. One can imagine that it would be very easy for an enterprising software engineer to create a 'random statement of case generator' to save the time and expense of drafting a narrative. The programming would be simple – petitioners could elect to have four to eight bullet points, with a drop-down list to select from a range of behaviours including spending too much time at work/on hobbies/with a different social group, not helping with cooking/cleaning/ironing/DIY, spending too much/too little money, etc, etc, with the effect of leaving the petitioner sad/hurt/disappointed/lonely/upset, and rounding off with a coda 'The parties separated on [insert a date] as a result of the respondent's unreasonable behaviour and the marriage has broken down irretrievably.' Or the programme could just generate the whole statement itself, without bothering the petitioner to select behaviours and impacts.

Whilst the idea of a random statement of case generator might seem fanciful, or disrespectful of the legal process, it is not far from what has been happening in practice. Tens of thousands of habitual narratives will have been submitted over

[58] Elston, Fuller and Murch (1975) 634.
[59] ibid 636.

the last decade, and the foregoing analysis suggests many of them might as well have been produced by a random statement of case generator (RSoCG). Nor would the court have been able to detect whether a RSoCG had been used, even if there had been any willingness or enthusiasm to do so. In a long history of ritualised stories to achieve a divorce, the habitual narrative represented a rather mundane and prosaic nadir.

Fortunately, the main lesson of this sad tale has already been learnt. The implementation of the Divorce, Dissolution and Separation Act 2020 will finally mean that petitioners (or applicants) and respondents will no longer have to construct stories to secure a divorce, and the court will no longer have to pretend to scrutinise them.

The research also underscores the importance of understanding context in any narrative analysis. The use of habitual narratives in divorce petitions can only be understood in the particular historical context, where the court simply required the petitioner to say something that could be construed as relevant. In contrast to research findings from other legal contexts,[60] that meant that lay petitioners were not necessarily significantly disadvantaged. As long as they had access to the internet, they were able to cut and paste someone else's draft into their petition and achieve their divorce through a form of legal plagiarism. That approach would be unlikely to work in almost all other legal contexts where what constitutes a competent story is more stringently policed. Narrative context is everything.

References

Brooks, P (1996) 'The Law as Narrative and Rhetoric' in P Brooks and P Gewirtz (eds), *Law's Stories: Narrative and Rhetoric in the Law* (New Haven, CT, Yale University Press).

Brooks, P (2006) 'Narrative Transactions – Does the Law Need a Narratology?' 18 *Yale Journal of Law & the Humanities* 1.

Chester, R and Streather, J (1972) 'Cruelty in English Divorce: Some Empirical Findings' 34 *Journal of Marriage and Family* 706.

Cretney, S (2003) *Family Law in the Twentieth Century A History* (Oxford, Oxford University Press).

Di Donato, F (2020) *The Analysis of Legal Cases: A Narrative Approach* (London, Routledge).

Ehrlich, S (2015) 'Narrative, Institutional Processes, and Gendered Inequalities' in A de Fine and A Georgakopoulou (eds), *The Handbook of Narrative Analysis* (London, Wiley).

Elston, E, Fuller, J and Murch, M (1975) 'Judicial Hearings of Undefended Divorce Petitions' 38 *Modern Law Review* 609.

Ewick, P and Silbey, S (1998) *The Common Place of Law: Stories from Everyday Life* (Chicago, IL, University of Chicago Press).

Gewirtz, P (1996) 'Narrative and Rhetoric in the Law' in P Brooks and P Gewirtz (eds), *Law's Stories: Narrative and Rhetoric in the Law* (New Haven, CT, Yale University Press).

[60] See Ehrlich (2015).

Herbert, AP (1934) *Holy Deadlock*, 1st edn (London, Methuen).
Johnston, J and Breit R (2010) 'Towards a Narratology of Court Reporting', 137 *Media International Australia* 47.
Labov, W (1972) *Language in the Inner City* (Philadelphia, PA, University of Pennsylvania Press).
Law Commission (1990) *The Ground for Divorce*, Report 192 (London, HMSO).
Law Society (2015) *Family Law Protocol*, 4th edn (London, The Law Society).
Love, J (1998) 'The Value of Narrative in Legal Scholarship and Teaching' 2 *Journal of Gender, Race & Justice* 87.
Olson, G (2018) 'On Narrating and Troping the Law: The Conjoined Use of Narrative and Metaphor in Legal Discourse' in M Hanne and R Weisberg (eds), *Narrative and Metaphor in the Law* (Cambridge, Cambridge University Press).
Probert, R (1999) 'The controversy of equality and the Matrimonial Causes Act 1923' 11 *Child & Family Law Quarterly* 33.
Resolution (undated) Code of Practice, available at https://resolution.org.uk/looking-for-help/code-of-practice/
Rheinstein, M (1972) *Marriage Stability, Divorce and the Law* (Chicago, IL, University of Chicago Press).
Riessman, CK (1990) *Divorce Talk: Women and Men Make Sense of Personal Relationships* (New Brunswick, NJ, Rutgers University Press).
Ryan, M (2004), *Narratives Across Media* (Lincoln, NE, University of Nebraska Press).
Stone, L (1990) *The Road to Divorce: England 1530–1987* (Oxford, Oxford University Press).
Trinder, L, Braybrook, D, Bryson, C, Coleman, L, Houlston, C and Sefton, M (2017) *Finding Fault? Divorce Law and Practice in England and Wales* (London, Nuffield Foundation).
Trinder, L and Sefton, M (2018) *No Contest: Defended Divorce in England & Wales* (London, Nuffield Foundation).

10

Royal Divorces and the Remaking of Marriage and Monarchy

DANIEL MONK

I. Introduction

Divorce is the thread that runs through the most well-known and endlessly retold stories of royal lives: from Henry VIII and his wives and Edward VIII's marriage to twice-divorced Mrs Simpson, to the romantic and marital troubles of Princess Margaret, and the tragic saga of Charles and Diana. But perhaps because it has been perceived as gossip, high intrigue and scandal, royal divorce has attracted little academic attention. With notable exceptions – and even then only in the context of remarriage[1] – legal and socio-legal scholarship on divorce has not mentioned it at all. This reflects Hazell and Morris's recent observation that 'in the academic disciplines of law and politics, monarchy is almost non-existent as a subject', a fact that they suggest has created 'not just a gap, but a gaping void'.[2]

There are several reasons for taking royal divorce seriously. From a constitutional perspective, royal divorces have played a key role in the evolving relationship between Church and State. And the manner, over centuries, in which they have been both resisted and enabled has helped redefine the institution of the monarchy. Moreover, as the power of constitutional monarchies has shrunk, 'new roles and new expressions of old roles have emerged to re-legitimate their existence',[3] and key here has been their role as exemplars of 'family' and symbolic reference points for debates about the institution of marriage.

Royal divorces are stories about the private lives of a very small number of people. But the enormous – some would say excessive – attention paid to them has transformed them into public events. Contemporary commentaries, from *Hansard* and newspaper headlines to public opinion polls, reveal the shifting of

[1] Probert (2011); Cretney (2000), (2008).
[2] Hazell and Morris (2020) 3. Exceptions Nash (2017), Probert (2011) and Whitty (1999).
[3] ibid 6.

attitudes about divorce, and family more widely, and, consequently, provide a rich source of social history. There is a paradox here, because the emergence of 'social history', with its emphasis on 'history from below', can be understood as a reaction against a perceived over-emphasis on the lives of Kings and Queens.[4] This may partly explain the silence about royal divorce in critical and sociological scholarship. In countering this oversight, Finch's concept of 'family display' is pertinent.[5] Introduced to identify how understandings of 'family' are contingent on display, through the active and shared observation and recognition of others, it takes on a particular significance in this context. The intensity and public nature of *royal* 'family display' is evident not only in the sources noted above, but also in countless costume dramas, with the global phenomenon of *The Crown* being but the latest in a long line.[6]

All family dramas in films, sitcoms and soaps take on a melodramatic quality, and in the context of the royal family this 'mode of excess' is even more pronounced. This may be another reason for the absence of academic research about royal divorces, as 'melodramatic' has become a pejorative term. Brooks' towering challenge to this too-quick-dismissal is particularly pertinent here:

> Melodrama starts from and expresses the anxiety brought by a frightening new world in which traditional patterns of moral order no longer provide the necessary social glue. It plays out the force of that anxiety with the apparent triumph of villainy, and it dissipates it with the eventual victory of virtue. It demonstrates over and over that the signs of ethical forces can be discovered and can be made legible.[7]

The institutions of monarchy and marriage have been invested with the ability to provide a reassuring and necessary social glue, and indeed they are intimately connected, and divorce has challenged and been a key source of anxiety for both. Taking the stories about royal divorces seriously then is to recognise that melodrama 'has the distinct value of being about recognition and clarification, about how to be clear what the stakes are and what their representative signs mean, and how to face them'.[8]

The main focus of this chapter is from the period just before the Divorce Reform Act 1969 to the present day. But it begins by taking a long view, identifying the wider significance of key royal divorces in British history from the twelfth century.[9]

[4] Samuel (1985).
[5] Finch (2007).
[6] Merck (2016). See also Cannadine (1983) for an analysis of the shifting importance of performance for the monarchy.
[7] Brooks (1976) 20.
[8] ibid 206.
[9] 'Royal divorces', with one exception, refers here to divorces where one of the parties is a member of the royal family (a status that is not always clear). For an analysis of remarriages by divorced royals, see Probert (2011).

II. Taking the Long View

'Divorced Beheaded Died. Divorced Beheaded Survived' is a rhyme used by generations of British school children to remember the fates of the six wives of Henry VIII. Described by d'Avray as 'the most famous divorce in history',[10] the ending of Henry's first marriage to Catherine of Aragon – and the ensuing Reformation – is undoubtedly one of the seminal moments in British history. But the legal details are misunderstood, and the focus on this one event has overshadowed later royal encounters with divorce that have also been of constitutional significance.

Despite the catchy rhyme, Henry VIII was never divorced: his first and fourth marriages to Catherine of Aragon and Anne of Cleves were in fact both annulled – that is, declared never to have existed in the first place. To a certain extent, the confusion is understandable: Catherine of Aragon's statement in her trial refers to '*divortium inter nos fieri*'. But '*divortium*' at that time referred to annulment or legal separation, and not to divorce in the modern sense of terminating a valid marriage.[11] The distinction is crucial, for confusing the two obscures the distinctiveness of Anglicanism. Henry VIII, never a Protestant, far from introducing the possibility of legal divorce, resisted such attempts. His battle with the Pope concerned disputes about papal dispensations,[12] and the break from Rome secured his preferred interpretation of existing Canon law. Indeed, if the recent, and not uncontroversial, reforms by the current Pope Francis had been in place, Cardinal Wolsey would have been able to provide Henry VIII with the desired annulment without papal approval.[13] Moreover, the longstanding Catholic pragmatic practice of 'separation of bed and board' (*divorce a mensa et toro*), fiercely rejected by the zealous Protestant theologians of the Reformation,[14] was retained by the post-Reformation church courts.

Acknowledging that Henry VIII was never divorced enables the saga of Catherine of Aragon to be understood as 'an instance of a structure with a long history',[15] for royal annulments were far from new. Indeed, d'Avray has argued that the 'easy availability of dispensations enabling remarriages was a factor favouring indissoluble marriage'.[16] The ending of King John's marriage to his first wife Isabelle of Gloucester in 1199 is an example of the flexibility the system provided for a wily monarch. The marriage had been within the prohibited degrees, and John had resisted calls at the time it took place to request validation by way of a papal dispensation.[17] This effectively enabled him to dispense with her at his

[10] d'Avray (2014) 227.

[11] d'Avray (2015) 234.

[12] ibid 227–38.

[13] Agnew (2015); McDonnell (2016); Morris (2017).

[14] Stone (1990) 301.

[15] d'Avray (2014) 1. See also Margaret of Scotland's second marriage to Earl of Douglas in 1515, and Henry III's annulment of his marriage to Jean of Ponthui in 1252.

[16] ibid 8.

[17] ibid 53–57.

will, as he did in 1200 to make a strategically beneficial marriage to Isabella of Angoulême. The faking of genealogies to enable annulments was also another established method.[18]

This early and often overlooked history of royal 'divorces' provides evidence of concerns and practices that re-emerge far later in debates about the introduction of, and practices under, the 1969 Act: ambivalence about whether the (relative) ease of ending marriages can be reconciled with women's best interests, and an awareness of the malleability and contrivance of facts to achieve a legal end.

In two further instances in British history, divorce functioned explicitly as a symbolic analogy for the relationship between the Monarch and the People.

The Roos Act 1670, while not strictly speaking the first parliamentary divorce by statute, undoubtedly laid the foundations for its possibility.[19] One reason for its success was the support of Charles II, and his attendance at the hearings was much noted. Whether this was because he was interested in the possibility of ending his own childless marriage has been much debated; it certainly indicated that inheritance and the transmission of property, rather than personal morality, was the motive for many supporting parliamentary divorce.[20] On Charles II's death, the removal of James II from the throne and the offering of the Crown to William and Mary in 1689 – the Glorious Revolution – challenged the Divine Right and introduced a contractual view of the relationship between the Monarch and the People. For both opponents and supporters, the position of the King was seen as analogous to that of a father in a family; and a sacramental approach was being challenged by a more functional perspective.[21] Whig aristocratic support for the potential dissolution of the contract between husbands and wives, aided by political theorists such as Locke, was explicitly referenced in support of James II's 'abdication'.[22]

However, arguments in support of divorce do not necessarily align neatly with an incremental, progressive view of history. George IV's attempt, in 1820, to divorce his wife Caroline of Brunswick, by the notorious Pains and Penalties Bill, demonstrates most clearly the contingent use of divorce in political debates about the monarchy. While the Bishops supported the Bill, opposition was led not only by Radicals, such as William Cobbett, but also by Whig peers, and was explicitly linked to political demands, which eventually resulted in the Great Reform Act 1832.[23] While enabling divorce suited the Whig cause in the 1690s, resisting this particular divorce now worked in the other direction. But the ability of divorce to function as a symbol of political relationships and straightforward power struggles is a recurring theme.

[18] ibid 3–4.
[19] Probert (2016).
[20] Probert (2016); Stone (1990) 312.
[21] Eekelaar (2006); Shanley (1979).
[22] Shanley (1979).
[23] Carter (2008); Melikan (2001); Fraser (1996).

The Trial of Queen Caroline was significant for two other reasons. First, as Carter demonstrates, it represented a landmark moment in gender relations, as it highlighted that the private marital behaviour of men, and not just women, could have an impact on public and political reputations.[24] Second, as Harris notes:

> For the first time, the collapse of a royal marriage unfolded in two-penny broadsheets that were accessible to members of all social backgrounds. The King's attempts to undermine the Queen's reputation to secure a divorce made him deeply unpopular with his subjects.[25]

Both set a pattern for the future, indicating the shifting nature of the monarchy and the extent to which royalty's response to divorce became a key part of its legitimacy.

III. Resisting Reform

While the Divorce Reform Act 1969 is – rightly – placed alongside other liberal reforms of that era, the calls for reform emerged in an earlier period. And both the monarchy as an institution and individual royalty played important roles in resisting reform.

A striking early example of this is a speech made in 1949 by the current Queen, three years before her accession to the throne and shortly after her own marriage (which had itself confirmed the 'invented tradition'[26] of royal marriages as nation-defining events). Addressing the Mothers' Union, a conservative Christian charity, she spoke scathingly of the 'current age of growing self-indulgence, of hardening materialism, of falling moral standards', and according to Pimlott:

> The young wives applauded warmly when she declared that broken homes caused havoc among children, and that 'we can have no doubt that divorce and separation are responsible for some of the darkest evils in our society today'.[27]

Strong words. Attlee's Labour Government had just passed the Legal Advice and Assistance Act 1949 and divorce work was 'the first target of the new scheme',[28] helping, in particular, ex-servicemen who had arguably been fighting something more worthy of the epithet 'darkest evil'. The speech 'plunged her into unexpected controversy'.[29] The chairman of the Marriage Law Reform Committee protested that it was inappropriate for a senior member of the royal family to take such a partisan position on what was a contested issue, and

[24] Carter (2008).
[25] Harris (2012).
[26] Hobsbawm (1983).
[27] Pimlott (1996) 160.
[28] Brooke (2017) at 7.
[29] Pimlott (1996) 161

counter-argued that '[t]he harm to children can be greater in a home where both parents are at loggerheads than if divorce ensues'.[30] Both the speech and the reaction provide an insight into shifting attitudes to both monarchy and marriage. As Smart reminds us, at that time, divorce was genuinely seen by many as being linked to the 'decline of Western civilisation'.[31] But the reaction is a reminder of how, far from being an age of deference and social conservatism, the post-war era in the 1950s was a time of explicit contestations about family life and personal morality.[32]

The royal family's opposition to divorce was also expressed directly by their pointedly attending the reception, but not the wedding, of a divorced cousin in 1950[33] and, until 1955, by refusing divorced people entry to the Royal Enclosure at Ascot.[34] Even where rules were changed, they throw a light on the deep-seated stigma attached to divorce; for example, it was only during the Second World War that divorced military officers were permitted to attend shooting parties at Sandringham.

A. The Coronation and the Royal Commission (the Morton Commission)

Ideals of moral and personal behaviour were clearly expressed at the coronation of the Queen in 1953. And in striking ways the messages mirrored the response to divorce expressed by the Morton Commission, which was set up in 1951 and reported in 1956.[35]

Contemporary mainstream commentary about the coronation – both the service and the prevailing atmosphere – emphasised the symbolic significance of the Queen's position.[36] The sociologists Shills and Young suggested in 1953, in the inaugural volume of *The Sociological Review*, that the coronation was an act of 'national communion' and that devotion to the royal family 'means in a very direct way devotion to one's own family, because the values embodied are the same'.[37] Fellow sociologist Birnbaum's response was that this was a highly romanticised position and suggested that the emotional responses to the Queen were akin to those felt towards film stars.[38] More brutally, Nairn described Shills and Young's account as 'the sociology of groveling'.[39] Read today, Pimlott argues that the essay

[30] ibid.
[31] Smart (2000) 5.
[32] See Bauer and Cook (2012); Rebellato (1999).
[33] Koenig (2009).
[34] See Graham (2015).
[35] Royal Commission (1956).
[36] Pimlott (1996) 216.
[37] Shills and Young (1953).
[38] Birnbaum (1955).
[39] Nairn (1988) 118.

> has the flavour of a period piece, but one which accurately perceived, without solving the mystery, that the coronation was more than mere flummery: and that it helped define, not just loyalty, but the British identity for the next generation.[40]

Projected on to the coronation were beliefs that were closely aligned to a commitment to post-war moral rearmament. From this perspective, monarchy and marriage represented mutually sympathetic and supportive institutions: national and domestic cohesion required and reinforced each other. They were linked not simply by a belief in tradition and social conservatism, but by a communitarian belief that the contractual relationships underlying both institutions were premised on prioritising duty over the individualistic pursuit of happiness.[41] And it is attitudes to divorce that demonstrate most clearly the alignment in this period of marriage and monarchy.

In rejecting calls for divorce to be made easier, the Morton Commission concluded:

> We are convinced that the real remedy for the present situation lies in other directions: in fostering in the individual the will to do his duty by the community; in strengthening his resolution to make marriage a union for life; in inculcating a proper sense of his responsibility towards his children.[42]

A lifelong commitment and putting duty first as a necessary defence of 'the family' mirrored the much-quoted speech to the Commonwealth in 1947 of the then Princess Elizabeth:

> My whole life whether it be long or short shall be devoted to your service and the service of our great imperial family to which we all belong. But I shall not have strength to carry out this resolution alone unless you join in it with me.[43]

Smart, commenting on Morton, made clear how its findings reflected not simply a traditional or religious view of marriage but a broader vision:

> [Morton] presumed (rightly or wrongly) that it was addressing an homogeneous society, albeit one which appeared to have started down a slippery slope of moral decline in family matters. The signs were identified in respect of the growing demand for personal fulfilment in relationships, rather than satisfaction with the virtuous reward of doing one's duty … Divorce seemed to be a carry over of war-time (im)morality and what the Commission wished to regenerate was pre-war decorum and duty.[44]

In the 1950s, divorce was 'a key issue, both for the nation and for royalty',[45] and the royal family, both explicitly and through the projection of others, was intimately

[40] Pimlott (1996) 217.
[41] Mort (2010).
[42] Royal Commission (1956) 14.
[43] 21 April 1947, quoted in Pimlott (1996) 117.
[44] Smart (2000) 368.
[45] Pimlott (1996) 372.

aligned with the opposition to reform. But there was a tension. For while Church doctrine and the family's 'traumatic encounters with non-royal divorcees' pulled one way, at the same time they were 'in danger of becoming beached – defending a code in which privately it had ceased to believe'.[46]

B. The Townsend Affair

> Think about this, I have a country that is for me, newspapers that sympathise with me. I represent what a growing majority want, the future not the past, a kinder more tolerant attitude to marriage and divorce.
>
> Princess Margaret to the Queen, *The Crown* (Series 1: 'Gloriana')

At the coronation, the removal of fluff by Princess Margaret, the Queen's sister, from the uniform of Group Captain Peter Townsend resulted in news stories that confirmed that they were in a relationship and contemplating marriage. The ensuing Townsend Affair – which concluded just before the publication of the Morton Report – was not a 'royal divorce' per se, for the question at stake was, as in the Abdication Crisis 20 years earlier, whether a member of the royal family could marry a divorced person. What is pertinent here is not Princess Margaret's eventual decision not to marry Townsend but the reactions of others. It was a public issue: as Mount notes, 'social historians neglect it at their peril', for the royal family was being 'deployed as an instrument of social control'.[47]

On 26 October 1955, *The Times* published a leader article penned by the editor Sir Michael Haley, which concluded that

> in her [the Queen] people saw their better selves ideally reflected … If the marriage … comes to pass, it is inevitable that this reflection becomes distorted. The Princess will be entering into a union which vast numbers of her sister's people … cannot in conscience regard as a marriage.[48]

Pimlott comments that this argument appears now to be 'not merely monstrous but almost incomprehensible', but that it demonstrates how seriously the issue was discussed and that it reflected 'a snapshot of royalty doctrine at the time'.[49]

Five days later, Princess Margaret publicly announced her decision not to marry Townsend, 'mindful of the Church's teachings that Christian marriage is indissoluble, and conscious of my duty to the Commonwealth'. The announcement interrupted radio programmes. Mount reminisces that '[y]ou need to be over 70 to remember the awful thrill of the announcement'.[50]

[46] ibid.
[47] Mount (2018) 92, 100. See Kynaston's full account (2010).
[48] Pimlott (1996) 237.
[49] ibid 238.
[50] Mount (2018) 92.

What is clear from the contemporaneous accounts and later commentaries is that the Establishment's opposition to the marriage was not simply a defence of tradition. As Pimlott comments:

> Liberal pressure to change the divorce law, so far from easing the path to royal acceptance of divorce, encouraged the Church hierarchy to react with even greater indignation against any behaviour that seemed likely to open the flood-gates.[51]

Further evidence of the dominance of reactionary thinking in the Church of England at that time, is the introduction, two years later, of measures that strongly discouraged priests from exercising their discretion to marry divorcees.[52]

That the Townsend melodrama was newsworthy reflected the extent to which the social order was being challenged and, crucially, the centrality of divorce in that narrative. A contemporary Gallop poll found that 59 per cent of the public approved of the marriage, against only 17 per cent who disapproved[53] – a snapshot of attitudes towards divorce and marriage 15 years before the Divorce Reform Act 1969. But it was also a key moment in the redefining of the institution of the monarchy.

C. 'The Family on the Throne'

Schama, commenting on royal portraiture, argues that as part of monarchy's survival in the twentieth century, it was 'important that the institution should be seen to be the family of families, at once dynastic and domestic, remote and accessible, magical and mundane'.[54] The inherent tensions go to the heart of a debate in the 1950s about the meaning of 'the family on the throne', the concept introduced by Bagehot in 1867 to explain the role of the monarchy in his classic account of the Constitution. While largely undeveloped ever since[55] and 'tamely repeated in public law textbooks',[56] the Townsend Affair brought to the fore its contested meanings.

On one side was Fisher, the Archbishop of Canterbury, who, like the editor of *The Times*, believed the Queen's example was key to upholding 'domestic fidelity' and 'united homes' as 'the pillars of society'.[57] This view was eloquently articulated by Dermot Morrah, a journalist and courtier, and the author of the Queen's 1947 speech noted in Section III.A.[58] In his influential 1958 text, *The Queen*

[51] Pimlott (1996) 201.
[52] Probert (2021) 201.
[53] Mount (2018) 98.
[54] Schama (1986) 183.
[55] Hazell and Morris (2020) 4.
[56] Whitty (1999) 94.
[57] Pimlott (1996) 210.
[58] Utley (2017).

at Work, Morrah argued that the 'family on the throne' had to be identifiable, visible and exemplary in the eyes of the people, as

> [t]hey proceed from the healthy fact that the people have before their eyes a picture not of an ideal woman but of an ideal group, so that families in mansion or cottage may be strengthened in their inward relationships by the feeling – it scarcely amounts to a thought – that the little social unit they are maintaining is also one that also lives and develops in its most admirable form in Windsor Castle or Buckingham Palace.[59]

However, this view was distinct from that of Bagehot, for whom Queen Victoria's personal behaviour was welcome but an exception, and not essential for the symbolic 'dignified' role of monarchy. Adopting a pragmatic approach, Bagehot was, according to Pimlott, aware that the temptations available to royalty in particular made them less likely to be privately respectable.[60] This alternative interpretation of 'the family on the throne' was best expressed by Lord Altrincham, a liberal Tory politician and journalist and editor of the *National and English Review*, who questioned several aspects of the tradition-bound court and described Morrah's views as 'British Shintoism'.[61] Together with Attlee and others, Altrincham believed modernisation was key to the survival of the monarchy.

In the end it was Morrah's views that most influenced the court. It proved to be a doomed project.

IV. After the Divorce Reform Act 1969

While attitudes in society were changing, for the royal family 'the word divorce continued to cause a tremor'.[62] Holding the line increasingly placed them at odds with their own aristocratic social milieu, within which divorce was far more acceptable.[63] It reflected a wider tension, noted by Cannadine, between the monarch's traditional role of being 'head of society' to the new more complex role of 'head of the nation'.[64] The post-war conservative position was reasserted in 1967 when the Queen's first cousin Lord Harewood was divorced by his wife Marion Stein. Arguably the first royal divorce of a member of the royal family,[65] it resulted in his becoming persona non grata at court. Reminiscing later, Harewood

[59] Morrah (1958) 37–44.

[60] Pimlott (1996) 294.

[61] ibid 278–79.

[62] ibid.

[63] Burgoyne et al (1987) 36 argue that, unlike for the middle classes, status for the aristocracy was not dependent on conventional conformity.

[64] Cannadine (1983) 133.

[65] Two possible earlier claims are the divorces of Princess Victoria of Edinburgh in 1901 from Ernst of Hesse, by the courts in Hesse (she had to wait until the death of her grandmother Queen Victoria, and it was commented at the time that 'death would have been much better'), and of Lady Iris Mountbatten, a great-granddaughter of Queen Victoria, in 1946 from a Captain O'Malley and then again in 1957 from a US jazz musician.

observed 'I doubt if it is possible to exaggerate the horror with which I initially looked upon divorce … which was less prevalent in England in those days and seemed to me at first … the refuge of despair'.[66]

In legal terms, his divorce raised no issues, although his status as the adulterer, the guilty party, increased the stigma. His remarriage as a divorced man did, however, raise legal questions because of the Royal Marriages Act 1772: permitting the marriage, but only on the basis of simply following Cabinet advice, avoided compromising the Queen's position as Head of the Church of England, which at that time refused to countenance the remarriage of divorcees.[67] According to Pimlott, '[b]y passing the buck, the Queen left the Monarchy's attitude murky'.[68]

The 1969 Act did not change the perception of the royal family as representing traditional 'family values'. Indeed, 1969 saw the broadcast of *Royal Family*, a fly-on-the wall documentary, described by Pimlott as the 'highpoint of domestication' of the royal family.[69] Later blamed for changing the relationship of the family with the media, it brought to the fore the tension between their being represented as an 'ordinary' family or a 'model' family. That the latter still held sway was evident at the time of the Silver Wedding anniversary of the Queen and Prince Philip in 1972. Coinciding with the procedural changes that made divorce considerably easier, the *Daily Telegraph* editorial took the opportunity to contemplate the nation's moral decline, observing that 'The Queen, the Duke and their children have set a standard of family life and family happiness that everyone must respect and many envy'.[70]

It is nonetheless possible to detect a subtle change in understandings of 'happiness' that cohered with the changing approach of the Church of England to divorce. A key moment was the publication in 1963 of *Honest to God* by John Robinson, the Bishop of Woolwich. According to Smart, it heralded

> an important shift away from a focus on status towards a recognition of the individual occupying the status … it became the quality of a relationship that became the yardstick of its moral worth, not simply the marital status of the parties.[71]

But while status and duty were less central to the institution of marriage, these qualities remained essential for the institution of monarchy. Consequently, the implications for royal marriages of the shift signified by divorce reform were more ambivalent.

Once again, it was Princess Margaret who tested the boundaries of acceptable behaviour. While tabloid stories about her marriage to Antony Armstrong-Jones, her relationships with Roddy Llewellyn and her lifestyle on the Caribbean island of Mustique abounded, the formal statement announcing her separation was carefully

[66] Harewood (1981) 218.
[67] Probert (2011).
[68] Pimlott (1996) 374.
[69] ibid 387.
[70] *Daily Telegraph* (21 November 1972).
[71] Smart (2000) 371.

stage-managed. It was released on 16 March 1976, the same day that the Prime Minister, Harold Wilson, announced his retirement. A supportive gesture from Wilson, based on his assumption that his resignation 'would blanket the separation', his press officer observed that 'Wilson didn't understand the tabloids … it was the other way round'.[72] While raising no distinct legal issues, the separation was newsworthy and perceived not simply as a private matter but as an event with potential implications for, at the very least, the popularity of monarchy. As Pimlott notes, 'the revelation that the perfect family suffered from the same tensions as many imperfect ones came as a shock'.[73] It was announced in the following way:

> HRH The Princess Margaret, Countess of Snowdon, and the Earl of Snowdon have mutually agreed to live apart. The Princess will carry out her public duties and functions unaccompanied by Lord Snowdon. There are no plans for divorce proceedings.[74]

The reference to divorce revealed a fear expressed at the time that 'if she divorced her example would upset the established principles of Christian family life of the Church of which her sister is head, and attract the disapproval of influential Church leaders'.[75]

Despite the initial disavowal, just over two years later, on 10 May 1978, a further formal statement, while discreetly avoiding the dreaded word, announced the plans to divorce:

> Her Royal Highness, the Princess Margaret, Countess of Snowdon, and the Earl of Snowdon after two years of separation have now agreed that their marriage should formally be ended. Accordingly, Her Royal Highness will start the necessary legal proceedings.

In a similar vein, and referencing the new law, the BBC announced:

> The two sides had agreed that their marriage should be ended with the minimum of formality in our new streamlined divorce system in exactly the same way that thousands of commoners choose to end their marriages in our courts each year.[76]

As a further indication of the changing times, the then Archbishop of Canterbury, Donald Coggan, in marked contrast to his predecessor Fisher, offered his sympathy and understanding. Reinforcing the shift in moral emphasis was the fact that it was not her separation or divorce that dominated tabloid criticism of her but, rather, her lifestyle and whether she was 'value for money': private behaviour still mattered, but not so much marital status.

Warwick has suggested that Margaret's most enduring legacy was establishing public acceptance of royal divorce.[77] Tolerance of marital discord, however, went

[72] Pimlott (1996) 435.
[73] ibid.
[74] BBC, *On This Day*, 19 March 1976.
[75] Pimlott (1996) 441.
[76] Warwick (2017).
[77] ibid.

hand in hand with greater freedom in discussing marital behaviour. Media coverage of the personal lives of the Queen's children was extensive and lurid. Princess Anne and her husband Mark Phillips announced their separation on 21 August 1989 and stated that 'there were no plans for divorce'.[78] The year 1992 – famously described by the Queen as her *annus horribilis* – saw their subsequent divorce, together with announcements of the separations of Prince Andrew and Sarah Ferguson and of Prince Charles and Diana. Four years later, in 1996, both couples divorced.

Despite the extensive media coverage, the issue of separation and divorce per se appeared no longer to be problematic. As *The Times* editorial noted in 1995, in marked contrast to its position 40 years earlier at the time of the Townsend affair, 'Despite the fulminations of moralists and sentimentalists a divorce carries no constitutional implications.'[79]

While undoubtedly a markedly different terrain, the process followed for ending these royal marriages demonstrates both change and continuity. All followed the precedent set by Princess Margaret: a formal announcement of a separation alongside a statement that divorce is not being considered, followed three or four years later by divorce using the fact of two years' separation as the evidence for establishing irretrievable breakdown of the marriage.

The very clear distinction made between separation and divorce indicates a degree of caution about the latter. It avoided addressing questions of remarriages, which would, and indeed did, raise distinct legal questions.[80] But it also represented an acknowledgement of and echoes the traditional legitimacy of separation under Canon law. As noted in Section II, the Catholic – and Anglican – condoning of formal separation (*divorce a mensa et toro*) was a practical device that deeply offended ardent protestants. Consequently, the modern royal separations (as they began life) were explicitly distinguished from divorce and can be understood as part of a longer tradition of pragmatic High Anglicanism. As Junor observed in relation to the announcement of the separation of Prince Charles and Diana, the reference to there being 'no intention of remarrying' was 'a gesture to bridge the divide between the two Palaces, a peace offering to the Queen, to the public and to the Anglican Church'.[81] In the cases of Sarah Ferguson and Diana, they also echoed a similarly longer royal practice of dispensing with troublesome women.

But alongside this nod to tradition, the use of the new no-fault fact of two years' separation represented a clear break with tradition. There are sound pragmatic reasons why this route has consistently been adopted. Most obviously, it avoids the need to provide potentially contentious and lurid details to satisfy the conduct-based facts. And with no quick remarriages and downplaying the actual

[78] BBC, *On This Day*, 21 August 1989.
[79] 21 December 1995.
[80] Princess Anne remarried in the Church of Scotland, and Prince Charles's remarriage in the Registry Office at Windsor was the subject of much debate: Probert (2011).
[81] Junor (2018) 140.

divorce suiting other agendas, the two-year delay had no drawbacks. But this is not to say that fault had no part to play in the wider narratives. On the contrary, the 'blame game' was played endlessly by the media, and in the context of the Wales's marriage by the parties themselves, to vast audiences encouraged and eager to judge and take sides.[82]

Despite the extensive coverage, the fact that in law the no-fault route was adopted has never been commented on – despite the partial introduction of 'no-fault' divorce having been the most controversial aspect of the 1969 Act and despite the conduct-based facts remaining overwhelmingly cited in practice. That the royal family, having been identified clearly with attempts to resist reform, felt no obligation or pragmatic need to divorce according to traditional religious doctrines premised on the finding of a guilty party indicated the legitimacy of no-fault divorce. But far from evidence of laissez-faire permissiveness, what this shift indicated – and what the divorce of Charles and Diana in particular demonstrated – was that a new set of moral standards was now firmly in place.

V. The Dianification of Divorce

Diana is an iconic, ambivalent and contested figure for cultural historians, psychoanalysts, media theorists and especially feminists. So much has been written about her that Benton has coined the phrase 'Dianology'.[83] The underlying fascination lies in exploring the responses to and projections onto Diana, rather than attempting to understand the actual woman herself. Attempting to explain this, Hilary Mantel suggests that 'something in her personality, her receptivity, her passivity, fitted her to be the carrier of myth'.[84] Similarly, from a public law perspective, Whitty notes that 'the boundaries of Britishness are sufficiently fluid to allow people to appropriate the Diana experience for multiple purposes'.[85] But despite her divorce being perhaps the most famous in recent history, the literature curiously says very little about divorce and the institution of marriage more widely. In filling that gap, what becomes clear is that there are significant parallels and connections between discussions about Diana and about divorce reform.

Some progressive commentators perceived in the reaction to Diana's death something more than individual grief that resonated with a deeper cultural and social change. Acknowledging this, Merck describes the event as 'a floral revolution'.[86] Darcus Howe, writing in the *New Statesman*, argued that the event

[82] A poll in the *Today* newspaper found that 84% of readers thought that Prince Charles's confession of adultery in his television interview with Jonathan Dimbleby damaged the monarchy: Junor (2018) 125.

[83] Benton (1998) 95. See eg Seidler (2013); Davies (2001); Merck (1998).

[84] Mantel (2018) 82.

[85] Whitty (1999) 41.

[86] Merck (1998) 3.

'removed the veil to reveal the New Britain'; that '[w]e swallowed and lived by the myths of how British people were: conservative, gradualistic, instinctively right-wing, the moral of middle England … we were monumentally wrong.'[87]

Will Hutton similarly suggested that the outpouring of grief represented a broader sense of 'freeing ourselves from the reigns of the past'.[88] Central to these interpretations was a valorising of the open expression of feelings. AL Kennedy saw in this evidence of 'Britain's newfound emotional maturity' and Susy Orbach of Britain's 'growing up as a nation'.[89]

Hyperbole aside, these projections cohered with a shift in understandings of divorce from a focus on establishing lapses in marital duties and a need to establish guilt, towards an emphasis on individual emotional growth and happiness; a move from formal justice to therapeutic justice. Even Mother Theresa, who had campaigned in Ireland in 1995 to keep the constitutional ban on divorce, expressed approval of her friend Diana's divorce in an interview with *Ladies' Home Journal*, because she had been so unhappy.[90] Within this framework the finding of fault is not a question of law – or justice – but rather a question purely of psychology. It was the underlying causes of the acts of adultery that mattered, not the facts. And in this context the therapeutic explanations inevitably looked to the childhoods of Charles and Diana. The son of a distant, cold mother and bullying father, and the daughter of an unhappy 'broken home', they were rendered not morally guilty but victims of Adverse Childhood Experiences (ACEs) – the increasingly fashionable, albeit contested, framework for early-years policy makers.[91] Truth is not unimportant here, but the emphasis is on being true to oneself. As Wilson observed, 'we no longer have fallen woman, we have confused woman, woman finding themselves, breaking free from restricting relationships … grief for Diana privileges the values of feeling over reason'.[92]

Coles, reviewing Diana's *Panorama* interview with Martin Bashir, commented:

> She finessed the forensic matter of guilt or innocence of infidelity by turning a cross-examination into a romantic soliloquy. She presented herself not as an adulteress, but as a romantic heroine, compelled by true love to finally throw off the shackles of a loveless marriage to a cruel and unfeeling adulterer.[93]

The marginalisation of religious and legal doctrines based on guilt are part of a broader – and widely commented on – secularisation of divorce law.[94] But notwithstanding that, Maitland argued that the response to Diana's death had a particularly Catholic tone, that she swiftly became in effect a 'secular saint'.[95]

[87] ibid 3.
[88] ibid 3.
[89] ibid 2.
[90] Hitchens (1998) 60.
[91] Macvarish and Lee (2019).
[92] Wilson (1998) 114, 124.
[93] Coles (1998) 180.
[94] Glendon (1989).
[95] Maitland (1998) 73.

There are echoes here of Catherine of Aragon – the Catholic Queen discarded by an adulterous husband, and indeed at the command of the Monarch; for it was the Queen who ordered Charles and Diana to divorce, a decision that overshadowed any formal legal process in the contemporary and subsequent accounts. There are echoes too of Caroline of Brunswick, another troublesome discarded consort, whose loyal supporters questioned the moral and political authority of George IV, as indeed Diana's fiercest advocates questioned Charles's fitness to rule. And as with Caroline,[96] responses to Diana also emphasised the significance of gender roles. Maitland acknowledges that Diana was a 'patron Saint of femininity whose lifestyle was precisely the opposite of that propagated by Catholicism', and in this new model, this new belief system, 'emotional sincerity [is] more important than truth; self-discovery superior to chastity; love to marriage'.[97]

While the impact of divorce reform on marriage and the impact of Diana on the monarchy are viewed by some as similarly modernising and progressive, there are, of course, more critical accounts of both. In her sustained analysis of the Family Law Act 1996 reforms, Reece identifies the move away from doctrinal fault as an example of 'post-liberalism'. Distinct from both conservative morality and laissez-faire liberalism, post-liberalism requires individuals not to obey juridical commands but to internalise a demanding model of 'responsibility'. In this account, divorce per se is no longer morally bad but has been replaced by an injunction to divorce responsibly: 'psychological norms have replaced social norms, and therapeutic correctness has become the new standard of good behaviour'.[98] For Rose, this represents a form of 'government at a distance' that, through concepts of 'empowerment' and 'self-esteem', serves to mask strategies of control.[99] These insights underlie much of the criticism – especially amongst feminists – of the assumptions about mediation and the removal of legal aid, which have gone hand in hand with the removal of 'fault' from divorce law.

The critique of divorce reform and the ambivalence about the wider shift from being 'governed' to 'self-governance' mirror exactly the critiques of the progressive and optimistic investments in Diana. Central to these critiques was the concern that the legitimation of individual feelings and demonstration of emotions coincided and was aligned with the rejection of a commitment to a social collective and the increasing privatisation of care. As Gilles et al have argued, the early feminist slogan 'the personal is political' has increasingly been articulated as 'the personal is the only political'.[100] Wilson, who confessed to being 'baffled' by the reaction to Diana's death, observed that 'as we wept for Diana we forgot how we kicked the momless and loathed the poor'.[101] Coles, who described Diana's death

[96] Carter (2008).
[97] Maitland (1998) 73.
[98] Reece (2003) 217.
[99] Rose (2000).
[100] Gilles, Edwards and Horsley (2013).
[101] Wilson (1998) 125.

as 'a paradigm shift', critiqued 'sincerity being mistaken for truth' and expressed concern that it mirrored something wider; that we had

> [l]ost sight of or lost the will to look for … the moral blindness which results from … the unquestioning belief in the rightness of acting in accordance with one's feelings … the smothering of cold hard responsibilities with a fluffy pillow of sentimentality.[102]

Similarly, Debray observed that 'the culture of public duty was as it were stepping down to meet the culture of intimacy'.[103] Paradoxically these concerns, from commentators all on the left, echo some of the fears of about unbridled individualism expressed by social conservatives in the post- war period.

Therapeutic justice for these commentators was not just distinct from formal justice but a barrier to social justice. Again, there are clear parallels with critiques of moves in other aspects of the law relating to marriage, in particular a willingness tentatively to condone a more individualistic contractual approach by the recognition of pre-nuptial agreements. Here too what is represented by its proponents as modernising and progressive has been critiqued by those wary of the uneven and gendered consequences of such moves and of the perceived rejection of collective values.[104]

Readings of Diana and her impact have been deeply contested, and other feminists responded with a counter-critique. Grant, for example, in reply to those who rejected the progressive or more supportive interpretations, suggested that 'the Left can't cope with beauty, is terrified of feelings and guilty of "sneering elitist condescension"'.[105] There are echoes here of the social historian Raphael Samuel's wider despair of the 'heritage baiting' within parts of the Left; an inability to comprehend and understand or respect ordinary people's attachments to and the pleasures derived from historic institutions.[106] And this in part explains the ambivalence about the social and cultural legacy of Diana, for her refusal to accept a traditional, unquestioning role in her marriage and in the royal family may have helped, provoked and cohered with a redefinition of both monarchy and marriage; but it was never a fundamental challenge to either and instead a form of 'conservative modernisation'.[107] As Linda Holt remarked, the 'most enduring fact about Diana may prove to be that she brought forth not a feminist warrior, but a true Prince Charming'.[108] As this quote from 1998 hinted, the debates and projections about Diana live on in the very public dissection of the personal lives – and marriages – of her sons.

[102] Coles (1998) 182.
[103] Debray (1998) 127.
[104] See Baroness Hale's dissenting judgment in *Radmacher v Granatino* [2010] UKSC 42; and Shanley (2003).
[105] Grant in Wilson (1998) 112.
[106] Samuel (1994).
[107] Merck (1998) 14.
[108] Holt (1998) 196.

VI. Conclusion

Monarchy and marriage, institutions with complex and entwined theological and cultural roots, have – in Britain – both proved to be remarkably resilient. They have defied predictions of their demise by both their adherents and their detractors. Perceived by the former as forces for stability and for collective and individual well-being, and by the latter as outdated, oppressive power structures that restrict imaginations of alternative personal and political development, they both attract deep attachments and polarised responses. Royal divorces, broadly defined, have throughout history been key moments of rupture not just for the relationship of the individuals involved but for both institutions, and taking royal divorces seriously provides a way of examining how both marriage and monarchy have both resisted and responded to change.

Starting with the long view, at a time of unquestioned patriarchal marriage and absolute monarchy, royal annulments enabled King John and Henry VIII to discard wives for reasons of political and dynastic efficacy. The contemplation and possibility of divorce more generally, and for Charles II and George IV specifically, played a role at key moments of the Whig ascendency from the Glorious Revolution to the Great Reform Act; parliamentary sovereignty gradually evolving alongside parliamentary divorce.

In the second half of the twentieth century, royal divorces became the trigger for crises, as both marriage and monarchy responded to secularisation, welfarism, social democracy and feminism. Prior to 1969, the emerging norm of companionate marriage premised on the pursuit of happiness rather than duty posed a particular challenge for a monarchy invested with a new function of exemplifying conservative 'traditional' family values. From fighting a losing battle, the frequency of royal divorces after the Act not only reflected the increase in divorce more widely but also legitimised it in its most radical (no-fault) form by rejecting legal fault and the doctrine of guilt. No longer a threat to monarchy, royal divorces have according to some merely shifted the theory of 'the family on the throne' from ideal to ordinary. In doing so, royal divorces have not only played a role in fundamentally challenging the indissolubility of marriage, but have also redefined the role of monarchy, as Paul Foot suggests:

> The influence of a monarchy which has long ago been stripped of real political power lies precisely in its absorption of people's aspirations, griefs, ambitions and endeavours. Weaknesses, therefore, are as adorable as strengths. Royal idiocies, divorces, selfishness, as detailed in the popular press, are not destructive of modern monarchy. On the contrary, they provide a vital link between the monarch and their subjects.[109]

In this new framework, the liberal acceptance of individual human frailties comes up against a far more amorphous code – but one arguably no less moral or

[109] Foot (2018) 27.

judgmental – premised on individual rights and therapeutic justice, albeit operating outside of formal law.

The move away from the certainties provided by a social order premised on status and duty makes the task of defining companionate marriage as complex as establishing the function of a constitutional monarch. In her landmark dissenting judgment in which she rejected a move towards the contractualisation of marriage, Lady Hale held that 'Marriage still counts for something in the law of this country and long may it continue to do so.'[110] The same could be said of the monarchy, but precisely *what* both institutions count for is a matter of ongoing debate. And it is precisely in this contested space that royal divorces continue to play a role.

The drama of a royal divorce, displayed for all in public, becomes a performance as significant as not only a royal marriage but ceremonial events such as the opening of Parliament or the Trooping of the Colour. Bagehot's confident assertion that '[w]e have to regard the Crown as the head of our morality'[111] is as true today as it was when he wrote those words, almost exactly a century before the 1969 Act. But in a more democratic age, in some if not in all respects, and in an age where the injunction to be true to oneself is a moral injunction as much as a liberatory practice, the national conversation – and the taking of sides and constructing of narratives – about royal divorces becomes more critical than ever before. Royal divorces have unquestionably challenged the divinity of marriage and monarchy; but far from being the death knell for the romanticism of both, have been essential to sustaining and redefining them.

References

Agnew, P (2015) 'The Francis Process: Moving from a Minor to a Major Key?' 104 (415) *Studies: An Irish Quarterly Review* 281.

Bagehot, W (1867) *The English Constitution* (London, Henry King and Co).

Bauer, H and Cook, M (2012) *Queer 1950s* (London, Palgrave/Macmillan).

Benton, S (1998) 'The Princess, The People and Paranoia' in M Merck (ed), *After Diana: Irreverent Elegies* (London, Verso).

Birnbaum, N (1955) 'Monarchs and Sociologists: A Reply to Professor Shills and Mr Young' 3 *The Sociological Review* 5.

Brooke, H (2017) *The History of Legal Aid* available at www.fabians.org.uk/wp-content/uploads/2017/09/Bach-Commission-Appendix-6-F-1.pdf (last accessed 8 July 2021).

Brooks, P (1995; first pub 1976) *The Melodramatic Imagination* (New Haven, CT/London, Yale University Press).

Burgoyne, J, Ormrod, R and Richards, M (1987) *Divorce Matters* (London, Penguin).

[110] *Radmacher v Granatino* [2010] UKSC 42 [195]. See also Shanley (2003) for an alternative progressive critique.

[111] Bagehot (1867) 52.

Cannadine, D (1983) 'The Context, Performance and Meaning of Ritual: The British Monarchy and the "invention of Tradition", c 1820–1977' in E Hobsbawn and T Ranger (eds), *The Invention of Tradition* (Cambridge, Cambridge University Press).
Carter, L (2008) 'British Masculinity on Trial in the Queen Caroline Affair of 1820' 20 *Gender and History* 248.
Coles, R (1998) "Feelin's' in M Merck (ed), *After Diana: Irreverent Elegies* (London, Verso).
Cretney, S (2000) 'The King and the King's Proctor: the abdication crisis and the divorce laws 1936-1937' 116 *Law Quarterly Review* 583.
—— (2008) 'Royal Marriages: Some Legal and Constitutional Issues' 124 *Law Quarterly Review* 218.
Davies, J (2001) *Diana, A Cultural History: Gender, Race, Nation and the People's Princess.* (London, Palgrave Macmillan).
d'Avray, D (2014) *Dissolving Royal Marriages: A Documentary History 860–1600* (Cambridge, Cambridge University Press).
—— (2015) *Papacy, Monarchy and Marriage 860–1600* (Cambridge, Cambridge University Press).
Debray, R (1998) 'Admirable England' in M Merck (ed), *After Diana: Irreverent Elegies* (London, Verso).
Eekelaar, J (2006) *Family Law and Personal Life* (Oxford, Oxford University Press).
Finch, J (2007) 'Displaying Families' 41 *Sociology* 65.
Foot, P (2018) 'The great times they could have had' in *Royal Bodies: Writing about the Windsors from* the London Review of Books (London, LRB).
Fraser, F (1996) *The Unruly Queen: The Life of Queen Caroline* (London, Macmillan).
Gilles, V, Edwards, R and Horsley, N (2013) 'Brave New Brains: Sociology, Family and the Politics of Knowledge' 64 *The Sociological Review* 219.
Glendon, MA (1989) *The Transformation of Family Law* (Chicago, IL, University of Chicago Press).
Graham, A (2015) 'Royal Ascot History and Traditions' *Eclipse Magazine* available at https://eclipsemagazine.co.uk/2015-royal-ascot-history-and-traditions/ (last accessed 12 July 2021).
Harris, C (2012) 'The Trial of Queen Caroline in 1820 and the birth of the British tabloid coverage of royalty' *Royal Historian* available at www.royalhistorian.com/the-trial-of-queen-caroline-in-1820-and-the-birth-of-british-tabloid-coverage-of-royalty/ (last accessed 8 July 2021).
Harewood, G (1981) *The Tongs and The Bones. The Memoirs of Lord Harewood* (London, Weidenfeld & Nicolson).
Hazell, R and Morris, R (2020) *The Role of Monarchy in Modern Society: European Monarchies Compared* (Oxford, Hart Publishing).
Hitchens, C (1998) 'Princess Di, Mother T and Me' in M Merck (ed), *After Diana: Irreverent Elegies* (London, Verso).
Hobsbawm, E (1983) 'Introduction: Inventing Traditions' in E Hobsbawn and T Ranger (eds), *The Invention of Tradition* (Cambridge, Cambridge University Press).
Holt, L (1998) 'Diana and the Backlash' in M Merck (ed), *After Diana: Irreverent Elegies* (London, Verso).
Junor, P (2018) *The Duchess: The Untold Story* (London, William Collins).
Koenig, M (2009) 'The marriage of Prince George of Denmark and Anne, Viscountess Anson' *Royal Musings*, 24 April 2009, available at http://royalmusingsblogspotcom.blogspot.com/2009/04/marriage-of-prince-georg-of-denmark-and.html (last accessed 12 July 2021).

Kynaston, D (2010) *Family Britain, 1951–57 – Tales of a New Jerusalem* (London, Bloomsbury).

Macvarish, J and Lee, E (2019) 'Constructions of Parents in Adverse Childhood Experiences Discourse' 18 *Social Policy and Society* 467.

Maitland, S (1998) 'The Secular Saint' in M Merck (ed), *After Diana: Irreverent Elegies* (London, Verso).

Mantel, H (2018) 'Royal Bodies' in *Royal Bodies: Writing about the Windsors from the* London Review of Books (London, LRB).

McDonnell, A (2016) 'Mercy Applied – Marriage Annulments' 67 *The Furrow* 92.

Melikan, R (2001) 'Pains and Penalties Procedure: How the House of Lords "Tried" Queen Caroline' 20(3) *Parliamentary History* 311.

Merck, M (1998) 'Introduction: After Diana' Me' in M Merck (ed), *After Diana: Irreverent Elegies* (London, Verso).

—— (2016) *The British Monarchy on Screen* (Manchester, Manchester University Press).

Morrah, D (1958) *The Work of the Queen* (London, William Kimber).

Morris, D (2017) 'Annulment reform seems to cultivate change of culture' *National Catholic Reporter* (5 June) available at www.ncronline.org/news/people/annulment-reform-seems-cultivate-change-culture (last accessed 11 July 2021).

Mort, F (2010) *Capital Affairs: London and the Making of the Permissive Society* (New Haven, CT, Yale).

Mount, F (2018) 'Always the Same Dream' in *Royal Bodies: Writing about the Windsors from the* London Review of Books (London, LRB).

Nairn, T (1988) *The Enchanted Glass: Britain and its Monarchy* (London, Radius).

Nash, M (2017) *Royal Wills in Britain from 1509–2008* (London, Macmillan).

Pimlott, B (1996) The Queen. Elizabeth II and the Monarchy (London, HarperCollins).

Probert, R (2011) *The Rights and Wrongs of Royal Marriages* (Kenilworth, Takeaway Publishing).

—— (2016) 'The Roos Act and Modern Family Law' in S Gilmore, J Herring and R Probert (eds), *Landmark Cases in Family Law* (London, Bloomsbury).

—— (2021) *Tying the Knot: The Formation of Marriage 1836–2020* (Cambridge, Cambridge University Press).

Rebellato, D (1999) *1956 and All That: The Making of Modern British Drama* (London, Routledge).

Reece, H (2003) *Divorcing Responsibly* (Oxford, Hart Publishing).

Rose, N (2000) 'Government and Control' 40 *British Journal of Criminology* 321.

Royal Commission (1956) *Report of Royal Commission on Marriage and Divorce*, Cm 9678 (London, HMSO).

Samuel, R (1985) 'What is Social History?' 35(3) *History Today* 34.

—— (1994) *Theatres of Memory: Past and Present in Contemporary Culture* (London, Verso).

Schama, S (1986) 'The Domestication of Majesty: Royal Portraiture 1500–1850' XVIII *Journal of Interdisciplinary History* (Summer 1986) 158.

Seidler, V (2013) *Remembering Diana: Cultural memory and the reinvention of authority* (London, Palgrave Macmillan).

Shills, E and Young, M (1953) 'The Meaning of the Coronation' 1 *The Sociological Review* 63.

Shanley, MA (1979) 'Marriage Contract and Social Contract in Seventeenth Century English Political Thought' 32 *Western Political Quarterly* 79.

Shanley, ML (2003) *Just Marriage* available at bostonreview.net/archives/BR28.3/shanley.html (last accessed 11 July 2021).

Smart, C (2000) 'Divorce in England 1950–2000: A Moral Tale' in S Katz, J Eekelaar and M Maclean (eds), *Cross Currents: Family Law and Policy in the US and England* (Oxford, Oxford University Press).

Stone, L (1990) *Road to Divorce: England 1530–1987* (Oxford, Oxford University Press).

Utley, C (2017) 'My grandfather wrote the Princess's Speech', *The Oldie* (June 2017) available at www.magzter.com/stories/Culture/The-Oldie-Magazine/My-Grandfather-Wrote-The-Princesss-Speech (last accessed 12 July 2021).

Warwick, C (2017) *Princess Margaret: A Life of Contrasts* (London, Andre Deutsch).

Whitty, N (1999) 'Royalty and identity in public law: Diana's Queen of Hearts, England's Rose and People's Princess' in S Milns and N Whitty (eds), *Feminist Perspectives on Public Law* (London, Cavendish).

Wilson, E (1998) 'The Unbearable Lightness of Diana' in M Merck (ed), *After Diana: Irreverent Elegies* (London, Verso).

PART FOUR

Contemporary Perspectives and Challenges

11

Divorced from Human Rights? English Divorce Law under Human Rights Scrutiny

CARMEN DRAGHICI

I. Introduction

In recent debates over the adequacy of divorce procedures under the Matrimonial Causes Act 1973 (MCA 1973), human rights considerations have been unduly overlooked. In *Owens v Owens*,[1] the Supreme Court acknowledged that, notwithstanding changes in social attitudes, the law left a woman in her mid-60s trapped in an unhappy nominal marriage for five years if her estranged husband neither agreed to the divorce nor engaged in conduct justifying a finding that she could not be reasonably expected to live with him. *Owens* showcased a reality seldom evident in litigation:[2] if none of the Section 1(2) MCA 1973 facts can be proved, a petition will fail even if the court is persuaded that the relationship has broken down irretrievably.[3] The Supreme Court regrettably rejected the submission made by the Intervener (Resolution) (counsel for Mrs Owens having withdrawn the Human Rights Act (HRA) ground for appeal), that Section 1 of the MCA 1973 was incompatible with the HRA 1998; the HRA argument was mentioned only by Lord Wilson, and merely to endorse the Court of Appeal's conclusion.[4] Nevertheless, the judgment questioned the desirability of current divorce procedures, and the Ministry of Justice launched a public consultation on possible changes. The proposals included replacing the 'conduct' and 'living apart' requirements by a notification of intent to divorce and removing the ability to contest the application.[5] This was the first attempt to reform divorce law since the failed implementation and repeal

[1] *Owens v Owens* [2018] UKSC 41. For an analysis, see Trotter (2019).
[2] Fewer than 1% of divorces are defended: Trinder and Sefton (2018) 15.
[3] See *Buffery v Buffery* [1988] 2 FLR 365.
[4] *Owens* [2018] UKSC 41 [29].
[5] Ministry of Justice (2018).

of Part II of the Family Law Act 1996 (FLA 1996) two decades earlier,[6] and resulted in the passage of the Divorce, Dissolution and Separation Act 2020 (DDSA 2020).

Given the lack of traction of HRA arguments in the courts, it was perhaps unsurprising that human rights concerns hardly featured in the public consultation. Supporters of reform (and the Government's response) highlighted the stressful, acrimonious and dishonest nature of the divorce system (with the potential for reverse-engineered facts and no court inquiry in undefended cases), its detrimental impact on children and the vulnerability of spouses trapped by domestic abuse. Those opposing reform expressed apprehension about higher divorce rates and diminishing the gravitas of marriage.[7] Similarly, academic criticism of the MCA 1973 focused primarily on the acrimony engendered by alleging fault, the lack of 'intellectual honesty' of the process in the absence of any genuine judicial inquiry into allegations in undefended divorces, and the unfairness to respondents, who cannot challenge the truthfulness of allegations against them unless they can afford to contest the petition.[8] However, the MCA 1973 also has far-reaching human rights shortcomings, affecting the right to respect for individual autonomy and family life, the right to marry and the enjoyment of property. It is the human rights concerns raised by restrictive divorce rules that this chapter addresses. In examining the human rights rationale for eliminating lengthy waiting periods, 'behaviour' thresholds or spousal consent to divorce, the chapter considers the lessons to be learned for other areas of family law in which the HRA 1998 may play a role, as well as stressing the importance of implementing the DDSA 2020 without further delays.

While acknowledging the reluctance of the European Court of Human Rights (ECtHR) to uphold a right to divorce, this chapter draws on principles emerging from Strasbourg decisions on the regulation and conduct of divorce proceedings in jurisdictions no longer characterised by the indissolubility of marriage: the applicability of the 'living instrument' approach to Article 12 of the European Convention on Human Rights (ECHR); the importance of personal status for individual autonomy and family life after relationship breakdown under Article 8; and the need for a fair balance between competing interests in designing divorce legislation. It argues that Section 1(2)(e) MCA 1973 is inconsistent with the ECHR owing to the disproportionate impact of excessive delays in dissolving marital ties on re-partnering, forming new marriages, the legal affiliation of children born to new *de facto* family units, property rights in the absence of a decree permitting financial remedies, and the freedom of testamentary disposition. The law's HRA-compatibility will be shown to be further undermined by the increased emphasis on individual autonomy within the marital relationship in other areas of family law (eg the enforceability of prenuptial agreements) and by domestic courts'

[6] For a discussion of Pt II of the FLA 1996 and the failed reform attempt, see Reece (2000).
[7] See Ministry of Justice (2019).
[8] Trinder and Sefton (2018) 16; Kay (2004) 898; Trinder (2018) 558.

stricter standards of assessment of primary legislation under the HRA 1998 when compared to the international (subsidiary) supervision under the ECHR.

II. The Limited Impact of Human Rights Arguments in Divorce Litigation, Legal Reform and Scholarship

Marriage is central to the organisation of human society and cannot be reduced to a private contract. For the ECtHR, 'support and encouragement of the traditional family is in itself legitimate',[9] and marriage is an institution 'singled out for special treatment under Article 12 of the Convention'.[10] Nonetheless, obstacles to the dissolution of marriage greatly impact an individual's self-determination rights. It is, therefore, in some ways astonishing that English divorce law has remained largely immune from the HRA 1998.

The marginalisation of the human rights discourse in the divorce literature and litigation seems to have its origins in the *Johnston v Ireland* ruling in 1979,[11] which held that the ECHR does not enshrine a right to divorce and that states do not overstep their margin of appreciation by setting an absolute bar on divorce or, *a fortiori*, lesser impediments.[12] The judgment invoked the ordinary meaning of the words 'right to marry' in Article 12 (covering the formation, not the dissolution, of marriage) and the drafters' intentions, as shown by the *travaux préparatoires*.[13] For the ECtHR, the 'living instrument' doctrine could not update the interpretation of a provision where the omission of a right had been deliberate.[14]

The *Johnston* decision was and remains controversial.[15] Assessing the then absolute Irish bar on divorce, the ECtHR accepted that 'in a society adhering to the principle of monogamy, such a restriction cannot be regarded as injuring the substance of the right guaranteed by Article 12'.[16] The argument is certainly underwhelming; monogamy only excludes multiple *contemporaneous* marital relationships and 'the possibility of divorce would precisely serve to avoid situations of factual bigamy'.[17] Moreover, the indissolubility of formal ties does not protect the stability of marriage, as it does not preclude estrangement and new intimate relationships.

[9] *Marckx v Belgium* (1979-80) 2 EHRR 330, para 40.

[10] *Shackell v United Kingdom* App no 45851/99 (ECtHR, 27 April 2000), para 1. See also *Quintana Zapata v Spain* App no 34615/97 (ECmHR, 4 March 1998).

[11] *Johnston v Ireland* (1987) 9 EHRR 203.

[12] See Kay (2004) 898 and *Owens v Owens* [2017] EWCA Civ 182 [77]–[79].

[13] *Johnston*, para 52.

[14] ibid, para 53.

[15] For a critical analysis see Dillon (1989).

[16] *Johnston*, para 52.

[17] van Dijk, van Hoof, van Rijn and Zwaak (2006) 852. The MCA 1973 does not support the emphasis on monogamy (understood as fidelity): adultery entitles a spouse to petition for divorce only if accompanied by intolerability (s 1(2)(a)) and subject to implied condonation (s 2(1)).

In addition, the unavailability of divorce generates precarious family situations. Leaving committed couples with children outside the protection of the law arguably goes against states' obligation to protect effective family relationships. The ECtHR recognised in *Johnston* that the applicants, who had cohabited for 15 years, raised a child and provided each other economic and emotional support, presented all the hallmarks of 'family life'; for the majority, however, Article 8 did not encompass a positive obligation to permit divorce in order to protect new family units.[18] Having excluded the right to divorce from the scope of Article 12, the ECtHR held that it would be inconsistent to derive it from the more general Article 8.[19] The Court thereby avoided the more difficult analysis under Article 8, a provision that, according to its own jurisprudence, requires positive measures in order to prevent hardship for *de facto* families and allow them to lead a normal family life.[20] This may entail an obligation to facilitate the dissolution of purely formal ties that fly in the face of social reality and benefit no one,[21] particularly where the unavailability of divorce also affects the private and family life of the (technically adulterous) couple's children, a situation *Johnston* did find to breach Article 8.[22]

The prohibition of divorce also raises issues under Article 14 taken together with Article 8 where a domestic law recognises foreign divorce decrees obtained by nationals elsewhere; divorce then becomes available to those with sufficient resources to establish residence abroad for the time required to fall within a more permissive jurisdiction.[23] The majority in *Johnston* dismissed Article 14 claims, holding that the applicants were not analogously situated to Irish nationals domiciled abroad.[24] However, this overlooks the inconsistency of the law's approach to purportedly core values; if divorce clashed with public policy, foreign decrees would not be recognised either. A partly Dissenting Opinion rightly lamented the 'unfortunate contradiction with the absolute character of the principle of indissolubility of marriage' and the irrationality of the distinction between Irish citizens according to their domicile.[25]

The bar on divorce was further challenged under Article 9 ECHR. The male applicant claimed that, by precluding him from divorcing his estranged wife, the law forced him to live in an extra-marital relationship, which was contrary to his conscience.[26] The majority rejected this claim, finding that the ordinary meaning

[18] *Johnston*, paras 56–57.

[19] ibid, para 57.

[20] See *Marckx*, para 31.

[21] See *Kroon v Netherlands* (1995) 19 EHRR 263, para 40 (regarding an irrebuttable *pater est* presumption).

[22] See *Johnston*, para 75. Difficulties included the lack of automatic parental authority for natural fathers, no retrospective legitimisation through marriage, less extensive succession rights for illegitimate children.

[23] To become habitually resident in a jurisdiction, one needs to work, own property, have children in school there. See, for instance, Art 3(1) of Council Regulation (EC) No 2201/2003.

[24] See *Johnston*, paras 59–61.

[25] *Johnston*, Separate Opinion Judge De Meyer, para 7.

[26] *Johnston*, para 62.

of Article 9 could not be taken to extend to the unavailability of divorce.[27] A similar complaint featured in *JG v Ireland*;[28] the applicant maintained that his religion did not ban divorce and therefore the law imposed the tenets of a different religious persuasion on him. Regrettably, the claim was discontinued after the *Johnston* ruling. However, the Separate Opinion in *Johnston* considered the Article 9 implications of the ban at length, deeming it inconsistent with religious liberty and coercive in relation to individuals whose religious views do not prohibit divorce.[29] Judge De Meyer noted that an absolute bar cannot be justified by the support of a substantial majority of the population: 'a balance must be achieved which ensures the fair and proper treatment of minorities and avoids any abuse of a dominant position'.[30]

Although subsequent case law did not overrule *Johnston*, *Piotrowski v Poland* recognised the need to read Article 12 in light of present-day conditions.[31] Moreover, reliance on *Johnston* was robustly discredited by Judge Sajó's Separate Opinion in *Babiarz v Poland* based on the living instrument doctrine.[32] The Opinion recalled the Grand Chamber's position in *Magyar Helsinki Bizottsag v Hungary*: the *travaux préparatoires* are not dispositive of whether a right falls within the scope of an ECHR article 'if the existence of such a right was supported by the growing measure of common ground that had emerged in a given area'.[33] Furthermore, Article 2 case law on capital punishment shows that a new European consensus can displace not only the preparatory works, but also the express wording of a provision, and create obligations for states lagging behind an overwhelming legislative trend.[34] In other words, state practice can create new ECHR rights, notwithstanding the drafters' intentions or even the text itself. The right to divorce, whilst not enjoying consensus in 1950, could be seen nowadays as part of ECHR rights.

In *Owens*, the Court of Appeal relied on *Johnston* and *Babiarz* in dismissing the HRA claims.[35] It did not discuss the impact of the living instrument doctrine or Strasbourg jurisprudence narrowing states' margin of appreciation in this area. It is this stream of case law that the following section will examine.

III. The Case for a Holistic Reading of Strasbourg Jurisprudence on Divorce

While *Johnston* and *Babiarz* are important authorities, what is needed is a holistic reading of Strasbourg jurisprudence. The ECtHR has recognised that the

[27] ibid, para 63.
[28] See *JG v Ireland* App no 9584/81 (ECmHR, 8 May 1987).
[29] *Johnston*, Separate Opinion of Judge De Meyer, para 5.
[30] ibid, para 6.
[31] *Piotrowski v Poland* (2017) 64 EHRR SE6, para 46.
[32] *Babiarz v Poland* [2017] 2 FLR 613, Separate Opinion of Judge Sajó, paras 3–4.
[33] *Magyar Helsinki Bizottsag v Hungary* (2020) 71 EHRR 2, para 125.
[34] Draghici (2017c) 23.
[35] *Owens* [2017] EWCA Civ 182 [77]–[81].

regulation of purely domestic rights[36] connected with existing ECHR rights may also breach the Convention.[37] Examples include domestic entitlements affecting status, such as the ability to adopt a child or to form a civil partnership. Although states have no obligation to legalise these institutions, they engage ECHR rights and their administration must be ECHR-compliant.[38] The UK Supreme Court has also accepted that Article 8 ECHR applies to civil partnerships, and access conditions must satisfy Article 14 requirements.[39] Accordingly, states permitting divorce must regulate access in conformity with ECHR principles.

Strasbourg case law on divorce confirms that the regulation and conduct of proceedings (duration, grounds for divorce, burden on laypersons) remain subject to human rights obligations (particularly under Articles 6, 8 and 12), and that any interferences with ECHR rights arising from such proceedings must pursue a legitimate aim and be necessary in a democratic society. Two streams of case law demonstrate that divorce laws are no longer exempted from ECHR constraints: that condemning the inefficiency of domestic courts dealing with divorce petitions; and that criticising substantive rules delaying the possibility of obtaining the divorce in the first place.

A. Unreasonable Obstacles or Delays in Divorce Proceedings as ECHR Violations

Strasbourg judgments have found that unreasonable delays or practical impediments in divorce proceedings breach the Convention, and have recognised the fundamental interest an individual has in dissolving a failed marriage and reacquiring the capacity to marry. In *Airey v Ireland*,[40] the ECtHR held that, by failing to provide an accessible judicial separation procedure for those unable to meet the costs of legal representation, Irish law violated Article 8 ECHR. Although a procedure for obtaining judicial separation from an abusive spouse existed and the authorities had not actively interfered with the applicant's rights, there had been a breach by omission.[41] Once domestic law recognises a person's right to secure judicial separation in certain circumstances, this 'means of protection' must be 'effectively accessible'.[42] Arguably, if a legal system recognises that protecting private and family life may require the dissolution of marital ties, a drawn-out process or one contingent upon the other party's consent[43] fails to satisfy the accessibility requirement.

[36] ie rights conferred by a state but not mandatory under the Convention.

[37] Draghici (2017b) 315–19.

[38] *EB v France* (2008) 47 EHRR 21, para 49; *Vallianatos v Greece* (2014) 59 EHRR 12, paras 75, 78.

[39] *R (Steinfeld) v Secretary of State for International Development* [2018] UKSC 32 [16]–[19].

[40] *Airey v Ireland* (1979-80) 2 EHRR 305.

[41] ibid, para 32.

[42] ibid, para 33.

[43] Although the respondent's rights are also at play, the balance between competing rights leans in favour of the spouse wishing to have the marriage dissolved (see Section III.B).

Furthermore, according to *F v Switzerland*, 'if national legislation allows divorce, … Article 12 … secures for divorced persons the right to remarry without unreasonable restrictions'.[44] A temporary prohibition on remarriage (three years since the last divorce, after three failed marriages) impaired the very substance of the right. The Court acknowledged states' wide margin of appreciation in matrimonial matters; a waiting period did not necessarily constitute a breach, even if other ECHR states no longer had an equivalent rule,[45] but it was not regarded as an appropriate means of achieving the legitimate aim of promoting the stability of marriage.[46] The Court dismissed the Swiss Government's concern to protect the prospective spouse and the divorcee himself, supposedly sheltered through a compulsory period of reflection; such arguments were seen as paternalistic and insufficient to justify the interference with the rights of mentally competent adults.[47] While *F* involved restrictions on remarriage after divorce had been obtained, it could be argued, *mutatis mutandis*, that restrictions on a person's capacity to remarry after a relationship breakdown, resulting from procedural hurdles to obtain the divorce, must also be necessary and proportionate.

The excessive length of proceedings for judicial separation was also found in breach of Article 6(1) ECHR in *Laino v Italy*, insofar as it was inconsistent with the right to have one's case heard 'within a reasonable time'.[48] The Grand Chamber highlighted that special diligence is required of state authorities in proceedings concerning civil status, given the importance of what is at stake for the applicant, namely the effective enjoyment of the right to respect for family life.[49] Disappointingly, the Court did not entertain the Article 8 claim separately.[50] Subsequently, however, in *Charalambous v Cyprus*, the length of divorce proceedings was examined as both an Article 6 and an Article 12 violation. Although on the facts the Court disagreed that the length of proceedings had been excessive, given the various appellate stages, the ruling firmly established that 'a failure of the domestic authorities to conduct divorce proceedings within a reasonable time could, in certain circumstances, raise an issue under Article 12'.[51]

The ECtHR did find an Article 12 breach on the facts in *VK v Croatia*,[52] where the duration of divorce proceedings had exceeded five years. The judgment consolidated the principle outlined in *Charalambous*:

> [A] failure on the part of the domestic authorities to conduct divorce proceedings with the required urgency may impair the right to marry of an individual who has, for

[44] *F v Switzerland* (1988) 10 EHRR 411, para 38.
[45] ibid.
[46] ibid, para 36.
[47] ibid, para 37.
[48] *Laino v Italy* App no 3158/96 (ECtHR, 18 February 1999).
[49] ibid, para 18.
[50] ibid, paras 23–25.
[51] *Charalambous v Cyprus* [2008] 1 FLR 473, para 56. See also *VK v Croatia* [2013] 2 FLR 1045, para 99.
[52] *VK v Croatia*, paras 100–107.

> example, sought to have his previous marriage dissolved in order to marry again, or who has acquired a serious and genuine opportunity to remarry after he had instituted divorce proceedings.[53]

Due to the lack of efficiency in the conduct of proceedings, 'the applicant was left in a state of prolonged uncertainty which amounted to an unreasonable restriction of his right to marry'.[54]

Two subsequent cases suggest, however, that the length of divorce proceedings breaches the Convention only if the applicant had concrete plans for a new family. No breach of Article 12 was found in *Truszkowska v Poland*, where 'the applicant ha[d] not shown that she actually wanted to and was prevented from re-marrying'.[55] Similarly, the absence of a new partner in *Berlin v Luxemburg* led the Court to conclude that no violation of Article 8 had occurred.[56] These cases are problematic because of the intrusiveness of the proposed judicial test, the failure to recognise that formal marital ties can affect a person's ability to embark upon new relationships, and the downplaying of the inherent interest one has in the clarification of one's civil status (upheld in *Laino*). This unfortunate development does not detract, however, from the principle that divorce proceedings are not free from human rights oversight: divorce, where available as a means to protect a person's private and family life, must be effectively accessible; Article 12 safeguards the right to remarry; and excessive delays or practical obstacles to securing a divorce may breach Convention obligations.

B. The Requirement for Divorce Grounds to Strike a Fair Balance between Competing Interests

A separate stream of case law has established that the grounds for divorce themselves must strike a fair balance between competing interests. The ECtHR indicated in *Ivanov and Petrova v Bulgaria* that an Article 12 breach may arise where, despite an irretrievable breakdown of marital life, domestic law regards the lack of consent of an innocent party as an insurmountable obstacle to granting a divorce to a guilty party.[57] Although Section 1(2)(e) of the MCA 1973 does not give the spouse opposing the divorce an absolute veto power, it does give them a temporary one; that imbalance between the parties' positions raises Article 12 issues and requires justification. Moreover, in *Piotrowski v Poland*, the Court recalled that, under

[53] ibid, para 100.

[54] ibid, para 106. Other indirect obstacles to remarriage, such as undue delays in providing a prisoner with the divorce certificate, may violate Art 12; see *Chernetskiy v Ukraine* App no 44316/07 (ECtHR, 8 December 2016).

[55] *Truszkowska v Poland* App no 52586/99 (ECtHR, 11 December 2001), para 3.

[56] *Berlin v Luxembourg* App no 44978/98 (ECtHR, 15 July 2003), paras 64–65.

[57] *Ivanov and Petrova v Bulgaria* App no 15001/04 (ECtHR, 14 June 2011).

Article 8, a fair balance had to be struck between competing interests, although in the area of divorce law that task was largely delegated to states (who enjoy considerable discretion as to where that balance should be struck).[58] The *Babiarz v Poland* judgment (invoked in *Owens* as evidence that the ECHR did not guarantee a favourable outcome in divorce proceedings[59]) further reiterated states' duty to reconcile competing interests in designing and applying divorce legislation:

> In the area of *framing their divorce laws* and implementing them in concrete cases, the Contracting Parties enjoy a wide margin of appreciation in determining the steps to be taken *to ensure compliance with the Convention* and *to reconcile the competing personal interests at stake*.[60]

Albeit finding against the applicant on the facts, in *Babiarz* the Court suggested neither that states enjoy unfettered discretion as regards divorce legislation nor that the ECHR did not apply to it. The Court's conclusion on the facts is questionable. The wife did not consent to the divorce, although the husband lived with another woman and had a 4-year-old daughter with her at the time of divorce proceedings. Domestic courts recognised the irretrievable breakdown of the marriage, but noted that Polish law did not permit a divorce to be granted to the party at fault if the innocent party refused to consent, unless the refusal was 'contrary to the reasonable principles of social coexistence';[61] they applied the Supreme Court's interpretation, that is, that the refusal was not unreasonable if motivated by the desire to reconcile rather than exact vengeance or frustrate the spouse's intention to re-marry. The ECtHR regrettably concluded that the applicant complained about the outcome of domestic proceedings (which was not a matter for the international judge), whereas in fact the case revolved around whether the Polish judicial test for unreasonably withheld consent met ECHR standards; this was a point of law, not of application to the facts, and did not warrant self-restraint. The test developed by the Polish judiciary evidently failed to strike a fair balance: the credibility of the declarations of motivations is doubtful, and the approach indulges deluded hopes for reconciliation (much like those of the husband in *Owens*). The ECtHR did reiterate the principle formulated in *Ivanov and Petrova v Bulgaria*: there is a potential Article 12 breach where the consent of the innocent spouse is an insurmountable obstacle to granting a divorce to a guilty party; problematically, it found that it did not apply to the circumstances at hand, because there was no bar in the law, and the applicant's petition had failed after a hearing examining individual circumstances. The ECtHR thus overlooked the lack of discretion for judges applying domestic rules on consent as interpreted by the Supreme Court, which had the same effect as a legislative proviso or bar.

[58] *Piotrowski*, para 44.
[59] *Owens* [2017] EWCA Civ 182 [80]–[81].
[60] *Babiarz*, para 47 (emphasis added).
[61] ibid, paras 24–31.

Consequently, while a right to divorce did not gather international support when the ECHR was adopted, it is no longer disputed that the regulation of divorce must accommodate Convention rights and that everyone has a fundamental interest in dissolving a failed marriage and reacquiring the capacity to marry. Even if the right to divorce at all is optional under the Convention, its administration must remain consistent with the rights engaged under Articles 8 and 12.

C. Unsuccessful Challenges as Product of the Subsidiarity of Strasbourg Supervision

The justifications underpinning the pro-state outcome in *Piotrowski* and *Babiarz* further confirm the human rights constraints on divorce laws. First, the ECtHR declined to act as a final court of appeal, since domestic courts had had the benefit of direct testimony and relevant legal context.[62] It is, in fact, a well-established principle in Strasbourg jurisprudence, derived from the general rule of subsidiarity of international courts, that the ECtHR is not an appellate jurisdiction and only provides broad-brush supervision of domestic courts' rulings, not a full retrial of the case.[63] The doctrine, however, risks reducing Strasbourg supervision to a 'perfunctory control of procedural propriety',[64] and supranational litigation involving divorce laws illustrates this difficulty. Where the alleged ECHR breach stems from acts of the judiciary (as opposed to legislative measures or administrative practice), the Court refuses to engage with the substance of the claim, lest it should act as an appellate court. This deprives applicants of any realistic opportunity for redress in Strasbourg proceedings when the failings are imputable to courts. Additionally, as seen in *Babiarz*, the Court sometimes conflates the interpretation of legislative acts by domestic courts (akin to law-making powers) with the application of the law to the facts (not warranting Strasbourg intervention save in cases of flagrant denial of justice).

Second, when assessing divorce laws (rather than their application to a particular case), the Court is deferential to the balancing exercise sought by the legislative scheme. In *Piotrowski*, it was readily satisfied that domestic law 'can be seen as intended to be a safeguard to protect one party, usually the weaker, against the machinations and bad faith of the other party'.[65] This wide margin afforded to domestic lawmakers and the superficial scrutiny of their balancing exercise are further problematic expressions of subsidiarity; the Court accepts any generic justification without carrying out a genuine assessment and focuses on the

[62] ibid, para 53. See also *Piotrowski*, para 50.

[63] *Kemmache v France (No 3)* (1995) 19 EHRR 349, para 44. See also *Kearns v France* (2010) 50 EHRR 33, para 75; *Winterwerp v Netherlands* (1979-80) 2 EHRR 387, para 46; *Bozano v France* (1987) 9 EHRR 297, para 58.

[64] Draghici (2017a) 24–25.

[65] *Piotrowski*, para 49.

(defendable) aims of the law more than on how it reconciles competing interests. Nonetheless, the way in which the Court rationalises its decision does confirm that divorce law is subject to ECHR obligations.

Third, in evaluating proportionality, the Court adopts a narrow focus on individual circumstances and deems the divorce regime reasonable where the applicant had no new prospect of marital life. In *Piotrowski*, this over-simplistic approach led the Court to conclude that no violation had occurred because the applicant did not mention 'any concrete marriage plans frustrated by the refusal to obtain a divorce'.[66] Equally unconvincing is the observation that nothing prevented the applicant from submitting a fresh divorce petition if/when circumstances changed. As noted previously, the interest in obtaining a divorce goes beyond remarriage; making access to divorce contingent upon proof of a planned marriage impinges on the petitioner's privacy and is potentially discriminatory (rights are differently safeguarded depending on an irrelevant characteristic, namely, whether the person is affianced).

However unsatisfactory in those specific cases, the Court's analysis nevertheless reinforces the notion that divorce laws must obey the same criteria as any other interference with fundamental rights, that is, pursue a legitimate aim and avoid a disproportionate impact on the individual rights concerned.

IV. Applying Strasbourg Jurisprudence to the English Divorce Regime

Taking stock of Strasbourg jurisprudence, this section considers whether the MCA 1973 interferences with Articles 8 and 12 ECHR pursue a legitimate aim and strike a fair balance between the public and private interests at stake. It examines the policy objectives of the MCA scheme, questioning whether it benefits the non-consenting spouse, the couple (as a family unit), any children of the family or society at large.

A. Balancing Private and Public Interests

i. Secularised Divorce and the Non-Justiciability of Marital Breakdown

The Christian heritage of European family laws made it difficult for ECHR drafters to include a right to divorce in 1950. As Eekelaar pointed out, the right could not take hold because of its clash with a widely held religious precept.[67] In *Johnston*,

[66] ibid, para 51.
[67] Eekelaar (2011) 236.

the indissolubility of marriage was seen as 'largely a religious matter',[68] which attracted deference. By contrast, in present-day England, divorce restrictions should be disconnected from religious sensitivities and expected to meet the usual criteria of necessity and proportionality.

Admittedly, the law's approach to divorce does not have exclusively religious foundations. Lady Hale, writing extra-judicially, explained the state's pragmatic interest in the stability of marriage: by strengthening family responsibilities, spouses look after one another and the children, and less state support is required.[69] Nonetheless, this goal can be achieved by cementing child and spousal support obligations after divorce. Keeping the parties married goes beyond that legitimate collective interest and is not logically connected to it.

Nor can it be assumed that the state is better placed than the spouses themselves to decide whether their marriage has failed. Writers have long queried if it is the law's task to determine when a marriage is no longer viable.[70] Whether the irretrievable breakdown of a marriage is a justiciable matter was a concern already raised before the 1969 reform, although doubts mainly focused on courts' workload.[71] Even though the MCA 1973 does not require courts to make an evaluative judgement about the breakdown themselves, it (erroneously) assumes that the five facts serving as proxy for that finding *can* be objectively determined.

According to *Frasik v Poland*, Article 12 does not permit state authorities to inquire into the intended spouses' reasons for wanting to marry.[72] Symmetrically, one could argue that the state should not inquire into the parties' reasons for wanting to dissolve the marriage. Whilst marriage is not an ordinary contract, rescindable according to the parties' wishes, it cannot be viewed as a primarily public interest; the state cannot have an overwhelmingly greater say in its termination than those who are directly affected, for reasons explored next.

ii. Still a 'Voluntary Union'? The 'Entry' and 'Exit' Discrepancy

Self-determination in the intimate sphere of family life is an important feature of human rights law. Article 23(3) of the International Covenant on Civil and Political Rights 1966 protects marriage as a commitment entered into 'with full and free consent'. English marriage law recognises the importance of choice, allowing a party to have the marriage annulled if he/she did not consent to it[73] and providing protection against forced marriage.[74] Yet once a person has validly entered a marriage, the principle of autonomy loses force: one cannot obtain a divorce

[68] Dillon (1989) 87.
[69] Hale (2011) 4.
[70] Welstead (2012) 36.
[71] Hall (1966) 185.
[72] *Frasik v Poland* App no 22933/02 (ECtHR, 5 January 2010), para 93.
[73] MCA 1973, s 12.
[74] FLA 1996, ss 63A–63S.

simply because one no longer consents to be married. Consent to the marriage appears to be only an 'entry' requirement, whereas the marriage should arguably be contingent upon its remaining voluntary.

iii. Recognition of Individual Autonomy within the Couple in Other Areas of Family Law

Under the ECHR, 'morals' and 'public order' justifications for restrictions are country-specific. The proportionality of the divorce regime must therefore be assessed in light of the evolution of other areas of English family law in a direction more respectful of individual autonomy within the married couple.

The law has abandoned the doctrine of unity between husband and wife,[75] and this is further demonstrated by the relaxation of affinity bars. Former step-parents and step-children can now intermarry in certain circumstances,[76] and no bars remain on the marriages of former in-laws.[77] Departure from the doctrine of unity is also evidenced by the special treatment reserved to non-marital assets in proceedings for financial and property remedy upon divorce in high-value cases. Courts have allowed pre-marital or inherited property to be ring-fenced by the owner where the needs of the other spouse could be met without including it in the pool of assets available for redistribution.[78] The presumptively binding nature of prenuptial agreements since *Radmacher v Granatino*[79] further promotes autonomy within the couple and limits the state's intervention in the regulation of the consequences of relationship breakdown. Additionally, although spouses are likely to be successful in an application under the Inheritance (Provision for Family and Dependants) Act 1975 (IPFDA 1975), courts have recognised that the testator can dispose of their estate as they please after making reasonable provision for their spouse.[80]

Family law has, thus, increasingly recognised that spouses maintain their individuality within the marital union, rather than being absorbed by it. Divorce law has lagged behind these developments. For the ECtHR, proportionality requires consistency between the various areas of domestic law; this is so even in matters of wide state discretion.[81] Treating consent to be bound in marriage as non-rescindable for five years (unless a judge or the other spouse supports the decision) is a reductive understanding of autonomy, which should exclude a self-binding element.

[75] As evidenced by the recognition of wives' capacity to own property, be sued in tort and make binding contracts in their own right.

[76] Marriage Act 1949, s 1(3).

[77] Marriage Act 1949 (Remedial) Order 2007 (SI 2007/438).

[78] *White v White* [2000] 2 FLR 981; *K v L* [2011] EWCA Civ 550; *P v P (Inherited Property)* [2004] EWHC 1364 (Fam).

[79] *Radmacher v Granatino* [2010] UKSC 42; see also *Kremen v Agrest (No 11)* [2012] EWHC 45.

[80] *Fielden v Cunliffe* [2005] EWCA Civ 1508. *Ilott v The Blue Cross* [2017] UKSC 17 reinforced the principle of testamentary freedom.

[81] See *Costa and Pavan v Italy* App no 54270/10 (ECtHR, 28 August 2012), paras 60–71 (inconsistency in abortion and embryo screening legislation).

B. Balancing Private Rights: Innocent Spouses and New De Facto Family Life

Strasbourg case law has shown that the Convention does not protect a person's desire to remain married against the other spouse's wishes. According to *Slimani v France*, the right to marry does not encompass a right to the indissolubility of the marriage or a right to immunity against nullity proceedings; thus, Article 12 does not assist a respondent wishing to contest an annulment action in which they had a fair opportunity to make representations.[82] The recognition that Article 12 does not guarantee the indissolubility of marriage is significant for the assessment of the balancing of rights: the spouse who wishes to stay married has no right to expect that the marriage will be shielded against dissolution, whereas the spouse who pursues the divorce has a right to respect for self-determination and the protection of the family life created with a new partner. A five-year wait does not adequately reflect this contrast; the weaker claim of the spouse wishing to stay married, unsupported by any discernible ECHR right, is disproportionately accommodated at the expense of the other party's well-established ECHR rights.

Moreover, as Judge Sajó noted in *Babiarz*, it is improper to speak of a balance between the competing rights of the spouses, as the party who does not wish to be divorced has a mere interest, rather than a right (understood as an enforceable ECHR claim), in maintaining the formal legal bond to an estranged spouse,[83] whereas the spouse who has formed a new *de facto* family unit has a right to its protection under Article 8, as well as a right to remarry without unreasonable obstacles under Article 12. Whilst the right to remarry only benefits individuals who have the capacity to marry, as defined domestically (and so it cannot be invoked until the conditions for divorce are met), states do not have unfettered discretion in defining capacity-to-marry conditions, as shown by Article 12 case law regarding former in-laws, divorced persons and detainees.[84] The regulation of divorce is part and parcel of the regulation of capacity to marry.

Even assuming that the legislator had to perform a balancing exercise between the two spouses' rights, greater weight would have to be afforded to 'the private life right not to be forced to live in a marital union with another person, whether as an instance of self-determination or as a precondition to family life'.[85] Compelling one person to stay married[86] merely to accommodate the 'innocent' spouse's wish to retain marital status is a questionable balancing exercise; the proportionality of this approach is considered in greater detail in Section IV.C.

[82] *Slimani v France* App no 33597/96 (ECmHR, 9 April 1997), para 2.

[83] *Babiarz*, Separate Opinion of Judge Sajó, para 6.

[84] See, inter alia, *B and L v UK* (2006) 42 EHRR 11; *F v Switzerland* (discussed in Section III.A); and *Jaremowicz v Poland* App No 24023/03 (ECtHR, 5 January 2010).

[85] *Babiarz*, Separate Opinion of Judge Sajó, para 7.

[86] Continuation of marital status is not tantamount to enforced cohabitation, but formally a person needs a decree of judicial separation to be relieved of the obligation to cohabit with their spouse (MCA 1973, s 18(1)), for which one of the same facts in s 1(2) must be proved (s 17).

C. Trapping Spouses in Unhappy Marriages: Necessary and Proportionate?

The five-year separation requirement and associated wait to commence divorce proceedings has potentially far-reaching consequences. An individual's private life is affected by their civil status, and any children with *de facto* partners are confusingly born under the *pater est* presumption.[87] When death occurs during the period of separation, the devolution of property benefits the estranged spouse;[88] intestacy rules apply even after a decree nisi,[89] let alone *de facto* separation. Nor can a will adequately safeguard the wishes of the deceased, as the law is protective of spousal claims.[90] Further knock-on effects include the potential ineligibility for assisted reproductive services with a new partner.[91]

The five-year wait is also a disproportionate interference with the right to remarry and affects the very essence of that right. A three-year delay in forming a new marriage after several failed marriages was condemned in *F v Switzerland*. While that case concerned a law that inhibited remarriage *after* the divorce had been obtained, it shows that even a short postponement of a new marriage may raise Article 12 concerns. Article 12 violations were also ascertained in cases involving the right to marry of prisoners detained for relatively short sentences.[92] If the ECHR does not permit states to postpone prisoners' exercise of their right to marry, however briefly, despite society's legitimate interest in preserving the punitive and deterring function of criminal law, it is equally unacceptable to compel individuals whose marriage has collapsed to wait several years before they can enjoy Article 12 rights again. That state discretion regarding capacity-to-marry requirements is not unlimited is further demonstrated by the condemnation of the bar on marriage between former in-laws in *B and L v UK*. One should thus avoid the temptation of trivialising the impact on Article 12 rights of a five-year wait to divorce a spouse who vetoes the legal dissolution of a failed marriage.

[87] The common law presumption can be rebutted by a declaration of parentage (FLA 1986, s 55A), supported by DNA evidence if necessary (Family Law Reform Act 1969, s 20(1)). It is unlikely that the husband would wish to assume financial responsibility for the wife's adulterine children, but he could conceivably raise further hurdles for her, out of spite or to prolong contact. A married woman wishing to register a third party to the marriage as the father on the child's birth certificate under Births and Deaths Registration Act 1953, s 10 faces difficulties that the alignment of marital status to social reality would avoid.

[88] Administration of Estates Act 1925, s 46.

[89] *Re Collins* [1990] 2 All ER 47.

[90] IPFDA 1975. See *Davis v Davis* [1993] 1 FLR 54; *Fielden v Cunliffe*; *P v G* [2006] Fam Law 179.

[91] Under the Human Fertilisation and Embryology Act 2008, s 38(2), the *pater est* presumption prevails over the 'agreed fatherhood conditions'. While the presumption could be rebutted (the husband is not the biological father and did not consent to his wife's insemination with donor sperm and to his treatment as the father *per* s 35) and ss 36–37 would ultimately allocate paternity, the fertility clinic might be reluctant to provide treatment in the circumstances, in light of the practice guidance in s 25(2) of the Human Fertilisation and Embryology Act 1990.

[92] *Hamer v UK* (1982) 4 EHRR 139; *Jaremowicz*. See further Draghici (2017a) 62–63.

Moreover, while the MCA 1973 scheme purports to ensure the stability of marriage, in practice it does not achieve that aim. The legal unavailability of divorce does not prevent spouses from living separate lives and forming new intimate relationships; even less so in recent decades, as the cultural, social or religious reservations that dissuaded many spouses from separating and forming non-marital relationships have largely fallen away. The five-year wait required for non-consensual divorce leads to estranged spouses, vulnerable *de facto* family structures, extra-marital re-partnering and adulterous children, benefitting neither the parties nor society. As the ECtHR held in *B and L v UK*, restrictions pursuing legitimate aims but incapable of achieving them are intrinsically disproportionate.[93] In that case, banning marriage between former parents-in-law and children-in-law did not prevent intimate relationships and confusion for children. The same discrepancy between aims and results taints the five-year ban on unilateral divorce.

D. 'Pressing Need'? A Comparison with Closely Related Jurisdictions

In Australia, a spouse can petition for divorce on the grounds that the marriage has broken down and there is no reasonable likelihood of reconciliation (itself a non-justiciable sop), and proceedings may be started after 12 months of separation (whether living apart or living separated under the same roof).[94] In Canada, divorce is available if the breakdown of the relationship is proved through adultery, cruelty or one-year separation (allowance being made for a period of resumed cohabitation of up to 90 days); proceedings may be introduced as soon as the parties cease living together or start living separate lives at the same address.[95]

In other European jurisdictions, such as Spain and Sweden, the law was amended so as to recognise as the sole ground for divorce the decision of one or both spouses to end the marriage, without any requirement to justify the reasons underlying that decision, in recognition of the petitioner's right to privacy.[96] Within the UK, the Family Law (Scotland) Act 2006 reduced the separation period to one year if there is consent to divorce and two years if there is not.

All these developments call into question the 'pressing need' for a five-year bar interfering with Convention rights in England and Wales.

[93] *B and L v UK*, para 38.
[94] Family Law Act 1975.
[95] Divorce Act 1986.
[96] Bernand (2015) 68–69.

V. European Minimum Standard and Enhanced Domestic Rights

Although the impact of divorce restrictions on private and family life is so significant as to raise human rights concerns, the impetus for legal reform in England and Wales did not proceed from Strasbourg adjudication. The ECtHR has been notoriously reluctant to intervene in matters pertaining to personal law – for example to read an obligation for ECHR states to introduce civil partnerships[97] or to recognise religious or traditional marriage.[98] As Choudhry and Herring pointed out, in family law cases, the ECtHR tends to apply the least strict standard of review, recognising socio-cultural diversity in Europe.[99]

By contrast, domestic scrutiny of primary legislation under Section 4 of the HRA 1998 was equipped to challenge the necessity and proportionality of the divorce regime under the MCA 1973. The scope of ECHR rights as interpreted and applied under the HRA 1998 can go beyond the minimum ECHR standard.[100] The distinction between an international claim of ECHR violation and a domestic claim of HRA-incompatibility was clarified in *Re G (Adoption: Unmarried Couple)*.[101] Lord Hoffmann pointed out that in cases where the ECtHR has declined to take a stand on a matter, deeming it within states' margin of appreciation, it is for the domestic courts to shape the understanding of rights under the HRA 1998.[102] Similarly, in *Nicklinson*, the Supreme Court recognised that its re-examination of assisted dying claims was not precluded by the Strasbourg finding that each state could decide how to reconcile the competing interests at stake.[103] Divorce legislation warranted the same approach. Although divorce is a sensitive area and attracts substantial deference to Parliament, courts had previously shown willingness to co-shape policy in relation to personal status (access to civil partnerships, legal parenthood following surrogacy arrangements, recognition of the acquired gender for marriage purposes).[104] The feeble engagement with the HRA 1998 in the divorce arena makes for a disappointing contrast.

VI. Conclusions

The limited impact of the HRA 1998 on divorce law apparently flowed from a superficial reading of ECHR jurisprudence and its relationship with domestic law.

[97] See Draghici (2017a) 198–209.
[98] ibid 43–47.
[99] Choudhry and Herring (2010) 32–34.
[100] Draghici (2014) 167–68.
[101] *Re G (Adoption: Unmarried Couple)* [2008] 3 WLR 76.
[102] ibid [36].
[103] *R (Nicklinson) v Ministry of Justice* [2014] UKSC 38 [76]. See also *Conway v Secretary of State for Justice* [2018] EWCA Civ 1431 [128].
[104] *Steinfeld*; *Re Z (A Child) (No 2)* [2016] EWHC 1191 (Fam); *Bellinger v Bellinger* [2003] UKHL 21.

On closer inspection, recent Strasbourg case law has recognised that divorce laws may breach Articles 8 and 12 ECHR and that their design and implementation require an adequate balancing of competing interests. Unsuccessful applications were typically the product of the ECtHR's light-touch international oversight of the balancing exercise undertaken by domestic legislators and of domestic courts' assessment of facts, in deference to states' wide margin of appreciation. A heightened degree of scrutiny was expected under the HRA 1998 and could have supported calls for reform.

The inability to dissolve marital ties without spousal consent or a lengthy period of separation is a serious interference with an individual's private and family life and their right to remarry; as such, it requires cogent justification, based on either societal interests or the rights of the non-consenting spouse. The formal preservation of failed marriages does not secure the stability or gravitas of the institution, admittedly a legitimate public goal; as to the competing private interests of the other spouse, Article 12 confers no right to have one's marriage treated as indissoluble. The five-year bar on unilateral no-fault divorce is, thus, ill-suited to address any superior need, and so unjustifiably curtails individual autonomy and the effective enjoyment of family life. Additionally, it unduly restricts Article 12 rights, preventing individuals from reacquiring the capacity to marry and formalising new relationships for a considerable period of time, without advancing anyone else's interests.

The lack of an unequivocal Strasbourg precedent asserting a right to divorce should not be seen as dispositive of human rights objections to the bar. The ECtHR has acknowledged that divorce proceedings must take place within a reasonable time and without insurmountable impediments, such as a veto right for innocent spouses. The latter aspect of Strasbourg jurisprudence confirms that ECHR requirements apply to substantive divorce rules as well, and not merely to procedures. While the ECtHR defers to states in matters affecting personal status, recognising their closer link with their communities and their ability to strike a fairer balance between the rights at stake, the case law reveals that that discretion must be exercised within certain common (substantive and procedural) parameters. Although the 'margin of appreciation' doctrine has been occasionally (mis)-interpreted as requiring domestic courts to defer to the legislature,[105] the discretion afforded to states in applying Convention norms is shared by all branches of government. The assessment of legislation under Section 4 of the HRA 1998, unencumbered by the subsidiarity of international tribunals or the absence of European consensus, can accommodate human rights concerns to a greater extent than Strasbourg litigation.

The domestic interpretation of Convention rights must also take into account the evolution of other areas of family law, such as the increased legal significance attached to prenuptial agreements, the ring-fencing of non-marital property where

[105] See eg *Conway* [132].

needs are otherwise satisfied, and the non-sharing of assets after short, childless, dual-income marriages in which finances are kept separate.[106] This changing landscape of English family law, prioritising individual autonomy within the marriage, casts doubt on the legitimacy of the MCA 1973 divorce restrictions. The comparison with other common law and European jurisdictions further suggests that the enduring bar on unilateral divorce (absent relevant conduct or five-year separation) does not respond to a pressing social need.

The inescapable conclusion, notwithstanding the mainstream approach to divorce in the literature, the courts and the public debate, is that the soon-to-be-replaced MCA 1973 divorce scheme is inconsistent with the HRA 1998, in that it disproportionately interferes with the rights protected by Articles 8 and 12 ECHR, as understood and applied domestically. Despite the ECtHR's cautious position, requiring divorce laws to achieve a fair balance between competing interests but deferring that exercise to states, overall, its jurisprudence invited more rights-protective domestic standards. The *Owens* litigation was a missed opportunity to affirm those standards in England and Wales. Nevertheless, the ensuing public consultation paved the way towards a historical transformation of divorce law into a more modern and rights-sensitive framework.

References

Bernand, Y (2015) 'Évolution de la place de la volonté des époux dans le divorce' in F Ferrand and H Fulchiron (eds), *La rupture du mariage en droit comparé* (Paris, Société de législation comparée).

Choudhury, S and Herring, J (2010) *European Human Rights and Family Law* (Oxford, Hart Publishing).

Dillon, K (1989) 'Divorce and Remarriage as Human Rights: The Irish Constitution and the European Convention on Human Rights at Odds in *Johnston v Ireland*' 22 *Cornell International Law Journal* 63.

Draghici, C (2014) 'The Human Rights Act in the Shadow of the European Convention: Are Copyist's Errors Allowed?' 2 *European Human Rights Law Review* 154.

—— (2017a) *The Legitimacy of Family Rights in Strasbourg Case Law: 'Living Instrument' or Extinguished Sovereignty?* (Oxford, Hart Publishing).

—— (2017b) 'Equal Marriage, Unequal Civil Partnership: A Bizarre Case of Discrimination in Europe' 4 *Child and Family Law Quarterly* 313.

—— (2017c) 'The Strasbourg Court between European and Local Consensus: Anti-Democratic or Guardian of Democratic Process?' 1 *Public Law* 11.

Eekelaar, J (2011) 'Naturalism or Pragmatism? Towards an Expansive View of Human Rights' 10 *Journal of Human Rights* 230.

Hale, B (2011) 'Equality and Autonomy in Family Law' 33(1) *Journal of Social Welfare & Family Law* 3.

[106] *Sharp v Sharp* [2017] EWCA Civ 408.

Hall, JC (1966) 'Divorce Reform?' 24 *Cambridge Law Journal* 184.
Kay, R (2004) 'Whose Divorce is it Anyway – the Human Rights Aspect' (2004) 34 *Family Law* 892.
Ministry of Justice (2018) *Reducing family conflict. Reform of the legal requirements for divorce* available at https://consult.justice.gov.uk/digital-communications/reform-of-the-legal-requirements-for-divorce/supporting_documents/reducingfamilyconflictconsultation.pdf (last accessed 8 July 2021).
Ministry of Justice (2019) *Reducing family conflict. Government response to the consultation on reform of the legal requirements for divorce, 'Summary of consultation responses'* available at https://assets.publishing.service.gov.uk/government/uploads/system/uploads/attachment_data/file/793642/reducing-family-conflict-consult-response.pdf (last accessed 8 July 2021).
Reece, H (2000) 'Divorcing Responsibly' 8 *Feminist Legal Studies* 65.
Trinder, L (2018) 'Divorce Reform in England and Wales: The Human Rights Perspective' 6 *European Human Rights Law Review* 557.
Trinder, L and Sefton, M (2018) *No Contest: Defended Divorce in England & Wales* (Nuffield Foundation) available at https://www.nuffieldfoundation.org/wp-content/uploads/2018/04/No-contest-final_Nuffield_Foundation.pdf (last accessed 8 July 2021).
Trotter, S (2019) 'The State of Divorce Law' 78 *Cambridge Law Journal* 38.
van Dijk, P, van Hoof, F, van Rijn, A and Zwaak, L (2006) *Theory and Practice of the European Convention of Human Rights*, 4th edn (Antwerp, Intersentia).
Welstead, M (2012) 'Divorce in England and Wales: Time for Reform' 24 *Denning Law Journal* 21.

12

British Muslim Communities, Islamic Divorce and English Family Law

SAMIA BANO

I. Introduction

At present, there are no data on marriage breakdown and divorce in England and Wales according to the parties' ethnic and religious background. There is, however, a wide body of sociological and anthropological literature detailing a rise in marital breakdown and divorce within British Muslim communities and the complex factors behind this, including the increasing economic independence of Muslim women and the use of religion as a source of female empowerment and control. Similarly, there is an established body of scholarship examining the relationship between law and cultural and religious diversity, and the experience of marriage and divorce within British Muslim communities. This scholarship, encompassing empirical research, covers a wide range of issues, including: the nature of transnational marriage; arranged marriage practices and strategies to combat the practice of forced marriage;[1] the formation in England and Wales of religious marriages that are not recognised by English marriage law; the recognition or not of divorces obtained in other jurisdictions; and the increasing emphasis on private ordering of the consequences of divorce and its impacts on religious communities. At the heart of this body of scholarship lie the important questions of identity, multiculturalism, law and rights.

This chapter draws upon some of this literature to trace and analyse divorce practices within British Muslim communities over the past 50 years. It begins by providing brief introductions to the issue of religious diversity and its accommodation (or not) by secular law, and to the sources of Sharia law, and then considers the practice of Muslim family law in Britain, around both the formation of marriage and divorce as forms of social and legal lived realities. Sharia Councils have a significant role in relation to divorce, and so these are also examined.

[1] Agarwal and Kapil (2014); Ahmed (2006); Anitha and Gill (2009).

It is necessary to consider marriage formation as well as divorce, as many Muslim couples do not create their religiously-recognised marriage in a way that will be recognised at all by English law. For these couples, Sharia law is the only pertinent marriage and divorce law, and so they reject civil law and procedure altogether, marrying and divorcing according to their faith via community mosques and Sharia Councils. Meanwhile, observant couples who did contract a marriage recognised by English law and so who do fall within the jurisdiction of the matrimonial court, may nevertheless still need or wish to engage with Sharia law to ensure that their legal status (under English law) and their status under religious law are congruent.

II. Religious Diversity and the Law

In 1986, Sebastian Poulter wrote:

> Should the ethnic minorities who have come to live here conform to English ways or should they be free to continue and practise their own customs in this country? More specifically, should English law adapt its principles and rules to accommodate foreign customs or should new arrivals bear the burden of any adjustments?[2]

Similarly, in his early work, Werner Menski detailed the ways in which Muslim communities were forging new ways of incorporating and developing Sharia and Western legal norms to describe what he termed (in Urdu) '*Angrezi Sharia*' ('English Sharia').[3] Menski, in particular, brought attention to the 'lived reality' that Muslim religious communities were creating new forms of 'personal law systems' based upon diverse religious and cultural traditions, while being clear that 'Western state law … obstructs and restricts the scope for Muslim law in a new diaspora to become part of the recognised official law.'[4] For Poulter, the marginalisation of 'ethnic minority customs' meant the law neither understood nor was able effectively to regulate practices that might be unfair and unjust, breaching principles of equality and respect. This early work raised important and fundamental questions for scholars, and continues to lay the template for much current academic research and policy work.

Debates across Britain and wider Europe have also examined policies of multiculturalism and the extent to which minority religious practices are tolerated and/or endorsed by national domestic courts. Further afield, debates in Canada, the United States and Australia highlight issues of conflict, equity and discrimination. Muslim women remain at the centre of these debates, while feminists from across the political spectrum seek to defend or resist calls for greater accommodation of

[2] Poulter (1986) iv.
[3] Menski (1993) 28.
[4] Pearl and Menski (1998) 50.

religious norms, values and practices in Western democratic societies. This has led to debates crossing political spectrums over the extent to which state law should recognise alternative systems of family law dispute resolution. As Marie Ashe and Anissa Helie explain:

> Civil governmental recognitions of jurisdiction in specifically-religious courts may be the most extraordinary of the accommodations currently being provided to religious organisations. The toleration of judicial autonomy in such bodies in itself manifests a striking sharing of sovereignty. And the ceding to religious bodies of a central feature of governmental sovereignty – the judicial power – becomes particularly problematic when that power is utilized in order to enforce religious law that conflicts with fundamental principles of the civil law.[5]

Examination of the British Muslim identity reveals important insights into the ways in which community formation, legal regulation and the rights of minority religious communities have taken shape over the past five decades. There has been significant debate about religious and cultural difference, and about whether minority groups should be afforded a different family law regime from regular English law to take into account specific cultural and religious norms.[6] This underpins debates on the role of religion in society, the limits of secularism and the extent to which the state should intervene in the private space of family life and personal relations to protect minorities within the groups against potential injustice, unfairness and abuse.

This chapter specifically addresses the validity of religious marriages and the use of Islamic divorce laws and process. But there are other examples in the marriage arena. In her early work, Jessica Jacobson[7] detailed the ways in which South Asian Pakistani communities in the 1980s and 1990s began rejecting culturalised forms of Pakistani identity in favour of a religious faith-based Islamic identity. Similarly, Robina Mohammad's research has traced the ways in which young Pakistani Muslim women enter into transnational marriages as ways to challenge patrilineal norms of marriage conventions in order to reflect 'new repertoires for remaking the self and women's assertion of modern, cosmopolitan, Muslim identities'.[8] Religious identity therefore provides an important context in which to understand the relationship between law, culture and identity. As Andrea Büchler explains, 'Religion is indeed experiencing some of a renaissance in the discourse of cultural diversity and is becoming an ever-important form of self-identification.'[9]

Research has also detailed the ways in which family expectations may influence marriage and divorce patterns within South Asian communities. For example, Katherine Charsley[10] has demonstrated how young British Pakistanis

[5] Ashe and Helie (2014) 142.
[6] Ahmed (2013).
[7] Jacobson (1998).
[8] Mohammad (2015) 599.
[9] Büchler (2011) 25.
[10] Charsley (2013).

take ownership of their marriages (as arranged and transnational kin marriages) while challenging parental assumptions and doing things in a different way. More importantly, Islam – not mere cultural expectations – provides the context within which young people are able to make choices that enable them to challenge parental power and control. In 2007, Pnina Werbner explained that 'being observant Muslims empowers these young men and women with the right to choose their own marriage partners, even against the will of their parents'. Their religiosity offers licence to 'accuse their parents of being ignorant, locked into false or mistaken parochial "customs" and "traditions" of the old country'.[11]

Collectively, this body of work not only raises important questions on the role of religion and faith in the lives of Muslims and British Muslim communities, but has also raised critical questions over the extent to which cultural diversity and religious practices should be recognised in English law.

III. Sources of Islamic Family Law

The term 'Sharia' in classical Muslim law refers to 'definition of practice'. In day-to-day usage it refers to the body of rules and principles that make up Islamic religious law. Wheeler observes that Sharia' determines how certain aspects of everyday life are to be practised according to the model provided by the canon', which includes both civil and criminal codes.[12] Its application is wider, however, than the word 'law' implies, as these precepts do not distinguish between public and private activities. Rather, Sharia covers a broad range of actions and obligations for Muslims. Washing, cleaning, eating, marriage, divorce, bank loans, business transactions and property purchases are all examples of areas of day-to-day life on which Sharia provides guidance.

Sharia has its roots in two key religious scriptures: the *Qur'an* and the *Sunna*. The *Qur'an* contains the religious scriptures of Islam, while the *Sunna* contains the actions and words of the prophet Mohammed.[13] Where issues or disagreements cannot be settled through religious texts, jurists look toward the *Ijma*, the body of principles arrived at through the consensus of Islamic scholars. Where neither the *Qur'an* nor *Sunna* provides the necessary authority, a jurist may apply *qiyas*: reasoning through analogy to provide the applicable Islamic principle to decide the issue at law.[14]

No single document or source gives a definitive list of every Sharia precept. Even to describe Sharia as a singular framework can be misleading, since there is no atypical model of Sharia in the Muslim world today, and therefore no one

[11] Werbner (2007) 134.
[12] Wheeler (1996) 34.
[13] Nasir (1990) 2–3.
[14] Hallaq (1999).

comprehensive Islamic legal system. Instead there is variation according to Islamic school of thought, ethnic background, local customs, cultural practices and local traditions. Notably, Sharia law is subject to interpretation by different religious scholars and communities, broadly divided into Sunni and Shia schools of thought.[15] As such, there is no cohesive body of Sharia, but differing strands based upon the *Qu'ran* and *Hadith* literature. However, common themes nevertheless emerge, and Islamic scholars aim to establish a cohesive body of Islamic jurisprudence, *Fiqh al-Aqalliyyat* (or, more simply, the *fiqh*).[16] Overall, Sharia is therefore perhaps best characterised as an evolving legal philosophy (jurisprudence).

Since the *Qur'an* is concerned predominantly with religious precepts, there are relatively few identifiably legal injunctions, covering perhaps only 3 per cent of the total text. However, as Badr notes, most of those legal provisions deal with family law and inheritance, and so we now turn to marriage and divorce.[17]

IV. Muslim Marriage Practice in Britain Meets English Law

As Vora points out, 'Islam prohibits adultery and restricts sexual relationships to within the framework of marriage. In order for a British Muslim couple to live together, they must marry in a form that is accepted by their community'.[18] His research emphasises the importance British Muslim communities place on the institution of marriage, and how this may shape their experience of using English family law. It is important, therefore, to examine how minority ethnic groups practise marriage and divorce, how different forms of marriage practices may be accepted or recognised in English law today and the kind of change that is taking place around marriage practices within South Asian Muslim families.

Under Sharia law, the Muslim marriage itself is simply a civil contract between an adult woman and an adult man who have the legal capacity to enter into such an agreement. In Arabic, a Muslim marriage is described as a *nikah* (meaning 'to tie a knot'). The marriage contract is not sacrosanct and is revocable. The requisites of a valid *nikah* contract include 'legal capacity' (individual to be of sound mind and to have reached puberty), consent, acceptance and the dower or *mahr*. The *mahr* is a key component of the Muslim marriage contract: for the contract to be valid, the groom must provide a sum of money that the parties have agreed, known as the *mahr*. This belongs to the wife. In her work, Ali notes that the significance

[15] The Sunni schools of Islam include: *Hanafi*, *Hanbali*, *Shafii* and *Maliki*. The dominant Shia school is *Twelvers* (sometimes also called *Jafari*, which excludes the *Ismaili* and *Zaydi* sects).

[16] Ali (2010) 28.

[17] Badr (1978) 188.

[18] Vora (2020) 53.

of the *nikah* to the institution of the 'Muslim family' cannot be underestimated, explaining:

> [T]he central idea in Muslim family law is the institution of nikah or marriage. Almost every legal concept revolves around the central focal point of the status of the marriage. It is through marriage that the paternity of children is established, and relationship and affinity are traced.[19]

Debates on Muslim divorce are closely connected to the initial validity of Muslim religious marriages. Marriage law today in England and Wales is regulated by the Marriage Act 1949, the Matrimonial Causes Act 1973 and the Marriage (Prohibited Degrees of Relationship) Act 1986, which determine who can marry, where they can marry and at what time. It is possible for a religious marriage ceremony conducted in England and Wales to create a marriage recognised in English law, but only if the normal civil preliminaries have been completed (ie appropriate notice given to the local registrar) and the marriage has been solemnised in an appropriately registered building in the presence of an authorised person. But, as the Law Commission has identified, very few mosques have been registered for this purpose.[20]

How the status of a religious marriage ceremony is to be assessed was clarified in *Attorney-General v Akhter and Khan*.[21] The couple in this case had entered a religious marriage. None of the formal requirements just outlined had been complied with, no attempt at all having been made to marry in a way that could be recognised by the Marriage Act 1949.[22] Indeed, it had been expected that the religious marriage would be followed by a civil ceremony (which the wife understood was essential to ensure a marriage recognised in English law). But despite the wife's repeated requests of the husband to arrange for this second, legal marriage ceremony, no such wedding occurred. Upon the breakdown of the relationship, the husband claimed the religious marriage had no legal effect, and so argued that he had no financial obligations to the wife of the sort that would follow divorce or nullity proceedings. At first instance, the High Court[23] applied a novel human rights approach based on Article 8 of the European Convention on Human Rights and the right to respect for family life (and the best interests of the child) to determine marital status, and recognised the marriage as a void marriage, thus giving rise to financial remedies. But this was overruled by the Court of Appeal in favour of a more orthodox reading of the law. The religious-only marriage was classified as a non-qualifying ceremony, leaving the wife (mother of four children) with no

[19] Ali (2010) 157.

[20] Law Commission (2015), (2020).

[21] *Attorney-General v Akhter and Khan* [2020] EWCA Civ 122.

[22] A wilful and knowing disregard of formal requirements will render a marriage void, but only where the parties were purporting to marry in accordance with the Marriage Act 1949, which was not the case here or in other 'non-qualifying ceremony' cases.

[23] *Akhter v Khan* [2018] EWFC 54.

financial remedies for her benefit in English law at the end of her 18-year religious marriage.

Data on the number of 'religious-only' or 'unregistered' Muslim marriages within British Muslim communities remain limited, but what data we have provide some important insights. In her small-scale study of unregistered Muslim marriages, Akhtar[24] found participants reluctant to contribute to the study, as 'enquiring about one's decision not to register a marriage appeared to infringe on the couple's privacy and those who were within higher ranking professions in particular were unwilling to engage'.[25] A principal reason given for not registering marriages related to time constraints and the 'busy lives of Muslims' to arrange a second (civil) ceremony alongside often lavish religious celebrations, rather than a strategy to circumvent formal civil marriage in order to enter into polygamous marriage relationships. Some couples reported perceiving no need to engage with the civil law; and some younger respondents deliberately avoided marrying in a way recognised by English law, in order that they could conduct their relationships in a way of which their parents would approve without taking on the legal status of spouse.[26]

Akhtar's study also found that the practice of having religious-only marriages could not be linked to the perceived rise in polygamy.[27] However, this can be contrasted with another short study recorded in a report produced by Habiba Jaan for 'Aurat: Supporting Women', a charity that supports female victims of honour and cultural-based abuse, based in Birmingham, UK.[28] The report focused on the predicament of Muslim women who found themselves in unregistered marriages and who lived in polygamous households with little state and/or community support. Of central concern was that many Muslim women were simply unsure of their rights in law when entering into a religious-only marriage. Of the sample of 50 women in unregistered Muslim marriages, two-thirds identified themselves as being 'married' but had received no financial support from their husbands. Husbands often took second wives and abandoned the first wife if she disagreed with what he understood as his marital choice.[29]

Whether or not polygamous in nature, religious-only marriages of this sort, not recognised at all by English law, leave the women in them (in particular) in a vulnerable situation in the event of relationship breakdown, with no access to the usual matrimonial financial remedies. So their only source of protection may lie in religious divorce and associated remedies, discussed in Section V. But before moving on to that issue, it is important to appreciate that the difficulties presented for Muslim women in this arena – the obstacles Muslim women may experience

[24] Akhtar (2015).
[25] ibid 175.
[26] Akhtar (2020).
[27] ibid 76.
[28] Jaan (2014).
[29] Akhtar (2020) 83.

in order to register their marriages – provide a key rationale for reform of English law's very complex marriage laws.[30] To this end, the Law Commission for England and Wales is currently reviewing the law of weddings, with a view to recommending reforms, and published its Consultation Paper in 2020, following an earlier scoping review in 2015.[31] The project considers whether the current law provides a fair and coherent legal framework for enabling people to marry, and identifies areas of the law that might benefit from reform. The problems raised by these religious-only marriages receive extensive attention in the Law Commission's work, and the proposals currently under consideration would go a long way towards avoiding the difficulties currently experienced, making it far more likely that religious ceremonies could create at least a void marriage.[32] If Muslims are more able to determine how and when they marry within a framework that meets the requirements of both English law and religious obligations, then the objectives of both state law and religious identity can potentially be met.

V. Muslim Divorce in Britain, and the Role of Sharia Councils

In her study, Kaveri Qureshi[33] details rich ethnographic research identifying an increase in marital breakdown in British Muslim communities. She finds that while the experience of divorce for Muslim women mirrors marital breakdown across all British communities, the experience of Muslim women living close to wider families can influence their decision making in divorce. Two key issues can be identified for Muslim women in Britain regarding the ending of their marriages: first, the extent to which Muslims are divorcing outside the civil law system and whether this creates a conflict-of-law scenario with English law; second, the problem of 'limping divorces', whereby a civil divorce has been obtained by the woman but her husband is refusing to grant her a Muslim divorce.[34]

A. Types of Muslim Divorce

There are several types of Muslim divorce and a diversity of approaches to these among the different schools of Islamic thought.

Muslim men have the right to terminate their marriage unilaterally. Such a divorce is known as *talaq*. Other forms of Muslim divorce include *tafwid*, *khula*,

[30] Parveen (2020) 85.
[31] Law Commission (2015), (2020).
[32] ibid.
[33] Qureshi (2016).
[34] Pearl and Menski (1998).

mubarah and *faskh*. Divorce may also be granted, in a sense, by mutual consent where parties have simply included a term in their nikah (marriage contract) that permits the wife to divorce if she wishes, the husband thereby effectively delegating the decision to divorce to the wife: this is known as *talaq at-tafwid*. The *khula* divorce can be instigated by a wife with her husband's agreement, on the condition that she forgoes her right to the *mahr* (excluding instances of neglect and abuse). *Faskh* permits the marriage to be ended if the wife can prove her husband has acted unreasonably. However, in order for the wife to access these other types of divorce where the husband refuses to pronounce a *talaq*, she must contact a Sharia Council, and so has to invoke the authority of religious scholars who will determine the kind of divorce to be issued.

B. Sharia Councils: An Introduction

The role and use of Sharia Councils are clearly important for a significant number of Muslim women seeking a Muslim divorce. Sharia Councils operate as unofficial legal bodies specialising in Muslim family law and providing advice and assistance to Muslim communities on these matters. They have developed their services to cater to the local and specific needs of British Muslim communities whilst fitting in with the wider framework of dispute resolution in Islam. They have three key functions: issuing Muslim divorce certificates; reconciling and mediating between parties; and producing expert opinions on matters of Muslim family law and custom to the Muslim community, solicitors and the courts.

Sharia Councils in Britain are not unified beneath any one overarching governance structure, and do not all adopt a single school of thought; instead, they are a collection of various different bodies representing the different schools of thought in Islam. They generally form part of a wider range of community services, rather than being distinct and separate bodies, and are often linked to a mosque, either occupying a room there or being based in a local community centre with weekly drop-in sessions for clients and panel meetings (see Section V.D) taking place on average once a month. While the nature and scope of Sharia Council activity in England and Wales remain relatively undocumented, it is likely that a fairly small number of key Councils operate in England: one report[35] in 2012 identified just 30 working on issues of Muslim family law and issuing Muslim divorce certificates.

Sharia Councils can be traced to a diverse set of social, political and religious developments in civil society as part of a Muslim identity. Yilmaz[36] identifies four key conditions that have led to the emergence of Sharia Councils in Britain. First, according to Muslim tradition, family issues are purposively left to 'extra judicial' regulation, and this continues within Muslim diasporic communities today, who

[35] For the Ministry of Justice, Bano (2012b).
[36] Yilmaz (2002) 349.

choose to resolve disputes in the private sphere. Second, Muslims do not recognise the authority and legitimacy of Western secular law as being on a par with Muslim law. Third, familial notions of honour and shame prevent family disputes from being discussed in the 'public sphere', which gives religious laws greater legitimacy within religious communities. And finally, the failure of the state to recognise plural legal orders has led to the development of 'alternative' dispute resolution processes in the private sphere. In his study, Warraich regards all of South Asian Muslim family laws, localised cultural practices in British Muslim communities and the inflexibility of English family law as contributory factors in the emergence of Sharia Councils. He argues that such bodies 'have appropriated for themselves the role and position of parallel quasi-judicial institutions', and attributes this to 'the lack of space in the English system for appropriate solutions to dilemmas facing people', leading to 'this confusing situation'.[37]

C. The Role of the Sharia Council in Relation to Divorce

There is very little variation between Councils in the procedure adopted in divorce cases, which can broadly be described as follows:

- Applicant makes contact with the Sharia Council to obtain a Muslim divorce certificate.
- A meeting takes place between the applicant and the religious scholar.
- The applicant is asked to fill in an application form citing the grounds for divorce and pays an administrative fee.
- A divorce notice is sent to the husband asking for his version of events.
- If there is no response from the husband, a further notice is sent out.
- Once contact has been made with all parties, a meeting is arranged to consider reconciliation.
- If contact is not made with the husband and his family then the religious scholar continues with the process to issue the divorce certificate.
- If reconciliation fails then a process of mediation begins, with a view to trying get the husband's consent to divorce.
- The religious scholar considers what type of divorce certificate can be issued.
- Once all meetings are completed and evidence has been collected, a copy of the file is passed to all members of the Council panel.
- A date is set for a meeting of the panel to discuss all cases, where all panel members make a collective decision as to whether a divorce certificate can be issued.
- If so, a divorce certificate is sent to the applicant *or* she is asked to collect it.

[37] Warraich (2001) 11.

The type of Muslim divorce granted to women by the Sharia Council raises important practical issues for those women. For example, if a *khul* is granted, the female applicant must give up her right to dower or *mahr* in return for a divorce, and this seems unfair given that this is the result of the husband's refusing to pronounce the unilateral *talaq*. As Menski explains, '[u]sually the wife will offer to pay a certain sum, normally the amount of the dower either given to her or promised to her, in return for the agreement of the husband to release her from the marriage tie'.[38] Again, this is a complex area and one that ensures some confusion as to the precise amount of dower the husband should receive for the *khul*.[39]

Sharia Councils also deal with how the wife can retrieve her *mahr* after her husband has willingly divorced her. Nasir points out that, in theory, Muslim women entitled to the *mahr* have an exclusive right to it under the terms of the marriage contract, though in practice this may vary 'according to the circumstances. She may be entitled to the whole dower, half of it or may have no dower at all.'[40] Furthermore, Afshar points out that 'What women are entitled to and what they get are very different. Married women are not expected to assert their proprietorial rights. They are not to bring conflict, but peace.'[41] Therefore in Muslim divorce we are dealing with a complex formulation, whereby 'legal discourse' in matters of religious marriage and divorce are reconfigured in the private sphere and privatised dispute resolution mechanisms such as Sharia Councils.

D. The Experience of British Muslim Women before Sharia Councils

So what are the experiences of Muslim women using religious mechanisms of dispute resolution in matters of divorce? Do religious tribunals promote patriarchy and gender inequality? Several significant pieces of research provide important insights into how Sharia Councils in Britain operate as alternative dispute resolution mechanisms, detailing the lived experience of British Muslim women and their use of Sharia Councils.

Gohir and Akhtar-Sheikh analyse several case files from their work with the national Muslim women's organisation, Muslim Women's Network (MWUK), and illustrate the problems Muslim women experience in their use of Sharia Councils. They found that, upon the breakdown of marriage, Muslim women seek to resolve disputes outside English courts, as Islam directs Muslims to seek conciliatory redress in the form of mediation and arbitration. This gives considerable power and influence to Sharia Councils. And of course, women who have a religious-only

[38] Pearl and Menski (1998) 284.
[39] Carroll (1997).
[40] Nasir (1990) 103.
[41] Afshar (1994) 29.

marriage are necessarily propelled towards Sharia Councils in order to obtain a Muslim divorce. The Councils' focus on reconciliation and mediation within these bodies remains a significant concern:

> [T]here is no evidence to suggest that Sharia Council members, mediators and case-workers have had any adequate training in mediation, arbitration, or even general counselling. They therefore have neither the skills nor the knowledge to deal with family and divorce matters, whether from an Islamic or UK perspective. It is also of concern the panelists can interchangeably act as mediators with no separation of role or procedure. The lack of training, lack of transparency, and lack of accountability and discriminatory processes make it essential that the issues surrounding certain Sharia Councils be addressed as soon as possible.[42]

Case-file analysis and interviews with women users of Sharia Councils also revealed several complaints by Muslim women of not being listened to, their grievances not being taken seriously or given due consideration, and being questioned by panel members in accusatory tones and made to feel guilty for pursuing a divorce. By contrast, the women felt that their husbands were given a disproportionate level of attention in the divorce process.

The ambivalent relationship between some Muslim women and Sharia Councils has also been documented in my research.[43] While on the one hand Muslim women identify as Muslims and therefore recognise the importance of Sharia Councils in helping them to obtain a Muslim divorce, they can also be critical of these bodies as mediation forums and critical of the attempts by the scholars to reconcile them with their husbands. The most obvious questions concern the autonomy and independence of the women during this process of dispute resolution, and their experience of mediation and reconciliation. Although not all women are marginalised and denied equal bargaining power during official mediation processes, there is evidence to suggest that there is deep anxiety amongst many women at the prospect of initiating both official and unofficial mediation in order to obtain a Muslim divorce, and this anxiety persists throughout the process.[44]

Parveen analysed 100 closed files in one Sharia Council based in Birmingham, UK, related to cases where wives had sought a religious divorce.[45] She found that no women were employed in the Council in any capacity, and that this made it an intimidating environment for the women users. Indeed, probably the most common criticism of Sharia Councils is that they refuse to allow Muslim women to act as religious scholars on a par with male scholars when issuing Muslim divorce certificates. For example, it is widely assumed within the Councils that Muslim women are simply forbidden under Islamic law and jurisprudence to act as religious scholars in family law matters, and this norm is rarely challenged.[46]

[42] Gohir and Akhtar-Sheikh (2017) 177.
[43] Bano (2012a), (2018).
[44] Bottomley and Conaghan (1993).
[45] Parveen (2017).
[46] Bano (2012a).

Parveen also found that the Sharia Council process and meetings can be confusing for Muslim women, explaining:

> [T]he objectives of the meetings were never entirely clear, and I share this view. The parties did not seem to be aware at the beginning of the meeting what its purpose was, nor were they sure at the end what was likely to happen next. Some of the women said they had expected a final decision at the end of the meeting and had not been aware that there was a process and the matter would need to go to a board.[47]

Despite this, Parveen concludes that Sharia Councils offer an important service to Muslim women, providing them with the essential service of issuing religious divorce certificates 'while remaining faithful to normative Islam'. Therefore, she argues, the state should neither ban nor ignore Sharia Councils but instead provide them with support and assistance.[48] Research also demonstrates that Sharia Council verdicts serve primarily to uphold the 'moral authority' of the Muslim community, and there are no mechanisms of enforcement, relying instead on the goodwill of the parties concerned.[49]

The debate on Muslim family law and 'alternative dispute resolution' has not yet developed satisfactory explanations of gender relations and power, nor the fact that the reality of women's connections to these bodies may be very complex, contested and subject to the contingent local variations of the Councils. While mediation has for many years now has a central place in the family justice system in England and Wales, and reconciliation practices emerging within all communities have been explored, there is very little analysis of the growth of religious bodies operating in privatised spaces and developing such services in Britain.

Douglas et al conducted research with three religious tribunals operating within Jewish, Christian and Muslim communities,[50] and found little if any formal conflict between these bodies and state law as the bodies deliberately and carefully sought to avoid any potential conflicts with law. However, the exercise of different forms of power and power relations within these frameworks of unofficial dispute resolution may affect the decision-making abilities of some female users. Clearly in this situation, the unofficial mediator is in an all-too-powerful position, potentially able to encourage or coerce the applicant into reconciling, making the potential consequences for women particularly disastrous. This argument is powerful, particularly if there is no screening process at these bodies to determine which cases are suitable for mediation and which are not.

[47] Parveen (2020) 154.

[48] ibid 162.

[49] Bano (2012a).

[50] Douglas et al (2011), examining the Birmingham Sharia Council, the London Beth Din of the United Synagogue, and the National Tribunal for Wales of the Roman Catholic Church.

In his research, Uddin makes an important finding relating to the continued use of Sharia Councils by Muslim women who had in fact registered their marriages according to civil law but still continued to pursue a religious divorce. He explains:

> [R]eligious divorce was important to them as it severed the religiously recognised marital relationship and contact with the husband and his family, removed any doubts as to whether the women were still married, and allowed women the freedom to move on, and remarry if they wished.[51]

He concludes, therefore, that while the Councils are imperfect in their current form, they currently fill a void in civil law provision by settling religious divorce, and this must therefore be supported by the state.

E. The 'Limping Marriage' Problem

The discussion so far has focused on the situation where the marriage is not recognised by English law. However, Sharia Councils may also have a role to play where the marriage *is* legally recognised, given the importance of obtaining a religious as well as a civil divorce. As Yilmaz explains:

> If the woman is not religiously divorced from her husband, it does not matter that she is divorced under the civil law, in the eyes of the community her remarriage will be regarded as adulterous and any possible offspring will be illegitimate since it is not allowed under the religious law. So, in reality, until the religious divorce is obtained, the civil divorce remains ineffective because one party is unable to remarry.[52]

Section 10A of the Divorce (Religious Marriages) Act 2002 enables a spouse concerned to ensure that a religious – as well as legal – divorce is obtained to apply to court for an order that will prevent a decree of divorce being made absolute unless and until both parties declare that they have taken the steps required to ensure the dissolution of the underlying religious marriage.[53] Specific religions need to be prescribed by secondary legislation for this provision to be available, and thus far only the Jewish faith has been covered.[54] But there is no reason why the Muslim faith could not also be included, in which case, as Gohir and Akhtar-Sheikh point out, 'where the couple have entered into a both civil and Islamic marriage, the courts can ensure that the husband grants the Islamic divorce by withholding the decree absolute'.[55] As in the Jewish context, an inherent limitation of this 'remedy' is that its efficacy depends on the husband's desire to secure a divorce recognised by English law – if he is not concerned about that, denial of that

[51] Uddin (2020) 121.
[52] Yilmaz (2001) 355.
[53] Matrimonial Causes Act 1973, s 10A.
[54] See Edge (2013).
[55] Gohir and Akhtar-Sheikh (2017) 179.

decree will not induce him to move in relation to the religious divorce. However, since Sharia law (unlike Jewish law) does – in theory – provide a route for wives to obtain a divorce without the husband's consent, albeit via the Sharia Council, the problem is arguably less acute in the Muslim context.

F. The Muslim Arbitration Tribunal

Another example of Muslim family law practice that aims to settle disputes in accordance with religious Sharia law is the Muslim Arbitration Tribunal (MAT), set up in June 2007. The authority of this tribunal derives from the Arbitration Act 1996, which permits civil matters to be resolved in accordance with Muslim law and within the ambit of state law. For many, this process of resolving disputes may provide the ideal forum, not only because it brings the usually claimed advantages of arbitration – granting parties some autonomy in the decision-making process, its informal setting, lower costs, flexibility and time efficiency compared to litigation through the courts – but more particularly, in this context, because it allows the arbitrating parties to resolve disputes according to English law while fulfilling any obligations under Islamic law.

Al-Astewani (2020) argues that the MAT represents a successful model of family arbitration in disputes involving religious marriages for three primary reasons. First, the Tribunal panel has access to a number of experts both in Islamic law and English law, which provides a body of expertise and an in-depth understanding of complex legal matters. Second, the Tribunal is run and managed by British Muslims, ensuring a cultural as well as religious understanding of the issues raised. And, finally, women are fully involved in the functioning and work of the Tribunal, ensuring no gender bias and an environment more suited to the needs of Muslim women.[56]

Consent to arbitration and the enforcement of any agreements reached can only take place under the principles of English law.[57] In a case in which the High Court approved a consent order that had been arbitrated and facilitated by a Beth Din under rabbinical law in New York,[58] Baker J reiterated in his judgment that resort to arbitration of any sort, religious or otherwise, could not oust the jurisdiction of English family court and family law, and the draft consent order was approved, pursuant to English law, as being in the best interests of the child. Bowen argues that this case signals 'a partial opening of courts toward private arbitration of divorce, and even to arbitration considered by religious bodies, but with the proviso that the court has the last word, and that principles of equity and the child's welfare prevail'.[59]

[56] Al-Astewani (2020) 140.
[57] Blackett (2009) 13.
[58] *AI v MT (Alternative Dispute Resolution)* [2013] EWHC 100 (Fam). See also Blackett (2009) 13.
[59] Bowen (2016) 178.

However, despite this, the establishment of the MAT has also been controversial for a number of reasons, and there remain real concerns over whether it restricts women's equality in family law matters. It has been claimed that such tribunals have allowed Sharia law in through the back door, directly challenging the superiority of the English legal system and undermining the principles upon which English family law is based. Patel argues that

> [t]he prime concern of the MAT is to achieve reconciliation between women seeking a divorce and their husbands even where there is evidence of abuse and violence. Indeed, reconciliation is viewed as a moral duty (to preserve the sanctity of religious values) and as a religious obligation (many claim that a divorce cannot be pronounced without reconciliation). But evidence shows that the MAT's approach to family matters flies in the face of established good practice and leads to profoundly unequal outcomes and violations of rights in which the state by its acquiescence is implicated.[60]

Since 2011, Baroness Cox has been promoting a Private Member's Bill, the Arbitration and Mediation Services (Equality) Bill. The Bill last received a Second Reading in January 2017, but, whilst it generated considerable media attention, it has made no further progress. It aims to clarify the limits of arbitration, seeking to make amendments to the Arbitration Act in order to ensure its compliance with the Equality Act 2010 and to outlaw discrimination on the grounds of sex. This Bill was widely believed to target Muslim communities and to attempt to limit the powers of organisations such as MAT and Sharia Councils. But for many scholars it also raised the question how far state law should intervene in religious Councils and tribunals. It was criticised for promoting the ideas that the practice of Muslim family law is based upon unfair and unequal principles, specifically targeting and discriminating against Muslim women as primary users of Muslim dispute resolution bodies.[61] Critics also objected to the Bill's formalist, top-down, state-interventionist approach for seeking to limit the powers of religious bodies and so being predicated on fixed and homogeneous notions of Islam and Islamic legal practice, which fails to recognise the dynamism and pluralism within the communities themselves.

VI. Conclusion

In his book *Muslim Families, Politics and the Law, A Legal Industry in Multicultural Britain*, Grillo[62] charts the very specific ways in which the law targets Muslim families, Islam and Islamic practices, a phenomenon underpinned by a general anxiety surrounding Muslims. He explains:

> Muslim families are caught up in socio-legal and political arguments and cultural and social disputes about meaning and practice, with issues such as marriage registration,

[60] Patel (2017) 89.
[61] Grillo (2015) 32.
[62] Grillo (2015).

> forced and arranged marriages, polygamy and divorce disputed among and between Muslims and non-Muslims, reviewed in consultations, discussed in Parliament, tested in the courts with Muslim religious leaders and their critics and supporters, increasingly prominent in public life.[63]

At present, a good part of the discussion of Muslim divorce relates to the prior question of whether the initial marriage is valid as a matter of English law. The Law Commission is shortly to publish its recommendations for reform of marriage laws in England and Wales in order to promote a simpler and fairer system for all, including Muslim communities and the problem of the recognition of religious marriages. In turn, in order to be legally effective, faith-based arbitration must comply with the requirements of the Arbitration Act 1996 and fall within the provisions of the Human Rights Act 1998. And in order for agreements to be recognised by the matrimonial courts, they will need to comply with relevant English family law principles. And in order to be approved – and so rendered enforceable – as a consent order by the matrimonial courts, the outcome will need to comply with relevant English law principles.

Nevertheless the issue of 'unofficial' mediation in forums such as Sharia Councils and the MAT remain of concern, in particular the question of their 'voluntary' use by Muslim women and the experience of Muslim women as directed through procedures laid down by Sharia Councils. The *Independent Review into the Application of Sharia Law in England and Wales*[64] found evidence of good and bad practice across Sharia Councils and made a series of recommendations, including: legislative changes to the Matrimonial Causes Act 1973 to ensure that civil marriages are conducted before or at the same time as an Islamic marriage; awareness campaigns to inform women of their rights and responsibilities, including the need to highlight the legal protection that civil registered marriages provide; to ensure that Sharia Councils operate with best practice and adopt non-discriminatory processes; and, finally, the regulation of Sharia Councils through the creation of a body to ensure good practice and continue self-regulation.[65] Such recommendations share ground with those put forward by Uddin, who concludes that 'while Sharia councils are imperfect in their current form, with great room for improvement, they currently fill a void in civil law provision by settling religious divorce and therefore fulfil a need in the Muslim community'.[66] He describes the need to establish 'a standard of practice' to ensure equality and justice for Muslim women, and calls for the implementation of the following measures: the recognition of a civil divorce as the basis of a religious divorce; equal fees applied to men and women respectively during the process; a complaints procedure incorporated into the Sharia Council process; and, finally, female representation at different levels of the application process, including on the Council decision-making boards.

[63] ibid 1.
[64] Siddiqui (2018).
[65] ibid 26–29.
[66] Uddin (2020) 128.

Such recommendations aim to both recognise and accommodate religious practices within the existing legal framework, supported by legislation, whilst ensuring adherence to existing legal rules and the consent of all parties in the religious dispute resolution process. Yet evidence presented by the research drawn upon in this chapter also clearly reflects the different treatment of women in the Sharia Council processes, leading to conflicts between women's equality and autonomy and the protection of family, culture and religion, as enshrined by the norms and values of Sharia Councils and the MAT. Manea describes Sharia Councils as 'inherently discriminatory'[67] and calls for them to be abolished.

Yet existing research also points to the diversity of women's experiences and the strategic and complex ways in which they utilise divorce and Sharia Councils. As Anitha and Gill point out:

> Women exercise their agency in complex and often contradictory ways, as they assess the options that are open to them, weigh the costs and benefits of their actions, and seek to balance their often competing needs with the expectations and desires. While there remains a need to recognise gendered power imbalances at the same time there also remains a need to respect women's exercise of agency … We need to give more support to those women who wish to express their subjectivity within the framework of the communities of which they perceive themselves to be such a fundamental part.[68]

There seems, therefore, an inherent conflict between recognising religious identities as diverse and plural, and formulating social policy initiatives that are based upon specific and fixed cultural practices, precisely because cultural and religious practices are open to change, contestation and interpretation. The practice of Muslim divorce within British Muslim communities challenges the mutually exclusive binaries of religious law versus state law, highlighting the dynamic and nuanced ways in which religious institutions as such Sharia Councils conduct dispute resolution work and how the goals and practices of dispute resolution work have complex implications both for the relation between the state and faith-based legal systems and for gender equality. The empirical research demonstrating the lived reality of Sharia Councils, religious arbitration and the experience of Muslim women highlights both the dangers and the emancipatory possibilities of such new forms of dispute resolution in the family law context. At the very least, we must therefore ensure that mechanisms are in place so that those who choose not to participate in such privatised mechanisms of dispute resolution are not compelled to do so.

[67] Manea (2016) 56.

[68] Anitha and Gill (2009) 168.

References

Afshar, H (1994) 'Muslim Women in West Yorkshire: Growing up with real and imaginary values amongst conflicting views of self and society' in H Adshar and M Maynard (eds), *The Dynamics of Race and Gender* (London, Taylor and Francis).

Agarwal, G and Kapil, G (2014) 'Arranged Marriage as an Example of Marginalised Relationships' 19(10) *Journal of Humanities and Social Science* 89.

Ahmed, F (2006) 'The Scandal of Arranged Marriages and the Pathologization of BrAsian families, in N Ali, V Kalra, S Sayyid (eds), *Postcolonial People: South Asians in Britain* (London, Hurst).

Ahmed, F (2013) 'Religious Norms in Family Law: Implications for Group and Personal Autonomy' in J Eekelaar and M Maclean (eds), *Managing Family Justice in Diverse Societies* (Oxford, Hart Publishing).

Akhtar, R (2015) 'Unregistered Muslim Marriages: An Emerging Culture of Celebrating Rites and Conceding Rights' in J Miles, P Mody and R Probert (eds), *Marriage Rites and Rights* (Oxford, Hart Publishing).

—— (2018) 'Modern Traditions in Muslim Marriage Practices. Exploring English Narratives' 7 *Oxford Journal of Law and Religion* 427.

—— (2020) 'Religious-Only Marriages and Cohabitation: Deciphering Differences' in R Akhtar, P Nash and R Probert (eds), *Cohabitation and Religious Marriage, Status, Similarities and Solutions* (Bristol, Bristol University Press).

Al-Astewani A (2020) 'Arbitration as a Legal Solution for Relationship Breakdown in the Muslim Community: the Case of the Muslim Arbitration Tribunal' in R Akhtar, P Nash and R Probert (eds), *Cohabitation and Religious Marriage, Status, Similarities and Solutions* (Bristol, Bristol University Press).

Ali, S (2010) 'Cyberspace as emerging Muslim discursive space? Online Fatawa on women and gender relations and its impact on Muslim family law norms' (2010) 24 *International Journal of Law, Policy and the Family* 338.

Anitha, S and Gill, A (2009) 'Coercion, Consent and the Forced Marriage Debate' 17 *Feminist Legal Studies* 165.

Ashe, M and Helie, A (2014) 'Realities of Religio-Legalism: Religious courts and women's rights in Canada, UK and US' 20 *UC Davis Journal of International Law and Policy* 120.

Badr, G (1978) 26 'Islamic Law: Its relation to other legal systems' *American Journal of Contemporary Law* 187.

Bano, S (2012a) *Shariah Councils and Muslim Women: Transcending the Boundaries of Community and Law* (Basingstoke, Palgrave Macmillan).

—— (2012b) *An Exploratory Study of Shariah Councils in England with Respect to Family Law* (London, Ministry of Justice).

—— (2018), 'Feminist Methodologies, Legal Pluralism and Muslim Family Law in Britain' in R Scarciglia and W Menski (eds), *Normative Pluralism and Religious Diversity: Challenges and Methodological Approaches* (Padova, Kluwer Press).

Blackett, R (2009) 'The Status of Religious "Courts" in English Law' in *Decisions, Decisions: Dispute Resolution & International Arbitration Newsletter* (December) 11.

Bottomley, A and Conaghan, J (1993) *Feminist Legal Theory and Strategy* (Oxford, Blackwell).

Bowen, J (2016) *On British Islam: Religion, Law, and Everyday Practice in Shari'a Councils* (Princeton, NJ, Princeton University Press).

Büchler, A (2011) *Islamic Law in Europe? Legal Pluralism and its Limits in European Family Laws* (London, Routledge).

Carroll, L (1997) 'Muslim women and "Islamic divorce" in England' 17 *Journal of Muslim Minority Affairs* 97.

Charsley, K (2013) *Transnational Pakistani Connections, 'Marrying Back Home'* (London, Routledge).

Douglas, G, Doe, C, Gilliat-Ray, S, Sandberg, R and Khan, A (2011) *Social cohesion and civil law: marriage, divorce and religious courts* (Cardiff, Cardiff University) available at https://orca.cardiff.ac.uk/26308/ (last accessed 27 July 2021).

Edge, I (2013) 'Islamic Finance, Alternative Dispute Resolution and Family Law: Developments towards Legal Pluralism?' in R Griffith-Jones (ed), *Islam and English Law, Rights, Responsibilities and the Place of Sharia* (Cambridge, Cambridge University Press).

Eekelaar, J (2013) 'Law and Community Practices' in J Eekelaar and M Maclean (eds), *Managing Family Justice in Diverse Societies* (Oxford, Hart Publishing).

Gohir, S and Akhtar-Sheikh, N (2017) 'British Muslim Women and Barriers to Obtaining a Religious Divorce' in S Bano (ed), *Gender and Justice in Family Law Disputes, Women, Mediation and Religious Arbitration* (Waltham, MA, Brandeis Press).

Grillo, R (2015) *Muslim Families, Politics and the Law, A Legal Industry in Multicultural Britain* (London, Routledge).

Hallaq, W (1999) *A History of Islamic Law Thought* (Cambridge, Cambridge University Press).

Jaan, H (2014) *Equal and Free? 50 Muslim Women's Experiences of Marriage in Britain Today* (Aurat: Supporting Women) available at www.secularism.org.uk/uploads/aurat-report-dec2014.pdf (last accessed 27 July 2021).

Jacobson, J (1998) *Islam in Transition: Religion and Identity among British Pakistani Youth* (London, Routledge).

Law Commission (2015) *Getting Married. A Scoping Paper* (London, TSO) available at www.lawcom.gov.uk/document/getting-married-scoping-report/ (last accessed 27 July 2021).

—— (2020) *Getting Married: A Consultation Paper on Weddings Law* (London, TSO) available at www.lawcom.gov.uk/project/weddings/ (last accessed 27 July 2021).

Manea, E (2016) *Women and Shari'a Law: The Impact of Legal Pluralism in the UK* (London/New York, IB Tauris).

Menski, W (1993) 'Asians in Britain and the question of adaptation to a new legal order: Asians in Britain?' in M Israel and N Wagle (eds), *Ethnicity, Identity and Migration: The South Asian context* (Toronto, University of Toronto Press).

Mohammad, R (2015) 'Transnational Shift: Marriage, Home and Belonging for British Pakistani Muslim Women' 16 *Social & Cultural Geography* 593.

Nasir, JJ (1990) *The Islamic Law of Personal Status* (London, Graham and Trotman).

Parveen, R (2017) 'Do Sharia Councils Meet the Needs of Muslim Women?' in S Bano (ed), *Gender and Justice in Family Law Disputes, Women, Mediation and Religious Arbitration* (Waltham, MA, Brandeis Press).

—— (2020) 'From Regulating Marriage Ceremonies to Recognizing Marriage Ceremonies' in R Akhtar, P Nash and R Probert (eds), *Cohabitation and Religious Marriage, Status, Similarities and Solutions* (Bristol, Bristol University Press).

Patel, P (2017) The Growing Alignment of Religion and the Law: What Price Do Women Pay? in S Bano (ed), *Gender and Justice in Family Law Disputes, Women, Mediation and Religious Arbitration* (Waltham, MA, Brandeis Press).

Pearl, A and Menski, W (1998) *Muslim Family Law* (London, Sweet & Maxwell).

Poulter, S (1986) *English Law and Ethnic Minority Customs* (London, Butterworths).

Qureshi, K (2016) *Marital Breakdown among British Asians* (London, Palgrave).

Siddiqui, M (2018) *Independent Review into the Application of Sharia Law in England and Wales* (London, OGL).

Uddin, I (2020) 'In Pursuit of an Islamic Divorce: a Socio-Legal Experience' in R Akhtar, P Nash and R Probert (eds), *Cohabitation and Religious Marriage, Status, Similarities and Solutions* (Bristol, Bristol University Press).

Vora, V (2020) 'The Case for Moving Away from "Non-Marriage" Declarations' in R Akhtar, P Nash and R Probert (eds), *Cohabitation and Religious Marriage, Status, Similarities and Solutions* (Bristol, Bristol University Press).

Warraich, S (2001) 'Migrant South Asian Muslims and Family Laws in England: An Unending Conflict' (unpublished MA Thesis, University of Warwick).

Webley, LC (1998) *A Review of Literature on Family Mediation in England and Wales, France, Ireland, Scotland and the United States* (London, Lord Chancellor's Advisory Committee on Legal Education and Conduct).

Werbner, P (2007) 'Veiled interests in pure space, honour, shame and embodied struggles among Muslims in Britain and France' 24 *Theory, Culture and Society* 117.

Wheeler, BM (1996) *Applying the Canon in Islam: The Authorization and Maintenance of Interpretive Reasoning in Hanafi Scholarship* (Albany, NY, State University of New York Press).

Yilmaz, I (2001) 'Muslim Law in Britain: Reflections in the socio-legal sphere and differential legal treatment' 20 *Journal of Muslim Minority Affairs* 353.

—— (2002) Challenge of post-modern legality and Muslim legal pluralism in England' 28 *Journal of Ethnic and Migration Studies* 343.

13

Dissolution, Divorce and Changing Practices of Commitment

BRIAN HEAPHY AND JAMES HODGSON

I. Introduction

Divorce has been central to the changes associated with marriage as a legal and social institution. Nowadays, in England and Wales, divorce itself is undergoing radical change that is linked to developments that have also enabled the introduction of civil partnership and same-sex marriage. Under various forms of legislation through the Matrimonial Causes Acts 1857, 1937 and 1973 (which consolidated the Divorce Reform Act 1969), divorce has gone from being seen as indicative of social decline and questionable moral character, and as the source of moral panic and personal stigma, to a relatively ordinary aspect of everyday relational life. The ordinariness of divorce can be grasped straightforwardly by the fact that between 2005 (when civil partnership came into force) and 2018 there were 1.6 million divorces. During the period 2005 to 2017, there were 2.9 million marriages, which attests to the continuing social and personal significance attached to legally sanctioned relationships.[1] Equally, 65,280 civil partnerships and same-sex marriages were formed between 2005 and 2017, often between couples who had already been in long-term relationships and viewed themselves as having 'marriage-like' commitments, but who had previously been legally forbidden to marry. Between 2005 to 2018, amongst same-sex partners, there were 8,740 dissolutions and divorces. While the figures for heterosexual divorce and same-sex separations cannot be compared in a meaningful way, not least because of the relatively short period during which civil partnerships and same-sex marriages have been in existence, they do indicate that as well as a shared enthusiasm for formalising relationships on the part of both

[1] As of 8 July 2020, the Office of National Statistics (ONS) only supplies data on marriage up to 2017. It supplies data on the formation of civil partnerships up to 2018. The ONS supplies information on divorce up to 2018, including the divorces of same-sex marriages, and also supplies data on the dissolution of civil partnerships up to 2018 (Office of National Statistics, 2020).

heterosexual and same-sex couples, divorce and dissolution will continue to be a common feature of marriage and civil partnerships for all kinds of couples.

Politically and legally, the extent to which divorce and dissolution are nowadays best viewed as an ordinary aspect of the changing institution of marriage, as opposed to being indicative of its ultimate demise, is reflected in the Government's enactment of the Divorce, Dissolution and Separation Act 2020, given Royal Assent on 25 June 2020. This legislation removes the need (and opportunity) to prove any basis on which divorce must be justified (removing the current law's five 'Facts': adultery; behaviour; desertion; separation of more than two years with spousal agreement; separation of five years without spousal agreement). The changes will (i) enable couples to give notice jointly; (ii) allow joint applications to become sole applications and vice versa; (iii) remove the ability of one person to contest the divorce; (iv) retain the two-stage process of decree nisi and decree absolute; and (v) introduce a minimum time frame of six months from petition to decree absolute. According to David Gauke, the Justice Secretary at the time the proposals were launched, the Government aimed to use this legislation to modernise the language used in the divorce process. The new law is due to come into effect in April 2022.

In 2018 alone, 56,141 women and 34,461 men in heterosexual marriages filed for divorce, while 838 women and 514 men in formalised same-sex relationships either filed for divorce or dissolved their civil partnerships. Efforts to modernise divorce come hot on the heels of the introduction of same-sex marriage in 2014, which followed the introduction of same-sex civil partnerships in 2005. Alongside these changes runs the introduction of mixed-sex couples'[2] access to civil partnership, which came into force through the Civil Partnerships, Marriages and Deaths (Registration etc) Act 2019. Thus, developments with respect to how heterosexual relationships can be legally formalised and dissolved can reasonably be thought to be entangled with developments in the legal recognition of same-sex couples. However, the nature of this entanglement, the social factors that have enabled it and its implications are so far generally unexplored, with the exception of a small number of studies. In this chapter we explore recent and promised legal developments in divorce and dissolution through the lens of some of the key sociological investigations of heterosexual divorce, as well as the very small body of existing research on same-sex divorce. We discuss some of the broader social developments that are shaping married and partnership life, and more specifically those that are influencing a convergence between heterosexual and same-sex couples' cultures of dissolved commitments. In doing so, we gesture towards future areas of study raised by the existing scholarship on divorce and dissolution.

[2] In this chapter we refer to mixed-sex and to heterosexual marriage interchangeably; we use 'heterosexual' to refer to mixed-sex marriage to underscore ways in which the institution of marriage has historically been inextricably linked to heterosexuality as a social institution.

II. The Sociology on Divorce: A Focus on Gender

The vast majority of sociological research has taken place in the United States, and typically concerns the 'risk factors' for heterosexual divorce, personal adjustment to it, and the impact on and consequences for children. The US social and cultural context cannot directly explain divorce and dissolution in England and Wales, even as similar narratives of divorce (as personally traumatic; as a high-stakes conflict; as morally significant) appear in both contexts. Gender differences tend to take centre stage in the US work. Amato provides a comprehensive summary of the field in the United States, focusing on studies that draw on large quantitative datasets.[3] One major strand identified in research is oriented towards developing divorce predictors: women's employment, for example, has often been framed in earlier literature as a risk factor for divorce,[4] an idea that presumes that greater independence for women destabilises marital relations. Contemporary studies on the risk factors or 'predictors' of divorce suggest that wives' employment may generate relational tensions that could, eventually, lead to divorce,[5] but more through an increase in the perception of unfairness over the division of household labour[6] than women's independence per se.[7] In an earlier study, Amato and Previti noted that in the US scholarship to date, there were key differences between men's and women's personal reasons for divorce: women in heterosexual marriages were more likely to report emotional and relational issues as leading to the breakdown in marriage (for example unhappiness, incompatibility, difficult personalities or lack of love), or they were likely to refer to men's negative behaviours, including physical and emotional abuse, substance use, and the neglect of home and children.[8] Men, on the other hand, were more likely to report what might be understood as 'external' factors as the cause of their divorce, including in-laws, former husbands and partners, or they were more likely than women to report 'unknown' causes.[9] According to Amato, these tendencies arise from the (gendered) notion that women monitor their relationships more closely and attend to relationship problems sooner, while men are more likely to withdraw from discussions about relationship problems.

[3] Amato (2010).

[4] Becker (1981).

[5] Amato et al (2007).

[6] Frisco and Williams (2003).

[7] Other risk factors that correlate with increased divorced rates listed by Amato include marrying as a teenager, living with one's spouse or another partner prior to marriage, having a pre-marital birth, marrying someone from a different race, being in a second- or higher-order marriage, and growing up in a household without two continuously married parents: Amato (2010). One could object to these conclusions based on normative grounds, insofar as they sustain ideas of a good marriage set against 'risky' deviations, although Amato himself notes that a predictor is not a cause. More than anything else, it is arguable that research into predictors does not tell us about the lives of the people who divorce in much depth.

[8] Amato and Previti (2003); Bloom et al (1985); Cleek and Pearson (1985); Kitson and Holmes (1992); Levinger (1966).

[9] Kitson and Holmes (1992); Levinger (1966).

This has been taken to mean that women are more likely to initiate divorce and men more likely to misrecognise their own role in the collapse of the marriage (and blame external factors more readily). The realities on the ground may be more nuanced than suggested, and Amato and Previti's own study (N=208) could not replicate some of these associations – for example, finding that men were no more likely than women to refer to external causes, nor less likely than women to report communication problems.[10] On the other hand, the findings of the study were more consistent with research indicating the reasons given for divorce tend to vary according to socio-economic status, where wealthier spouses tended to report expressive and relationship-centred reasons for divorce (for example, lack of emotional support, excessive emotional and material demands), while poorer spouses tended to report instrumental reasons (for example, disagreements over finances, neglect of household duties, or employment problems).[11]

An additional issue to consider as regards the 'reasons' for divorce is linked to the connection that Amato notes between causal attribution and post-divorce adjustment. While individuals in general tended to attribute the cause of the divorce to their former spouses rather than to hold themselves responsible, he notes that more strongly attributing blame to the ex-spouse also correlated with a low level of adjustment and a higher degree of emotional attachment to the ex-spouse after the divorce. Conversely, individuals who blamed 'the relationship' itself for failing, rather than their ex-spouse, were also better adjusted to life post-divorce. Here Amato encounters an obstacle that returns in much of the more-qualitatively oriented divorce scholarship, that is, the difficulty of disentangling cause and effect. Just as establishing who or what is to blame for a divorce is thought to determine adjustment to life after the divorce (whether or not they remain attached to the ex-spouse, for example), post-divorce adjustment is seen as shaping the degree of blame individuals attribute to themselves, the relationship or their spouses. Amato and Previti's analysis falls short of deciding whether the reported reasons for divorce represent the actual causes of marital breakdown or are 'simply' post-hoc reconstructions.[12] This alerts us to the need to treat such reasons as based on narrative truths, as expressed by research participants, as opposed to literal ones, and to explore the work they do in the life of divorcees, the audiences that they are told to and the broader society, as opposed to taking them as uncontested fact.[13]

Amato's work, and the literature to which he largely responds, is quantitative in approach, and thus often fails to grasp the nuances of divorcees' narratives of their experiences and practices. Another major US study of divorce, Catherine Riessman's *Divorce Talk*, in contrast, focused on divorce from a qualitative perspective, and her analysis of interviews with divorced spouses revealed the continuing

[10] Amato and Previti (2003).
[11] ibid.
[12] ibid.
[13] See also Plummer (2002).

importance of gender and gender roles to personal narratives of how divorce is experienced.[14] Many of her respondents understood divorce as stemming, ultimately, from a failure on their or their spouse's part to perform the role allotted by gender within the marriage – perhaps the husband was unable or unwilling to provide the financial support expected, or the wife could or would not provide the degree of domestic work or emotional care demanded. Gender 'failure', Riessman suggests, appeared in respondents' narratives just as much to describe their own failings as the failings of their partner. According to Riessman, the prevalence of this tendency can be explained by commonly held ideology, or cultural narrative, of 'the companionate marriage', the gendered idea of what marriage is supposed to be, wherein husbands perfectly complement wives and vice versa, such that marriage is the harmonious union of two opposites.[15] In making sense of their divorces, Riessman's respondents often mourned the failure to meet the standards set by the companionate marriage, and only rarely viewed it in a critical light.

Riessman's account of her qualitative research is of importance to the sociological understanding of divorce for a number of reasons. First, it alerts us to the sheer complexity of the post-hoc rationales given for divorce, where 'blame', 'fault' and the 'facts' of divorce can be attributed to a mix of personal, partner and socio-cultural factors. Second, many of her respondents expressed a number of often contradictory emotions around the divorce process (joy, relief, elation, as well as and simultaneous to loss, anger and grief). Third, she rejects research that aims to calculate the 'effects' of divorce for failing to register suffering beyond overt displays of distress – men, she argues, have an incentive to conceal and minimise their distress based on gendered expectations around strength and vulnerability. Fourth, and importantly, Riessman found her respondents were frequently able to see positive aspects to the divorce process, which tend not to be widely recognised in the literature. This, might include, for women, the development of financial independence and, for men, learning basic self-care tasks like housekeeping and cooking. Finally, Riessman directly draws our attention to the value of seeing the process of divorce as a process of narrative construction: one story about how a marriage had ended. Her participants worked hard through the telling of stories to make sense of this ending and integrate it into a new story. Even though gender differences inflected the accounts men and women gave about the ending of a marriage, she suggests, both men and women's stories tended to be contradictory and messy. They are best viewed as work-in-progress rather than complete.

Joseph Hopper's article 'The Rhetoric of Motives in Divorce' has built on Riessman's insights into divorce talk and brought gendered power dynamics to the fore in his study of divorce in the United States.[16] Rather than understanding

[14] Riessman (1990).

[15] See also Fisher (2013) for a further discussion of 'the companionate marriage', with particular attention paid to the varying, contested ideas that have shaped this term.

[16] Hopper (1993).

divorce narratives as a factual reporting of events, Hopper took them to be a form of 'account' or, phrased in interactionist terms, as an effort to make sense of social interaction rather than a statement of objective fact. So, while a respondent might present a clear narrative in which they were left by a spouse who initiated the divorce, the events of the divorce itself might be opaque, and it could be that the respondent in fact 'left the marriage' in an emotional sense long before their spouse made their request for a divorce known. Building on his argument, Walzer and Oles argue that gender significantly influences these accounts, limiting and defining the claims made around the divorce narrative itself:

> For some initiating women, there may be a tension between claiming control and accounting to a socially constructed definition of themselves as women. And for non-initiating men – a population that has been referred to in clinical literature as 'angry, abandoned husbands'[17] – there may be a tension in not having had the control that men are supposed to have.[18]

In short, gendered power dynamics inflect not only the unfolding divorce process but also the stories through which that process comes to be reported, made sense of and understood.

Vanessa May, in her research on divorced mothers in Finland (2008), develops these points where she argues that the gendered dynamics of a divorce narrative can be further compounded by the moral weight of other related issues, such as parenting and motherhood. In her study, she found divorced mothers tended to downplay their own personal wellbeing as a justification for divorce and foreground instead the wellbeing of their children. This, May argues, is a consequence of the powerful cultural stigma attached to the 'bad mother' who puts her own interests above her family. Divorce narratives not only help the women in her study to make sense of divorce, as suggested by Riessman, Hopper, and Walzer and Oles, but also contribute to sustaining and even repairing the mothers' sense of moral self, which might have otherwise been threatened by the end of their marriages. Riessman, Hopper, Walzer and Oles, and May all show that divorce talk emerges though the complex weaving together of socio-cultural, interpersonal and personal narratives, some more successfully than others, for a range of purposes beyond straightforwardly determining who is to blame for the termination of a formalised relationship. These are productive of a range of relational identities and social positions, such as 'the initiator', 'the good mother', the 'innocent husband' and so on.[19]

Some of this complexity in weaving the divorce narratives together is taken up by United Kingdom-based scholar Shelley Sclater.[20] Following a review of the psychological/psychosocial literature, Sclater writes that positivist scholarship

[17] Myers (1986).
[18] Walzer and Oles (2003) 346.
[19] See also Walzer (2008) for a persuasive argument about how heterosexual divorces provide an opportunity for both men and women to renegotiate gender roles.
[20] Sclater (1997), (1999).

often frames divorce as a process of gradual acclimatisation to new circumstances, the 'success' or 'completion' of which can be measured through psychological testing and conceptualised as post-divorce 'adjustment'. Sclater traces the impact of this ideology within the Family Law Act 1996 (which was never brought into force and was eventually removed from the statute book), which in part aimed to minimise the emotional impact of divorce by reducing conflict between the involved parties through the removal of the 'fault'-based system, and by placing extensive emphasis on and encouragement of mediation (and reconciliation). Sclater challenges the expert discourse of adjustment, finding that it cannot manage the many different ways people come to make sense of their experiences and that it overlooks the contextual specificities in which peoples' lives are lived. She notes that efforts to reduce conflict can end up framing otherwise ordinary emotions as pathological. This point leads her to suggest that a conflicted divorce may not be a social bad but rather a healthy, even necessary, response to the end of a marriage:

> It is only when the emotions associated with divorce are read through the framework of the dominant discourses that divorce appears as personal and social disaster. It is only through an appeal to the 'child as victim' (Piper, 1996) that emotions such as anger can be marginalized, and conflictual situations rendered inappropriate.[21]

Aside from a welcome focus on divorce as an ordinary (if painful) emotional experience, Sclater provides two key insights. First, through attending to divorce as a process of psychological and social separation, she is able to argue that gender becomes significant for divorcing heterosexual couples because gender itself is a major way by which those couples make sense of difference (particularly difference between romantic or sexual partners). In other words, as a couple disentangle themselves from each other, they come to view their spouse as more distinct from them than familiar, and gender works as an easy toolkit or resource on hand to help make sense of that difference. This might further explain why gender features so prominently in Riessman's narrative study, and in divorce literature around motivations more broadly. Second, Sclater helps shift divorce away from the realm of court drama and social disintegration and instead emphasises the primacy of everyday or ordinary emotions, as well as emphasising the social processes of self- and intersubjective negotiation, as important features of divorce rather than undesirable outcomes. We would go one step further and suggest that divorce can be better viewed as a relatively ordinary relational experience, involving ordinary emotions and administrative processes, but one to which extraordinary significance is attributed in the cultural, expert and political discourse. We also suggest that the study of same-sex divorce and dissolution is likely to bring the ordinariness of divorce and dissolution to the fore, but also the ways in which this ordinary experience is shaped by factors that are not always reducible to gender. This is an argument we return to following a discussion of the existing research on same-sex divorce and civil partnership dissolution.

[21] Sclater (1997) 435.

III. Same-Sex Divorce and Dissolution

In theory, the dissolution of legally formalised partnerships should at least legally be 'just the same' for same-sex couples as it is for heterosexual couples, because the laws governing same-sex civil partnership dissolution and same-sex divorce are essentially facsimiles of heterosexual divorce. This assumption appears to be borne out in some scholarship of same-sex divorce, but only to a limited degree. Rosemary Auchmuty, in her UK study, carried out qualitative interviews with a small number of same-sex partners (N=19) who had dissolved their civil partnerships.[22] Participants were recruited through convenience sampling, advertising the study in magazines, newsletters, websites, and gay and lesbian venues. She points out that most civil partnerships were dissolved for reasons not easily distinguished from those provided by different sex couples in divorce: relationships had broken down as a result of issues like infidelity, mental health and substance abuse, career divergence and falling out of love, and a dissolution was eventually sought in order to resolve the situation. A similar finding was also reported in a US study of lesbian couples (N=20) who divorced: Balsam et al found their participants divorced after their relationships had deteriorated over time and for similar reasons as listed by Auchmuty.[23] Both Auchmuty and Balsam et al noted the significance of catalysts or stressful life events[24] in triggering divorce, or that life stressors like the death of a parent might lead to what Balsam et al describe as 'growing apart'. This, they suggest, had in turn lead to an affair, failing out of love and so on, and that the relationships ended after a cascade of such events. Both authors also acknowledge that, in this respect, same-sex divorces had geneses comparable to heterosexual ones.

For Auchmuty, differences between same-sex and heterosexual couples emerged due to the context in which civil partnerships were legalised. Civil partnerships represented the promise of legal parity with heterosexual couples, and heralded broader social acceptance of same-sex relationships. However, same-sex couples had few 'models of failure' against which they might compare themselves. The fact that cultural narratives of divorce were limited to heterosexual couples, Auchmuty suggests, could lead to a heightened sense of failure when same-sex relationships ended. Put another way, there were few models for same-sex couples to refer to regarding formalised divorce or dissolution. While this may be true to some extent, we should not ignore that many same-sex partners will also have had the experience of witnessing their parents', relatives, friends and colleagues' divorces, even their own failed heterosexual marriages, so may, in fact, have 'experienced' divorce at a distance. Nevertheless, Balsam et al noted a strong and complicated sense of failure expressed by the women in their study. Their

[22] Auchmuty (2016).
[23] Balsam et al (2017).
[24] ibid 37.

participants held their marriages to a higher standard than heterosexual marriages – they had fought hard to demonstrate their relationships were as dignified and as worthy of respect as heterosexual relationships – and dissolution was experienced as a failure to meet their own standards. Linked to this, they expressed a sense of shame that divorce had come so soon after the victories of legal recognition for same-sex relationships, and worried that they had simply confirmed societal stereotypes around their brevity and instability. Thus, Balsam et al's work suggests that formalised same-sex couples face a unique set of pressures.

Other distinctive features of same-sex partnership dissolution stem from different cultures of relating. Before civil partnerships came into force, many same-sex couples made carefully planned legal and financial arrangements in order to protect their shared assets as part of the couple. These ranged from the creation of wills, the nomination of partners as beneficiaries of a pension in the event of death, and the creation of mutually-agreed funds and trusts for their partners' children. In short, planning for the end of the relationship, whether by separation or death of a partner, was negotiated and tailored to the particular needs and interests of the individuals, in ways that they believed were egalitarian.[25] This often reflected a broader egalitarian ethos that was a prominent feature of same-sex relational cultures in the 1980s and 1990s.[26] According to Auchmuty, bespoke arrangements around property and other assets were displaced by the financial remedy provisions of the Civil Partnership Act, which left the respondents feeling let down by the law, or, as Auchmuty puts it, experiencing legal 'shock'.[27] Auchmuty also notes the impact of generation. Many of her older respondents entered into civil partnerships after having spent many years in committed but non-formalised relationships. They were more likely to feel dismayed when legal arrangements 'failed' or, indeed, when their relationships ended in ways that reflected the acrimonious heterosexual separations that they had previously sought to avoid. Younger people, she notes, appeared less affected by the dissolution process – less troubled by the conflict it produced, and less upset by the consequences of legal separation. Citing Heaphy et al,[28] Auchmuty argues this is because younger lesbians and gay men felt more similar to heterosexual couples than different, both in the status of their legal unions and in terms of dissolving that union. As a consequence, younger same-sex couples appeared to share similar experiences of divorce and dissolution with different-sex couples more often than not.

Other scholars focus on the legal practices that develop when a court system accustomed to handling heterosexual divorce cases must resolve same-sex civil partnership dissolutions. Charlotte Bendall,[29] and later with Rosie Harding,[30]

[25] Auchmuty (2016); Heaphy et al (1999).
[26] Weeks et al (2003).
[27] Auchmuty (2016) 15.
[28] Heaphy et al (2013).
[29] Bendall (2016).
[30] Bendall and Harding (2018).

carried out qualitative interviews with lawyers (N=14) who handled same-sex civil partnership dissolution cases, as well as clients (N=10) who had experienced same-sex civil partnership dissolution, their participants largely recruited through snowball sampling. They found that lawyers tended to apply a general heteronormative approach to same-sex dissolutions that actively ignored distinctive features of same-sex relationships, like egalitarian practices around property division. Partly, she argues, this is strategic. Presenting clients as 'normal [heterosexual] members of society' to the judges, clerks and other personnel involved in the legal process was a tried-and-tested way to reduce risks and maximise the chance of a successful outcome, at least in the view of the legal practitioners.[31] One such 'risk' comes through non-monogamy, which may be a fairly common practice among gay men[32] but, as Bendall and Harding report, was seen by one lawyer assisting with a dissolution case to be 'fairly shocking stuff'.[33] On the one hand, same-sex partners expressed desires for lawyers who had an understanding of the sexual and relational norms of same-sex cultures, in order to feel comfortable with their legal team, and for that team to work with an accurate picture of the relationship. On the other hand, they signalled a notable degree of distrust towards legal systems and institutions, largely due to fact that in attempting to treat same-sex dissolutions as identical to marriages, courts failed to capture and respond appropriately to sexual difference.

Bendall sheds light on some of the possible implications of handling same-sex dissolution as if it were heterosexual divorce. This leads to circumstances where familiar heterosexual stories around marriage, divorce and gender are awkwardly, and sometimes cynically, rehashed. For example, Bendall recounts the case of a man who, when dissolving his civil partnership, found to his surprise that his partner (who had been unemployed for some time) cast himself as the dependant, 'the wife', in their legal negotiations.[34] This played into arguments about financial remedies. Rather than reflect a particular truth about the relationship, the casting of one partner as the 'man' and one as the 'woman' was understood by Bendall's respondent to be a highly strategic move made on the part of the partner's legal team to secure a better financial settlement. Bendall argues that the capacity for gendered narratives around divorce (for example, paternalistic frames that place women as always vulnerable and men as always independent) to be become dislodged or transformed when same-sex couples separate, is blunted by strategic efforts to secure the best outcome for clients, and, moreover, by the persistence of those narratives in wider cultures of legal practice. Partly for this reason, Bendall and Harding found a significant degree of resistance amongst same-sex couples to

[31] For the approach of the courts, see *Lawrence v Gallagher* [2012] EWCA Civ 398, discussed in Monk (2015).

[32] Heaphy et al (2004); Klesse (2016); Weeks et al (2003).

[33] Bendall and Harding (2018).

[34] Bendall (2016) 226–27.

reaching financial settlements through the legal process; they preferred, instead, to establish things like division of assets outside of court, despite the vulnerability of these arrangements to the law (without a consent order, bespoke arrangements are not guaranteed to be legally binding).

Aside from material arrangements, scholars have also explored same-sex difference from the perspective of kinship and parenting. The US scholars Abbie Goldberg and Katherine Allen carried out qualitative interviews with young adults (N=20) whose lesbian, gay and bisexual parents had dissolved their relationship with a same-sex partner.[35] Their sample was recruited through school- and university-based LGBT organisations. Most of their participants had been born into and raised by lesbian-parent families. Several features of the divorce and co-parenting arrangements are worth noting. First, children of women in relationships with other women tended to report the separations as non-acrimonious, and most of the study participants reported that their parents' dissolutions were relatively amicable. This fits with research that notes how many gay men and lesbians sustain close friendships with their ex-partners after romantic relationships have ended.[36] It also chimes with the assessment made by Bendall and Harding that the complexity of gay and lesbian relational lives (specifically, remaining close friends with ex-partners) are often not factored in during divorce negotiations, and can be completely misunderstood.[37] The young adults in Goldberg and Allen's study tended to report continuity in the contact they had with both gestational and non-gestational mothers, and that equal contact with both parents was sustained partly through both parents living close by during their childhood. Furthermore, most recounted that both mothers worked to ensure mutual involvement in their upbringing, and conducted co-parenting negotiations outside of the court system rather than formally establishing where the child should live (as is the case with most mixed-sex parents).[38] Goldberg and Allen speculated that an out-of-court arrangement was preferable to engaging with a court system that would not understand the specificities of their relationship. In this case, the validity of the non-gestational mother could be considered as a risk: couples feared the courts might view one woman as the 'real mother' and one as 'irrelevant', and organise the child's living arrangements accordingly. This parallels the sense, emergent in Auchmuty's study, that the law was inept in handling same-sex dissolutions. It also

[35] Goldberg and Allen (2013).

[36] Nardi and Sherrod (1994); Weeks et al (2003).

[37] Bendall and Harding (2018).

[38] It is worth pointing out here that Goldberg and Allen's study examines US-based parents. According to their study, where the child should live, and with which parent, in the case of a same-sex separation is not straightforwardly determined, because the law around parentage varies State by State. In some States a 'de facto' parentage is recognised 'based on parental conduct and significant bonding with the child', which makes some provision for same-sex parents. However, about half of States recognise parentage on the basis of the completion of a formal adoption process alone, and otherwise only recognise the gestational mother as the sole parent.

echoes Bendall's findings[39] that some same-sex couples did not trust the existing legal system on the ground that the nuances of lesbian and gay relational life would be lost, preferring still to make informal arrangements. Taken together, this research underscores that while the law may be valued as a route to recognise the social validity of same-sex relationships, it is not always trusted to represent the everyday experiences and realities of them, especially when it comes to divorce and dissolution. It is worth enquiring into the extent to which this also the case for contemporary heterosexual relationships, particularly in the context of heightened concerns about recognising the realities for domestic abuse.

IV. Distinctive and Ordinary

The notion that divorce or relationship dissolution inevitably involves an 'intimate battle'[40] is in many ways linked to its cultural construction as both a personal and social disaster. However, this does little to illuminate the experience of divorce and dissolution in everyday life. In contrast, we argue that divorce can be viewed as an ordinary experience that, despite the historic legal incentives to construct it negatively and social incentives to attribute 'blame' and 'victimhood', can have multiple and often conflicting emotions (including a sense of sorrow, loss, anger, freedom, relief) and practices (including abusive, disruptive, caring, empathetic, democratically negotiated ones) associated with it.[41] In principle, divorcing partners can separate in the spirit of friendship and mutual concern (even applying for divorce jointly, as they will be able to under the Divorce, Dissolution and Separation Act 2020), and in reflective and reflexive ways, as is implied by the much-maligned notion of 'conscious uncoupling', as much as they might do in the heat of disappointment and anger. However, in a cultural context where dissolution is consistently associated with acrimony, betrayal, failure to live up to gendered roles and the couple ideal, less disastrous personal narratives of divorce and dissolution struggle to be heard.

Our argument is in many respects in line with the arguments of socio-legal scholars like Robert Dingwall. Dingwall criticised the impetus toward mediation and conflict reduction in the Family Law Act 1996, focusing instead on the contradictory political tensions that shaped divorce law during the Family Law Act's conception, development and eventual passing.[42] Such tensions included, on the one hand, efforts to make divorce easier to obtain (working towards a 'no fault divorce') and, on the other hand, countervailing drives to encourage men and

[39] Bendall (2016); Bendall and Harding (2018).

[40] Beck and Beck-Gernsheim (1995).

[41] See the aforementioned reform of divorce law by the Divorce, Dissolution and Separation Act 2020.

[42] Dingwall (2010).

women to remain married (emphasising 'reconciliation'). He points out that 'most families do not have enough assets to fund an all-out, knock-down conflict'.[43] While the notion of divorce being a high-stakes legal battle is a key cultural trope, he argues that in everyday life it is most often a relatively ordinary administrative experience. He also dissociates the legal process of divorce from the breakdown of the marriage, noting that '[d]ivorce applications tend to come some way after the breakdown of a marriage, when parties are seeking to formalize this in legal terms'.[44] The studies by Reissman, Dingwall and Slater all suggest that to get a clear picture of same-sex divorce, how it feels, the practices involved and its personal implications, future sociological studies should examine the everyday life contexts within which it is experienced. People's experiences are as much about working through ordinary feelings and navigating the changing nature of relationships as they are about the division of assets and what happens in a court.

Most of the literature and research so far has focused on divorce and dissolution in a heterosexual context. This is understandable in light of the only recent legal formalisation of same-sex relationships. Given the focus of recent studies of same-sex relationship breakdown on civil partnership dissolution, studies that also take same-sex divorce into account are warranted. It is worth asking, therefore, about ways in which the insights of the existing research on heterosexual divorce might apply to current practices of same-sex divorce and dissolution. Heterosexual couples might well make sense of the ending of their relationships in recognisably gendered ways.[45] To what extent might this also be the case for same-sex couples, or do they script their experiences of separation in different or less straightforwardly gendered ways? What cultural resources do same-sex couples have access to in such scripting, and what different and similar intersubjective and reflexive dynamics are at play? How are self- and moral identities managed by divorcing same-sex couples, and what relational ethos and 'personal-political' expediencies are at play? What existing and new dynamics of stigma linked to divorce are at play in shaping new feelings of shame and disappointment that might originate from same-sex couples' having fought for entry into the institution of marriage, and heterosexual couples' for access to civil partnerships, only for their relationship to be deemed as having 'failed'?

The question of same-sex relational distinctiveness can be located within a series of broader debates around relationships and identities in modern society. To make sense of this, it is worth briefly considering the broader sexual and socio-political context of same-sex marriage and partnership recognition. The legalisation of civil partnerships and same-sex marriage, while long desired by some activists, academics and campaign groups, was viewed with a degree of suspicion by activists and academics who equated legal recognition with assimilation into

[43] ibid 107.
[44] ibid 109.
[45] Sclater (1999).

heteronormative regimes of power.[46] The term 'homonormativity' was formulated to capture the privileges now accrued by gay and lesbian people at the expense of those who less easily acceded to social norms. Questions have been raised about how relevant such analyses are given they are produced and consumed most easily by metropolitan elites.[47] Given that gay and lesbian people living outside of major metropolitan centres live far less comfortable or privileged lives, the legal and social recognition of same-sex relationships can be key to disrupting what Blasius has term the 'heterosexual panorama' that works to make same-sex relationships invisible, vulnerable to hostility, violence and social inequality.[48] Furthermore, the homonormative angle has been argued ironically to burden gay men and lesbian women with a new set of morally-weighted binary positions (normative/queer), which by virtue of their abstraction from material and social practices do not account for variations in class or capital and social standing, nor capture the complexities of how power is lived and experienced at a micropolitical level.[49] In these respects, as the sub-title of Brown's article suggests, we should be alert to the notion that homonormativity can be 'A metropolitan concept that denigrates "ordinary" gay lives'.[50]

From our own perspective, we suggest that it is worthwhile considering how 'the ordinary' speaks to how greater social, legal and political recognition has had significant consequences for many gay men and lesbians in their everyday lives. Ordinariness, as a concept, not only captures the sense that legal recognition was seen by some as powerful strategic victory won for gay and lesbian rights campaigners (and one which brought tangible improvements to the lives of many gays and lesbians), but also mutes some of the 'associated triumphalism'[51] by pointing out ways in which the differences between heterosexual and non-heterosexual relational arrangements are increasingly diminished.[52] While some have linked this to 'late modern' developments that increasingly enable women's financial and social independence, others have more explicitly linked this to the ways in which the urban homosexual experience has become more generalised in relatively recent times. This implies that heterosexual couple arrangements have come to resemble longstanding non-heterosexual urban arrangements.[53] It is not so much (or at least not only) that gay men and lesbian women have assimilated to a dominant norm, but that heterosexual relational cultures have shifted in the other direction and become more like non-heterosexual ones, in sense that they: can more often involve the realisation of both partners' projects of the self (and not just the male's); are more open to negotiation in terms of couple's family practices; can involve

[46] Duggan (2002); Puar (2007); Ruskola (2005); Warner (2000).
[47] Brown (2012).
[48] Blasius (1994).
[49] Heaphy (2017); Heaphy et al (2013).
[50] Brown (2012), See also Wiegman and Wilson (2015).
[51] Weeks (2007); Weeks et al (2003).
[52] Bech (1997), 1992; Weeks et al (2003).
[53] Bech (1992).

flexible financial arrangements; in principle, are based on agreed sexual practices, including monogamy and non-monogamy; and so on.[54] Ordinariness has thus become a prominent feature of accounts of relational life told by legally committed same-sex partners: as the broader relational culture becomes less dissimilar to same-sex ones, many same-sex married or civil partners claim to experience their relationships (and it is likely their dissolutions) in ways that are 'just like' everyone else.[55]

V. Conclusion

Taking as a starting point developments in how heterosexual relationships can be legally formalised and dissolved, and their entanglement with developments in the legal recognition of same-sex couples, this chapter sought to explore aspects of the nature of this entanglement. It aimed to do this by critically engaging with existing literature and research on heterosexual and same-sex divorce and dissolution, and by analysing the legal practices and social factors that are at play. In doing so, we discussed the specific (and some of the broader) social developments that are influencing a possible convergence between heterosexual and same-sex couples' cultures and experiences of divorce and dissolution.

First and foremost, there is need for research that examines the socio-biographical and relational context in which both mixed and same-sex couples legally dissolve their relationships. By this we mean the legal, social, cultural, gender, sexual and generational contexts that shape attitudes, experiences and narratives of divorce, alongside partners' personal history of relationships and their ending. Second, key to contextualised study is avoiding a sole focus on the divorce process itself and including a focus on the 'biography' of the relationship at hand, focusing as much on the 'life' and deterioration of the commitment to the formal marriage or partnership as much as on the period that commenced when the formal process of dissolution began. Third, in terms of the formal processes, it is important to examine the influences on how the divorcing relationship and its history are narrated, by focusing on negotiations between partners themselves, their support networks and their legal advisers. Fourth, and finally, it crucial not to conceive the formal granting of the divorce or dissolution as the end of the couple's relationship; rather, key to understanding contemporary divorce is the manner in which divorcees and ex-partners continue the relationships, in ways that can be experienced as positive *and* negative, as members of personal communities or 'chosen' families, and as co-parents, adversaries, friends, co-residents and so on.

On the one hand, if it is the case that heterosexual relationships are becoming more like the same-sex ones documented in the 1990s, as might be suggested

[54] Heaphy (2017), (2015); Heaphy et al (2013).
[55] Heaphy et al (2013).

by the success of efforts to reduce the adversarial aspects of divorce law and to foster an egalitarian or at least more mutually negotiated approach to separation, then our currently dominant cultural frames for understanding divorce are seriously at odds with how people experience the ending of their formal marriages and partnerships in everyday life. Studies of those same-sex relationships testified to the possibility of maintaining strong, mutually supportive and satisfying relationships with ex-partners, in ways that seem especially difficult for heterosexual divorcing couples, largely because expectations, practices and experiences of the latter seemed framed in adversarial terms. On the other hand, if, as some suggest, same-sex relationships are subject to 'homonormalisation' through their inclusion within the institution of marriage, it could be that same-sex divorce and dissolution follow the historically dominant heterosexual 'norm' of adversarial legal separation, rather than the 'queer' sub-cultural norms of negotiated informal dissolution. Either way, the entanglement of developments in divorce and partnership law with same-sex marriage and partnership law is worthy of further in-depth examination.

References

Amato, PR (2010) 'Research on Divorce: Continuing trends and new developments' 72 *Journal of Marriage and Family* 650.

Amato, PR, Booth, A, Johnson, DR, Johnson, DR and Rogers, SJ (2007) *Alone Together: How marriage in America is changing* (Cambridge, MA, Harvard University Press).

Amato, PR and Previti, D (2003) 'People's reasons for divorcing: Gender, social class, the life course, and adjustment', 24 *Journal of Family Issues* 602.

Auchmuty, R (2016) 'The experience of civil partnership dissolution: Not "just like divorce"' 38 *Journal of Social Welfare and Family Law* 152.

Balsam, KF, Rostosky, SS and Riggle, ED (2017) 'Breaking up is hard to do: Women's experience of dissolving their same-sex relationship' 21 *Journal Lesbian Studies* 30.

Bech, H (1997) *When Men Meet: Homosexuality and Modernity* (Chicago, IL, University of Chicago Press).

—— (1992) 'Report from a rotten state: marriage and homosexuality in Denmark' in K Plummer (ed), *Modern homosexualities. Fragments of lesbian and gay experience.* (Abingdon/Oxford, Routledge).

Beck, U and Beck-Gernsheim, E (1995) *The Normal Chaos of Love* (London, Blackwell Publishers Ltd).

Becker, G (1981) *A Treatise on the Family* (Cambridge, MA, Harvard University Press).

Bendall, C (2016) 'A "Divorce Blueprint"? The Use of Heteronormative Strategies in Addressing Economic Inequalities on Civil Partnership Dissolution' 31 *Canadian Journal of Law and Society/ La Revue Canadienne Droit et Société* 267.

Bendall, C and Harding, R (2018) 'Heteronormativity in dissolution proceedings: Exploring the impact of recourse to legal advice in same sex relationship breakdown' in E Brake and L Ferguson (eds), *Philosophical Foundations of Children's and Family Law* (Oxford, Oxford University Press).

Blasius, M (1994) *Gay and Lesbian Politics: Sexuality and the emergence of a new ethic* (Philadelphia, PA, Temple University Press).

Bloom, BL, Niles, RL and Tatcher, AM (1985) 'Sources of marital dissatisfaction among newly separated persons' 6 *Journal of Family Issues* 359.

Brown, G (2012) 'Homonormativity: A metropolitan concept that denigrates "ordinary" gay lives' 59 *Journal of Homosexuality* 1065.

Cleek, MG and Pearson, TA (1985) 'Perceived causes of divorce: An analysis of interrelationships' 47 *Journal of Marriage and Family* 179.

Dingwall, R (2010) 'Divorce mediation: should we change our mind?' 32 *Journal of Social Welfare & Family Law* 107.

Duggan, L (2002) 'The new homonormativity: The sexual politics of neoliberalism' in R Castronovo and DD Nelson (eds), *Materializing Democracy: Toward a revitalized cultural politics* (Durham, NC, Duke University Press).

Eekelaar, J (1991) *Regulating Divorce* (Oxford, Oxford University Press).

Fisher, L (2013) 'Marriage and Companionate Ideals Since 1750' in S Toulalan and K Fisher (eds), *The Routledge History of Sex and the Body, 1500 to the Present* (London, Routledge).

Fouzda, M (2020) 'Divorce reform swiftly returns to parliament', *The Law Society Gazette*, 7 January 2020 available at https://www.lawgazette.co.uk/law/divorce-reform-swiftly-returns-to-parliament/5102641.article [last accessed 8 July 2021].

Frisco, ML and Williams, K (2003) 'Perceived housework equity, marital happiness, and divorce in dual-earner households' 24 *Journal of Family Issues* 51.

Goldberg, AE and Allen, KR (2013) 'Same-sex relationship dissolution and LGB stepfamily formation: Perspectives of young adults with LGB parents' 62 *Family Relations* 529.

Hasson, E (2006) 'Wedded to "fault": The legal regulation of divorce and relationship breakdown' 26 *Legal Studies* 267.

Heaphy, B (2015) 'Civil partnership and ordinary marriages' in N Barker and D Monk (eds), *From Civil Partnership to Same-Sex Marriage* (London, Routledge).

—— (2017) 'Ordinary Sexuality' in A King, AC Santos and I Crowhurst (eds), *Sexualities Research: Critical Interjections, Diverse Methodologies, and Practical Applications* (Abingdon/Oxford, Routledge).

Heaphy, B, Donovan, C and Weeks, J (1999) 'Sex, money and the kitchen sink: power in same-sex couple relationships' in J Seymour and P Bagguley (eds), *Relating Intimacies: Power and Resistance* (London, Palgrave Macmillan).

—— (2004) 'A different affair? Openness and nonmonogamy in same sex relationships' in J Duncombe, K Harrison, G Allan and D Marsden (eds), *The State of Affairs: Explorations in infidelity and commitment* (Mahwah, NJ, Lawrence Erlbaum Associates Publishers).

Heaphy, B, Smart, C, and Einarsdottir, A (2013) *Same Sex Marriages: New generations, new relationships* (London, Palgrave Macmillan).

Hopper, J (1993) 'The Rhetoric of Motives in Divorce' 27 *Journal of Marriage and Family* 801.

Kitson, GC and Holmes, WM (1992) *Portrait of Divorce: Adjustment to marital breakdown* (New York, NY, Guilford Press).

Klesse, C (2016) *The Spectre of Promiscuity: Gay male and bisexual non-monogamies and polyamories* (Abingdon/Oxford, Routledge).

Levinger, G (1966) 'Sources of marital dissatisfaction among applicants for divorce' 36 *American Journal of Orthopsychiatry* 803.

Maclean, M and Eekelaar, J (2016) *Lawyers and Mediators: The brave new world of services for separating families* (Oxford, Hart Publishing).

May, V (2008) 'On being a "good" mother: the moral presentation of self in written life stories' 42 *Sociology* 470.

Michelmores (2019) 'Grounds for Divorce in a Same Sex Marriage' available at www.michelmores.com/news-views/news/grounds-divorce-same-sex-marriage (last accessed 8 July 2021).

Monk, D (2015) 'Judging the Act: Civil partnership disputes in the courtroom and the media' in N Barker and D Monk (eds), *From civil partnership to same sex marriage: Interdisciplinary reflections* (Abingdon/Oxford, Routledge).

Myers, MF (1986) 'Angry, Abandoned Husbands: Assessment and Treatment' 9(3-4) *Marriage & Family Review* 31.

Nardi, PM and Sherrod, D (1994) 'Friendship in the lives of gay men and lesbians' 11 *Journal of Social and Personal Relationships* 185.

Office of National Statistics (2020) *Births, Deaths and Marriages* available at www.ons.gov.uk/peoplepopulationandcommunity/birthsdeathsandmarriages (last accessed 8 July 2021).

Plummer, K (2002) *Telling Sexual Stories: Power, change and social worlds* (Abingdon, Routledge).

Puar, JK (2007) *Terrorist Assemblages: Homonationalism in queer times* (Durham, NC, Duke University Press).

Riessman, CK (1990) *Divorce Talk: Women and men make sense of personal relationships* (New Brunswick, NJ, Rutgers University Press).

Ruskola, T (2005) 'Gay Rights versus Queer Theory: What is left of sodomy after Lawrence v Texas?' 23 *Social Text* 84.

Sclater, SD (1997) 'Narratives of divorce' 19 *Journal of Social Welfare and Family Law* 423.

—— (1999) *Divorce: A psychosocial study* (London, Ashgate Publishing).

Trinder, L, Braybrook, D, Bryson, C, Coleman, L, Houlston, C and Sefton, M (2017) *Finding Fault? Divorce law and practice in England and Wales* available at www.nuffieldfoundation.org/sites/default/files/files/Finding_Fault_full_report_v_FINAL.pdf (last accessed 8 July 2021).

Walzer and Oles (2003) 'Accounting for Divorce: Gender and Uncoupling Narratives' 26 *Qualitative Sociology* 331.

Walzer, S (2008) 'Redoing gender through divorce' 25 *Journal of Social and Personal Relationships* 5.

Warner, M (2000) *The Trouble with Normal: Sex, politics, and the ethics of queer life* (Cambridge, MA, Harvard University Press).

Weeks, J (2007) *The World We Have Won: The remaking of erotic and intimate life* (Abingdon/Oxford, Routledge).

Weeks, J, Heaphy, B and Donovan, C (2003) *Same Sex Intimacies: Families of choice and other life experiments* (Abingdon/Oxford, Routledge).

Wiegman, R and Wilson, E (2015) 'Introduction: Antinormativity's Queer Conventions' 26 *differences* 1.

Afterword

JOHN EEKELAAR

The reasons why power structures decay are various. One does not have to think only of political power, including that of such international behemoths like the Roman and British Empires, and smaller political entities, such as the variety of 'vanished' European kingdoms recounted by Norman Davies[1] and those that survive only as an empty shell like the 'Holy Roman Empire' but also of institutions within polities. This can occur when a dictatorship suddenly ceases to function, as happened dramatically in Romania in 1989. What must have gone through the mind of Nicolae Ceausescu when he addressed the crowd on 22 December and it became apparent to him that it was not there to cheer but to jeer him? But power can be lost in other ways. Think of the shifts in economic power when industries decline because of economic and technical change (a recent example being in high street retail trading). Such fluctuations can be rapid, or emerge relatively slowly, and can be very disruptive. Or they may be managed in some way.

The institution of marriage has been an important manifestation of the exercise of power, and those able to determine its nature and the law governing the means by which it is entered and (if possible at all) exited, and the consequences of bearing children without the parents being married, had an apparatus which gave them significant control over the structure of society as a whole. The consequences for people's lives have been immense.[2] As recently as 2020, in Ireland an extensive and detailed report catalogued the horrific conditions undergone by women and children in mother and baby homes in that country to which large numbers of mothers were driven to give birth as a consequence of their transgression of the legal and social expectation that children should be born within marriage.[3] Less dramatically, the legal consequences for adult parties who enter and leave cohabitation without marrying are still under discussion in most jurisdictions.[4]

Although the Protestant concession against its indissolubility in cases of adultery could be seen as weakening the institution, it could also be presented as

[1] Davies (2012).

[2] Some of the literature is discussed in Eekelaar (2017) ch 1.

[3] *Mother and baby homes, Commission of investigation, Final Report*, 30 October 2020: https://assets.gov.ie/118565/107bab7e-45aa-4124-95fd-1460893dbb43.pdf.

[4] See for example, UK Parliament, Women and Equalities Committee: *The Rights of Cohabiting Partners*: https://committees.parliament.uk/work/1196/the-rights-of-cohabiting-partners/.

underwriting it by treating divorce as a punishment for breaking the obligations of marriage, a factor reinforced by the imposition of the death penalty in some cases.[5] Thus the doctrine of fault-based divorce became firmly entrenched as a necessary means to ensure both that the bonds of marriage could not lightly be overthrown and also that, if they were to be removed, this would only be at the behest of someone who had been seriously wronged or (as in the case of adulterous wives) whose family's property interests were threatened. In this way the fundamentals of the institutional structure could be safeguarded even where its objectives had failed. But if they failed because *both* parties disregarded their obligations, they were to remain locked into the institution because allowing exit in such cases would seem to empty the structure of any real content because that would allow it to be departed from simply if both parties wished to move to different relationships.

An alternative view of marriage as being a framework whose fundamental purpose is to support a special kind of relationship between two people, created by themselves for their mutual benefit, and which also created optimal conditions into which children could be born, seems to be at the opposite pole to the one described above. Under such a dispensation, it would follow that the marriage should fall with the relationship: divorce should be allowed for irretrievable breakdown of the relationship. This would seem to transfer the power whether or not couple were to live their lives within the institution of marriage from those holding authority in the community to the individuals themselves. The Divorce Reform Act 1969 appeared to accept that principle, although this was not a clean break from the past as elements of the older view clung on in the new dispensation, which could be seen as commencing a lengthy period of transition from the former to the latter view of marriage.

Each chapter in this book opens a window revealing details of various aspects of the history of this transformation. They are referred to below by the names of the authors. We encounter those who exercised power through the institution of marriage, from politicians and churchmen[6] to judges[7] and even members of the British Board of Film Censors.[8] Even the apparent victory of the irretrievable breakdown principle in the 1969 Act was partly justified by the Law Commission and others (such as Leo Abse MP)[9] on the ground that it would support marriage by enabling substantial numbers of separated people who could not divorce under the existing law and were living together unmarried now to dissolve their first marriage and produce legitimate children, which to some extent did happen.[10]

[5] See Eekelaar (1991) 7–13.

[6] See chapters by Auchmuty, Sinclair, Miles and Monk, adding further detail to the account by Cretney (2003) ch 9.

[7] See Miles, this volume.

[8] See Brown, this volume.

[9] See Auchmuty, this volume.

[10] See Haskey, this volume.

However, the proposal threw up new problems, in particular the economic vulnerability of a divorced wife.[11] In accepting irretrievable breakdown as the basis for divorce, the Act put it into operation in two different ways: one through the two separation grounds (two years with consent; five without consent) and the other by allowing quicker dissolution but with a requirement of fault, as in desertion and adultery, or where 'the respondent has behaved in such a way that the petitioner cannot reasonably be expected to live with the respondent' – where 'expected' was clearly meant, and (as Miles vividly demonstrates) was used in the judgmental, not predictive, sense. This perpetuation of fault was justified as providing some kind of protection for a wife's economic interests. As the Law Commission observed: 'At present, the economically weaker party (normally the wife) has the safeguard that she cannot be divorced against her will so long as she does not commit a matrimonial offence (or become insane)'.[12] So this 'safeguard' would be retained, except for the five-year separation ground, which was provided with its own safeguard where the divorce might create 'grave financial hardship'. That attention was moving away from upholding the institution of marriage and towards providing better financial protection on breakdown appears in the debates at that time about changing the law on financial and property provision on divorce[13] which came into effect at the same time as the divorce reform did in 1971.[14] Unfortunately, despite this effort, women still usually suffer greater economic detriment after divorce than men do.[15]

It turned out that this residual retention of fault in the divorce law was soon undermined by procedural developments, especially the introduction of the Special Procedure in 1973 (extended in 1976) which significantly reduced the scrutiny courts could give to petitions, and there could be little confidence that the 'facts' alleged were true, or represented the whole story, or indeed that this was not divorce by consent under another name. Indeed, at one time it was proposed that the need to give any information about the facts upon which an application based on 'unreasonable behaviour' might be based should be abolished in undefended cases.[16] This would indeed have recognised the reality that the Special Procedure had effectively introduced divorce by consent, yet granting a divorce for the reason that someone behaved in such a way that one person cannot reasonably be expected to live with the other, without requiring any mention of what the behaviour consisted in, would be to contradict the terms of the substantive law.

But the general effect of the new system was an increase in divorce, accompanied by what Probert calls its 'normalisation'. The empirical evidence on the dynamics of relationship breakdown (both for opposite and same sex couples) is discussed by Heaphy and Hodgson, but this was not reflected in the legal process

[11] See Thompson, this volume.
[12] (1966), para 112.
[13] See Auchmuty, this volume.
[14] Matrimonial Proceedings and Property Act 1970; later Matrimonial Causes Act 1973.
[15] See Eekelaar (2018).
[16] Matrimonial Causes Procedure Committee, HMSO 1985, para. 4.22. See Eekelaar (1986).

of divorce. The literature in the period following the reform surveyed by Probert shows attention (unsurprisingly) moving away from courtroom conflict, but also reveals a degree of bemusement at the artificiality of the new process. Interestingly, Trinder's description of the 'habitual' narratives found in 'behaviour' petitions shows that they followed a fairly standard pattern, mainly referring to a cooling off of the marital relationship, and no mention of abuse. But this may simply reflect that these are constructed by the parties together, sometimes with legal advice, and are designed precisely to avoid provoking conflict and possible defence of the petition. The fact that wives, especially in less well-off economic circumstances, used the 'unreasonable behaviour' ground much more than husbands[17] could indicate the extent of abusive behaviour by men in marital relationships. However, its increasing use by husbands could also suggest that both frequently used it for strategic reasons and they are unlikely to be telling the full story. However, the literature also mentions the possibility of the process provoking conflict, and empirical research by Trinder and colleagues[18] involving (inter alia) interviews with people involved in the process, found that 'producing evidence of fault can create or exacerbate unnecessary conflict with damaging consequences for children and contrary to the thrust of family law policy'. An attempt to break with the system was made in 1996, but failed because policy remained too strongly focused on the objectives of diverting the parties from the courts and saving the marriage.[19] And even after the enactment of the Human Rights Act 1998, which Draghici argues could have made the system vulnerable to challenge on human rights grounds, a scheme that fully replaced fault with the breakdown ground was introduced only in 2020 by the Divorce, Dissolution and Separation Act of that year.

Under this Act either or both the parties may apply for a divorce order on the basis of irretrievable breakdown, which the court must take as being conclusive, and if confirmed by the applicant(s) after 20 weeks, the court must make a conditional order. This can only be made final after 6 more weeks have elapsed. This is very similar to an approach I advocated in 1975, whereby

> a spouse, at any time during the marriage, could lodge with a court notice of intention to institute divorce proceedings. This would be informal and in no way the actual institution of proceedings since … it is a common view among marriage counsellors that, once proceedings have started, they gather a momentum that could jeopardise prospects of reconciliation. … The notice could be informally withdrawn at any time. … The hope would be that, when notice was lodged, the attention of both spouses would be drawn to the assisting agencies … At the effluxion of a fixed period (preferably one year) from lodging the notice, the party who lodged it would decide whether to proceed with the divorce. Should (she) wish to do so, (she) would be entitled to a decree by

[17] See Haskey, this volume.
[18] Trinder et al (2017).
[19] For a full analysis see Reece (2003).

> virtue of the sole fact of the effluxion of that period since the lodging of notice irrespective of the state of cohabitation or of anything which happened between the parties during that time.

This was based on a view of divorce as being

> an adjustive process guiding the parties through a natural (if unfortunate) re-orientation of their relationship … It is essential that, in the interests of all parties, divorce should be a transitional, forward-looking process, unconcerned (in the main) with events of the past, bringing the parties and their children to terms with their new relationships and working out the most satisfactory basis upon which they may operate.[20]

It may be that this goal has now been achieved. Power has moved to the parties, but power imbalances (mainly but not only economic) between them remain and attention should be sharply focused on what institutional provision, including advice and support, should be available to ensure relationship breakdown does not impact unfairly on either party, or the children. The legal process still has an important part to play in this.[21]

References

Cretney, S (2003) *Family Law in the Twentieth Century: A History* (Oxford, Oxford University Press).

Davies, N (2012) *Vanished Kingdoms: The History of Half-Forgotten Europe* (London, Penguin).

Eekelaar, J (1975) 'The Place of Divorce in Family Law's New Role' 38 *Modern Law Review* 241–53.

—— (1986) Divorce English Style – A New Way Forward?" *Journal of Social Welfare Law* 226–36.

—— (1991) *Regulating Divorce* (Oxford, Oxford University Press).

—— (2017) *Family Law and Personal Life* (2nd ed) (Oxford, Oxford University Press).

—— (2018) 'The Financial Consequences of Divorce: Law and Reality' 32 *Australian Journal of Family Law* 28–42.

Law Commission (1966) *Reform of the Grounds of Divorce: The Field of Choice*: Cmnd. 3123 (London, HMSO).

Maclean, M and Eekelaar, J (2019) *After the Act: Access to Family Justice after LASPO* (Oxford, Hart Publishing).

Reece, H (2003) *Divorcing Responsibly* (Oxford, Hart Publishing).

Trinder, L, Braybrook, D, Bryson, C, Coleman, L, Houlston, C and Sefton, M (2017) *Finding Fault? Divorce Law and Practice in England and Wales* (London, Nuffield Foundation).

[20] See Eekelaar (1975) 250–51.

[21] See the discussion in Maclean and Eekelaar (2019).

INDEX

Lightning Source UK Ltd.
Milton Keynes UK
UKHW020746270322
400660UK00003B/82

9 781509 947881